SINGLENESS, MARRIAGE,
and the
WILL OF GOD

J. Robin Maxson
with Garry Friesen

HARVEST HOUSE PUBLISHERS
EUGENE, OREGON

Cover design by Dugan Design Group, Bloomington, Minnesota

Back cover photo by sjharmon.com

The author is represented by MacGregor Literary, Inc. of Hillsboro, Oregon.

Singleness, Marriage, and the Will of God
Copyright © 2012 by James Robin Maxson
Published by Harvest House Publishers
Eugene, Oregon 97402
www.harvesthousepublishers.com

Library of Congress Cataloging-in-Publication Data
 Maxson, J. Robin, 1947-
  Singleness, marriage, and the will of God / J. Robin Maxson with Garry Friesen.
   p. cm.
  ISBN 978-0-7369-4549-3 (hardcover)
  1. Marriage--Religious aspects--Christianity. I. Friesen, Garry, 1947- II Title.
  BV835.M29 2012
  248.4--dc23
                  2011050762

To my friend, colleague, and advisor
Garry Friesen,
a worthy model of a single man
who has faithfully fulfilled the stewardship of his singleness
with fruitfulness and joy.
Unmarried Christians would do well to
"follow his example, as he follows the example of Christ"
(1 Corinthians 11:1 NIV).

CONTENTS

Prologue   7
Introduction   13

Part 1: God's Design for Decision Making
Modern Myth 1: As a Christian, you can expect God to tell you
whether to marry and whom to marry.

Introduction to Part 1   27
Chapter 1: Obeying God's Moral Will   33
Chapter 2: Trusting God's Sovereign Will   47

Part 2: God's Design for Marriage
Modern Myth 2: Marriage is fundamentally a "couples relationship"
designed to meet the sexual and emotional needs of the spouses.
Therefore, the key to a successful marriage is to find and marry
one's soul mate.

Introduction to Part 2   65
Chapter 3: Marriage in a Perfect World   75
Chapter 4: The Marring and Makeover of Marriage   89
Chapter 5: Balancing Marriage   103
Chapter 6: The Ultimate Marriage   115

Part 3: God's Design for Singleness
Modern Myth 3: Singleness should be regarded as a transitional
state en route to the ultimate destination of marriage. Problems
stemming from the incompleteness of singleness are resolved
by marriage.

Introduction to Part 3   127
Chapter 7: Eunuchs for Yeshua   135
Chapter 8: Singleness and the Will of God   143
Chapter 9: Single Choices.   161

Part 4: God's Design for Sex

Modern Myth 4: The best way to determine compatibility with a prospective mate and reduce the likelihood of marital failure is to live together prior to marriage.

Introduction to Part 4 181
Chapter 10: God's Purposes for Sex(uality) 187
Chapter 11: Sex and the Moral Will of God 203
Chapter 12: Sex and the Single Christian 211
Chapter 13: Cohabitation: A Dangerous Liaison 229

Part 5: Looking for a Mate

Modern Myth 5: The most important criterion for a good marital match is chemistry.

Introduction to Part 5 251
Chapter 14: Top Ten Missteps to a Miserable Marriage 257
Chapter 15: Profile of a Keeper 275
Chapter 16: Calculating Compatibility 285
Chapter 17: Courtship: Getting Our Bearings 303
Chapter 18: Courtship: Devising the Plan 317

Afterword 333
Appendix: Divorce, Remarriage, and the Moral Will of God 337
Acknowledgments 345
Endnotes 349

Prologue

Chris and Debbi, both in their junior year in college, had been going together for about a year. Chris grew up in a Christian home and was attending Bible school; Debbi came to faith through a campus ministry at her university, which was nearby. They appeared to be quite compatible and were very much in love. So in due course, when Chris broached the subject of marriage, Debbi sounded cautiously enthusiastic about the idea. They agreed to pray that God would make his will clear to them.

As they talked, they found that a lot of indicators pointed toward marriage. In fact, there was only one red flag. Chris had the sense that he should consider vocational Christian ministry. He had begun researching seminaries and verbalizing his emerging vision to Debbi. Her reaction was less than enthusiastic. She wasn't so sure she was cut out to be a missionary or a pastor's wife. She expressed openness to the idea, but it seemed to Chris that her reluctance ran pretty deep.

Were they getting different messages from the Lord? Was God's guidance for one decision in conflict with his leading for another? How could that be? Would this guidance clarify with the passing of time? What was wrong with this picture?

❖ ❖ ❖

On paper, Carl's rating as a prospective mate was high. Claudia had spent a year in recovery from her breakup with Steve when she signed up for the mission trip to Honduras. Carl was a fellow short-termer, and over the span of the two-week project, they formed a genuine friendship. Claudia was drawn to Carl's empathetic nature; he was easy to talk to. He was also hardworking and congenial, a great team member. He seemed to have a servant's heart expressed in an eagerness to help others.

When these qualities came to be focused on her, Claudia responded with an openness that surprised her. When they began dating on their return to the States, Claudia appreciated Carl's respect for her boundaries. The contrast with Steve was striking.

Claudia had met Steve and Jesus at about the same time. Steve was exciting, a lot of fun, and frankly arousing. But when Claudia established sexual limits because of her faith in Christ, Steve dumped her for somebody less restrictive. So Claudia was much more comfortable and secure with Carl.

But when the topic of marriage eventually surfaced, it was the contrast with Steve that gave Claudia pause. The level of passion she had experienced with Steve didn't seem to be there with Carl. Carl ranked high on caring, character, and commitment to Christ—and her. He was more than a friend. But did they have enough chemistry? Wasn't that important in marriage? Would it grow? How could she know?

❖   ❖   ❖

Lorraine was a graduate student who was just three months shy of completing her degree. Coming down the homestretch, she was pouring most of her time and energy into her studies. The remainder was shared with Josh, her boyfriend of eight months. She had met him at church, and their romance had become electric. Her two passions—academics and Josh—maxed out her physical and emotional circuits.

So she felt overwhelmed when Becky, her apartment-mate, announced that she was going to have to leave by the end of the month to go care for her cancer-afflicted mother. The lease was in Becky's name, and the apartment owner had agreed to release her from the remaining three months on the contract. But Lorraine could neither afford to pay for the apartment by herself or pay the deposits required to assume the lease. And the prospects of finding someone to share housing midterm were remote.

She was also unprepared for Josh's suggestion: "Why don't you just move in with me? You're going to have to relocate in a couple of months anyway. And who knows how things might play out?"

Lorraine was stunned. What did he mean by that? Was this a hint of deepening commitment? Isn't that what she wanted? But at what price? And how would she explain such a move to her parents? Maybe they wouldn't have to know…

❖   ❖   ❖

Nancy was grading papers on the dining room table when she overheard her mother talking on the phone in the kitchen: "Honestly, Fran, I don't think I'm ever going to have grandchildren."

Nancy sighed. Living at home was saving money, but was costly in other ways. Her mother meant well. Her mom tried to avoid nagging in her efforts to prod Nancy into taking action to find a husband. But her exasperation was thinly disguised. "At least find a church singles' group that has some men in it." And it only added to Nancy's frustration.

For years, she had clung to the promise of Psalm 37:4 (ESV): "Delight yourself in the LORD, and he will give you the desires of your heart." Her operating assumption, drawn from sermons and reinforced by Christian articles and books, was that her task was to focus on her relationship with Christ. And he would either give her a heart that was satisfied with single life, or a husband (which, she had to admit, was still her preference). In either event, "finding a husband" was not her job. After all, her parents had met serendipitously at a friend's wedding. Wouldn't the same thing happen to her, at the right time, if it was God's will? That's how it was supposed to work.

And yet, she couldn't help but wonder: did it really need to take so long? Was she somehow obstructing the process? Was her "delight in the LORD" insufficient?

Sigh. She hated to admit that her nagging mother was giving voice to her own nagging question: was there something else she should be doing?

❖   ❖   ❖

"You want a beer?"

"Uh, no thanks," Tom replied as he settled into the couch opposite the TV in Sherry's parents' den.

Sherry had just introduced him to her father, Hank, who shook Tom's hand without getting out of his recliner. The Cowboys were playing the Giants on the flatscreen, and Hank was halfway through his second Bud. Sherry disappeared into the netherworld of her parental home leaving the two men to bond; her mother was nowhere to be seen.

It's a good thing I like football, Tom mused, *'cause it looks like that's the agenda for the afternoon.*

The contrast with his own family could hardly be more pronounced. They had embraced Sherry like a daughter; and she loved joining them for meals, family activities, or just hanging out. Tom noticed that she was reluctant to talk about her family—especially her parents—and had put off taking Tom home as long as possible. He had intended to follow his father's counsel: "When you court a woman, you should court her entire family." But this family was proving elusive. Sherry joked about "swapping families," but now it wasn't sounding so humorous. What was going on? Tom really liked Sherry, but he couldn't help but wonder how her history might affect their future.

❖   ❖   ❖

"So how's it going with that boyfriend of yours? What's his name? Jeff?"

It was Mary's turn to check in with her accountability group. The leader, Scott, was offering her the chance to share from her life and receive input from the other members. At her invitation, they had been monitoring the progress of this relationship.

"It's going OK, I think," she said. "But I wish he showed more interest in spiritual things."

At least this time, the man who was pursuing her was a believer. Jeff was handsome, athletic, interesting, gainfully employed, and aggressively interested in her. He hadn't been a believer very long, so he hadn't acquired the spiritual disciplines of a more mature Christian. His church attendance was pretty regular—it tended to coincide with hers. Their interaction on spiritual matters occurred at her initiative, and he mostly asked questions. She had invited him to join her small group, but he "didn't feel comfortable" around people who had so much more knowledge of the Bible. Well, she didn't feel all that comfortable with the friends he liked to hang with on Friday nights. And she admitted to wondering if he was always completely truthful in his reports of his activities when they weren't together.

"I believe this relationship has lots of potential," Mary continued. "I think that as I model what it means to be a committed Christian, Jeff will want to grow more in his relationship with Christ."

Scott turned to the other members of the group. "Does anyone have any words of wisdom for Mary tonight?"

Introduction

*The purpose of this book is to equip unmarried Christians
to make wise marital choices according to the will of God.*

As a young man, David LeVine wanted to get married. So he set out to find a wife. He narrates his search in the audio series, *Get the Ring*:

> When I embarked on my search, I started by looking at all the dating and relationship data that was available. Then I came across the national divorce-rate statistic of over 50 percent. Now imagine for a second that you're going to get a nose job. And you go in to the doctor and he sits down and says, "Dave, there's a 50 percent chance I'm going to get your nose right." You're going to say, "Hey, doc, this is my nose. I can't hide my nose—and fifty-fifty is not going to cut it." And you would get out of there pretty quickly. Marriage, I thought, is a far more major life decision; yet less than half of the people were getting it right. I knew there had to be a better way.[1]

Why This Book Was Written

The experience of David LeVine highlights three noteworthy points: 1) The outcomes of one's decisions regarding marriage are hugely important; 2) it is difficult to get it right; therefore, 3) it would be wise to get some direction from a reliable source.

My guess is that if you are reading this book, you get those three points. I was aware of them when I got married over thirty-five years ago. Through the intervening years, I've had the sense that what was challenging enough for my generation has become even more complicated for the succeeding ones. But when I began serious research for this book, I was stunned by what I learned.

Coffee or Sex?

I don't think I'm engaging in hyperbole if I describe the situation in which contemporary single adults find themselves as "the perfect storm." The scenarios narrated in the Prologue represent just the tip of the iceberg. When all the factors are considered, it's hard to escape the conclusion that the circumstances confronting single adults today make the venture of marital decision making *more complex than it has ever been.*

One of the major contributors to this perfect storm is the cultural environment in which marital decision making is carried out. Societal perspectives on marriage, singleness, dating, and sex have undergone tremendous changes in an incredibly brief span of time. How dramatic have these changes been? Historian Stephanie Coontz summarizes: "The current rearrangement of both married and single life is in fact without historical precedent."[2] And in another place she says, "The role of marriage in society and personal life has changed more in the past 30 years than in the previous 3,000."[3]

You might want to reread that last sentence.

I will survey the history and nature of these changes later. For now I will simply note that the fairly uniform view of courtship and marriage that existed in our culture during my youth has given way to chaos and confusion. Marriage has become deinstitutionalized and alternative patterns of mating have emerged alongside traditional arrangements. As a result, many single adults who would like to have a life partner aren't clear about what form that relationship ought to take. Furthermore, established mating rituals of the past have been jettisoned, but no definitive system has arisen to replace them. As one young man described the current dating scene, "You don't know whether you're going out for coffee or sex." So unmarried people are perplexed not only about the destination, they are also bewildered about how to get there.

Programmed for Failure

One might think that *Christian* singles, who have the benefit of the Bible and the instruction of the church, might avoid being swept up in this squall. And for some, the circumstances might not be so dire. But from my vantage point, it appears that far too many believers are ill-equipped to competently deal with these circumstances. This is worse than being up a creek without a paddle. This is more akin to riding out a typhoon in a life raft.

There are two dominant reasons why so many are ill-prepared to make wise marital choices. The first is a combination of *ignorance and ambivalence*. One of my presuppositions in writing this book is that God has supplied the information we need for navigating life, including our marital decisions. But many single Christians are not accessing or applying that guidance in their choices. Some are simply unaware of God's design for marriage, singleness, sexuality, and decision making. Others have a partial understanding of biblical guidelines; so they attempt to make grown-up decisions with the comprehension level of a child. Some have a hard time imagining that scriptural instruction, authored in antiquity, could provide relevant and reliable direction for the complexities of a modern world. So it doesn't occur to them to consult the Owner's Manual for directions. As a result, they confront life-determining choices without the benefit of insight from the ultimate Source of wisdom—their Creator.

A second reason so many are poorly equipped for constructive decision making has to do with *personal experiences*. Consider two sobering ramifications of an astronomical divorce rate. The first is that the dominant model of marriage for those growing up in broken homes is one of dysfunction and failure. Our strongest perceptions of marriage are forged in the experiences we have in our families. For a significant percentage of those now considering marriage, that perception is skewed, but those affected are often unaware of that fact. Furthermore, adult children of divorce are usually emotionally and relationally scarred by that experience. That damage is not irreversible—indeed, God's grace can heal and strengthen those who turn to him for recovery and growth. The problem is that so few address the effects of those traumatic experiences, until the consequences start to surface within subsequent adult relationships, such as marriage.

In short, as they address marital decisions, too many unmarried Christians are *underinfluenced by the Scriptures and overinfluenced by their personal experiences and their culture*. A frequent result is unwise choices. And foolish decisions are hugely consequential—rippling outward in fractured relationships, inward in broken hearts, and downward, generationally, into the souls of wounded children.

When David LeVine considered the seriousness of the choices he was confronting and the unfavorable odds of a good outcome, he wondered where he could get reliable guidance that would improve his chances of success. In his research, he found one group of people that had an amazingly low divorce rate—Orthodox Jews. So he turned to them for advice. And when he put that counsel into practice, it worked.[4]

Whether they know it or not, Christian singles already have a reliable source of guidance for navigating single life and the choices that must be made. The apostle Peter affirmed that God's "divine power has bestowed on us everything necessary for life and godliness" (2 Peter 1:3). His provisions include the Holy Scriptures, the teaching of the church, the wisdom of godly counselors, and the illuminating presence of his Spirit.

To address the current situation, I am attempting to provide a resource that draws together in a single volume those biblical truths that address the issues confronted in marital decision making. That's why this book was written.

What This Book Is About

This book is about marital decision making on the part of single Christian adults. It aims to identify what those decisions are, explain biblical principles of decision making, and apply those principles to those decisions. *The purpose of this book is to equip unmarried believers to make wise marital choices according to the will of God.* Such decisions will be honoring to God and beneficial to those making them and to everyone related to them.

My statement of purpose raises two questions:

1. What are marital decisions?

2. What constitutes wise choices according to the will of God?

To Marry or Not to Marry...

So what are marital decisions? Well, first of all they have to do with one's relationship to marriage. Everyone starts out single; most people get married. I do not assume that everyone will get married or should get married. I do believe that virtually all single adults *think about* marriage.

Whether singles remain unmarried or get married, they make decisions that either maintain the status of singleness or attempt to change it. In that sense, even those decisions that perpetuate singleness are marital in nature—that is, the individual is choosing to not pursue marriage (at this time).

To be specific, the really big issues that must be addressed are *whether* to marry and, if so, *whom* to marry. But to come to conclusions on these questions, one should grapple with a host of intermediate decisions, such as:

- Do I want to get married? Why or why not?
- What is marriage about?
- Are there good reasons to remain single?
- What sort of person should I consider as a potential spouse? What characteristics should I insist on? Which ones are unacceptable? Negotiable?
- How do I go about looking for a mate? Should I take initiative or wait for our paths to cross? How hard should I look? How long?
- If I find a person of interest, how should we carry out a courtship? Should we date? How long?
- How should I prepare for marriage?
- What should I do if no spouse materializes?
- What is God's role in the decision-making process?

Your answers to these questions (and others yet to be discussed) constitute the marital decisions addressed in this book.

In Harmony with Design

To explain what I mean by "wise choices according to the will of God," it will help to tell a personal story.

When my kids were growing up, our neighbors had an only child, a boy, who was the same age as our daughter, Rachel, and two years older than our son, Michael. (Because his identity needs protecting, I'll call him George.) Lacking siblings, George was disadvantaged when it came to acquiring social skills. Our kids had enough opportunity for social development to get on each other's nerves. So Michael would seek relief from his sister by escaping across the street to play with George. (Also, George had lots of neat stuff to play with.)

In a partnership that could only have been divinely orchestrated, George became my ally in the impartation of wisdom to my son. Whenever Michael came home crying, I knew that class was in session. George would do something mean, selfish, or (mostly) clueless, and Michael would get hurt. Most of the time, it was his feelings that were injured; but often enough there was an actual gouge or lump newly applied to some unprotected part of his anatomy. (We couldn't talk Michael into wearing a helmet and pads when he visited George.) So I would hear myself saying things like, "When George is swinging a rake around his head, you need to put more distance between the two of you."

George taught Michael many useful lessons, often by demonstrating the consequences of foolish behavior. Most lessons were reinforced by repetition, one of which was *use a thing only for the purpose it was designed for*. For example, don't use a toy airplane as a hammer—or, worse, vice versa. If you insist on pounding on things with an airplane or launching a hammer through the air, sooner or later something bad is going to happen.

This book is based on a very simple premise: God created human beings according to a design. He had specific purposes in mind for us and he made us to function in accordance with a particular pattern. It follows that *our lives will be successful to the degree that we live in harmony with the Creator's design*.

When I speak of "wise decisions according to the will of God," I am talking about choices that apply God's instructions and principles that explain how we can live in harmony with God's design. As Dr. Joe Aldrich used to put it, "Get on the right side of how things work." The task at hand, then, is to unveil and understand God's design for *marriage, singleness, sexuality*, and *decision making*. In my opinion, Christian single adults need to have a sufficient grasp of God's direction for all four of these categories to make wise marital decisions. That's what this book is designed to provide.

A grasp of the divine design will provide solid footing for the Christian who must make decisions in the midst of the perfect storm. One benefit of understanding the biblical paradigm is that it provides a basis for exposing the fallacies of the conventional wisdom of our time. So as we unpack the elements of God design, we will be debunking *modern myths of singleness and marriage*. Here are some of the more prominent ones:

- As a Christian, you can expect God to tell you whether to marry and whom to marry.

- Marriage is fundamentally a "couple's relationship" designed to meet the sexual and emotional needs of the spouses. Therefore, the key to a successful marriage is to find and marry one's soul mate.

- Singleness should be regarded as a transitional state en route to the ultimate destination of marriage. Problems stemming from the incompleteness of singleness are resolved by marriage.

- The best way to determine compatibility with a prospective mate (and thus reduce the likelihood of marital failure) is to live together.

- The most important criterion for a good marital match is chemistry.

While some of these ideas contain a measure of truth, there is something wrong with each of them—as judged by the biblical framework. So the believer who follows any of these assumptions uncritically is vulnerable to undesirable outcomes. I hope this book will help readers to avoid them.

Start Here

You are now in a position to understand what this book is *not* about. It does not explain "How to Find Your Ideal Mate in Three Easy Steps." There is no guarantee that every reader will actually find a mate, whether ideal or not. On the other hand, I do devote several chapters to the process of *looking* for a *suitable* mate. That, I believe, is biblically appropriate, and I hope you will find that material to be useful. Neither is this a book on premarital counseling, though I strongly recommend structured marriage preparation with a qualified counselor for engaged couples.

No, this book is designed to precede those steps. It is about how to *approach* the decisions pertaining to singleness and marriage. What I want to say to every Christian single adult who is contemplating marriage is: "Start here." If you were taking a course on "How to Prepare for Marital Decision Making," this volume could be the textbook. It is intended to be a tutorial on the application of biblical principles to the issues you are confronting as a single person who is interested in marriage. As such, it would be a good resource for *pre-engagement* counseling.

How to Read This Book

I conclude this introduction with what may be a shocking confession: *I do not believe that reading this book, in and of itself, will equip you to make wise marital choices according to the will of God.* Surveying this book may be helpful, but it will not be enough. For most readers, the deceptive influences of a hostile culture and personal experience will remain stronger than the influence of this book. Your vulnerability to foolish choices will remain strong.

Readers who truly benefit from this material will be those who read it, learn the concepts that are explained, and *internalize the principles* to be applied. As I said, this is not a self-help book containing "three easy steps." It is an introduction to those biblical truths that must shape your decision making at every step on the journey.

What is required of you, the reader, is serious *engagement* with each chapter. You can accomplish this in two simple (though not necessarily easy) steps.

- *Step 1*: Read this book in partnership with a friend who will interact with you on the content. Better yet, work through the book with several friends in a small group. The value will be even greater if some of the members of the group are mature mentors who can serve as role models of wise decision making.

- *Step 2*: Make good use of the "Questions for Reflection and Group Discussion" at the end of each chapter. You don't have to restrict yourself to the questions in the book, but let them provoke your thinking and expand your understanding. Listen carefully to the insights of others and write notes in your book. Better yet, obtain a notebook or open a file on your computer where you can record the thoughts, questions, and ideas provoked by your interaction with this material.

Don't just read—internalize!

You can start with the questions at this end of this introduction.

Three Things You Might Find Interesting

About the Authors

This book is the second major writing project on which Garry Friesen and Robin Maxson have collaborated. The first effort was *Decision Making and the Will of God: A Biblical Alternative to the Traditional View* published in 1980 and revised and updated in 2004 (Multnomah Publishers). That book was an extreme makeover of Garry's Th.D. dissertation (Dallas Theological Seminary, 1978). In it, Dr. Friesen challenged the prevailing notions about divine guidance and provided a better paradigm for decision making that more accurately reflects biblical instruction (see Part 1 of this book). *Decision Making* was a landmark publication that changed how evangelical Christians think and talk about the will of God. In that writing project, Robin played a supporting role as writer.

Singleness, Marriage, and the Will of God is a sequel to *Decision Making and the Will of God*. It is also a collaborative effort; only this time our roles were reversed. Robin wrote the original version of this book as the centerpiece of his doctor of ministry research project (Dallas Theological Seminary, 2009). The responses from thirty-five readers in ten states (and Azerbaijan!) were incorporated into two major revisions culminating in this present volume. Garry served as one of my advisors in the DMin project and directly contributed many insights to the final product as a contributing author. For the record, the "I" and "my" references in this book are made by Robin.

Dr. Friesen (www.gfriesen.net) is professor of Bible at Multnomah University where he has taught since 1976. He also serves as an elder at Imago Dei Community, Portland, Oregon. And he is resident advisor and mentor to six male students of Multnomah University living in community at *Aslan's How.*

Dr. Maxson (www.uefc.org) is senior pastor of United Evangelical Free Church in Klamath Falls, Oregon, where I have served since 1976.

Garry Friesen is a lifelong single man. Robin Maxson is married to Louise. We have two adult children, Rachel Maxson and Michael Evans-Maxson.

Neither Robin nor Garry is female, which, for the purposes of this book, is a liability. But it can't be helped.

The Book Within the Book—Endnotes

Sir Isaac Newton famously said, "If I have seen further it is by standing on the shoulders of giants."[5] The first purpose of endnotes is to identify the giants on whose shoulders I am standing—to identify the sources of facts and insights included in the text.

But my favorite use of endnotes is to smuggle additional content into the book. This device is especially useful in a work that seeks to summarize and condense more extended treatments of the topics addressed. So amplifications, illustrations, quotations, and technical details are tucked away in endnotes for the edification of inquiring minds. Such spillover may prove useful to any reader who wants to explore a particular idea or topic further. But this bonus material may be of greatest benefit to teachers and others who are engaged in ministry to single adults and want to know where to go for additional information.

The Book Beyond the Book—Webpage

Believe it or not, a lot of relevant material was excluded from this book. Entire chapters have been culled from previous drafts. But one of the benefits of living in the electronic age is that potentially useful information considered surplus by the publisher can still be accessed on the Internet. The portal for this book's parallel universe is: www.TheMarriageDecision.com.

Already catalogued at this site are carefully crafted responses to some Frequently Asked Questions, such as:

- Doesn't Psalm 37:4 promise that if I delight myself in the Lord, he will give me a spouse (the desire of my heart)?

- Is it necessary to have the gift of celibacy in order to enjoy long-term singleness?

- Dating, courtship, or betrothal—is there a biblically prescribed method for mate selection?

In addition, those who choose to lead small group studies of the material in this book will find supplementary discussion questions for each chapter at this location.

The existence of a webpage devoted to marital decision making allows for continued exploration, presentation, and discussion of issues related to this area of critical concern for single adults.

❖ ❖ ❖

Questions for Reflection and Group Discussion

1. What is the stated purpose of this book? What do you hope to gain from your study of this book?

2. How do you respond to the assertion that "many Christian single adults are actually ill-prepared to make wise marital decisions"? What reasons does the author give? Can you think of other reasons why this might be true?

3. How would an understanding of God's design be helpful in decision making? What four categories of God's design are explored in this book? What is the relevance of each one for marital decision making on the part of Christians?

4. When it comes to marital decisions, which approach do you think is preferable: 1) intentional and anticipatory, or 2) spontaneous and go with the flow? Why? Do you know of examples that illustrate why one approach might be more advisable? Which decisions can or should be made prior to romantic involvement?

Part 1

God's Design for Decision Making

Modern Myth 1

As a Christian, you can expect God to tell you whether to marry and whom to marry.

Introduction to Part 1

The genesis of *Singleness, Marriage, and the Will of God* was a letter my daughter, Rachel, wrote to me when she was a freshman at Wheaton College. She was exercised about the circumstances of one of the girls in her dorm who had become engaged to a young man she had met scarcely one month before. "Sandee talks about how she feels 'convicted' to marry Tom, and she just knows this is God's will, because she feels totally at peace about it. Just about everyone on this floor thinks she's making a huge mistake, but when she walks up we smile and say, 'Congratulations.'"

The case of Tom and Sandee (not their real names) illustrates at least three things about marital decisions. The first is that *Christian singles who are contemplating marriage must answer three questions*: 1) Who decides? 2) How are the decisions to be made? 3) What is God's role in the process?

It is apparent that Tom and Sandee had received instruction on guidance that was similar to what Garry Friesen and I had been taught. This theology espouses the idea that God chooses each person's ideal mate, and then reveals his will to the man and woman who are to marry. In this paradigm, God is the one who ultimately chooses (question 1). So his role (question 3) is to reveal his will to the individuals involved. The task of the divinely matched pair is to discern this leading from God (question 2).

Is God a Matchmaker?

This view continues to shape the perspectives of many Christians.[1] In his book *Finding the Right One for You*, Christian marriage counselor H. Norman Wright devotes six pages to the question: "How Do I Determine God's Will?"[2] For part of his explanation, he cites some paragraphs from the late Derek and Ruth Prince in their book *God Is a Matchmaker*:

> If marriage is part of God's plan for you, then you can trust Him to work out every detail, both for you and for the mate He has destined for you. He will bring you together with a person who is exactly suited to you that, together, you may experience marriage as God originally designed it. This will be on a level higher than the world has ever dreamed of...Remember from now on you do not make your own decisions. You find out God's decisions and make them yours.[3]

However, within the evangelical Christian community, there are differences of opinion on this question. Several Christian writers believe that the prerogative for decision making lies with each person (question 1). In *Your Single Treasure*, Rick Stedman writes:

> Many Christian teachers believe that God has one particular person picked out for you; I do not agree...The notion that God has already chosen a certain, specific person to be one's mate diminishes the role of personal choice and free will. Instead, it fosters the idea that each person must try to find God's perfect will in its absolute and inflexible specificity...God does not want us to act like children in this most important area of life. He wants us to make wise decisions about whom we should marry, using our own resources and the wisdom and insight He has given us through godly counsel and the Word.[4]

In *The One: A Realistic Guide to Choosing Your Soul Mate*, Ben Young and Samuel Adams concur: "We believe that God delights in our ability to choose and exercise responsible judgment within the context of His greater will for all mankind...When we understand that mate selection is our choice, it causes each of us to take personal responsibility for that choice once we're married."[5]

As you will see, this latter viewpoint reflects my understanding of the Bible's teaching on the first question: *Who decides?* These books I've just cited are mostly devoted to question 2: *How are marital decisions to be made?* And they give excellent counsel. But because it lies beyond the scope of their purpose, they say little or nothing about *God's role in the process* (question 3). One might infer from this silence that believers are left to their own devices in making marital decisions. But that is not what the Bible teaches. So further exploration of the third question is necessary. (We will explore all three questions in the following chapters.)

The second thing that Tom and Sandee's case illustrates is that *there are consequences stemming not just from the choices made but from the approach that is taken to decision making.* In their immaturity, Tom and Sandee's implementation of the "ideal will" view of guidance led to a foolish decision. This was apparent to everyone but them. But because their friends shared their theology of the will of God, they were hard pressed to know how to respond when Sandee played her trump card, "We just know that this is God's will." The proof? Perfect peace. So anyone who might contest the wisdom of their decision would be arguing against God. End of discussion. "Congratulations!"[6]

The third reality demonstrated by Tom and Sandee is that *the approach we take in decision making is determined prior to the act of choosing.* Before they came to college, Tom and Sandee had adopted a framework for decision making in which they expected God to reveal his plan for them through inward impressions and outward circumstances. When they met and fell in love, it was not difficult to interpret these circumstances as the leading of the Lord. The difficulty in this scenario is that there were problems with their theology of guidance that set them up to make decisions they might later regret.

Deciding How to Decide

When you approach decisions as important as the choice of a mate and the timing of a wedding, you need to be confident that the manner in which you go about making such decisions is sound. The process of decision making needs to begin further back. It needs to start with the determination to examine, with an adult mind, biblical principles of decision making.

Rachel's clarity on this subject, including her conviction that her friends were applying a flawed theology, stemmed from the fact that she had grown up with a different framework for decision making.[7] She was a toddler when Garry and I were working on the manuscript of *Decision Making and the Will of God.* Her inculcation in the Way of Wisdom enabled her to recognize the roots of Tom and Sandee's misguided choices. What she lacked was some way to constructively address the situation with Sandee. What she wished for was a more concise book that applied the principles of the Way of Wisdom to marital decision making.

This, belatedly, is that book.

[*Note to the reader:* You may be tempted to skip over this section on God's design for decision making to get to the material on marriage, singleness, and sex. Please don't. Everything that follows is built on the foundation of the next two chapters. Please stay with me through this section as we lay that foundation. It's really important.]

So what is this Way of Wisdom that contains the biblical instruction concerning decision making and the will of God? At its simplest, it can be summarized in four succinct principles:

The Way of Wisdom[8]

1. Where God commands, we must obey (chapter 1).

2. Where there is no command, God gives us freedom (and responsibility) to choose (chapter 1).

3. Where there is no command, God gives us wisdom to choose (chapter 1).

4. When we have chosen what is moral and wise, we must trust the sovereign God to work all the details together for good (chapter 2).

As I expand on the meaning and application of these four principles in the chapters that follow, you should be asking two questions: 1) Is this really what the Bible teaches? and 2) How do these principles work in real life?

Questions for Reflection and
Group Discussion

1. What is problematic about Tom and Sandee's announced decision? How do you think you might have responded to them?

2. Do you think God is a matchmaker?

1
Obeying God's Moral Will

When my children were small, we were driving home from church one Sunday when four-year-old Michael abruptly declared, "I want to be God."

"What?" I asked.

"I want to be God," he repeated.

"Why?"

"Well, Josh is Superman, and Lindsay is Wonder Woman. So I want to be God."

I was relieved that we were dealing with a simple power struggle between superheroes. And I was gratified to know that Michael knew which one would ultimately triumph. Drawing upon all of my theological expertise, pastoral experience, and fatherly wisdom, I said, "Good luck with that."

Mike has since traded his quest for deification for less ambitious (and less idolatrous) goals. But not everyone does. A tenet of faith for most Americans is that the "pursuit of happiness" is an inalienable right. Each individual occupies the center of his own universe, and all other features and persons orbit around him. And this self-centered orientation governs the process of decision making. The goal of our decisions is success—an outcome that is personally beneficial, as defined by me.

"Christian" Decision Making

So how is decision making to be different for Christians? When we are thinking straight, we choose in pursuit of a different, higher goal. "We make it our ambition," wrote the apostle Paul, "to please [the Lord]" (2 Corinthians 5:9). We pursue that goal because we have been dislodged from our imaginary stance at the hub of everything and relocated to a place of humble submission before the throne of the rightful King. We have embraced the undeniable truth that *it's not about us*—it's about him. Everything is ultimately about him. So we find ourselves willingly managing resources that belong to Someone Else advancing a mission defined by Someone Else.

In the Sermon on the Mount, Jesus said that his disciples are not to be like the unbelievers who are scrambling to attain material things. "But above all pursue [God's] kingdom and righteousness, and all these things will be given to you as well" (Matthew 6:33). That is, *my dominant preoccupation is to be the expansion of Christ's rule and righteousness in my own life (spiritual growth) and in my world (mission).*

In our decision making, then, the ultimate ambition of the Christian will not be self-advancement but kingdom advancement; not self-pleasure but "to please the Lord."

Now if we want to choose in ways that are pleasing to God, what will be required? We must learn what pleases the Lord. That is exactly what the apostle Paul says in Colossians 1:9-10: "we…have not ceased praying for you and asking God to fill you with *the knowledge of his will* in all spiritual wisdom and understanding, so that you may live worthily of the Lord and *please him in all respects*."

The first task in Christian decision making, then, is to learn what God wants us to do ("the knowledge of his will"), and then do it ("please him in all respects").

So far so good. The obvious question becomes, how is the Christian to learn what God wants him to do as he is confronted with life's decisions?

To answer that question, we must distinguish between two categories of decisions: those that are directly addressed by the Bible and those that are not. For instance, the modern reader will look in vain for any verse commanding her to get married (or to remain single). And only a blatant misuse of the Bible would be construed as pointing out God's choice for a spouse. On the other hand, the Bible has a lot to say about how single persons should behave and how husbands and wives should treat each other. So there are some features of singleness and marriage that the Bible provides guidance for, but there are also many specific decisions that are not addressed in Scripture.

Later on, we'll deal with the matter of what we should do about the decisions not directly addressed by the Bible. First, we need to acknowledge our responsibility in those areas where God has already spoken: *Where God commands, we must obey.*

This is where the biblical expression "will of God" becomes relevant. In the Bible, this most often refers to *all the commands, principles, and promises that God has revealed in the Scriptures.*[1] This usage is well described as God's *moral* will.[2]

The Nature of God's Moral Will

The guidance God provides through his already-revealed moral will is more pervasive than many realize. The abundance of this provision is more keenly appreciated when we explore two facets of the moral will of God.

First, in its *scope,* God's moral will touches every aspect and moment of life. That is true because the directives of God's will encompass more than overt behavior; they prescribe the believer's goals[3] and attitudes[4] as well as his actions.[5] To put it differently, God is not concerned simply with *what* we do; he cares equally about *why* we do what we do, as well as *how* we do it. In fact, while we tend to focus our attention on our actions, Scripture indicates that God is more concerned about our goals and attitudes. So when we face multiple options, one criterion of a good decision ought to be to determine the choice by which we can best glorify God with Christ-like attitudes.

Second, in its *impact,* the moral will of God is able to equip believers for every good work (2 Timothy 3:16-17). Furthermore, God's moral will points the way to fullness of life. It functions as a kind of owner's manual for human beings. Because it reflects God's character (Romans 7:12; Luke 6:35-36) and is provided "for our good" (Joshua 1:8; Deuteronomy 10:12-13), obedience brings blessing (Psalm 1:1-6, 19:7-11; John 13:17).

Because God's moral will touches every aspect and moment of life (in its scope), and leads to fullness of life (in its impact), it follows that *the believer's understanding of and proper response to the moral will of God are two of the most important components of decision making that is truly Christian.*

That's two things: understanding and response.

The first requirement is to *learn* what constitutes the moral will of God.[6] I hope that one of the main reasons you are reading this book is to understand God's will as it pertains to marital decisions. I have worked hard to identify and explain as clearly as possible the teaching of the Scriptures in the areas you need to consider. Having finished my task, I pray that you will be diligent as you undertake yours. Borrowing from the apostle Paul, the first half of my prayer comes from Colossians 1:9: I am "asking God to fill you with *the knowledge of his will* in all spiritual wisdom and understanding."

As you encounter this direct guidance, you will have some decisions to make. As you weigh your options, consider this observation from a veteran pastor: *one major reason why people (even Christians) make poor decisions is that they elevate their own reasoning and desires over God's revealed will* (see Proverbs 3:5-7). When it comes to responding to the moral will of God, the right thing is also the smart thing. So the second half of my prayer for you comes from Colossians 1:10: "so that you may live worthily of the Lord and please him in all respects—bearing fruit in every good deed, growing in the knowledge of God."

The Way of Wisdom

1. Where God commands, we must obey.

Commander's Intent

On the field of battle, the actions of U.S. soldiers are guided by rigorous training and meticulous planning. The orders that direct an operation are specific enough to map out the actions of every fighting unit and every member within each unit. The directives specify the equipment to be used, the route to the target, the schedule for intermediate checkpoints, the lines of communication, the plan of attack, the means of resupply—every detail of the anticipated engagement. Everybody knows what they're supposed to do.

There's just one drawback: the plans often turn out to be useless.

Colonel Tom Kolditz, the head of the behavioral sciences division at West Point, gives this explanation:

> The trite expression we always use is *No plan survives contact with the enemy...* You may start off trying to [execute] your plan, but the enemy gets a vote. Unpredictable things happen—the weather changes, a key asset is destroyed, the enemy responds in a way you didn't expect. Many armies fail because they put all their emphasis into creating a plan that becomes useless ten minutes into the battle.[7]

So what keeps an army unit on target when some aspect of the battle plan unravels? In the 1980s the Army adapted its procedures and came up with the concept of Commander's Intent (CI). Authors Chip and Dan Heath explain: "CI is a crisp, plain-talk statement that appears at the top of every order, specifying the plan's goal, the desired end-state of an operation." This is the Army's way of saying, "Here's what we're trying to accomplish; do whatever it takes (within approved conventions) to make that happen."

Commander's Intent serves to guide the actions of soldiers at all levels without requiring detailed instructions from their leaders. When people understand the desired outcome, they're free to improvise, as needed, to accomplish it.[8]

The concept of Commander's Intent provides a useful analogy for the biblical paradigm of decision making. The Commander's Intent for Christian soldiers is the moral will of God. The fact that the directive comes from the Commander carries the expectation that the orders will be carried out. (Principle 1: "Where God commands, we must obey.") But the moral will of God does not address every detail of life. Within the larger framework of the Commander's Intent, we are given latitude in how we execute the assignment. And so the second principle of biblical decision making is: *Where there is no command, God gives us freedom and responsibility to choose.*

Freedom Within Limits

This principle of freedom of choice within revealed limits was clearly part of the Creator's design from the very beginning. For it was explicitly declared in one of the very first recorded commandments:

"Then the LORD God commanded the man, 'You may freely eat fruit from every tree of the orchard, but you must not eat from the tree of the knowledge of good and evil, for when you eat from it you will surely die'" (Genesis 2:16-17).

In a demonstration of God's goodness, the Creator began this directive with a declaration of the extent of Adam's *freedom* of choice: "You may *freely* eat fruit from *every* tree of the orchard." Then he added the single restriction ("the tree of the knowledge of good and evil") with a clear explanation of the consequence of violation ("you will surely die").

This early direction by God set the pattern for the revelation of his moral will in the centuries that followed. There are many instances in the Bible where we encounter freedom within specified limits.[9] Of particular interest to single Christians is the example we find in the only passage in the New Testament that directly advises a single person in marital decision making: "A wife is bound as long as her husband is living. But if her husband dies, she is free to marry anyone she wishes (only someone in the Lord)" (1 Corinthians 7:39).

This verse illustrates both of the first two principles in the Way of Wisdom. It begins and ends with two commands that are part of God's moral will. The first is that the marriage covenant is to be a lifelong commitment: "A wife is bound as long as her husband is living." The second command concerns the spiritual status of any man who might become a future spouse: "only someone in the Lord." So these directives fall under the first principle of decision making: "Where God commands, we must obey." A Christian wife is to remain married; but if her husband dies, and she chooses to remarry, she must find a husband who is also a believer.

In between these two limits are two expressions of freedom. As the widow considers the option of remarriage, she can choose to marry—but is not obligated to do so: "she is *free* to marry." And the choice of a spouse is up to her: "anyone she wishes." What we have here are two choices for which there is no biblical command: 1) whether to marry; and 2) whom to marry. (How interesting—these are the very decisions this book is concerned with!)

When we speak of freedom within the moral will of God, our terminology suggests a diagram. God's moral will can be represented by a circle. Whatever is commanded by God lies within the circle; whatever is forbidden by God is outside that perimeter. Within the larger circle of God's moral will is a smaller circle signifying an area of freedom.

BIBLICAL VIEW OF FREEDOM WITHIN GOD'S MORAL WILL

Now in the command given to Adam, the tree of the knowledge of good and evil is outside the circle of God's will—it is forbidden. The rest of the trees of Eden are not only inside the larger circle, they are within the area of freedom. In Paul's counsel to widows about remarriage, all single men who are not believers are outside the circle—not part of the acceptable pool of prospects. Christian single men are within the circle, and the choice among them lies within the area of freedom.

In the course of our life, we are faced with thousands of decisions that are not directly addressed by the Bible. (We call these "non-commanded decisions" because no passage of Scripture directly tells us what to do about them.) Many of them—such as which car to buy or what television program to watch—could not be addressed by a Bible written so long ago. Others are too specific to the life of the person who has a choice to make. So how are believers to make decisions that honor God when he does not tell us specifically what to do in those situations?

I have already noted that some Christians maintain that God *will* tell us what to do if we listen for his guidance. They do not usually mean that God will speak to us in an audible voice the way he spoke to Moses in the burning bush. God's guidance today, they say, is imparted through inner impressions that represent the "still small voice" of the Spirit. Such inner impressions are supported and confirmed by other signs such as circumstances, passages from the Bible, the counsel of other Christians, personal desires, and even common sense.

Without intending any disrespect for fellow Christians who hold this view, I do not find this explanation taught in the Bible.[10] In fact, at the very point where one might expect a biblical writer to instruct his readers to "seek God's will" for the decision in question, the author offers different counsel. As noted above, the apostle Paul declined to advise the widow to ask God to reveal whether she should remarry or to indicate which man should become her husband. The apostle clearly indicates that those decisions were up to her. Whenever we encounter the freedom to make a decision, we must accept the assignment to exercise that freedom responsibly. "Where there is no command, God gives us the freedom and responsibility to choose."

This second principle has three important ramifications. First, in non-commanded decisions, the freedom that the Christian has to make a choice is real—God should not be expected to dictate (micromanage) what she must do. Second, when such a decision is made, it must not violate God's moral will in any respect—purpose, attitude, or execution. And third, some decisions have multiple options, any number of which may be acceptable to God.

The Way of Wisdom

1. Where God commands, we must obey.

2. Where there is no command, God gives us freedom and responsibility to choose.

Criteria for God-Approved Choices

Within the military doctrine of Commander's Intent, provision is made for officers and soldiers to improvise the means by which they carry out their assignments. But this stipulation raises a question: Are the troops expected to act in accordance with their own best ideas conceived on the spot, or are there other criteria governing their options?

For Christians, the principle of freedom within the moral will of God raises similar issues. For if believers are free to choose in non-commanded decisions, we are also *required* to choose. So, on what basis is the believer to make such decisions? This question assumes that if God has granted the privilege of choice and the dignity of accountability, he has also given appropriate instructions for the exercise of our responsibility. In our study of the Bible, that assumption has been proven true.

When Garry was doing research for the doctoral dissertation that became the basis for *Decision Making and the Will of God*, he repeatedly read through the book of Acts and the epistles asking specific questions:

- When the apostles were not responding to direct commands from God, how did they make their decisions?

- How did they explain their actions, whether in process or in retrospect?

- Further, when they gave instructions to Christians and churches, what directions did they give for decision making in the area of freedom?

The results of that study were eye-opening. What he found was a consistent pattern—and it wasn't the framework we had been taught in our youth.

When the apostles gave explanations for their non-commanded decisions, here is the terminology they used: "we thought it best" (1 Thessalonians 3:1-2 NIV); "I considered it necessary" (Philippians 2:25-26); "if it seems advisable" (1 Corinthians 16:3-4); "it is not desirable" (Acts 6:2-4 NASB); "I have decided" (Titus 3:12). When they gave directions in decision making, the apostles' exhortations were consistent with their practice. Some choices were commended on grounds of being "good," while others were "better" (1 Corinthians 7:1,9,26,38 NIV).[11]

All of the decisions referred to have two things in common: 1) since they were not determined by God's moral will, they each qualified as a matter of freedom, and 2) the terms utilized in the explanations (*good, better, best, fitting*) imply some standard—a specific basis for decision making. While the terminology varies, it is apparent that that criterion is *wisdom*. Paul makes this guideline explicit in Ephesians 5 and Colossians 4:

> Therefore be very careful how you live—not as unwise but as wise, taking advantage of every opportunity, because the days are evil (Ephesians 5:15-16).

> Conduct yourselves with wisdom toward outsiders, making the most of the opportunities (Colossians 4:5; see also Acts 6:2-3; 1 Corinthians 6:1-6).

We can sum up apostolic practice and instruction with this principle: *In non-commanded decisions, the believer's goal is to make wise choices on the basis of spiritual usefulness.*

To flesh out this principle, we need some definitions.

- "Spiritual" means that the ends in view, as well as the means to those ends, are governed by the moral will of God.

- "Usefulness" refers to the quality of being suitable or advantageous to the end in view. Put simply, it means whatever works best within God's moral will to get the job done.[12]

- "Wisdom is the power to see, and the inclination to choose, the best and highest goal, together with the surest means of attaining it."[13] Wisdom is the ability to figure out what is spiritually profitable in a given situation.[14]

Of course, it isn't just the New Testament apostles who model the pursuit of wisdom in decision making. The examples and exhortations of godly men and women in the Old Testament as well as the teaching of Jesus himself presage the pattern of the apostles in pointing to wisdom as the guiding principle for decisions that are beneficial to the individual and pleasing to God.[15] Scholars describe Job, Psalms, Proverbs, Ecclesiastes, and Song of Solomon as "wisdom literature." These writings underscore the value of wisdom for everyday living and decision making.

In our consideration of non-commanded decisions, then, we have established two biblical principles. First, where there is no command, God gives us freedom and responsibility to choose. Second, in non-commanded decisions, the believer's goal is to make wise choices on the basis of spiritual usefulness.

Acquiring Wisdom

Earlier in this chapter, I raised a question about the implementation of Commander's Intent that I haven't yet answered. When officers or individual troops find it necessary to develop their own plan in the fight to accomplish the mission, how do they go about choosing the most effective course of action? The key for soldiers in the U.S. Army is their training and experience. Knowledge acquired from the study of centuries of warfare, lessons extracted from modern-day theaters of operation, and the experiences of veteran warriors are translated into drills for almost every conceivable battle scenario. Combat procedures and situation reactions are ingrained in these troops through hands-on instruction and disciplined repetition. This training is reinforced and refined by on-the-ground engagement with the enemy. These soldiers are not left to their own devices to figure out solutions. The controlling element of their decision making is combat wisdom acquired by training and experience.

As Christian "soldiers" who strive to implement the Commander's Intent encoded in the moral will of God, we too need wisdom. Ultimately, this spiritual wisdom comes from God: "For the LORD gives wisdom, and from his mouth comes knowledge and understanding" (Proverbs 2:6; see Romans 11:33; 16:27). But this wisdom is not imparted to those who are passive. It is instilled in those who value it enough to *pursue* it with the godly attitudes of reverence, humility, teachableness, diligence, uprightness, and faith (Proverbs 2:4-7; 9:9-10; 11:2; 15:31-33; 19:20; James 1:6).

While the quest for wisdom requires effort, it is never strictly academic. We gain wisdom through a partnership with God who engages with us hands-on. He mediates his wisdom through a variety of channels: the Bible, our own research, wise counselors, and the applied lessons of life.[16] And as we practice wisdom in the experiences of life, we are *trained* in it (Hebrews 5:14).

Accordingly, the third principle of Christian decision making is: *Where there is no command, God gives us wisdom to choose.*

The Way of Wisdom

1. Where God commands, we must obey.

2. Where there is no command, God gives us freedom and responsibility to choose.

3. Where there is no command, God gives us wisdom to choose.

Conclusion: A simple, practical application issues from these three principles. The believer must ask two questions of every option in a given decision: "Is it moral?" and "Is it wise?" Using A.W. Tozer's terminology, "Is this decision in harmony with 'sanctified common sense'?"

To help us remember that we are seeking *godly* wisdom we might ask: "How can I best love God and man?" "Which decision will best promote God's kingdom?" "How can I most skillfully serve God and his people?"

❖ ❖ ❖

Questions for Reflection and Group Discussion

1. How does the moral will of God "touch every aspect and moment of life"?

2. The "ideal will" view of guidance teaches that in non-commanded decisions, God will tell the believer what to do. How does the perspective of the Way of Wisdom differ?

3. Identify a particular decision you have made recently. Would any of the three ramifications of Principle 2 have applied? How?

4. How does the quest for a wise choice rather than the right choice change one's approach to decision making? Are there any implications for mate selection?

5. What was the most significant insight you gained from reading this chapter?

For additional questions, go to www.TheMarriageDecision.com.

2

Trusting God's Sovereign Will

H is story is one of the oldest, and best, in literature. And his commentary, given at the climactic conclusion, continues to provide insight into the mysterious ways of God for believers living centuries later.

You probably know the plot. The eleventh son born to a nomadic patriarch, Joseph was his father's favorite. If his dreams were to be taken seriously, it appeared that he was also favored by God. As a young man, he sought to live uprightly. His future was certainly promising, which is precisely the thing that galled his older brothers. Jealous of the special esteem he enjoyed from their father, and fearing that he would usurp their inheritance, they kidnapped him and sold him as a slave. So much for his promising future!

In Egypt, he was acquired by an officer of Pharaoh's court. Making the best of his situation, Joseph worked with industry and integrity, and rose through the ranks to become his master's most trusted manager. But his refusal to submit to the sexual advances of the officer's wife and her subsequent charges of sexual harassment against him got him thrown in prison.

Even there, Joseph maintained his moral standards and applied himself. When one of his dreams revealed the cupbearer's return to his position in Pharaoh's court, Joseph had reason for hope of release from imprisonment. But his kindness was not returned, and he remained in confinement for two long years.

The only hopeful clue in the narrative of Joseph's long descent into oblivion is a cryptic phrase, recorded three times: "the LORD was with Joseph and gave him success in whatever he did" (Genesis 39:2-3,21,23 NIV).

After a long time, at a point of impending crisis for the region, Joseph was suddenly plucked from obscurity and promoted to the highest position in Pharaoh's kingdom. Joseph's promising future was fulfilled—far beyond his wildest dreams! In the end, his divinely revealed inside information about the future and the wisdom of his counter-famine measures saved not only the Egyptian population, but his own family as well. And he had the satisfaction of providentially arranged encounters with his older brothers where past issues were resolved.

To get from the pasturelands of Canaan to the court of Pharaoh, Joseph was required to experience a sequence of reversals and the anguish of unfair treatment from individuals who should have been on his side. In the biblical text, there is no indication that he ever violated the moral will of God. He seemed to get punished, repeatedly, for persisting in doing the right thing. And then, almost overnight, he rocketed from the nadir of prison to the apex of power and authority. And he changed history—and preserved the Messianic line.

It was in a final confrontation with his brothers that Joseph gave his explanation for the downs and ups of his remarkable career: "As for you, you meant to harm me, but God intended it for a good purpose, so he could preserve the lives of many people, as you can see this day" (Genesis 50:20).

The biography of Joseph illustrates that our lives unfold along two tracks. The one is visible; the other is hidden. The one concerns our decision making and actions as we play out our roles; the other concerns the work of God behind the scenes to bring about his purposes. The one presumes our freedom to make real decisions; the other takes for granted God's sovereign control over all things—including our choices.

In the introduction to this section, we observed that the Christian decision maker must answer three questions: 1) Who decides? 2) How are decisions to be made? and 3) What is God's role in the process? In our survey of the first three principles of the Way of Wisdom in the previous chapter, we have found answers to the first two questions. In the beginning, human beings were created in the image of God. Part of that *imago dei* is the capacity to freely make real decisions. Who decides? We do. And how are we to choose? Christians are called to make wise decisions within the moral will of God.

The remaining part concerns God's role in the process. And here we must avoid two opposite mistakes. The first, as we have seen, is to assume that in non-commanded decisions, we can expect God to tell us what to do. Of course, he *could* do that. And he *has* done that—though rarely. When God actually speaks, we call that divine revelation. But as I have noted, that's not what most people mean when they assert that God told them what to do. They are rather referring to the various hints and whispers that God supposedly gives to nudge people in the direction of his ideal will.

But what the Bible actually teaches is that Christians are given the freedom and responsibility to apply wisdom within God's moral will as we make choices not directly addressed by the Bible. When Adam decided what to name the animals, those names didn't come from God. Similarly, when we make decisions in the course of our lives, we shouldn't *expect* God to tell us what to do. We should follow the instructions he has given us for decision making and get on with it.

The opposite mistake, however, is to infer that God is not involved in our decision making at all. It turns out that he is more engaged with our choices than we would ever have imagined. For starters, he actively responds to our prayers for wisdom (James 1:5). And he works behind the scenes to govern both the process and the outcome of our decision making through the implementation of his *sovereign* will.

While most biblical references to God's will relate to his *moral* will, there are also numerous instances where this second category of God's will is in view. For instance, when Paul expressed his intentions to visit the church in Rome, he gave this explanation:

> God…is my witness that I continually remember you and I always ask in my prayers, if perhaps now at last I may succeed in visiting you *according to the will of God*. For I long to see you, so that I may impart to you some spiritual gift to strengthen you, that is, that we may be mutually comforted by one another's faith, both yours and mine. I do not want you to be unaware, brothers and sisters, that I often intended to come to you (*and was prevented until now*), so that I may have some fruit even among you (Romans 1:9-13; emphasis added).

In contrast to the so-called Macedonian Call (Acts 16:9-10), Paul's determination to visit Rome was not dictated by God. The idea for the visit emerged as Paul was developing long-term ministry goals. So he approached the decision-making process the same way he did other non-commanded decisions. First, he adopted spiritual objectives that were based on God's moral will. Next, he devised plans that gave him a strategy for accomplishing his goals.[1] And throughout the process, his planning was accompanied by prayer.

But even as Paul made his plans, he was aware of another dynamic at work. This is evident in his prayer that "now at last I may succeed in visiting you *according to the will of God*." What Paul understood is that his efforts to get to Rome would succeed only if his plans were in harmony with, and brought to fulfillment by, God's *sovereign* will.[2]

By way of definition, the sovereign will is *God's secret plan that determines everything that happens in the universe*.[3] God's moral will concerns what he wants the believer to do; his sovereign will is what he himself is doing. God's moral will is prescribed; his sovereign will is hidden. The former expresses Commander's Intent; the latter effects the Commander's Purpose.

The biblical writers both believed in the reality of God's sovereign will and factored it into their decision making. Their experience and instruction are the basis for the fourth principle of Christian decision making: *When we have chosen what is moral and wise, we must trust the sovereign God to work all the details together for good.*

The Nature of God's Sovereign Will

Before we can understand how God's sovereign will affects our decision making, we have to do some theology. This is not easy. For the doctrine of God's sovereignty takes us beyond the limits of our human comprehension. The outworking of God's sovereign will is a genuine mystery that is not fully explained to us on this side of eternity.[4] Nevertheless, Christian decision makers need to recognize what is revealed about God's sovereign will in Scripture. Then we will be in position to appreciate how Christ's apostles responded to it as they sought to honor God with their decisions.

As we look, then, at the full scope of biblical teaching, we affirm five things about God's sovereign will.[5]

First, it is *certain of fulfillment*. God "does according to his will among the host of heaven and among the inhabitants of the earth; and none can stay his hand or say to him, 'What have you done?'" (Daniel 4:35, ESV). His sovereign will cannot be frustrated by men, angels, or anything else (Acts 2:23; 4:27-28). To Paul's challenging question: "Who resists his will?" we are humbly compelled to agree, "No one!" (Romans 9:6-29).

Second, God's sovereign will is *detailed*—it encompasses all things. The scope of its governance ranges from the intergalactic to the infinitesimal. God's sovereign will ultimately determines the outcome of our plans, the existence of creation, a king's decisions, the result of rolled dice, the believer's experience of suffering, and our personal salvation (James 4:13-15; Revelation 4:11; Proverbs 16:33; 21:1; 1 Peter 3:17; Romans 8:29-30; 2 Thessalonians 2:13-14). In a word, the sovereign God "accomplishes *all things* according to the counsel of his will" (Ephesians 1:11; emphasis added).

Third, God's sovereign will is *hidden*. "Secret things belong to the LORD our God" (Deuteronomy 29:29). Older theologians often referred to God's sovereign will as his "secret will," in contrast to his revealed will in the Bible. God hides his sovereign will until it happens. Would you like to know God's sovereign will for next Tuesday? Read next Wednesday's newspaper. Only God knows what will happen in advance, and he's not telling (Psalm 115:3; Romans 11:33-34; James 4:15).[6]

Causation—Secondary and Ultimate

The revelation about God's sovereign will creates tensions in our minds with other biblical teachings.[7] In the context of decision making, one glaring conundrum emerges: If God sovereignly determines everything that happens, how can human decisions have any meaning? Isn't fatalism the natural, logical conclusion of sovereignty?

The Bible does not concur with such thinking. Scripture presents humans as moral agents who make real decisions for which we are responsible. At the same time, biblical writers affirm God's sovereign control of all things. Without apology, without explanation, without any effort to remove the tension, God's sovereignty and man's responsibility are sometimes asserted side-by-side in Scripture.

> "Jesus the Nazarene...who was handed over by the predetermined plan and foreknowledge of God, you executed by nailing him to a cross at the hands of Gentiles" (Acts 2:22-23).

> "For indeed both Herod and Pontius Pilate, with the Gentiles and the people of Israel, assembled together in this city against your holy servant Jesus, whom you anointed, to do as much as your power and your plan had decided beforehand would happen" (Acts 4:27-28).

We must accept that the nature of causality is complex. Who was responsible for Job's troubles? Was it Satan who moved against Job? Was it the Sabeans and Chaldeans who attacked his servants? Or was Job right when he said, "The LORD gives, and the LORD takes away"? All three are correct. God is the ultimate determiner, but he acts without taking away the causal roles of either humans or Satan (Job 1:12-21).

While I cannot resolve this mystery, the analogy of Commander's Intent points to a way of thinking about it. I can imagine a scenario in which a supreme commander issues orders to his army in the field, including statements of Commander's Intent. But he also has at his disposal secret weapons and special forces that he deploys in operations that parallel those of his main army. The soldiers in the regular army know that these resources exist and that they are being deployed, but they do not know how they are being utilized and they never see them in action. These weapons and forces operate by stealth, moving beneath the radar. Even though conditions in the midst of a battle may create confusion, the knowledge that these resources are operational gives great confidence to members of the regular army. For the engagement of these forces gives assurance of ultimate victory.

Like every analogy, this one is too simplistic. But there is some correspondence to the picture portrayed in Scripture. For instance, God does have special forces that operate, invisibly, alongside human beings. They are called angels, and they are agents that effect God's sovereign will. In at least one instance, the assurance of their presence gave God's servant Elisha the confidence to act decisively to break the siege of the Syrian army. As he explained to his incredulous aide, "Do not be afraid, for those who are with us are more than those who are with them" (2 Kings 6:16 ESV). (The whole story, recorded in 2 Kings 6:8-23 is well worth reading.)

Of course the outworking of God's sovereign will is much more involved and complex than the operations of angelic forces. By his Spirit, God is himself engaged. And his activity is not only parallel to our own, but he is at work ahead of, behind, around, over, under, and through us. Our own behaviors and choices are governed by his sovereign will. And yet, God is not a cosmic puppeteer, and we are not marionettes that jump when he jerks our strings. No one can excuse his (mis)behavior with the assertion, "God made me do it," or "The devil made me do it." A person's decision constitutes a real cause, produces genuine effects, and brings accountability. God is the ultimate determiner, but humans produce real secondary causes with their decisions and actions.

Whether we can put them together in our minds, we must accept both truths. And so we acknowledge a fourth characteristic of God's sovereign will: it is the *supreme* determiner of all things without violating human responsibility.

The Problem of Evil

But there's another conflict—one that is both doctrinal and personal. What connection am I to make between God's sovereign will and all the bad things that happen? If God has determined in advance everything that happens, doesn't that make God responsible for sin?

That was the conclusion reached by the Hebrew prophet Habakkuk when he was informed by God of his plan to use the Babylonians to punish Judah. "You can't do that," Habakkuk protested. "You are too just to tolerate evil…Why do you say nothing when the wicked devour those who are more righteous than they are?" (Habakkuk 1:13).

But he was wrong. Just as God used the evil actions of Joseph's brothers and Potiphar's wife to position Joseph for his role of rescuer, so he used the Babylonians to discipline the Jews. And he did so without compromising his holy character: "The LORD is just in all his actions, and exhibits love in all he does" (Psalm 145:17; Isaiah 6:3). God is truly sovereign, even over sinful acts of men, but he is not himself a sinner (James 1:13).

I went to seminary to find the resolution to this issue. And I thought, as I came to study Romans 9, that I would get my answer. For in that passage, the great theologian Paul unequivocally affirmed God's sovereign control even over the decisions of men like the Pharaoh who resisted Moses. And then Paul raised the question: "You will say to me then, 'Why does he still find fault? For who has ever resisted his will?'" (Romans 9:19). Precisely! And then Paul gave God's answer: "But who indeed are you—a mere human being—to talk back to God? *Does what is molded say to the molder, 'Why have you made me like this?'*" (9:20).

Paul ruled my question out of court. Part of what it means to be submissive to the sovereign will of God is humbly accepting the mystery inherent in those truths that are beyond the capacity of my finite mind to fully understand.

Often, when we reach the limits of our comprehension, we are directed away from our philosophical quandaries (which one day will be resolved, 1 Corinthians 13:12) to the cross. For there we see the ultimate instance of God's sovereign will being effected by wicked humanity: "Jesus the Nazarene…delivered up according to the definite plan and foreknowledge of God, you crucified and killed by the hands of lawless men" (Act 2:22-23 ESV).

The most heinous crime in human history—the willful murder of the Son of God, Israel's Messiah—accomplished the central requirement in God's glorious plan of redemption. If the worst thing that ever happened could also be the best thing that ever happened, everything else is a footnote.

For me, these inquiries are more than an exercise in frustration. They serve the useful purpose of pointing to the fifth characteristic of God's sovereign will: it is *good*. This is the term that stands out in two prominent passages.

> "As for you, you meant to harm me, but God intended it for *a good purpose,* so he could preserve the lives of many people, as you can see this day" (Genesis 50:20; emphasis added).

> And we know that all things work together *for good* for those who love God, who are called according to his purpose (Romans 8:28; emphasis added).

By now, we should recognize that we must have a grown-up conception of "good." The goodness that characterizes the sovereign will of God is good because it accomplishes his good purposes and ultimately brings the greatest glory to him (Ephesians 1:3-14; Romans 11:30-33). The classic passage in Romans 8 does not say that all things *are* good, for they are not. Rather, all things *work together* for good.

This is an important concept for single adults who are facing marital decisions. One of the reasons why individuals wish that God would tell them what to do is that such decisions would then be perfect. If God were to choose my spouse, she would be ideally suited for me (and me for her). We would be true soul mates and we would live happily ever after. I call this "Disney theology." A moment's reflection should expose this idea as a fantasy. (Are you *really* ideally suited for anyone else?) God's approach treats us as adults who live in a real, though fallen, world.

Here's the wonder of God's sovereign will: often our experience of the hard things of life leads to the accomplishment of what is truly good. Not only does sin not negate the sovereign will of God, he actually uses sinful people and difficult experiences (including those problems we bring on ourselves) to produce good outcomes—when we respond properly. This is a persistent theme of Scripture (Acts 14:21-22; Romans 5:1-5; 2 Corinthians 12:7-10; James 1:2-6; 1 Peter 1:3-9; 2:19-24; 3:13-17; 4:12-19; Hebrews 10:32-39; 11:32–12:14).

God can use the hardships we encounter as a result of living in a fallen world to produce at least three benefits:

1. We can gain a deeper experience of God's presence and grace that comes from greater dependence upon him (because of our need).

2. We can grow in spiritual character as we are cured of our self-centeredness and become more like Christ.

3. We can become equipped, through the process of healing and growth, to minister to others who experience similar difficulties.

These are all good purposes accomplished by God's sovereign will.

This does not mean we will always recognize God's good purposes in our difficulties. All our why questions ultimately must have the same answer—our loving God in his sovereign wisdom willed it so. Os Guinness has wisely observed: "As believers we cannot always know why, but *we can always know why we trust God who knows why*, and this makes all the difference."[8]

Our confident expectation is that when we arrive at our eternal destination, we will be able to see what God has wrought through the slings and arrows of our journey. In his classic exposition on "The Adequacy of God," J.I. Packer refers us to Paul's statement in Romans 8:32: "He who did not spare his own Son but gave Him up for us all, will he not also give us all things with Him?" Then he explains:

> Paul is telling us that there is no ultimate loss or irreparable impoverishment to be feared; if God denies us something, it is only in order to make room for one or another of the things He has in mind...The meaning of "He will give us all things" can be put thus: one day we shall see that nothing—literally nothing—that could have increased our eternal happiness has been denied us, and that nothing—literally nothing—that could have reduced that happiness has been left with us. What higher assurance do we want than that?[9]

God's sovereign will is...

1. *Certain* of fulfillment

2. *Detailed*—including all things

3. *Hidden*—it cannot be known in advance

4. *Supreme*—without violating human responsibility or making God the author of sin

5. *Good*—working all things together for God's glory and our good.

The Impact of God's Sovereign Will

As we move from our articulation of a theology of sovereignty to our application of that theology, we find some of the most practical instruction in the Bible. For whatever they may have thought of the tensions between human initiative and divine sovereignty, the biblical writers took both into account in their decision making.[10]

In their efforts to integrate the reality of God's sovereign will into our daily practices, some contemporary Christians fall prey to two fundamental mistakes. Both are the result of faulty inferences from the biblical theology.

Planning

The first conclusion may be expressed in this way: If God controls everything that happens, what point is there in making any plans? From the human perspective, this inference may make sense. But it overlooks an overriding consideration: the Bible tells us that planning is a legitimate and necessary enterprise (Proverbs 16:3; 20:18; 21:5). In the New Testament, James 4:13-16 expounds the biblical viewpoint:

> Come now, you who say, "Today or tomorrow we will go into this or that town and spend a year there and do business and make a profit." You do not know about tomorrow. What is your life like? For you are a puff of smoke that appears for a short time and then vanishes. You ought to say instead, "If the Lord is willing, then we will live and do this or that." But as it is, you boast in your arrogance. All such boasting is evil.

This paragraph contains a rebuke from the apostle James. But he does not condemn planning. The reprimand is directed at arrogant, self-assured presumptuousness that does not recognize God or his sovereignty. The corrective is, "You ought to say instead, 'If the Lord is willing, then we will live and do this or that.'" Once God's sovereign control is properly acknowledged, planning ("we will do this or that") is appropriate.

What James prescribed, Paul practiced. He humbly made both short-range (Acts 20:16; 1 Corinthians 4:19) and long-range plans (Acts 18:21; 19:21; 1 Corinthians 16:5-7). In the end, most of Paul's plans did come to pass, just as most of our well-laid plans are accomplished (Acts 18:21; 1 Timothy 1:3; Proverbs 16:3). Each time a carefully devised plan is successful, two truths are reinforced:

1. the importance of wise, orderly planning

2. the effectiveness of God's sovereign will in accomplishing the plans of men and the purposes of God

The failure of a plan should prompt the believer to reevaluate the strategy and to correct it if appropriate. When Paul encountered roadblocks in his efforts to go to Rome, he did not regard them as indicators that something was wrong with the attempt. All kinds of worthwhile projects have been accomplished (according to God's sovereign will) on the second, third, or fourth effort. Even an unfulfilled plan should remind us that God is working in all things, including our uncompleted or aborted projects, to accomplish his divine purposes for good (Proverbs 20:5; Romans 8:28; 1 Kings 8:18-19).

"Reading Providence"

The second error moves in the opposite direction: If God is in control of all things, I ought to be able to discern what he wants me to do by detecting his hand in my circumstances. This is a pervasive assumption. It is not uncommon to hear Christians say, "The Lord led me to do thus and such." When asked about the means and details of this leading, they list a series of circumstances that pointed the way to God's will. But this approach overlooks an important tenet of the theology we surveyed above: God's sovereign will is hidden. Therefore, we cannot know it in advance.

Nevertheless, people (Christian and non-Christian) persist in looking for signs in their circumstances. (This is sometimes described as "reading providence.") Not only is there no biblical warrant for this approach to decision making, no valid hermeneutic exists for interpreting circumstances. They may be taken to mean almost anything. And circumstances may be cited to justify almost any decision.

Some of the most ingenious stories of interpreted providence come from those who have fallen in love. Every detail is further confirmation to them of God's approval of their relationship. They ask, "What is the chance that out of a hundred people, we would sit next to each other and both be wearing blue?" Sane observers recognize coincidence when they see it. But the infatuated are sure they have been brought together by the hand of God.

Solomon made it clear that attempts to read providence make life confusing at best and futile at worst (Ecclesiastes 1:1-11). Accordingly, biblical characters who attempted to interpret providence failed in their efforts. When a viper clamped onto Paul's hand, the Malta natives concluded he was a murderer and waited for him to swell up or drop dead. When he was unaffected by the venom, they determined that he must be a god. They were sincere, but wrong both times (Acts 28:3-4).[11]

Jesus declared that the disciples were incorrect in attributing a certain man's blindness to sin. Popular opinion erred in thinking that a group of Galileans killed by Pilate were greater sinners than others (John 9:2-3). When the tower of Siloam collapsed killing eighteen victims, the tragedy wasn't proof that they had it coming due to the severity of their sin (Luke 13:1-5). From the human perspective, some things should simply be viewed as happening by chance, just as the Bible does (2 Samuel 1:6; Luke 10:31; see also Ruth 2:3; 1 Kings 22:34). Such events are determined by God, to be sure, but they are not to be viewed as signs to be read.[12]

God's sovereign will is truly hidden. We cannot legitimately read providence as a means of ascertaining what God wants us to do. Circumstances *do* have a role to play in decision making. They frame the context we now live in. The believer should not try to read messages in the circumstances, but judge the wisdom of a course of action in light of the current situation.[13]

So when we ask what bearing the sovereign will of God has on our decision making, the answer has two parts: (1) believers should make plans humbly, remembering that God is the final sovereign determiner of every plan; (2) believers should trust the sovereign God to always work things together for good—even though he does not reveal his sovereign plan ahead of time.

God does not expect us to discern what he has not clearly explained. He requires us only to be moral and wise. He will secretly guide in everything else. Accordingly, the fourth principle of Christian decision making asserts: *When we have chosen what is moral and wise, we must trust the sovereign God to work all the details together for good.*

The Way of Wisdom

1. Where God commands, we must obey.

2. Where there is no command, God gives us freedom and responsibility to choose.

3. Where there is no command, God gives us wisdom to choose.

4. When we have chosen what is moral and wise, we must trust the sovereign God to work all the details together for good.

Our Partnership in Decision Making

What we are able to recognize from an overview of these principles is that *Christian decision making involves a partnership* between the individual and God. In each of the principles, there is a provision by God and a response by the believer.

The human side of the equation is perhaps easier to understand. We are to obey the moral will of God. And we are to make responsible choices according to wisdom when there is no explicit biblical command.

What I want to underscore, by way of conclusion, is the variety of ways that God is engaged with us as we make decisions that are pleasing to him.

First, *he has provided the resources* for making decisions that are acceptable to him. He has revealed his moral will in its totality. He has instructed us in his Word to seek wisdom for making decisions, and he has informed us how to do it. Further, he has given us a new nature that makes obedience of his moral will possible. As a loving Father, he has equipped us with everything we need to make decisions that are pleasing to him (2 Peter 1:3).

Second, as we work through the process of arriving at a decision, *God is continually present and working within us.* The words of Paul remind us that "the one bringing forth in you both the desire and the effort—for the sake of his good pleasure—is God" (Philippians 2:13). Specifically, his grace enables us to trust in him (Acts 18:27); he gives us the desire to obey his will; and by his Spirit, he enables us to keep his commandments

(Romans 8:5-8). So every single act of obedience is proof of God's personal involvement in our lives.

Furthermore, *he gives us wisdom,* when we ask for it, through the channels he has established for our benefit (James 1:5). He also answers our prayers about our decisions. And he brings to successful completion those of our plans that are within his sovereign will.

Along the way, he utilizes the circumstances and the very process of decision making to *change our character and bring us to maturity.* As we depend on him, he blesses our obedience to his moral will and produces his spiritual fruit in our lives.

Finally, he works through our decisions *to accomplish his purposes.*

> **Here, then, is the essence of the Way of Wisdom: Christians are called to make wise decisions within the moral will of God, trusting in the sovereign will of God to accomplish his good purposes in and through us.**

As we turn now to God's design for marriage and singleness, we will see how this partnership is fleshed out in the decisions that single adults make about their marital status.

❖ ❖ ❖

Questions for Reflection and Group Discussion

1. What was the most significant insight you gained from reading this chapter?

2. What are the differences between God's moral will and God's sovereign will?

3. Read the Scripture passages that tell believers how to respond to life's difficulties (page 55). What are some of the "good purposes" of trials in our lives? If it is true that "often our experience of the hard things of life leads to the accomplishment of what is truly good," what are the ramifications of this dynamic for our experiences of singleness and marriage?

4. If Christian decision making "involves a partnership between the individual and God," what is the believer's responsibility and what is God's role?

5. Review the first case history in the prologue concerning Chris and Debbi. Based on what you have read in the chapters in part 1, what counsel would you offer them?

For additional questions, go to www.TheMarriageDecision.com.

Part 2

God's Design for Marriage

Modern Myth 2

Marriage is fundamentally a "couples relationship" designed to meet the sexual and emotional needs of the spouses. Therefore, the key to a successful marriage is to find and marry one's soul mate.

Introduction to Part 2

The Mess We're in and How We Got Here

Once upon a time, not so very long ago, everybody understood what marriage was about. They knew how to go about getting married, and they knew what to expect once they were married.

In the quest to find "the right one," boys asked girls out. Guys were looking for Cinderella; girls were hoping for Prince Charming. They dated, fell in love, went steady, got engaged, and had a wedding. Throughout the courtship process, they tried to resist the temptation to "go all the way" sexually—and many succeeded. Couples were motivated to pursue this ideal of premarital virginity by widely accepted moral and religious prohibitions against sex outside of marriage, reinforced by fear of pregnancy. Just about everyone got married and did so before they were twenty-four years old. The husband went to work as the family breadwinner; the wife took over domestic responsibilities as a homemaker. They started having babies and raising a family.

That was the script when I was growing up. Some call it "the Golden Age of marriage," and just about everyone in America followed it. I'm not suggesting that it was the right script; it was, in fact, flawed. But everyone seemed to be on the same page.

And then, in my teenage years, all hell broke loose. (And I don't think it was just a case of raging hormones.) My peers launched the Sexual Revolution. We were moving through adolescence into young adulthood during the turbulent decade of the sixties when student radicals and hippies conspired to overturn the prevailing standards, worldviews, and lifestyles of the Establishment. The development and accessibility of the Pill secured the freedom undergirding "free love," and a seismic shift occurred in the ethical perspective of a generation. It took a while for the ramifications to permeate the culture, but the dominant viewpoint has shifted 180 degrees in my lifetime. I can recall when there was a stigma attached to nonmarital sex, when girls who put out were considered loose.[1] Out-of-wedlock pregnancy was a cause for shame. Now virginity is stigmatized.

These societal changes erupted suddenly, and they were truly revolutionary. But in retrospect, we can see that their emergence should not have been so surprising. For forces were already at work, like molten magma flowing beneath the surface, that converged to undermine the stability of marriage as an institution.

It's Thomas Jefferson's Fault

One of those forces had been set in motion some two hundred years before. For thousands of years, marriage was viewed as an established institution that contributed to the propagation and stability of the extended family and society at large.[2] Virtually all marriages were arranged by the parents of the prospective husband and wife. The array of choices confronting contemporary singles could not have been even imagined.

Do you remember reading about the Age of the Enlightenment of the eighteenth century? It was a time when people began to challenge the prevailing authority of religious and political institutions. One expression of this challenge took the form of *individualism*.[3] For centuries, order had been preserved by requiring people to subject themselves to the social structures of the day. The survival and advancement of the extended family took precedence over the desires of spouses.

But gradually, a new appreciation for the value of individuals began to take hold. As it was famously propounded in the American Declaration of Independence, "the pursuit of happiness" came to be regarded as an inalienable right of each person. When applied to mate selection, a criterion that had not been given much weight—namely, mutual emotional fulfillment—was now being given consideration.

It didn't happen all at once, but over time the arranged marriage was replaced by individual freedom to choose or refuse a partner. "For the first time in five thousand years, marriage came to be seen as a private relationship between two individuals rather than one link in a larger system of political and economic alliances."[4] This represented a fundamental shift in the way that people perceived the very nature of marriage.

And over time, the role of romantic attraction grew in importance until it became the dominant factor in the choice of a spouse.

This change was surely welcomed, even championed, by marrying couples. But this novel approach to mate selection was not without its drawbacks. In the evolution of courtship patterns in the United States in the twentieth century, this elevation of romantic passion as the primary criterion for choosing a spouse is the first of two changes that *undermined the quality* of mate selection.

The problem with sexual attraction is that it tends to short-circuit objectivity in one's consideration of a prospective husband or wife. As historian Lawrence Stone put it, being in love is "a mild form of insanity, in which judgment and prudence are cast aside, all the inevitable imperfections of the loved one become invisible, and wholly unrealistic dreams of everlasting happiness possess the mind of the afflicted victim."[5]

The second detrimental change was the gradual exclusion of all parties other than the prospective spouses from the selection process. For a long time, even when parents were no longer arranging the marriages of their children, their permission was still required. But by the middle of the twentieth century, parental blessing was becoming optional. The pendulum had swung to the opposite extreme from arranged marriages wherein a whole community was often engaged in the process. Now a couple relies on their limited knowledge and experience with each other to make the most important and far-reaching decision of their adult life. And they often do this without consulting those whose wisdom could provide helpful guidance and even protection. This combination of *isolation* and *impaired judgment* is a prescription for poor decision making.

So the seeds of the Sexual Revolution were sown in the era of the American Revolution. Inevitably, the increasing value of individualism came into conflict with the value of preserving a social institution. Something had to give. And what gave was the cultural consensus that had defined and supported the bonds of marriage.

Who Wants to Live in an Institution?

This change in the way many people came to view the very nature of marriage was a really big deal. It amounted to what some experts describe as the deinstitutionalization of marriage. Social scientists David Popenoe and Barbara Dafoe Whitehead give this explanation:

> The deinstitutionalization of marriage is one of the chief reasons why it is more fragile today. For most Americans, marriage is a "couples relationship" designed primarily to meet the sexual and emotional needs of the spouses. Increasingly, happiness in marriage is measured by each partner's sense of psychological well-being rather than the more traditional measures of getting ahead economically, boosting children up to a higher rung on the educational ladder than the parents, or following religious teachings on marriage. People tend to be puzzled or put off by the idea that marriage has purposes or benefits that extend beyond fulfilling individual adult needs for intimacy and satisfaction. In this respect, marriage is increasingly indistinguishable from other "intimate relationships" which are also evaluated on the basis of sexual and emotional satisfaction.[6]

So what happens when rising individualism prompts couples to make poor marital choices while eroding the stability of marriage as an institution? What happens when spouses, who view marriage primarily as a contract for mutual emotional and sexual satisfaction, find that their needs are not being met? We all know what happens: divorce. Lots of divorce.[7] In the decades following the Sexual Revolution, the divorce rate shot up to 40-50 percent, where it has held steady.[8]

But even that statistic doesn't tell the whole story. Neil Clark Warren gives this assessment:

> The state of marriage is downright alarming in the United States. Nine out of every ten people in the U.S. will marry at least once during their lifetime. But of the 90 percent of Americans who marry, 50 percent will divorce. Another 20 to 25 percent will remain married though miserable. Did you catch that awful statistic? Putting it bluntly, nearly 75 percent of the marriages that take place this year will eventually turn sour. *Seventy-five percent!* (italics his)[9]

Divorce is horrible. The devastation experienced by former lovers whose marital fantasies have convulsed into nightmares is bad enough. But the divorce wars inflict collateral damage on innocent bystanders— the children. Their experience is also traumatic, and the emotional and relational damage they suffer often carries over into subsequent relationships. One of the oft-cited risk factors for marital failure is having divorced parents.[10] That is, the likelihood of divorce is significantly greater for those whose parents are divorced than it is for those who grow up in intact families.[11]

That statistic is ironic because it is the children of divorce who most want to avoid it themselves. Many offspring of divorced parents reason thusly: (1) The primary cause of divorce is marriage; therefore, (2) the surest way to avoid the pain of divorce is to refrain from getting married.[12]

This aversion to marriage creates a dilemma. For the very ones who are committed to avoiding divorce at all costs still desire the intimate relationship with another person that marriage offers. The solution: skip (or at least postpone) marriage and just live together.

This alternative, which was not a live option in my youth, is made possible by one of the results of the Sexual Revolution: cultural standards no longer restrict sexual activity to marriage. Lauren Winner summarizes: "What's unique today is society's utter acceptance of premarital sex. The key change is not simply that premarital sex is common, but that it's good—it's not just normal but normative. Today something is considered wrong with you if you're *not* having sex."[13]

The convergence of these factors has produced the emergence of an alternative to marriage that has exploded in popularity: *cohabitation*. From 1960 to 2006, the number of couples who lived together in the U.S. mushroomed from 430,000 to 5,368,000—a twelvefold increase![14] Cohabitation precedes marriage over 50 percent of the time. This makes cohabitation the most common way couples in America begin life together.[15] This arrangement wherein a couple can experience the sexual and emotional closeness of marriage while maintaining the autonomy of singleness provides an attractive alternative to the permanent commitment that rightly belongs to matrimony.

A Parallel Universe

Now *two* parallel *mating/dating patterns* are practiced in our culture. Some singles continue to pursue a modified version of the traditional courtship and marriage paradigm that prevailed during the first two-thirds of the twentieth century. But an alternative framework that is much less well-defined has arisen alongside the established one. Social historian Barbara Dafoe Whitehead calls it a "Relationships System." It is marked by flexibility and lack of commitment. It accommodates "a variety of intimate pair-bonded arrangements, from marriage to living together to serial monogamy to sexual partnerings without any strings attached."[16] The signature union of this alternative system is cohabitation, which may be viewed as a stage en route to marriage, or a less-committed replacement. (It is not unusual for cohabiting partners to have divergent viewpoints, often without knowing it, on whether their current arrangement is preparatory or ultimate.)

The punch line to our story is this: the environment in which contemporary single adults are making marital decisions is nothing less than chaotic. As I stated in the introduction to the book, the business of marital decision making is probably more complicated today than it has ever been. The traditional rules that used to provide moral guidelines and patterns for male-female relations have been largely abandoned, and no accepted protocol for appropriate behavior has arisen in their place. The result is widespread confusion and frustration.

And this confusion intrudes into specific encounters between men and women. Two individuals who find a spark of interest between them may not know which paradigm is shaping the other's perspective. Figuring it out will take time and may be awkward; not figuring it out could result in seriously clashing expectations (coffee or sex?). Further, the emerging Relationships System lacks the kind of structure from which rules might be constructed. So those who operate within that framework are required to make it up as they go along with every relationship.

So now, single adults encounter a state of affairs that is unique in human history. First, due to the tendency of never-married singles to postpone marriage until their late twenties,[17] the prevalence of cohabitation, and the ongoing epidemic of divorce, the sheer number of unmarried adults in our culture has reached unprecedented proportions. At this writing, "Barely half of all adults in the United States—a record low—are currently married."[18]

Second, the cultural acceptance of cohabitation and its central place in the emerging mating system is also unprecedented. Throughout human history, cohabitation has been taboo. Virtually every society around the world has had a way of marking off the beginning of a marriage relationship, a way of saying, "This man and this woman are going to live together permanently in a relationship that is exclusive, and they are going to relate to one another in ways that they do not relate to any other persons." The message to outsiders has been, "Keep your hands off." The idea that it is permissible for a man and a woman to live together in a sexually active but uncommitted arrangement is radically novel.[19]

And third, there probably has never been a social environment in which unmarried adults are so confused about the appropriate protocols for seeking out a spouse. The mating rituals that have served previous (and non-Western) societies so well are hard to come by, existing only in subcultures with identifiable historical roots.

Such is the social environment in which Christian single adults engage in marital decision making. And we are naïve if we believe that Christians are somehow immune to cultural influences. I am not the only pastor who has been put in the awkward position of responding to wedding requests from cohabiting adults connected with the church.

Christine Colón and Bonnie Field report:

> Sexual activity before marriage is common [in church singles groups], as is a couple living together without the bonds of marriage. Research from the Barna Group[20] shows that 25% of born-again Christians have cohabited, and research from the Centers for Disease Control[21] shows that approximately 45% of unmarried men raised in Fundamentalist Protestant homes are sexually active.[22]

Converging Elements in the Perfect Storm

- Commitment to individualism
- Deinstitutionalization of marriage
- Evaporation of constraints on premarital sex
- Increased sexual temptation due to later age for marriage
- The divorce epidemic
- Increasing acceptance of cohabitation
- Rise of alternative "relationships systems"

Getting Our Bearings

In the face of the buffeting forces that comprise the perfect storm, is it possible for Christian singles to somehow rise above the turbulence—to make good marital decisions with an expectation of favorable outcomes?

One advantage of understanding a problem is that it sometimes points to a solution. If we establish, for instance, that a fundamental cause of our present disarray is our society's determination to reinvent marriage, that conclusion implies that there was once an established, and correct, definition of marriage. It follows that the first step in getting our bearings is to acquire a solid grasp of that definition.

And so we turn our attention to the Creator's divine intent for marriage—and, yes, singleness. In the chapters of part 2 that follow, I'm going to attempt to set out an overview of God's design for marriage.[23]

It may seem ironic that chapters addressed to single adults begin with an exposition of marriage. But within the biblical framework, God's design for singleness can be understood only in reference to marriage—not the other way around. This sequence was affirmed by one of my favorite pastors and Bible teachers, the late Dr. John R.W. Stott.[24] Like Garry, he was a lifelong celibate.[25] In an interview, he was asked, "What is your view of singleness?" His reply:

> I wonder if you would allow me to postpone my answer to this question. The reason is that I think we need to discuss marriage before we discuss singleness…God's general will for his human creation is marriage. We single people must not resist this truth. Marriage is the norm, singleness is the abnorm.[26]

With that provocative observation, we turn to God's design for marriage.

❖   ❖   ❖

Questions for Reflection and Group Discussion

1. As you read the historical narrative in this introduction to part 2, what did you learn that you did not previously know?

2. Of the changes that have occurred in our cultural perceptions of marriage, which ones do you think have the greatest impact on the marital decision making of Christian singles? What is the nature of that impact?

3. If you had the option of choosing between a parentally arranged marriage and a personally arranged marriage, which would you prefer? What are the advantages of each approach? The risks? How could you mitigate the risks of your preferred approach?

4. The stated purpose of this book is to equip unmarried Christians to make wise marital choices according to the will of God. How does the story narrated in this introduction shed light on that purpose?

3

Marriage in a Perfect World

(Genesis 1-2)

Every April, one of the rites of spring that captures the attention of gridiron fans is the Player Selection Meeting of the National Football League (a.k.a. the NFL Draft). Over a two-day span, officials of the thirty-two NFL teams select new players from the ranks of college upperclassmen to join their rosters. The preparations made by each team for this event are prodigious. Countless hours, exhaustive research, millions of dollars, and the undivided energies of the most-talented scouts and executives in football are devoted to making the personnel choices the fortunes of each team will ride on in the years to come.

The decisions involved in player selection are quite complex. The basic objective of each team is to identify and draft the most-talented players to fill specific positions on the squad. The needs of a given team are identified on the basis of an intimate knowledge of the game of football, the style of play determined by the philosophy of the head coach, and the strengths of the veterans already on the roster. The specifications defining the ideal player for each position are very exacting. The trick is to find a match between the profile for each position and the best available candidate—before another team grabs your preferred choice.

"OK, I see where you're going with this," you say to me. "You're making the point that one's choice of a spouse is at least as important as the selection of a football player. So I should give a lot of consideration to the kind of person who would be a good match for me and carefully evaluate potential mates by a thoughtfully crafted set of criteria."

Very good!

But no, that's not my point.

To get to my point we must create an imaginary scenario. Suppose you were offered a job to become director of player personnel for a professional sports team. Let's assume that you are athletically inclined and avidly interested in sports, so this would be a dream job. For the record, you are also energetic and perceptive. Your first assignment would be to oversee the team of scouts and coaches preparing for the upcoming player draft. Even though the task appears daunting, the position is just too good to pass up. Just as you are about to sign on the dotted line, you read one last but extremely important detail in your contract. The sport in question is *cricket*.

Since I'm the one making up this fantasy, you don't get to tear up the contract. Instead, you're intrigued. *Why*, you wonder, *would anyone want to recruit you to this position?* And the very first thing you say to the general manager who has offered you this job is, "I don't know anything about cricket.[1] Why, I wouldn't know a googly from a grubber."

"I know," the general manager says. "We're looking for someone with your energy and perceptiveness, but who will bring the fresh perspective of a novice to the game."

And now we are closing in on my point. If you were hired to draft players for a sport you know nothing about, what is the first thing you would do? Surely you would set about to learn everything you could about that sport. You might go so far as to read the forty-two rules in *The Laws of Cricket*. Only then would you begin to have a clue about what sort of players you should be looking for.

You don't evaluate the players until you understand the game.

So how well do you understand the "game" of marriage?

If you read the preceding introduction to this section, you know that our culture is trying to rewrite the rules. But there is no governing consensus, so the players are engaging in differing versions of the same game without the benefit of umpires. Good luck with that.

My recommendation is that you consult with the Person who invented the game in the first place. Get back to original design. And ask a very basic question: *What is the purpose of marriage?* (What is the point of the game?)

Do you know the answer to that question?

Ironically, in spite of all the diverse ideas on related issues, our culture has a fairly uniform opinion on that point: the purpose of marriage is to meet the sexual and emotional needs of the spouses.[2] And so the *function* of marriage is *companionship*. The success of a marriage is measured in terms of intimacy and mutual satisfaction. Therefore, in the search for player personnel, the primary criterion for evaluation is compatibility. The best teammate will be a soul mate.

Is our society's judgment about the purpose of marriage correct? You probably suspect that the answer is no. But do you know why it is wrong? It's time to consult the Owner's Manual.

The Marriage Symphony

Though I describe the Bible as the Owner's Manual, God's design for marriage is not set out for us in a sequence of laws. It is unfolded in a kind of story—a historical narrative in which adaptations are made to the original prototype. To me it appears to be arranged like a symphony that is presented through four movements. I discuss the first movement in this chapter and subsequent movements in the chapters that follow.

The First Movement: The Institution of Marriage

The opening movement of the symphony, in which marriage is first established, is played out in Genesis 1–2. This movement itself has four parts:

1. The *mission* of the first couple[3] (Genesis 1:26-28)

2. The *creation* of the first couple (Genesis 2:7,18-22a)

3. The *wedding* of the first couple (Genesis 2:22b-25)

4. The *pattern* established by the first couple (Genesis 2:24)

The Mission of the First Couple

In order to understand God's purpose for marriage, we need to recognize his purposes for human beings. For marriage was established to assist the humans in carrying out their mission.

The creation narrative in Genesis is given to us in two installments. Genesis 1 gives an overview of the panorama of creation. Genesis 2 is like a telephoto lens zeroing in on the process by which the man and woman were brought into being.

In the first segment (Genesis 1), we are told that the creation of the first human beings was the culmination of the agenda for the sixth creative day.

> Then God said, "Let us make humankind in our image, after our likeness, so they may rule over the fish of the sea and the birds of the air, over the cattle, and over all the earth, and over all the creatures that move on the earth."
>
> God created humankind in his own image,
> in the image of God he created them,
> male and female he created them.
>
> God blessed them and said to them, "Be fruitful and multiply! Fill the earth and subdue it! Rule over the fish of the sea and the birds of the air and every creature that moves on the ground" (Genesis 1:26-28).

Our introduction to the first couple is given to us in summary fashion that emphasizes their place in the creative order—in relation to other living creatures on the one hand and in relation to the Creator himself on the other. In the context of Genesis 1, it is clear that the formation of human beings is the crowning climax of God's creative work. Not only were they the final living creatures to be set in place on the stage of planet Earth, but they were put in charge of all the others. This delegated responsibility is a central aspect of their mission.

This brief text is a treasure trove of information about God's plan for human beings, and we need to mine it carefully. For while it sets out God's original mission for the first couple, it reveals at least four related facts that should profoundly shape our understanding of the nature of marriage.

First, this passage establishes the unique *identity* of the first couple—they were created as image-bearers—"in the image and likeness" of God (1:26-27). Unlike the other creatures who were made "according to their kinds"[4], the point of reference for humanity (*adam*) was strikingly different.[5] Rather than comparing human beings with other created beings, they are described as somehow corresponding to the Creator.[6]

What does "the image of God" mean? The text doesn't give any further explanation. But we gain some insight from the practices of people who lived in the ancient Near East who used statues to represent deities or kings. These images were thought to embody the *essence* of the beings they represented and to somehow *act* on their behalf.[7]

The likeness that human image-bearers were to reflect was not physical—God is invisible. They were like him in his spiritual nature (Genesis 9:6; James 3:9; Colossians 3:10). And so, in contrast to the other creatures, human beings would have the component parts of personality—intellect, emotion, and volition (the ability to make decisions); they would have moral sensitivities embodied in a conscience; and they would possess a spiritual nature enabling them to relate to God, who is spirit. This was their shared identity.

But, *second*, the first humans were *different* from each other in a distinctive way—their sexuality: "male and female he created them" (1:27; 5:1-2). Of course the other creatures were also made male and female. But the narrator is calling attention to that fact about humankind. The reader is being told that both genders participate fully in the divine image. In fact, it takes male and female together to adequately represent that image and carry out the mission assigned to the image-bearers. And one expected outcome of this sexual differentiation is the reproduction of other image-bearers who will carry on and expand the mission (Genesis 5:1-3).

Third, these sexually differentiated image-bearers were to carry out a shared *role*. They were to function as vice-regents, acting on behalf of the sovereign Creator with delegated authority to rule over every creature (Genesis 1:28). "Be fruitful and multiply!" they were told. "Fill the earth and subdue it!" (Genesis 1:28). As the Creator had brought order to the cosmos, so his image-bearers were to subdue and rule the earth, bringing order to their world as well.[8]

Fourth, in their exercise of this assignment, they must not lose sight of a crucial *priority of allegiance*. That is, their relationship to the Creator was to take precedence over any responsibility they might have to one another. Before they were spouses, they were image-bearing creatures.[9] And their shared assignment entailed recognition of the authority of the King. There was thus a hierarchy of relationship.[10]

What we learn about the first couple from Genesis 1 is:

1. Their *identity*: they were image-bearers who reflected the nature of their Creator.

2. Their *differentiation*: it takes two genders to properly represent God's image and carry out the mission assigned to the image-bearers.

3. Their *role*: they were to rule over the sphere of earth as God's vice-regents.

4. Their *allegiance*: their first and ultimate accountability was not to each other but to their Creator.

From these four factors we are able to identify the essential *mission* of the first couple: *to serve God by advancing his rule over the earth*.[11] The covenant of marriage was established to facilitate the accomplishment of this mission.

The Creation of the First Couple

I wish I could somehow re-create for you the experience of reading the opening chapters of the Bible for the first time. I wish you could revert to a time of childlike innocence where you ask God, "Where did we all come from? How did it all begin?" And he would hand you Genesis 2 and say, "Here, read this." I think that you might be astonished by the story. For one thing, you would be surprised to learn that the first humans were not created simultaneously, in the same way.

The LORD God formed the man from the soil of the ground and breathed into his nostrils the breath of life, and the man became a living being (Genesis 2:7).

The LORD God took the man and placed him in the orchard in Eden to care for and maintain it. Then the LORD God commanded the man, "You may freely eat fruit from every tree of the orchard, but you must not eat from the tree of the knowledge of good and evil, for when you eat from it you will surely die."

The LORD God said, "It is not good for the man to be alone. I will make a companion for him who corresponds to him." The LORD God formed out of the ground every living animal of the field and every bird of the air. He brought them to the man to see what he would name them, and whatever the man called each living creature, that was its name. So the man named all the animals, the birds of the air, and the living creatures of the field, but for Adam no companion who corresponded to him was found. So the LORD God caused the man to fall into a deep sleep, and while he was asleep, he took part of the man's side and closed up the place with flesh. Then the LORD God made a woman from the part he had taken out of the man, and he brought her to the man (Genesis 2:15-22).

In the more detailed narrative of Genesis 2, we learn that God created the man first; then some time later he created the woman. This distinctive process of human formation was intended to convey foundational truths.

The man (Hebrew: *adam*) came into being as God formed his body from the earth (*adama*) and animated him with "the breath of life."[12] Then the Lord God placed the man in the Garden of Eden "to care for it and to maintain it."[13] In the context of this assignment one limitation was given: "you must not eat from the tree of the knowledge of good and evil, for when you eat from it you will surely die" (2:17). Thus the man's moral nature (part of the divine image) was engaged and put to the test. All of this was done before the woman appeared on the scene.

Now the Creator set about to bring the whole project to completion. He begins with an announcement that shocks the reader: "It is *not* good for the man to be alone" (2:18). On the heels of the seven-fold refrain of Genesis 1—"and it was good"—the statement of Genesis 2:18 is alarming. In a perfect world, what could possibly be "not good"? What's wrong with a man-by-himself? At one level, nothing; the man was not defective. But there was something about him that was incomplete. That is a point worth noting: Adam, as he was in himself, was incomplete *by design*. Human beings were not created to be solitary creatures. We have a built in capacity and need for relationship. Adam needed help.

But he didn't know it yet, or so it would appear. So God put him to work assigning names to the animals. And as he explored the animal kingdom, Adam noticed that something was missing—a companion corresponding to him (Genesis 2:20). Only when Adam became aware of his need was such a helper provided.

What sort of help did he need? We are prepared for the explanation by the vocabulary used to describe his companion and by the process by which she was created.

The first thing that reveals the nature of the woman's purpose is the terminology used to describe her: "corresponding companion" (*'ezer kenegdo*). Basically, the word *companion* (traditionally translated "helper") describes someone who comes to the aid of or provides a service for someone.[14] Throughout history, readers of the English text have inferred a kind of inferiority or subservience on the part of the woman. But the error of such a notion is exposed by the fact that the word *helper* in the Old Testament is overwhelmingly used to describe God as Israel's "help" or "strength."[15] Carolyn Custis James notes that the term is masculine in gender and indicates military assistance. Far from describing some sort of junior assistant, *companion* connotes a person of great strength.[16] The wife is not, however, more powerful than her husband. He is the one to whom the assignments were initially given. She comes alongside to give him aid, not to take over.[17]

The descriptive term *corresponding* (often translated "suitable") means "opposite" in the sense of "complementary." So the woman was not a clone of her husband, but an equally human person with complementing differences.[18]

Further clarification of God's intent for the woman is supplied by the manner of her construction. Rather than duplicating the process by which he created the man from the dust of the ground, God used a dramatically different approach—he formed the woman *from* the man. While most English translations speak of a "rib" as the raw material from which she was fashioned, the Hebrew terminology points to the area of the ribs that includes the flesh and muscle as well.[19] What the reader visualizes, then, is the Creator taking a handful of bone and flesh out of Adam's side to use in the construction of Eve.[20] Accordingly, she "corresponded" to him precisely.

The Wedding of the First Couple

The reader of the closing verses of Genesis 2 becomes a witness to the first wedding. The bride was created *from* the man. Then she was presented *to* the man. (The Creator in this instance took his place as "the father of the bride."[21])

> And the rib that the LORD God had taken from the man he made into a woman and brought her to the man. Then the man said,

> "This at last is bone of my bones
>   and flesh of my flesh;
> she shall be called Woman,
>   because she was taken out of Man."

Therefore a man shall leave his father and his mother and hold fast to his wife, and they shall become one flesh. And the man and his wife were both naked and were not ashamed (Genesis 2:22-25 ESV).

Adam's reaction to this wonder of a creation was an "outburst of love poetry"[22] (2:23). Nonpoetic paraphrase: "Wow! She's just like me—only different!" God had provided what Adam had been searching for—a companion perfectly suited to him.[23] The very process of her creation leaves no doubt that the woman shares the very nature of the man as an image-bearer. Nor can there be any question about her essential equality with her husband. It was long ago observed, and oft repeated, that woman was taken not from man's head to be ruler over him, nor from man's foot to be his servant, but from his side to be his companion.[24]

Why was the woman created for the man? In what sense was she a "companion who corresponded to him"? Relational togetherness is clearly one purpose. Because of her company with him, not only would he no longer be solitary, he would not be lonely.

But there's one other way the woman's help was needed. The assignment to "be fruitful and multiply, to fill the earth and subdue it" was not a one-man job. The woman was necessary for the task of reproduction. And by extension, her purpose was to assist Adam in carrying out all of his God-given responsibilities, of which procreation was only one. It is highly significant that the expression of God's determination to "make a companion for [the man] who corresponds to him" (Genesis 2:18) immediately follows (1) God's assignment to Adam to care for and maintain the Garden of Eden (2:15), and (2) God's commandment forbidding him to eat from the tree of the knowledge of good and evil (2:17). Adam needed more than company. *He needed help in fulfilling his responsibilities and keeping God's commandments.*[25]

What we see, then, is that in God's original design there are *two functions* for marriage: relational companionship and vocational partnership. The first couple was given a *relationship* to cultivate and a *work* to share (which included procreation). Dan Allender and Tremper Longman III have captured God's design for husbands and wives with this apt description: *intimate allies.*[26] "Intimate" pertains to the relational dimension; "allies" is a great term for the collaborative partnership envisioned.

(Procreation is such an essential component of the original design of marriage that a strong case can be made for recognizing reproduction as a third function, on a par with relational companionship and vocational partnership. My conclusion that procreation should be subsumed under the broader category of a couple's shared work may appear to minimize its importance in our understanding of what marriage is about. By God's design, most husbands and wives become fathers and mothers. Children are "a gift from the LORD" [Psalm 127:3], and the parental assignment is to strive to raise up "godly offspring" [Malachi 2:15 ESV].)

The Pattern Established by the First Couple

> Therefore a man shall leave his father and his mother and hold fast to his wife, and they shall become one flesh (Genesis 2:24 ESV).[27]

There can be only one first couple, only one first wedding. By the time Genesis was written, grooms and brides were not directly created by God. They came from different families. But God wanted them (and us) to understand the essential connection between the first marriage and all that followed it. The epilogue to this story (2:24) tells us that the first marriage provided a pattern for all others: "Therefore…" (ESV) or "That is why…" (NET, NIV).[28] And here is the main idea: *if a man and a woman are going to become lifelong vocational partners and relational companions, they must forge the strongest possible bond of commitment between them from the very beginning of the marriage.*

This bond consists of two elements: (1) "a man shall leave his father and his mother and hold fast to his wife," and (2) "they shall become one flesh."[29]

Leave and *hold fast* are two very strong verbs. *Leaving* often has the sense of "forsaking" or "abandoning." This is what the husband is told to do with regard to his parents. In point of fact, in Israelite society it was the woman who left her parents and joined her husband, becoming a part of his family's clan.[30] But the husband is given this directive because, even though he might not physically leave his father's household (that is, the extended family), he was to abandon his emotional attachment and loyalty to his parents and transfer them to his wife.[31]

This demand placed upon the husband signals that a new marriage dissolves a bond that would otherwise be the strongest human connection. "For it is the father and the mother whose very bodies give a man his life."[32] The loyalty of marriage, accordingly, is elevated above all other commitments, under God.

Holding fast is the positive complement to *leaving*. The word connotes a very strong bond—much like glue.[33] The verb appears repeatedly in Deuteronomy, where it is translated "remain loyal" or "hold fast," to describe Israel's covenant relationship to Yahweh (4:4; 10:20; 11:22; 13:4; 30:20).[34] In this decisive commitment, husband and wife together establish a new family unit that takes precedence over all others.

Taken together, "leaving and holding fast" (or "leaving and *cleaving*" in the quaint terminology of the King James Version) comprise the *public commitment* to faithfulness that historically has been the function of the wedding. In the progressive revelation of the Old Testament, this commitment came to be defined in terms of a covenant[35] (Proverbs 2:16-17;[36] Ezekiel 16:8; Malachi 2:14-16). A covenant is the most binding of human agreements—stronger in its intent than a contract.[37] The marriage covenant entailed a guarantee of lifelong loyalty that offered security to both parties in the relationship because of the extreme level of commitment promised.

At the moment the marital pledge is made, the marriage is established.[38] But while the groom and bride, by virtue of their public vows, are thereby legally *bound*, they are not yet physically and emotionally *bonded*.[39] For the pattern to be completed, the "leaving and cleaving" must issue in becoming "one flesh." This clearly points to the sexual union in which the couple literally and physically experiences a one-flesh connection.[40] But in this context it is equally clear that the sexual aspect is a sign and expression of a union that joins husband and wife at every level. More than a union of two bodies, "one flesh" connotes the joining of two lives.[41] Hence, the NET Bible translates the statement: "That is why a man leaves his father and mother and unites with his wife, and they become a new family."[42]

So while "leaving and cleaving" speak of the *public covenant* in which faithfulness is promised, "becoming one flesh" refers to the *private consummation* in which faithfulness is kept and expanded into a fully shared life. These two aspects together constitute the essence of marriage.

There is one more aspect to the pattern that was established in the marriage of the first couple. Just as God brought the first husband and wife together and rejoined them into a dynamic unity, so he similarly unites every groom and bride who pledge loyalty to one another in marriage. Jesus said, "What God has joined together, let no one separate" (Matthew 19:6).[43] So when a man and woman commit themselves to be faithful to the covenant of marriage, God is a partner in the creation of their union. And every wedding is a sacred event.[44]

Based on the revelation narrated in Genesis 1–2, John Stott supplies this biblical definition of marriage: "Marriage is an exclusive heterosexual covenant between one man and one woman, ordained and sealed by God, preceded by a public leaving of parents, consummated in sexual union, issuing in a permanent mutually supportive partnership, and normally crowned by the gift of children."[45]

Conclusion

At the beginning of this chapter, I suggested that we consult with the Inventor of marriage and ask a basic question: What is the purpose of marriage? We are now positioned to supply a definitive answer to that question.

> In God's original design, marriage was given to men and women to help them accomplish their shared *mission* of serving God in the advancement of his rule on the earth. This purpose is achieved as the husband and wife fulfill the marital *functions* of vocational partnership and relational companionship.

When we compare this original design for marriage with current conceptions, we immediately recognize two glaring differences.

The first is the *absence of one of the primary functions*—vocational partnership. Our culture is fixated on relational companionship, but has lost the notion of shared work. The reasons for this omission are not hard to fathom. In contrast to the biblical vision, the mission of most contemporary adults is personal fulfillment and happiness. Accordingly, the purpose of marriage could be said to be the advancement of "*my* kingdom."

In this scenario, there is no shared commitment to a higher calling, no unifying mission to which the spouses are committed. In the best marriages operating on this paradigm, husband and wife are mutually supportive of their respective agendas. But if their goals diverge, or if the primary function of relational satisfaction is not fulfilled, the marriage may well become expendable.

The second glaring difference is the *autonomy of married couples* in relationship to God. In the beginning, marriage was designed to operate within the framework of a hierarchy of relational priorities. At the end of the week, human beings are not primary—the Creator is. The first couple rules over all the other creatures, but in relation to God, everything about them has a *secondary* status. He is the Reality to which they bear a likeness. He is the King; they are *vice*-regents. He is the Owner; they are the caretakers. He is the Lawgiver; they are required to obey. In this context, the marital relationship is secondary (and intended to contribute) to the primary allegiance to the King. So long as the husband and wife discharge their shared assignments and carry out their relationship within the framework of a larger mission and a higher loyalty, their marriage fulfills its purpose.

If Adam and Eve had done that, there would be only one movement in the symphony of marriage. But they didn't. The second movement, which introduces and elaborates a discordant theme, was definitely written in a minor key.

Questions for Reflection and Group Discussion

1. What is the most significant insight you have gained from reading this chapter?

2. What was the point of the opening analogy with the sport of cricket? Did this chapter help you to understand the "game" of marriage? What ideas stood out to you?

3. In what ways does the narrative convey the distinctive purposes of the woman? What are they? What kind of help did the man need?

4. What are the component parts of marriage as instituted by God? Why is it important to understand a biblical definition of marriage?

5. On a sheet of paper (or computer file), complete each of the following sentences:

   • According to contemporary culture, the purpose of marriage is…

   • According to God's design, the purpose of marriage is…

   How would these divergent points of departure affect the process of mate selection on the part of a single adult?

6. Dedicate some pages of a journal (or computer file) to the creation of a profile of a prospective mate. Based on what you learned in this chapter, what qualities would you look for in a potential spouse? (Note: You will be adding content to this profile as you respond to future chapters.)

For additional questions, go to www.TheMarriageDecision.com.

4

The Marring and Makeover
of Marriage

❦

When I was very small, my father was a student at Dallas Theological Seminary, and we lived with my grandparents in Fort Worth. We didn't have much money, so treats were simple and rare. One of the best was an occasional visit to a drive-in on Rosedale Avenue where they served root beer in a frosted mug.[1] That root beer was the best thing I have ever tasted. The combination of froth, bouquet, carbonation, and frostiness created a taste sensation that can only be described as exquisite. On my list of life's simple pleasures, it's near the top.

This supreme enjoyment came to me when I was about four years old. When I was five, we moved to Kansas and the visits to the root beer stand faded away. So did the drive-in itself. And to this day I have not found any place else that serves that particular recipe—the quintessential root beer.

It's not that I haven't tried. So far A&W comes closest—probably because of the mugs. My children, for whom the fabled elixir has become part of the family lore, have scoured the country in search of the real thing. I get root beer for my birthday and root beer for Christmas—brands from the East Coast and microbreweries. With each new candidate we are always hopeful, always disappointed. I don't know what they want more—to see the look on my face when we strike gold or to taste the stuff themselves.

The eerie thing is that, half a century later, I still have a memory of perfection. An aroma or an experience will activate some part of my brain where flavors are stored and I'll catch a whiff of the brew. I can't really conjure it up at will, but I believe that if I were to taste the original again, I would recognize it. But until that happens, those mental sensations will evoke a nostalgic recollection that creates a kind of ache in my taste buds.

I think that a lot of people have similar feelings about marriage. We have a kind of memory of what it once was. We read Genesis 1–2, and we remember what it could have been. Sometimes, in real life, we feel like we've gotten close to the original, a glimpse of paradise, a whiff of Eden. But there is an ache for what has been lost, a longing for what is yet to be.

Yes, the pristine perfection of marriage as originally designed has been lost. It was lost when the first couple rebelled against the Designer and aborted their mission. When humanity fell, marriage fell. And nothing's been the same since.

The Fall of mankind is a painful part of the story. It ruined the ideal relationship that once was. But by the grace of God, it didn't completely ruin everything. Even in a fallen world, marriage can be good, and I can enjoy root beer. And the Fall didn't disrupt the ultimate purposes of God. But we need to understand some of what happened if we are to align ourselves with God's design for marriage in this marred environment.

The Second Movement: The Corruption of Marriage

You are perhaps familiar with the catastrophe the second movement begins with. In their disobedience of God's command to refrain from eating the forbidden fruit (as recorded in Genesis 3:1-7), the couple violated every component of their assignment. Instead of ruling over the creatures, they submitted to one—the serpent. Instead of helping her husband, the woman contributed to his downfall. Instead of trusting in God's provision, they believed the lie that he was holding out on them. Instead of being satisfied with being like God as image-bearers, they became dissatisfied with their station and lusted for more. Instead of serving him through their obedience, they rebelled.

And, as God had promised, they moved from the realm of life into the realm of death. The deadly consequences began to unfold in short order.

> Then the man and his wife heard the sound of the LORD God moving about in the orchard at the breezy time of the day, and they hid from

the Lord God among the trees of the orchard. But the Lord God called to the man and said to him, "Where are you?" The man replied, "I heard you moving about in the orchard, and I was afraid because I was naked, so I hid." And the Lord God said, "Who told you that you were naked? Did you eat from the tree that I commanded you not to eat from?" The man said, "The woman whom you gave me, she gave me some fruit from the tree and I ate it." So the Lord God said to the woman, "What is this you have done?" And the woman replied, "The serpent tricked me, and I ate" (Genesis 3:8-13).

To the woman he said,
"I will greatly increase your labor pains;
with pain you will give birth to children.
You will want to control your husband,
but he will dominate you."[2]
But to Adam he said,
"Because you obeyed your wife
and ate from the tree about which I commanded you,
'You must not eat from it,'
cursed is the ground thanks to you;
in painful toil you will eat of it all the days of your life.
It will produce thorns and thistles for you,
but you will eat the grain of the field.
By the sweat of your brow you will eat food
until you return to the ground,
for out of it you were taken;
for you are dust, and to dust you will return."
(Genesis 3:16-19)

And the Lord God said, "Now that the man has become like one of us, knowing good and evil, he must not be allowed to stretch out his hand and take also from the tree of life and eat, and live forever." So the Lord God expelled him from the orchard in Eden to cultivate the ground from which he had been taken. When he drove the man out, he placed on the eastern side of the orchard in Eden angelic sentries who used the flame of a whirling sword to guard the way to the tree of life (Genesis 3:22-24).

Before the fall, the first couple enjoyed unhindered communion with their Creator. The greatest blessing Adam and Eve experienced was not their marriage; it was their fellowship with God. This blessing was forfeited by their rebellion. The worst thing that happened to them was their expulsion from his presence (Genesis 3:23-24). As exiles, they were cut off from the Life-Source they should have relied on to carry out their assigned responsibilities. To repeat, *this is the worst thing that could happen to human beings.* No other problem even comes close.

Before the Fall, the first couple enjoyed the benefits of the marital functions designed by God: vocational partnership and relational companionship. Now every aspect of the marriage relationship was corrupted.

- *Companionship*: the intimacy of a one-flesh relationship was immediately fractured by alienation and blaming (3:12). Subsequently, spousal harmony was replaced by a competitive power struggle in which the stronger dominates the weaker (3:16).

- *Procreation*: childbirth will now be attended by pain and sorrow (3:16).

- *Shared vocation*: the domain they were to rule over now rebels against them, turning meaningful labor into life-sapping toil (3:17-19).

Before the Fall, the first couple enjoyed the dignity of participating in a divinely granted mission that gave meaning and significance to their work. They had been vice-regents in charge of everything else. Now they were unemployed, homeless nomads. And their lives were filled with regret and frustration as their efforts were turned toward the mission of survival—a mission doomed to ultimately fail.

As the themes of this second movement repeat through the generations to follow, they haunt the soul like the strains of a funeral dirge. The shadow that sin cast over marriage is all too apparent in the subsequent history recorded in Genesis where marital abuse is a recurring motif: "the violence, egotism and polygamy of Lamech (4:19, 23-24); the cowardice of Abram (12:10-20; 20:1-18) and Isaac (26:6-11); the rivalry and heartache of Sarai in relation to Abram and Hagar (16:1-6); the deceiving of Isaac by Rebekah and Jacob (27:5-29); Shechem's rape of Dinah (34:1-31); and Judah's disgraceful relations with his daughter-in-law Tamar (38:13-18)."[3] Indeed, the heavy-handed subjugation of women by men and the manipulative intrigues of scheming wives figure prominently in the centuries-long soap opera that comprises the history of marriage.

As you reflect on the nature of marriage and contemplate the possibility of finding a mate, you must not regard this invasion of our world by sin and death as a matter of passing theological or historical interest. The infection of sin extends to you and any future spouse (Romans 3:23; 5:12; Ephesians 2:1-2). If you marry, the person you marry will be a sinner. And the person that he or she marries will be a sinner. That's two sinners in close proximity to each other for long stretches of time. Your spouse will undoubtedly have many fine qualities, as do you. But you will need to pay attention to the fact that *you are both sinners*. (Will it help if I repeat myself?)

What's the big deal about sin? Broadly speaking, there are two problems: (1) Our acts of sin disqualify and disconnect us from fellowship with God (Colossians 1:21); and (2) our condition of sinfulness corrupts our character, infecting us with chronic self-centeredness (Jeremiah 17:9; Mark 7:20-23). In our foolishness, we live out our commitment to making life work on our own terms (Psalm 14:1; Isaiah 53:6). Our spiritual death (separation from God) produces social death (separation from others) and psychological death (separation from ourselves).

So even if you and yours have an accurate grasp of the purpose and nature of marriage (as described in chapter 3), you will inevitably experience frustration (at least) in your efforts to make it work. Because of the sinful condition of both spouses, every marriage has within it the seeds of its own destruction.

That's not to say that all married people are perpetually miserable. The image of God was damaged, but it was not destroyed. Husbands and wives are still capable of creating meaningful partnerships and enjoying loving companionship.[4] But the struggle, so glaringly absent from pristine Eden, is real. Too many marriages don't survive the conflict, and it tinges the best of them.

The Third Movement: The Redemption of Marriage

In the unfolding Symphony of Marriage, the third movement opens with all the hope attending the birth of a Baby, and all the promise attached to fulfilled prophecy regarding a virgin mother.

> An angel of the Lord appeared to [Joseph] in a dream and said, "Joseph, son of David, do not be afraid to take Mary as your wife, because the

child conceived in her is from the Holy Spirit. She will give birth to a son and you will name him Jesus, because he will save his people from their sins." This all happened so that what was spoken by the Lord through the prophet would be fulfilled: *"Look! The virgin will conceive and bear a son, and they will call him Emmanuel,"* which means "God with us" (Matthew 1:20-23).

The Good News is that even though we have turned away from God, he has not abandoned us. In the person of his Son, God has come to us—to be with us ("Emmanuel") and to deal decisively with our problem of sin ("Jesus" = "Yahweh saves"). The New Testament contains the third movement in the story of marriage because there has been another dramatic development in human history: Jesus has come!

Just as the establishment of marriage occurred within the larger framework of the original creation, so the rehabilitation of marriage is but one aspect of a more encompassing enterprise undertaken by God. Jesus did indeed bring about changes in the status of marriage. But to fully appreciate how things are different, we need to see those modifications in the context of the larger campaign.

Extreme Makeover, Cosmic Edition

If someone were to ask you, "What is God's current project in the universe?" what would you say? The answer may not be obvious, but we have been told. (I gave a hint in the heading.) God is currently working to bring all things in heaven and earth under one head, namely, Christ (Ephesians 1:10). *He is acting to restore what was ruined* (Acts 3:21; Romans 8:20-21) *and to reconcile what was alienated* (Colossians 1:19-20; 2 Corinthians 5:17-19)—*especially human beings* (Ephesians 1:3-14). The end result of this enterprise will be the establishment of a redeemed community of people inhabiting a renewed, perfected earth, dwelling in eternal fellowship with and service to him (Revelation 21–22). This is the current project, and when it is accomplished it will take our breath away.

Like most remodels, this venture is being carried out in stages. In Phase One, God dealt decisively with the core problem of sin. This work was done by Christ.

> For God was pleased to have all his fullness dwell in the Son and through him *to reconcile all things to himself* by making peace through the blood

of his cross—through him, whether things on earth or things in heaven (Colossians 1:19-20, emphasis added).

In order to reestablish the connection between man and God (severed by our transgression and guilt) and restore the marred image of God in man's nature (caused by our corruption), the penalty of sin had to be paid. This was accomplished through Christ's atonement—his sacrificial death on the cross validated by his resurrection and exaltation.[5]

Phase Two is the creation of the community of faith, the church, to embody the rule of God and to recruit others to repent and join the fellowship of faith (Acts 2). Those who are reconciled to God through faith in Christ become "new creatures" (2 Corinthians 5:17). Not only are we born again, but we undergo a process of renewal by which we are progressively transformed by the Holy Spirit into the *likeness* of our Creator (2 Corinthians 3:18; 4:16; Colossians 3:9-10; Titus 3:5). Then we are deputized as ambassadors of reconciliation, taking the invitation of God's gospel to the rest of the world: "Be reconciled to God!" (2 Corinthians 5:19b-20). If you hear echoes of the activity of the original creation in this description, then you are correctly recognizing that this project is about the *re-creation* of what was so damaged by the Fall.

So how does marriage fit into this scenario? Just as the marital covenant was given to facilitate the mission of image-bearers in the original creation, so it has been retrofitted to advance the mission of disciples in the re-creation. To this end, through his example, instruction, and sacrifice, Jesus has made two major contributions to the transformation of marriage during the third movement: (1) he has modified the status of marriage itself; and (2) he transforms believing spouses, enabling them to fulfill the functions of Christian marriage and accomplish its purpose for the sake of the kingdom.

Marriage: From Obligatory to Optional

When Jesus launched his public ministry he rocked his world. "Amazed" is the word the Evangelists use to describe the reaction of the people.[6] But one aspect to Jesus' career that must have been striking to his contemporaries receives little notice in the record: Jesus never married! His determination to carry out his ministry as a single man was the first flare fired across the bow of Jewish culture signaling a major shift in God's intent for marriage in a fallen world.

In the beginning, prior to the Fall, marriage was the only human social institution in existence. In the generations that followed, it retained a central place in the structure of societies as the nuclear family expanded into an extended family, and then into clans, tribes, and nations.

When God inaugurated his plan to redeem fallen mankind, he chose a man, Abraham, and promised that he would make from him and his offspring a great nation through which he would bless the world (Genesis 12:1-3). Throughout the era of the Old Covenant, the people of God were biologically defined. The advancement of the kingdom and the maintenance of the messianic line occurred through physical procreation. Accordingly, Israelite men and women were virtually *obligated to marry* and beget children. The genealogical record the New Testament opens with (Matthew 1:1-17) underscores the significance of the family connections through which God's covenant was maintained.

But when the One who fulfilled the promises to Abraham was born, and the Messianic Goal to which generations of Jewish couples had contributed was accomplished, things began to change. And Jesus' abstention from marriage was a stunning first clue that the status of marriage in the scheme of God's social order was under reconstruction.

Jesus' viewpoint was made explicit by the things he said. One of his most provocative statements was made in the context of an encounter with some religious opponents.

> Then some Pharisees came to him in order to test him. They asked, "Is it lawful to divorce a wife for any cause?" He answered, "Have you not read that from the beginning the Creator *made them male and female,* and said, 'For this reason a man will leave his father and mother and will be united with his wife, and the two will become one flesh'? So they are no longer two, but one flesh. Therefore what God has joined together, let no one separate." They said to him, "Why then did Moses command us *to give a certificate of dismissal and to divorce her?"* Jesus said to them, "Moses permitted you to divorce your wives because of your hard hearts, but from the beginning it was not this way. Now I say to you that whoever divorces his wife, except for immorality, and marries another commits adultery" (Matthew 19:3-9).

Jesus' disciples, who were often a little slow on the uptake, immediately grasped the implications of this pronouncement. "If this is the case of a husband with a wife," they emoted, "it is better not to marry!" (Matthew 19:10). If a man were to unwittingly wed a contentious woman (Proverbs 21:9), he could be trapped in an intolerable situation from which there was no escape.

In his startling reply, Jesus agreed with their conclusion, but submitted a different reason.

> He said to them, "Not everyone can accept this statement, except those to whom it has been given. For there are some eunuchs who were that way from birth, and some who were made eunuchs by others, and some who became eunuchs for the sake of the kingdom of heaven. The one who is able to accept this should accept it" (Matthew 19:11-12).

This declaration constitutes an announcement by Jesus that, in the kingdom he is inaugurating, it is appropriate for some of his disciples to follow his precedent in remaining unmarried in order to devote themselves more completely to the advancement of God's rule. We will explore the significance and ramifications of this statement in more detail in chapter 7, but for now we note this striking implication: the marital state, which had formerly been regarded as *obligatory,* has become *optional.* In Christ's kingdom, there are now two conditions in which his disciples may legitimately serve him—married or unmarried.

Marriage: From Primary to Secondary

The reasons for this change emerge in other statements Jesus made about his "family" relationships.

> Someone told him, "Look, your mother and your brothers are standing outside wanting to speak to you." To the one who had said this, Jesus replied, "Who is my mother and who are my brothers?" And pointing toward his disciples he said, "Here are my mother and my brothers! For whoever does the will of my Father in heaven is my brother and sister and mother" (Matthew 12:47-50).

> "Do not think that I have come to bring peace to the earth. I have not come to bring peace but a sword. For I have come to set *a man against his*

father, a daughter against her mother, and a daughter-in-law against her mother-in-law, and a man's enemies will be the members of his household.

"Whoever loves father or mother more than me is not worthy of me, and whoever loves son or daughter more than me is not worthy of me" (Matthew 10:34-37).

And Peter said, "Look, we have left everything we own to follow you!" Then Jesus said to them, "I tell you the truth, there is no one who has left home or wife or brothers or parents or children for the sake of God's kingdom who will not receive many times more in this age—and in the age to come, eternal life" (Luke 18:28-30).

In contrast to the physical family that is entered by means of natural birth, Jesus came to establish a spiritual family that one enters by means of regeneration through faith (John 1:11-12; 3:3; Galatians 3:7,26; 1 Peter 1:3-4), in which all distinctions of race or tribe are transcended (Ephesians 2:11-19; Colossians 3:11). "More important than physical ancestry—who one's parents are—is one's spiritual ancestry—who one's heavenly Father is (e.g. Luke 3:7-8; John 8:31-59)."[7] Accordingly, loyalty to Christ supersedes all family connections.

This does not mean the extinction of marriage. It does mean that marriage has been relocated from the place of primacy in human relationships to a secondary level of status within the larger framework of the family of Christ, the kingdom of God.[8] This, in turn, means that God's design for marriage must be understood in accordance with the role it plays in the fulfillment of the mission and purposes of the church.[9]

Marriage: A Ministry Institution

In the first movement of the symphony, we were able to discern the connection between the mission of the image-bearers on the one hand and the functions and purpose of marriage on the other. When we come to the third movement, there is a striking symmetry between the features of the original creation and those of the re-creation undertaken by God through Christ and the Spirit.

Let's start with mission. In the Sermon on the Mount, Jesus contrasted the priorities and attitudes of disciples with those of the Gentiles—the unconverted pagans. The latter are obsessed with getting their own needs met (sound familiar?) and are therefore anxious. Disciples, by contrast, are to trust in the provisions of their heavenly Father. And they are to reflect this confidence by a life-shaping focus: "But above all pursue [God's] kingdom and righteousness, and all these things will be given to you as well" (Matthew 6:33).

The words "above all" point to an ultimate priority: for the disciple of Jesus, the dominant preoccupation is to be the advancement of Christ's rule and righteousness in one's own life (spiritual growth) and in one's own world (ministry). That seems to be a succinct statement of our mission.

Now what are the functions of the spiritual family of Christ through which this mission is to be executed? I believe these are well-summarized in the Great Commandment and the Great Commission.

> Now one of the experts in the law came and heard them debating. When he saw that Jesus answered them well, he asked him, "Which commandment is the most important of all?" Jesus answered, "The most important is: 'Listen, Israel, the Lord our God, the Lord is one. Love the Lord your God with all your heart, with all your soul, with all your mind, and with all your strength.' The second is: 'Love your neighbor as yourself.' There is no other commandment greater than these" (Mark 12:28-31).

> "Therefore go and make disciples of all nations, baptizing them in the name of the Father and the Son and the Holy Spirit, teaching them to obey everything I have commanded you. And remember, I am with you always, to the end of the age" (Matthew 28:19-20).

These two functions correlate well with those given to the first human family. The Great Commandment (love) corresponds to the function of *relational companionship*; the Great Commission (make disciples) matches up with the assignment of *vocational partnership*. And in both cases, one's allegiance to Christ is primary.

What we find, then, when we compare the features of the first movement (original creation) with those of the third movement (new creation) is both continuity and change.

GOD'S DESIGN FOR MARRIAGE

	In a Perfect World (Genesis 1–2)	In a Fallen World (NT)
Ruler:	Creator God	Redeemer God (Re-Creator)
Environment:	Pristine	Fallen/Hostile
Participants:	Image-bearers	Disciples
Human Nature:	Innocent	Fallen/Redeemed
Family	Physically related	Spiritually related
Purpose:	To facilitate the mission (through the implementation of the functions)	To facilitate the mission (through the implementation of the functions)
Mission:	To serve God by advancing his rule throughout the world	To serve God by advancing his rule in my life and throughout my world
Functions:	Relational companionship (RC) Vocational partnership (VP) (including procreation of godly offspring)	RC and VP in service to the Great Commandment and the Great Commission
Priority of Allegiance:	A prior and higher commitment to the lordship of the Creator	A prior and higher commitment to the lordship of Christ
Placement in Institutional Hierarchy:	Primary	Secondary (part of the church)

Summary

While the original design for marriage still has validity in a fallen world (Matthew 19:4-6), Jesus has retrofitted the institution to serve his larger campaign to reconcile and restore all things to God. Two changes are noteworthy.

First, since the primary human institution through which Jesus is carrying out his program is the church, marriage is now regarded as a subset (alongside singleness) of that spiritual family. Accordingly, marriage is a *ministry institution* contributing to the mission of the church.

Second, the mission of advancing God's kingdom now focuses on the *spiritual* dimension of his rule not only externally (in the world) but also internally (within the individual disciple). The physical reign of God on earth will be established by Christ's triumphant return.

Earlier I said that Jesus has made *two* major contributions to the transformation of marriage during the third movement. We have just seen how he modified the status of marriage itself. Next we will consider the ways he works in the lives of believing spouses, enabling them to fulfill their assignments for the sake of the kingdom.

Questions for Reflection and Group Discussion

1. What is the most significant insight you have gained from reading this chapter?

2. How does sin damage marriages? What are the ramifications of the Fall for single adults who are contemplating marriage?

3. How did the coming of Jesus change how we are to regard the institution of marriage?

4. Take some time to track the ways that God's design for marriage has been adapted to life in a fallen world. As you consider the chart on page 100, at what points does God's design differ from the perspectives of our culture?

5. Of what value is this chart for Christian singles who are considering marriage?

6. Based on what you learned in this chapter, make appropriate additions or amendments to your "Profile of a Prospective Spouse."

For additional questions, go to www.TheMarriageDecision.com.

5

Balancing Marriage

❦

just made a tuna salad sandwich for lunch. It was pretty good. Turns out, I have enough fixin's left over to make another one tomorrow. But that's not what I intended to do.

My recipe for tuna salad blends three ingredients: tuna (from a can), mayo, and sweet pickle relish. Tuna, all by itself, is too…*something* (salty? fishy? tuna-y?). The relish is required to offset the overpowering flavor of the tuna. The mayo contributes more to consistency than taste. The trick is to apply the right quantities of each ingredient to the mix to create an appetizing combination. But I put in too much relish. There was nothing to do but open another can of tuna. Then add more mayo…and just a little relish. And voila! Just right (or close enough).

When it comes to combining complementary opposites, it's not always easy to strike the right balance.

But that's what God did, in the beginning. When the Creator launched humanity, he started with a single man to whom he gave assignments. Then, because the man needed help, God fashioned a woman to be his "corresponding companion." Within the shared life of marriage, the original pair was given a *work* to share and a *relationship* to cultivate.

But notice, when God provided a helper, he didn't just clone the man. (He didn't just add more tuna.) He created a female human who had built-in strengths and capabilities that were different from those of the male. Modern-day researchers have documented all sorts of contrasts between men and women. But within the framework of marriage, one dissimilarity stands out: "You'll always find exceptions to the rule, but research and experience consistently point to a fundamental and powerful distinction between the sexes: Men focus on *achievement*, women focus on *relationship*."[1] It can hardly be coincidental that the innate gender differences recognized to this day complement each other in ways that correspond to the divinely ordered functions of marriage.

But now, as we have noted, the natural balance that existed in Eden between labor and companionship has been corrupted by the Fall. Throughout human history, one of those functions has been predominant at the expense of the other. And we have seen the pendulum swing from one extreme to the other. We started out with too much tuna; now we've got too much relish. And when the recipe is out of whack, the consequences are distasteful.

For centuries, vocational partnership (a *work* to share) dominated society's conception of marriage. From antiquity until the eighteenth century AD, mate selection was based more on physical strength, skills, and material assets than attractiveness or affection. This was due in part to the curse pronounced upon our physical environment (Genesis 3:17-19), requiring countless families to struggle for survival. But it was reinforced by patriarchal social structures (Genesis 3:16b) in which the authority of the husband/father over his wife and children was virtually absolute. The head of the household was in charge of a kin-based labor force that worked together to eke out a living or, under better circumstances, to advance the economic and social standing of the family. Companionship took a backseat to productivity or was sought (especially by men) outside the confines of marriage.

The conception of marriage as an economic unit profoundly affected priorities in mate selection. "Few individuals of modest means had either the inclination or the opportunity to seek a soul mate. What they really needed was a work partner."[2] This perspective prevailed into the mid-1800s in the American West, as illustrated by this ad placed by a bachelor in an Arkansas newspaper:

> Any gal that got a bed, calico dress, coffee pot, and skillet, knows how to cut out britches, can make a hunting shirt, and knows how to take care of children, can have my services till death parts both of us.[3]

Today, by contrast, through the historical processes narrated in the introduction to this section, Western culture has moved to the opposite extreme—viewing marriage almost exclusively in terms of *companionship*. While the former imbalance perpetuated male domination, the current over-correction has produced its own detrimental consequences, including the destabilizing of marriage as a social institution.

The Christian single adult who is considering marriage should pay attention to two points. First, the cultural influences on mate selection today are the polar opposite of those shaping the marital landscape for centuries previous. The social environment in which you make your decisions is dramatically different from that of prior generations. But second, both extremes represent a distortion of the harmony between work and love that characterized the original marriage. Apart from God, fallen humanity just can't seem to get it right.

The calling of married Christians during the third movement is to substantially reestablish the original balance that existed between marital functions in ways that are appropriate to our changed (fallen) environment. To this end, Jesus has retrofitted the design of marriage (as spelled out in the previous chapter). And he transforms redeemed husbands and wives to carry out their respective roles in this endeavor.

This renovation entails two steps. First, we must correct our culture's distorted preoccupation with the quest for the ideal soul mate. And second, we must properly restore the dimension of vocational partnership to a Christian picture of marriage.

Debunking the Soul-Mate Myth

I don't know when the term *soul mate* became the vocabulary-of-choice to describe a potential spouse, but it has become the nearly universal designation for the desired ideal.[4] In the landmark survey conducted by the Gallup Organization for the National Marriage Project of Rutgers University in 2001, 94 percent of never-married single adults, ages twenty to twenty-nine, agreed that "when you marry you want your spouse to be your soul mate, first and foremost." Furthermore, 88 percent believe that "there is a special person, a soul mate, waiting for you somewhere out there"; and 87 percent fully expect to find that special someone when they are ready to get married.[5] (I wish a follow-up survey could be conducted with those very same people to see what they think today.)

So what is a soul mate? It is seldom defined. Young and Adams are no doubt correct in their recognition that it means "different things to different people. Most assume that a soul mate is the one 'true love' who represents the missing half of your soul; the special one who automatically and infinitely knows, loves, accepts, and adores you." They go on to label this conception as a "fantasy," an "illusion," a "false hope that actually works against people in their efforts to create a healthy, lasting, committed relationship."[6]

Neal Clark Warren noticed the prevalence of the term and, after considerable research, "discovered that 'soul mate' was not only a universal term to which everyone can relate, but that everyone is looking for a soul mate when considering a person for a long-term match." So he and his team at eHarmony adopted the term and gave it their own meaning: "At eHarmony when we speak of soul mates, we are talking about two people who enjoy broad-based compatibility; they fit together."[7]

I confess to a certain aversion to *soul mate* as an apt description of the sort of person a single Christian adult should be hoping to find as a spouse. My reluctance stems from connotations of terminology that are not biblically valid. I fear that the concept of a soul mate may inadvertently lead people to perceptions and conclusions that are actually counterproductive to wise decision making. Words mean something, and we have to be careful how we use them. So here are some of my concerns.

The first misleading implication of *soul mate* is the idea that there is only one such person out there for each individual—as was the case for Adam and Eve. But that notion is based more on Disney theology than biblical theology. In chapter 1, we saw that the Bible's guidelines for decision making presume that there are potentially multiple candidates who would make an acceptable mate (see 1 Corinthians 7:39).

In their book, ironically titled *The One*, authors Ben Young and Samuel Adams agree that several possible partners exist for the unmarried single. They explicitly debunk the notion that there is only one true soul mate per person:

> This assumption will help put you in an endless and frustrating quest for that one special person. As long as you hang on to the illusion that your "missing half" exists out there somewhere, you'll be distracted and miss out on many other potential relationships...Of course, when it comes to marriage, there should be many potential soul mates and your goal would be to wisely choose one out of many potential candidates.[8]

Neal Clark Warren concurs. In an article titled "Is There One Perfect Person for You?" Warren speculates that "there are five hundred—probably more—women with whom I could be extremely happily married."[9]

Second, the picture that many have of a soul mate is a fairy tale fantasy of the ideal mate. "If I can find my perfect match," the reasoning goes, "we will live happily ever after." This scenario puts the onus for the marital outcome on the other person being the right sort of partner. Duke professor Stanley Hauerwas injects a dose of reality with Hauerwas's Law: "You always marry the wrong person." Even the most compatible mate will be flawed—as are you! Instead of seeking to be matched to the ideal person, each individual should determine to become a godly spouse who will build up the soul of another. "The adventure of marriage is learning to love the person to whom you are married."[10]

A different version of the ideal mate fallacy looks for a partner who will "complete me." But this requirement puts too great a burden on the other person and misconstrues the purpose of marriage. *Complementing* the other person is not the same as *completing* them. Only God can do that. It is OK to say that a husband and wife are each half of a marriage—a one-flesh relationship. But they are not each other's "other half." The practical consequence of this way of thinking is that it can actually destabilize the marriage. At the eventual point where the partner fails to complete me, that person may well become expendable. Instead of working on the problems that inevitably arise in a marriage in order to make the relationship stronger, the solution that is often explored is to find a new (better) soul mate.

Finally, the underlying premise of the search for a soul mate seems to be that marriage is fundamentally an arrangement for getting one's sexual and emotional needs met. On this scenario, the ultimate goal of marriage is the mutual happiness of the participants.[11] But to make mutual happiness the primary purpose for marriage is to run the risk of idolatry. And idols inevitably fail to deliver on their genie-like promises.

Toward the beginning of his writing ministry, Larry Crabb gave this now-classic description of how this misconception often plays out. Imagine a bride and groom, each expecting the other to fulfill their needs, reciting their vows during their wedding. If we could employ a tape recorder to somehow broadcast the couple's unconscious intentions, we might hear words like these:

> *Bridegroom*: I need to feel important and I expect you to meet that need by submitting to my every decision, whether good or bad; by respecting me no matter how I behave; and by supporting me in whatever I choose to do. I want you to treat me as the most important man in the world. My goal in marrying you is to find my significance through you...
>
> *Bride*: I have never felt as deeply loved as my nature requires. I am expecting you to meet that need through gentle affection even when I'm growling, thoughtful consideration whether I am always sensitive to you or not, and in accepting, romantic sensitivity to my emotional ups and downs. Don't let me down.

Crabb points out that a marriage bound together by commitments to exploit the other for filling one's needs can legitimately be described as a "tick on a dog" relationship. Like a hungry tick that bores through the hide of a hound to suck nutrients from Fido's blood, each partner gloms on to the other in order to extract what is needed for a happy life. "The rather frustrating dilemma, of course, is that in such a marriage there are two ticks and no dog!"[12]

What I am critiquing here is our society's distortion of the companionship function of marriage. The marital union is indeed *one* of the means by which God meets the emotional, social, sexual, psychological, physical, and spiritual needs of his children (Philippians 4:19). But the biblical corrective to cultural narcissism is to remember that marriage is primarily a *ministry* institution. When the apostles addressed the subject of marriage, the focus of their instruction was not on what spouses should do to get their needs met; their emphasis was on the ways that husbands and wives should *serve* to meet the needs of others (See Ephesians 5:15-33; 1 Peter 3:1-7).

During the third movement, the function of relational companionship is expanded to include, even emphasize, the constructive influence that Christian spouses have on each other in the process of spiritual growth (sanctification). In the previous chapter, I underscored the bad news about our fallen condition: that within marriage, two sinners are placed within close proximity to each other for long stretches of time—with predictable and destructive consequences. The good news is that a *Christian* marriage places two redeemed and *recovering* sinners into close proximity for long stretches of time. If these two individuals, who are strongly committed to one another, utilize the means of grace at their disposal, they can actually help each other grow! Indeed, by virtue of the intimacy afforded through marriage and the sheer quantity of time available for mutual edification, the marital relationship should enable each of them to be the *greatest human influence* for spiritual advancement in the life of the other. Whenever this happens, marriage serves as a vehicle for transformation—which is clearly a major part of God's design for marriage in a fallen world.

Interlude
(excerpted from *Mortal Lessons* by Richard Selzer, M.D.)

I stand by the bed where a young woman lies, her face postoperative, her mouth twisted in palsy, clownish. A tiny twig of facial nerve, the one to the muscles of her mouth, has been severed. The surgeon had followed with religious fervor the curve of her flesh; I promise you that. Nevertheless, to remove the tumor in her cheek, I had cut the little nerve. Her young husband is in the room. He stands on the opposite side of the bed, and together they seem to dwell in the evening lamplight, isolated from me, private. Who are they, I ask myself, he and this wrymouth I have made, who gaze at and touch each other so generously, greedily? The young woman speaks. "Will my mouth always be like this?" she asks. "Yes," I say, "it will. It is because the nerve was cut." She nods, and is silent. But the young man smiles. "I like it," he says. "It is kind of cute." All at once I know who he is. I understand, and I lower my gaze. One is not bold in an encounter with a god. Unmindful, he bends to kiss her crooked mouth, and I am so close I can see how he twists his own lips to accommodate hers, to show her that their kiss still works.[13]

Reclaiming Vocational Partnership

Pastor Ben Patterson supplies the transition from our consideration of *relational companionship* to that of *vocational partnership* with this insight:

There are two images of marriage in the Bible. One is very popular today, the other has all but been ignored. The first is of two people gazing into each other's eyes. It speaks of intimacy and deep personal encounter and dominates the modern imagination. Its fullest expression in the Bible is in the lovely Song of Solomon.

There is a second message, equally biblical, and much in need today to balance the first. It is of two people gazing, not at each other, but in the same direction, shouldering the same burden. It speaks of work to do together that simply cannot be done well alone. Its fullest expression is found in the second chapter of Genesis.[14]

This outward gaze reflects a couple's commitment to vocational partnership. So what is it?

Most folks probably equate *vocation* with a person's job, occupation, career. In today's world, the idea that a married couple might have some sort of partnership in their work sounds farfetched. With both spouses often employed outside the home, most of a couple's productive hours are spent in separate spheres of activity. Far from promoting a sense of partnership, the demands of work more often compete with the interests of the family. Some workaholics are even said to be "married to their careers," and are thus guilty of vocational adultery.

For Christian spouses, *vocation* encompasses more than one's job. The word comes from the Latin term *vocare*, which means "to call." (Stick with me here.) This corresponds to the Greek word *kaleo*, which is used by Peter to describe the people of God: "But you are *a chosen race, a royal priesthood, a holy nation, a people of his own*, so that you may *proclaim the virtues* of the one who called [*kaleo*] you out of darkness into his marvelous light" (1 Peter 2:9). Believers are called to be God's servants and priests—that is our vocation. Indeed, the Greek word for church in the New Testament is *ekklesia*, a compound word consisting of *ek* ("out of") plus *klesis* ("calling"). "The church is the fellowship of the called. In the strictest sense of the word, the church is a vocational institution."[15]

The first step in understanding *vocational partnership*, then, is to make a distinction between *vocation* (our calling to be God's people) and *occupation* (the work we do to make a living). In the course of your life, you will likely have many occupations but only one vocation. And just as Christian marriage finds its proper meaning within the larger framework of the church, so our occupations are secondary to and become one avenue through which we carry out our vocation.

The next step is to identify more specifically the nature of our vocation. And here, the key word is *steward*. A steward is someone who has been given responsibility for the productive management of someone else's property. The resources belong to the owner; the steward is trusted to administer them in the best interests of the owner. So Peter tells believers, "Just as each one has received a gift, use it to serve one another as *good stewards* of the varied grace of God" (1 Peter 4:10, emphasis added). Biblical examples include Joseph in the Old Testament (Genesis 39:1-6; 41:39-44) and the apostle Paul in the New Testament (1 Corinthians 4:1-2).[16]

Adam and Eve were stewards whose assignment was to act on behalf of the Creator in the management of his creation, and specifically the Garden of Eden (Genesis 2:15). And that work had a spiritual dimension to it, as though they were carrying out priestly functions. Further, they were to expand God's rule throughout the earth (Genesis 1:28).

By extension, we too are stewards of God's creation; we too are "a holy priesthood" (1 Peter 2:5). But our stewardship extends to God's re-creation; and our call to expand God's rule relates primarily to the kingdom of God: "But above all pursue his kingdom and his righteousness" (Matthew 6:33). As we noted in the previous chapter, our dominant preoccupation (vocation) is to be the expansion of Christ's rule and righteousness internally in our own lives (spiritual growth) and externally in our world (ministry).

If our vocation, then, is to be steward-priests over God's creation and God's kingdom, what does vocational partnership look like in a Christian marriage? I can identify at least three "gardens" in which this partnership can be meaningfully carried out.

First, should God grant them the blessing of children, spouses can be partners in *parenthood*. In today's world, teaming up to disciple children is countercultural at two points. For self-focused marriages, children are an intrusion that detracts from the primary goals of intimacy and self-actualization.[17] Further, in some families, the care of the children is consigned to only one of the parents, usually the mother. Christian couples, by contrast, share in the *privilege* of parenting. And they view it as a means of fulfilling the Great Commission—first, in leading their children to faith in Christ, and then in making them part of the team that reaches out in ministry to the world around them.

Second, Christian spouses can be partners in *ministry* as they exercise their gifts and fulfill their commitments to the mission of the church. In some cases, they may work together as colaborers in a shared venture. At other times, they will find ways to facilitate each other's distinctive contributions to the overall enterprise of the gospel.

Finally, Christian spouses can be partners in their *occupations*. The workplace is one sphere where Christians are to exercise their stewardship; marriage is another. The trick is to manage these two spheres so that our efforts are mutually contributive rather than competitive. This balancing act requires two commitments.

The *first* is the determination by each spouse to keep their job subservient to the mission of the marriage. This means, negatively, that the occupational tail will not be allowed to wag the marital dog. Put differently, the individual who is a success at work but a washout at home has failed in the mutually accepted mission. And it also means, positively, that every effort will be made by each spouse to utilize the opportunities provided by their job (whether within or outside the home) to advance the mission of the marriage—to be salt and light in the workplace.

The *second* commitment accepted by each spouse is to be, and to encourage one's mate to be, a good Christian worker.[18] This begins with the recognition that our occupation is to be an expression of our vocation as stewards of God's creation and kingdom. It includes a conscious awareness that the Boss we are ultimately accountable to is none other than Christ himself. So our effort will be characterized by integrity and diligence.[19] And because our work is offered in service to Christ, we recognize that it has a sacred quality to it. As Johann Sebastian Bach did with each of his compositions, we aspire to sign our work with the inscription: *Soli Deo Gloria* ("to the glory of God alone").

If Adam and Eve provide the prototype for God's original design for marriage, perhaps the model for marriage in the fallen world would be Priscilla and Aquila (Acts 18:1-3,18-19,24-26; Romans 16:3-5; 1 Corinthians 16:19). When this Jewish couple was evicted from Rome by the edict of Emperor Claudius, they set up shop in Corinth. There they provided hospitality for the apostle Paul, a fellow tentmaker. Their partnership in ministry with Paul deepened to the point where they risked their own necks for him. When Paul moved on to Ephesus, they went with him. While there, they brought corrective instruction to the eloquent apologist, Apollos. When Paul departed Ephesus, Priscilla and Aquila stayed on providing hospitality and leadership for the house-church that met in their home.

Here was a husband and wife who dedicated themselves to a calling greater than mutual satisfaction or tentmaking. They are always referred to together, never individually; they functioned as a team, as partners in a shared mission. Far more than soul mates, they could be described as "mission mates." The scope of their influence ranged from hospitality to biblical instruction to church leadership. Together they were good stewards of the gospel. In their marriage we see a pattern for God's design for vocational partnership.

> Without this...image of [vocational partnership] guiding us, marriages become narcissistic and self-absorbed; and they often collapse under the weight of expectations heaped upon them. With it, our marriages can have the balance of both the inward and the outward perspective. When couples realize that there is more to marriage than personal fulfillment— that they have a work to do together for the glory of God—a fresh wind blows into their relationship. Happily, personal fulfillment is then given as a by-product of a larger activity; not the ever-elusive pot of gold to be sought at the end of the rainbow.[20]

❖ ❖ ❖

Summary: Contrary to popular opinion, marriage was not established simply for the mutual satisfaction of a husband and wife. *It was designed to be a ministry institution.* Its mission is to advance God's purposes—both in the lives of the partners (and their offspring) and in the world within which the spouses (and their family) are to live as salt and light.

Accordingly, those who marry are called to serve God by serving one another. As intimate allies, they are to invest in each other's personal growth and forge a partnership that makes an impact for good in others' lives. God's intention is that each spouse be spiritually transformed by their mutual ministry. At the same time, they are to fulfill their shared vocation by serving others together—through their family, their work, and their personal engagement in the mission of the church.

❖ ❖ ❖

Questions for Reflection and Group Discussion

1. What is the most significant insight you have gained from reading this chapter?

2. What issues does the author have with the concept of a *soul mate*? Do you think his critique is legitimate? Why or why not? Can you think of other problems with the concept?

3. What is the biblical corrective to our culture's obsession with soul mates?

4. How has the extended presentation on vocational partnership affected your understanding of marriage?

5. Why is a good balance between vocational partnership and relational companionship important to a healthy marriage? How does each of these functions contribute to the achievement of the other?

6. How should the content of this chapter shape the process of "player selection" for Christian singles? Based on what you have just learned, make appropriate additions or amendments to your "Profile of a Prospective Spouse."

For additional questions, go to www.TheMarriageDecision.com.

6

The Ultimate Marriage

⚜

Will you be married when you are in heaven?

If you suspect that this is a trick question, I confess that it is. But it is the good kind of trick question in the sense that no matter what answer you give, you will be correct even if you don't actually know the answer.

It is not, however, a hypothetical question. Nor is it irrelevant to Christian singles. The answer is part of the dramatic theme of the fourth movement in the symphony of marriage. And if you have been guessing the answer at this point, by the time you finish reading this chapter, you will know it—and why it matters.

But we're not quite done surveying the score of the third movement. There is one final detail that we need to explore if we are to fully appreciate the climax that lies ahead.

A Bonus Function

If you were to enter the Maxson home, the first thing you would likely notice is all the art on the walls. The living room, in particular, functions as a kind of gallery for the paintings our daughter created during her "elementary period." Over a span of four years (first through fourth grades), Rachel took private lessons from a gifted teacher. Most of her oil paintings are landscapes, several of which won awards, including "Best of Show," at the local county fair. By my count, there are ten originals hanging on the walls of our house. When people see them for the first time, their typical reaction is "Wow!"[1]

Good art has intrinsic value. It initiates an experience on the part of the viewer that touches the soul and evokes an emotional response.

Part of art's impact stems from the fact that it points beyond itself at two levels. First, this kind of portrayal connects the observer to an ultimate reality that actually exists someplace in three dimensions. The interpretive representation stimulates the imagination in a way that transports the observer to a setting otherwise inaccessible. Second, an artistic creation reveals certain attributes of the artist—her creativity, aesthetic aptitude, skill, values, and the like. By viewing her handiwork, the beholder encounters the artist and comes to understand significant aspects of her personality.

The communicative nature of art is also evident when the artist is God. The products of his creative genius and power—whether the universe at large (Psalm 19:1-6; Romans 1:19-20), human beings (Genesis 1:26-28), or Spirit-born children (Matthew 5:16; 1 Peter 1:14-16)—point beyond themselves to their Maker, giving him glory. So it should not surprise us to learn that this is true of marriage as well.[2]

From the very beginning of the first movement, God did in fact intend for human marriage to represent and reflect a more ultimate reality. And yet, in the unfolding revelation of God's design for marriage, he did not disclose—indeed *could not* disclose—this specialized function of marriage until the third movement. It was only when Christ had activated his mission to restore all things under God that the picture function of marriage could be explained.

The assignment to divulge this bonus function of marriage was given to the apostle Paul. The context for this revelation is Ephesians 5:15-33—Paul's most comprehensive instruction to Christian husbands and wives on the nature of Spirit-filled marriage in a fallen world. His announcement of this previously undisclosed role for marriage was given as an unexpected punch line to his marital counsel:

> Husbands, love your wives just as Christ loved the church and gave himself for her…In the same way husbands ought to love their wives as their own bodies. He who loves his wife loves himself. For no one has ever hated his own body but he feeds it and takes care of it, just as Christ also does the church, for we are members of his body. *For this reason a man will leave his father and mother and will be joined to his wife, and the two will become one flesh.* This mystery is great—but I am actually speaking with reference to Christ and the church (Ephesians 5:25, 28-32).

As he wraps up his instructions to Christian spouses, Paul returns to God's original design for marriage as recorded in Genesis 2:24. Then he says two remarkable things. First, he asserts that he is talking about a "great mystery." We all know that marriage is mysterious. (I think that is because women are mysterious—but I digress.) That is not what Paul means. Whenever he speaks of a "mystery," he is using that term in a technical sense to refer to a truth previously hidden in God (undecipherable to humans on their own) that has now been revealed by God through his apostle.

Second, in this case the previously hidden truth is that the definition of marriage recorded in Genesis 2:24 is *actually describing the covenantal relationship between Christ and the church*. From the very beginning—before anyone knew that humanity would need a Savior, centuries before that Savior actually came—God intended that the institution of marriage would be a picture of the relationship between the Savior and his people. Marriage was designed to point beyond itself to something more ultimate. And the supreme reality on which human marriage is patterned is the marriage of Christ and his church.[3]

John Piper's explanation of Paul's mystery is as clear as anything I've read:

> If you want to understand God's meaning for marriage, you have to grasp that we are dealing with a copy of an original, a metaphor of a greater reality, a parable, and a greater truth. The *original*, the *reality*, the *truth* refer to God's marriage to his people, or now in the New Testament we see it as Christ's marriage to the church. And the *copy*, the *metaphor*, the *parable* refer to human marriage between a husband and a wife...That's the deepest meaning of marriage. It's meant to be a living drama of the covenant-keeping love between Christ and the church.[4]

We can see a correlation between the functions of Christian marriage and that of Christ to the church, for in both cases there is *vocational partnership* and *relational companionship*. Jesus called the church into being to be the human agency through which he is carrying out his mission to restore all things to God.[5] This vocational partnership is summarized in the Great Commission and expanded upon in Ephesians 1–3 and 6. That partnership is enhanced and enabled by the mutual love expressed between Christ and his Bride, prefigured in the Great Commandment and described in Ephesians 4–5. When Christian spouses, in reliance upon the Holy Spirit, minister *with* each other (vocational partnership) and *to* each other (relational companionship), they both emulate and reflect the marriage between Christ and the church.

This is God's intention for human marriage, but the connection between picture and reality is subtle. It reminds me of those 3-D stereograms wherein a three-dimensional image is hidden within a two-dimensional pattern. At first, the target image is invisible to the observer. But as one stares *through* the surface pattern, the latent object emerges into focus.

With this analogy in mind, consider the marriage of a godly couple you admire. Or look once again at the partnership of Priscilla and Aquila. Do you see in those relationships a reflection of Christ and his bride? When you know what you're looking for, it's not really that hard.

The thing about stereograms is that some are easier to decrypt than others. The reason we have been told about the picture function of marriage is to challenge us to establish and develop partnerships that point to our Savior's marriage with as much clarity as possible.

Using a similar metaphor, Noël Piper (John's wife) sets before us a fitting goal:

> I love using my tiny digital camera. But the larger and more complex a subject, the more nearly impossible it is to represent it well and completely. No single photograph can show someone how magnificent the Grand Canyon is. It's true that my shortcomings as a photographer do nothing to change the majesty of that natural wonder. Still, some snapshots do give a better idea than others of the grandeur. I want to take that clearer kind of picture of the Grand Canyon. And that's the kind of image of Jesus I want our marriage to portray.[6]

When I am helping an engaged couple prepare for their wedding, my greatest contribution is to get across this biblical perspective: Even when you are standing "before God and these witnesses" in all of your nuptial glory, it's not ultimately about you. Our culture has been deceived by the idolatrous lie that the purpose of marriage is the mutual satisfaction of the respective partners. The truth is that every individual marriage is intended to participate in something much larger. And there is more at stake in the faithfulness of the groom and bride to their marital covenant than the mere survival of the marriage.

Paul's instruction in Ephesians 5 does not exhaust the scope of the picture function of marriage. But it prepares us well for the rest of the story that unfolds in the fourth and final movement.

The "Surprise" Symphony

On March 23, 1792, world-renowned composer Franz Joseph Haydn conducted the premier of his Symphony No. 94 in G major at the Hanover Square Rooms in London. The concert venue was packed and the audience was filled with anticipation. Haydn did not disappoint and, at the end of the first movement, the patrons gave enthusiastic applause. The second *andante* movement opened simply, gently. The melody resembled the children's tune "Twinkle, Twinkle, Little Star"—until the second beat of the sixteenth measure, which consisted of a one-beat, very loud, cymbal-crashing chord. The adrenaline-inducing explosion jolted the audience out of their reverie and provoked great delight. Today there are probably a handful of music historians who could tell you the official title of Haydn's Symphony No. 94 in G major without looking it up (as I had to do). But virtually every lover of classical music is familiar with its unofficial name—"The Surprise Symphony."

As we have been listening to God's symphony of marriage, we have encountered several surprises along the way. But none, by my estimation, compare with the Big One—the climactic surprise of the fourth movement. We've covered a lot of ground since the opening strains of the first movement. To fully appreciate the impact of the conclusion, it will be helpful to briefly replay the themes from each of the three movements encountered thus far.

First Movement:
The Institution of Marriage

The harmony and fruitfulness of the Edenic marriage was a product of the Creator's craftsmanship in fashioning two image-bearers perfectly adapted to one another, plus the initial obedience of the vice-regents who carried out their assignments in service to God. No doubt Adam and Eve loved each other, but that was a secondary reason for the compatibility and productivity they experienced. Genesis 1–2 gives us the first movement in the symphony of marriage.

Second Movement:
The Corruption of Marriage

The discord that came to be part and parcel with marriage is a result of the Fall. Husbands and wives don't purposely set out to give one another grief. But in their defective condition, having lost their primary connection with God, they act selfishly and inflict damage. In the first instance, marriage worked because of the spouses' right relationship to God. In the second instance, marriage falls short because that vertical relationship has been severed, and the participants' natures are corrupted.

Third Movement:
The Redemption of Marriage

But now, Jesus has come. By his intervention, he brought transformation to believing husbands and wives. Through his atoning sacrifice, resurrection, and exaltation to heaven, he has dealt decisively with the sin that infects all of us and our relationships. In paying the penalty for our sin, he has opened the door for us to receive forgiveness for our sins and to return to fellowship with God through faith in Christ. By breaking the power of sin and supplying us with the resources of grace, he has begun the process of renewing us into the image of our Creator, restoring us to our original design, and enabling us to fulfill his purposes for marriage as Christian spouses. All of this is part of his larger campaign to reconcile all things to God—a project that will be completed at the consummation of human history.

Further, Jesus reconstructed the institution of marriage itself, relocating it within the larger framework of the church. He also elevated the significance of marriage by completing the reality it was intended to portray—the marriage of Christ and his church. So, in contrast to the placement of marriage within the Old Covenant, Jesus declared marriage to be *optional* (alongside singleness), *secondary* (now a subset of the church), yet *significant* (pointing to the ultimate realities of the nature of God on the one hand and the relationship of Christ and the church on the other).

Fourth Movement:
The Culmination of Marriage

But there's more. For not only does the third movement look back to the beginning, it also looks ahead to the climax. There is another aspect to the picture-function of marriage. For it prefigures the ultimate expression of marriage—the wedding of the exalted Christ and his glorified bride, the church.

And when that happens, human marriage will no longer be optional. It will be *obsolete*!

The Best Is Yet to Come!

About the final movement in the symphony of marriage, there is less to say. Pretty much all we know about it is based on a single sentence by Jesus: "For in the resurrection [people] neither marry nor are given in marriage, but are like angels in heaven" (Matthew 22:30).

Just as his instruction on marriage in the present age was prompted by trap-setting Pharisees (Matthew 19:3), this time his baiters were Sadducees, a different religious party. Disbelieving in the resurrection, these academic posers sought to demonstrate the absurdity of resurrection by creating a hypothetical scenario in which one woman, through the law of levirate marriage (Deuteronomy 25:5-10), could end up married to seven brothers. "In the resurrection," they smirked, "whose wife of the seven will she be?" (Matthew 22:28).

Like a veteran astronaut explaining to children that the moon is not made of cheese, Jesus gave them enough information to demonstrate that they were out of their league (verse 33). And from that exchange we learn what we would not otherwise know—that marriage belongs to earthly life only.[7]

So if your answer to my opening question was no, you were right. You will not be married to an individual husband or wife when you are in heaven.[8]

I don't know how the Sadducees reacted to this information, but I have to admit that the first time I heard it, I was disappointed. As a happily married man who really enjoys his wife, I didn't relish the prospect of that relationship coming to an end. And it seemed inappropriate to be reacting to information about heaven with a feeling of loss.

I subsequently learned three things that changed my perspective. The first is that my love for my wife and hers for me will be in no way diminished. Quite the opposite—our love will be set free from the limitations of living in a fallen world. And I can see how this resolution solves a potential problem for my friend Chris, who just remarried after losing his first wife to cancer. Michael J. Wilkins gives this explanation:

> While the state of relationships will be altered at the resurrection, this does not imply that prior earthly relationships are eliminated completely, nor does it imply that resurrected relationships are without special attachment. The wife (or husband, for that matter) of multiple spouses in this life will have an equally altered capacity and understanding of love, which will enable her (or him) to love all without measure or jealousy or possessiveness.[9]

Is that cool or what?

The second corrective comes from factoring in what I've just been writing about the picture-function of marriage. To repeat, human marriage is designed to point beyond itself to something more ultimate—the relationship between God and his people. In human experience, marriage is the concrete thing, the known from which we gain insight into the unknown. But in the fourth movement, we will encounter the real thing. What we will learn is that we have been living all along in marital "shadowlands."[10] We will see that human marriage, at its very best, was giving us only the slightest glimpse of the glory that is to come in the true marriage (Ephesians 5:31-32). And when that happens, we will not be reluctant to lay aside earthly marriage—"the way a picture is no longer needed when you see face to face."[11]

The third factor in the reversal of my attitude was the dawning realization that when the wedding supper of the Lamb actually takes place, those of us who are participating in it will be giving no thought to our former state. We will be preoccupied with our engagement in an entirely different marital relationship. For the wedding alluded to in Ephesians 5 (where Christ is said to be preparing his bride) will be celebrated as the believers of this age are collectively presented to Christ as his bride (2 Corinthians 11:2; Revelation 19:7-9; 21:2,9-11). "There will be no human marriages in heaven...for heaven will be *the* marriage."[12]

> The people of God will be 'like angels in heaven', in that the centre of their existence will be undivided communion with God. Then the beautiful and delicate interplay of man and woman with one another will give way to the ultimate reality of Christ and his church for ever at one (Revelation 21:2, 9-10).[13]

And so if you answered yes to my opening question, you were right. For you will enter in fully to that marriage of which all earthly unions are but a dim reflection. Jesus himself will be the bridegroom and we will be the bride.

Apart from giving us something spectacular to look forward to, I see two major benefits of knowing how the symphony culminates. The first is the reminder that human marriage is not the ultimate relationship. Sometimes, as we exercise our stewardship during the third movement, we need help keeping marriage in its place. Recognizing that earthly marriage is optional, secondary, pictorial, and *temporary* can help us maintain the priority of our allegiance to the Lordship of Jesus Christ.

The second value comes from knowing and believing this promise: even if you never experience human marriage in this life, you will not be denied the fullest blessings of marriage in the age to come.[14] In the glorified community of the redeemed, every one of us will be single, and all relational restrictions that separated the married from the unmarried on a fallen planet will be removed. And all of us, together, will be married to King Jesus. I do not know how much of our former marital status we will remember; but I am confident that we will feel no more loss than a butterfly feels having shed its cocoon.

And although the fourth movement is the culminating passage in the symphony of marriage, it will never end.

The Symphony of Marriage

First Movement: The *Institution* of Marriage

Second Movement: The *Corruption* of Marriage

Third Movement: The *Redemption* of Marriage

Fourth Movement: The *Culmination* of Marriage

❖   ❖   ❖

Recommended Reading

The Meaning of Marriage: Facing the Complexities of Commitment with the Wisdom of God by Timothy and Kathy Keller (Dutton, 2011).

Questions for Reflection and Group Discussion

1. What is the most significant insight you have gained from reading this chapter?

2. Were you aware that marriage was designed to point to something "more ultimate"? Of what value is knowledge of this dimension of marriage to the Christian single who is contemplating marriage?

3. "There is more at stake in the faithfulness of the groom and bride to their marital covenant than the mere survival of the marriage." What else is at stake?

4. Why is it a good thing that there will be no human marriage in heaven?

5. The author said, "Sometimes we need help keeping marriage in its place." What do you think he meant by that? How would the content of this chapter help Christian singles to do that?

6. Based on what you learned in this chapter, make appropriate additions or amendments to your "Profile of a Prospective Spouse."

For additional questions, go to www.TheMarriageDecision.com.

Part 3

God's Design for Singleness

✦

Modern Myth 3

*Singleness should be regarded as a transitional state
en route to the ultimate destination of marriage.
Problems stemming from the incompleteness of singleness
are resolved by marriage.*

Introduction to Part 3

I believe that most people in Western culture come into young adulthood with a scenario in their mind about how their life is going to play out. The first order of business is to prepare for serious adulthood through education, apprenticeship, military experience, and the like. There may also be opportunities for adventures in travel, volunteer work, or missionary service. Somewhere along the line, one will encounter a suitable mate and marriage will follow. In the course of time, children will be born and a family will begin to grow. Within that same time frame, careers will be launched and the responsibilities of adult living will be assumed.

Sometimes life works out that way. It did for me. When I left my parental home, I went first to college, then to seminary. During my senior year of graduate school, it dawned on me that if I was going to be a pastor, I should think about getting married. I prayed about it, surveyed the terrain, determined that the one woman who was interested in me would be a suitable partner, and got married. I became a pastor, we had two children, and we have lived happily ever after. (That's the short version; the longer one appears in chapter 15.)

Sometimes it doesn't work out that way. My writing partner, Garry Friesen, pursued two serious courtships—one during college, one during his professional career—neither of which ended in marriage. He didn't set out to be a lifelong celibate; that's how things turned out. And so, of course, he has not lived happily ever after but rather has been doomed to a pitiful, second-rate life of loneliness and deprivation.

No, wait! That was Chandler's nightmare on *Friends*.[1] Garry has actually lived a life of joy and fruitfulness; he just didn't expect to be single for the duration.

A lot of people get married. But everyone starts out single. And well over half of those who get married spend some segment of their adult lives single again. In today's world, *single* is the primary adjective describing significant stages in the life of an adult. In fact, we happen to live at a juncture in history where, for the first time, the number of single adults in American culture is almost equal to the number of married adults.[2]

But what are we to make of the single condition? Already in the pages of this book I have used the word *abnormal* to describe it.[3] Is that a disparaging term? I don't intend for it to be. But given that the original design for the sexes entailed marriage, and that marriage has been the norm in most cultures throughout history, it is small wonder that many are ambivalent about the relative virtues and drawbacks associated with singleness. Vera Stinton puts our dilemma this way:

> A key issue for Christian theology is what emphasis to give to singleness in relation to the state of marriage. Is it to be treated as pathological: something abnormal that requires either a cure or at least the alleviation of pain? Or should we emphasize it as a privilege: the special vocation of the truly devoted follower of Christ?[4]

Albert Hsu is one of many writers who complain that the pathological attitude is all too prevalent in Christian circles. In the preface to his book *Singles at the Crossroads,* he explains his reasons for writing with these observations:

> The marriage books [from Christian publishers] never argue that marriage is a good thing. That is presupposed. They accept the reality that marriages often have problems, so that's what these marriage books are for: dealing with the problems. But books on singleness usually have a different approach. Instead of dealing with problems that singles might face, these books seem to think singleness *is* the problem. They instruct the reader on how to bide one's time until the right person comes along. In other words, they imply that the one solution to the problem of singleness is to get married. Then one can have marriage problems and read all those marriage books.[5]

A Little History

This attitude toward singleness has a long history, going all the way back to the ancient Hebrews. As we noted in chapter 4, Israelite culture was organized around family clans, so marriage and children played a key role. Rodney Clapp says, "The Old Testament provides no real place for single people. Even ascetics such as the priests and the Nazirites were not single (Leviticus 21:1-15; Numbers 6:1-21). In fact, for a Hebrew not getting married was catastrophic."[6]

That's because an individual who had no spouse or children would be without inheritors and guardians in old age. So marriage was the norm and the bearing of children, a blessing to any couple, was expected.[7] In fact, there is no word for *bachelor* in the Old Testament.[8]

One other component of the Hebrew mindset is connected to God's redemptive purposes for the Jewish race. "For Messiah was destined to come through the seed of Abraham (Genesis 17:8; Galatians 3:16) and the line of David (Matthew 1:1-16; Luke 1:32-33,68-70; 2:4; 3:23-28; John 7:42)."[9] So procreation was seen as a double-duty for Jewish couples—fulfilling the creation mandate (Genesis 1:28) and preserving the Messianic line.

At other times, though, the pendulum swung in the other direction. Church leaders in the early and medieval church tended to view celibacy[10] as more spiritual than marriage. Their thinking was that in a fallen world, sexual intercourse, even within marriage, is inevitably fueled by a measure of sinful lust, which corrupts a person's communion with God.[11]

Most commentators find the roots of this view outside of Hebrew or Christian teachings—usually in the Platonic dualism that viewed spirit as good and matter as evil. This perspective was championed by the gnostics, a heretical group that threatened Christianity in the second and third centuries. A similar worldview may have influenced the ascetic group[12] within the Corinthian church that prompted Paul's discourse on singleness and marriage (1 Corinthians 7).[13]

The idea of the spiritual superiority of celibacy began to emerge in the writings of the church fathers such as Clement of Alexandria, Jerome, and Augustine (second through the fifth centuries AD). They were not immune to "the tension between the physical and the spiritual…that pervaded the ancient world." This worldview influence was reinforced by the threat of martyrdom, which would result not only in the death of a devoted Christian but devastate surviving family members. "It is not surprising, then, that many Christians chose not to marry."[14]

As the threat of persecution was replaced by societal acceptance of Christianity, those Christians who wished to express a higher allegiance to Christ replaced martyrdom with monasticism. Before long, celibacy was required of all clergy, and the doctrine of the superiority of the single state over marriage became entrenched in the Western Catholic Church.

> For a thousand years, the single, celibate life had been upheld as the Christian ideal. Sex, though grudgingly permitted inside marriage, was not to be enjoyed. As Jerome declared in the fourth century, "Anyone who is too passionate a lover with his own wife is himself an adulterer."[15]

As the Reformation was launched in reaction to the doctrinal and ecclesiastical abuses within the medieval Western church, the pendulum swung back again. Luther and his fellow Reformers rejected the notion of the superiority of asceticism, both in their doctrine and in their practice. This repudiation was as great a reversal of medieval church tradition as their opposition to the church's dogma on faith, works, and the sacraments. The higher spiritual status previously conferred upon the pious residents of monasteries and nunneries was redirected to husbands and wives and parents.[16]

The influence of the Reformers and their exaltation of marriage seems to dominate the current evangelical perspective. Historian Ruth Tucker observes: "We [Protestants] view the emphasis on celibacy in the Roman Catholic church as misdirected, and we can see the problems that have resulted from it. But it is entirely possible that we have gone to the other extreme, so that subconsciously we view singles as somehow defective."[17]

Second-Class Singles?

My own observations confirm the conclusions of Albert Hsu, Ruth Tucker, and others.[18] The prevailing consensus within the evangelical church, generally supported by the culture at large, is that singleness is to be viewed as a temporary condition, a transitional stage en route to the ultimate destination of marriage. The nearly universal scope of this viewpoint is not difficult to understand, for it is reinforced by several supporting factors.

First, we are collectively under the impression that while the Bible speaks favorably of marriage, it treats singleness as, well, undesirable. At weddings especially, we read the passage from Ecclesiastes 4:9-11:

> Two people are better than one,
> because they can reap more benefit from their labor.

For if they fall, one will help his companion up,
but pity the person who falls down and has no one to help him up.
Furthermore, if two lie down together, they can keep each other warm,
but how can one person keep warm by himself?

In sermons from Genesis 2, preachers drive home the point that while the first man was a bachelor, his status was "not good" and hence temporary. I have pointed out in this very book that Adam was incomplete by design. He needed a helper. So God gave him a spouse. Marriage was created to be the norm and, though the institution has been corrupted by the Fall, a Spirit-filled marriage is a great blessing—a picture, even, of Christ and his church.

If you've been doing your homework, you have been applying insights gained from the last four chapters to the construction of a profile for a potential mate. In the face of such a full-court press, it is hard to escape the conclusion that the single journey is destined to find its fulfillment in marriage.

The inclination to adopt this perspective is further motivated by the unmarried person's intense desire—produced by the combination of their biological makeup and a yearning for the blessings inherent in a healthy marriage—to get married. This desire easily morphs into an *expectation* that is all too eager to believe the mythical promise that "someday my prince(ss) will come."

And it seems to work out that way for many people. The idea that everyone who truly wants to get married will do so is reinforced by the statistic that, historically, most adults do marry. So singleness actually culminates in marriage much of the time.

And yet there are two serious flaws with the notion that singleness finds its fulfilling destination in marriage.

The first is conspicuously obvious to single believers who remain unmarried as they enter their third decade (or so). A question begins to take shape in the minds of friends, family members, and even the single persons themselves. Tactful people do not verbalize the question; less sensitive people frame it in the guise of a joke. It starts out as an irritant, graduates to the level of nagging, and eventually begins to define the individual, like a chronic illness: "What's wrong with you? When are you going to get married?" Like Nancy (the school teacher profiled in the prologue), the single person may well turn to God in honest frustration and ask, *Are you ever going to give me the desire of my heart?*

Now it is bad enough when one person suffers from the widespread perception that due to their unmarried condition they are somehow defective. But when the impact of this assumption is multiplied across the lives of the growing number of single adults among us, the injurious effects of the "marriage expectation" are compounded:

- It consigns single adults to second-class status within the family of Christ.

- It makes an external condition (marriage) the standard by which the achievement of viable adulthood is measured.

- It fans a legitimate desire into a demand.

- When the expectation is not fulfilled, it intensifies disappointment and inevitably raises the question of blame, casting aspersions on the worthiness of the individual or the goodness of God.

Such a detrimental consequence should be a clue to us that our accepted construct is out of sync with God's design. And that is, in fact, the second flaw. The good news is that we have been wrong. We have inflated a widespread pattern into a universal one—taking what is commonly desired and frequently experienced and making it *normative* for everyone—without biblical warrant. And we have overlooked important biblical instruction on singleness that would give us a more balanced perspective. The pervasive view that the state of singleness is inferior to that of marriage flies in the face of the teaching (to say nothing of the example) of both Jesus and Paul.

Jesus not only redefined the role of marriage in a fallen world, he also elevated the status of singleness to a place of significance equal to that of marriage within the family of God. (Perhaps you noticed that point made in passing in chapter 4.) And Paul, the apostle who revealed to the church the mystery that Spirit-filled marriage portrays the relationship between Christ and his bride, actively *recruited* unmarried Christians in Corinth to remain single.

Maybe we don't have to feel sorry for Garry Friesen.

❖ ❖ ❖

Questions for Reflection and Group Discussion

1. What is the most significant insight you have gained from reading this chapter?

2. The author suggests that "most people in Western culture come into young adulthood with a scenario in their mind about how their life is going to play out." Do you agree with his description of that scenario? How would you modify it? How does the unfolding of your life compare with that template?

3. Consider the questions posed by Vera Stinton near the beginning of this introduction to part 3. How do you think most Christians of your acquaintance would answer them? Do you have evidence for your opinion?

4. The author listed four injurious effects of the widely shared perception that singleness finds its fulfilling destination in marriage. Have you encountered any of these consequences directly or indirectly? Can you think of any others?

5. Have you thought of your own singleness as being inferior to marriage? How would you respond to the reasons people give for this conclusion?

For additional questions, go to www.TheMarriageDecision.com.

Eunuchs for Yeshua
(Matthew 19)

When was the last time you had a discussion about eunuchs? Yeah, me neither. Even among guys—especially among guys—any contemplation of castration is so distressing, the only time it surfaces as a topic for conversation is when it is served up as the punch line of a bad joke.[1]

So when Jesus referenced eunuchs as the punch line of a point he was making with his guys, you can imagine that it got their attention. And it should get ours too. Even though it was an unexpected postscript to a debate about divorce, the Lord's comments about eunuchs introduced a dramatic change in the status of single adults in the kingdom ruled by Messiah.

Marriage Is Seriously Permanent

Let's return to the episode recorded in Matthew 19:3-9.

> Then some Pharisees came to him in order to test him. They asked, "Is it lawful to divorce a wife for any cause?" He answered, "Have you not read that from the beginning the Creator *made them male and female,* and said, *'For this reason a man will leave his father and mother and will be united with his wife, and the two will become one flesh'*? So they are no longer two, but one flesh. Therefore what God has joined together, let no one separate." They said to him, "Why then did Moses command us *to give a certificate of dismissal and to divorce her*?" Jesus said to them, "Moses permitted you to divorce your wives because of your hard hearts, but from the beginning it was not this way. Now I say to you that whoever divorces his wife, except for immorality, and marries another commits adultery."

The people of Israel were sharply divided on the question of when divorce was permitted. Some followed the stricter school of Rabbi Shammai in holding that sexual immorality was the only legitimate grounds for divorce. But many agreed with the looser interpretation of Rabbi Hillel that a man could divorce his wife if she displeased him "for any cause."

In his reiteration of the Creator's design for marriage, Jesus stressed the intended permanence of marriage. But his detractors would not be put off, pressing him to explain the ramifications of the Mosaic legislation "commanding" a certificate of divorce. It was not a command, Jesus explained. Rather it was a provision "permitted…because of your hard hearts." Bottom line: "Whoever divorces his wife, except for immorality, and marries another commits adultery."

As I noted in chapter 4, Jesus' disciples reacted to this conclusion with a combination of shock and dismay: "If this is the case of a husband with a wife, it is better not to marry!" (19:10). If divorce was ruled out except for immorality, a man could be permanently locked into an intolerable situation. Jesus' startling reply served notice, once again, that a new day was dawning:

> "Not everyone can accept this statement, except those to whom it has been given. For there are some eunuchs who were that way from birth, and some who were made eunuchs by others, and some who became eunuchs for the sake of the kingdom of heaven. The one who is able to accept this should accept it" (Matthew 19:11-12).

The first thing that was startling about this response is that, in a way, Jesus was agreeing with his disciples: it is better for *some* not to marry. This assertion defied orthodox convention, as we have seen. Not only did the rabbis insist that it was the duty for every Israelite to marry, they were themselves married.[2] Both in his teaching and in his practice, Jesus was an anomaly.[3]

But Jesus corrected his disciples' *reason* for considering a single life. Rather than a negative fear of imprisonment in a miserable marriage, Jesus posited a constructive reason: "for the sake of the kingdom of heaven" (19:12). Messiah has come, so the promises to Abraham and David of a kingly heir have been fulfilled (Romans 9:5; Galatians 3:16, 26-29; 6:15); the goal of physical procreation has been accomplished. The third movement of the symphony of redemption has begun.[4] So not only are the mission and purposes of the institution of marriage retrofitted to advance the objectives of the new age, an alternative path for kingdom service is opened up.[5] Just as "Jesus' singleness enabled him to focus on his messianic task,"[6] so some of his followers would choose to follow his example to advance his kingdom.

To return to our military metaphor, we might say that the army of Christ is made up of two battalions composed of those who are married and those who are single. Like artillery and infantry contingents, each of these battle groups has distinctive strengths and limitations, and they complement each other. The Commander's Intent for singleness and marriage is subsumed under the strategic umbrella of the Commander's Intent for the entire army. The roles of singleness and marriage are now identified by how they might advance the cause in the spiritual warfare.

Eunuchs: An Apt Figure

The manner in which Jesus opened the door to celibate life is as striking as the point he was making. He didn't just say, "Some people choose not to marry for the sake of the kingdom" (as some English versions paraphrase). He got their attention by talking about eunuchs. I imagine that the conversation may have unfolded like this:

> *Jesus*: There are some eunuchs who were that way from birth, and some who were made eunuchs by others… (pause for effect)
>
> *Disciples* (thinking to themselves): OK, that's true enough. Men who can't reproduce don't get married.
>
> *Jesus*:…and some who became eunuchs for the sake of the kingdom of heaven.
>
> *Disciples* (alarmed): What? Is he suggesting that we cut off…? No, that can't be right.[7]

Of course this third reference to eunuchs was figurative—Jesus was talking about disciples who voluntarily chose a celibate life.[8]

If we were able to hear Jesus' words through the ears of his first-century Jewish listeners, we would be better able to appreciate the impact of his imagery. Two things about eunuchs make them an apt metaphor for Christian celibates.

First, eunuchs were barred from inclusion in the community of the covenant (Deuteronomy 23:1), just as single people were excluded from a place of legitimacy within the culture. While their disqualification from participation in the assembly of Israel may have stemmed more from the linkage of castration to pagan rites than to the defilement of physical deformity, eunuchs were regarded as objects of revulsion by Jewish people. "A metaphor of such shame and sacrifice testifies to the value of the kingdom of God for which anyone would pay such a price."[9]

On the other hand, in royal courts, eunuchs were of great service to kings because their "physical state of perpetual celibacy provided them the opportunity to serve their king with wholehearted devotion and loyalty."[10] In a similar manner, Jesus is saying, some will recognize that they can better advance the cause of the kingdom by remaining single than by getting married. Such individuals are in a position to provide great service to the King.

Ironically, for Jesus' listeners the two dominant perceptions of eunuchs were polar opposites. Within Judaism, eunuchs were disdained, relegated to a position outside the blessings of the covenant—like foreigners. Within royal courts, by contrast, eunuchs were granted positions of trust, power, and prestige—like the Ethiopian eunuch encountered by Philip in Acts 8.

There is one place, in a prophecy of Isaiah, where these two seemingly incompatible pictures are brought together. Speaking of the changes that will come about in the coming day of deliverance (Isaiah 56:1), God declares:

> Let not the foreigner who has joined himself to the LORD say,
>   "The LORD will surely separate me from his people";
> and let not the eunuch say,
>   "Behold, I am a dry tree."
> For thus says the LORD:
> "To the eunuchs who keep my Sabbaths,
>   who choose the things that please me
>   and hold fast my covenant,
> I will give in my house and within my walls
>   a monument and a name
>   better than sons and daughters;
> I will give them an everlasting name
>   that shall not be cut off."
>   (Isaiah 56:3-5 ESV)

From the perspective of Isaiah, in a future time eunuchs who were faithful to God's covenant would receive blessing from God in the form of an "everlasting name" that (1) "is better than sons and daughters" and (2) "shall not be cut off." During the Old Covenant, the only way a man's name could be perpetuated ("not cut off") was through physical procreation. But that was impossible for eunuchs—to their great loss.

Question: How could eunuchs acquire such a legacy?

Answer: By participating in and serving the New Covenant family established by Messiah, who was himself celibate.

In his description of the Servant of Yahweh in chapter 53, Isaiah passes along surprising information:

> Yet it was the will of the LORD to crush him;
> he has put him to grief;
> when his soul makes an offering for guilt,
> *he shall see his offspring*, he shall prolong his days;
> the will of the LORD shall prosper in his hand.
> (Isaiah 53:10 ESV, emphasis added)

This passage, as we know, was describing Jesus, a celibate man. In what sense did he produce offspring through his death and resurrection? This has to refer to his spiritual children—the family of Christ, the church that is born in the New Testament. This is that family that Jesus himself referred to in the passages I cited in chapter 4 (Matthew 12:47-50 and Luke 18:28-30). This is that family that comes into being not through physical procreation but through regeneration by faith.[11]

If Jesus had Isaiah's prophecy in mind in the eunuch statements of Matthew 19, he would be implying that those spiritual eunuchs who choose to forgo marriage for the sake of the kingdom of heaven contribute to the birth of spiritual offspring—a mission, and a blessing, greater than the physical begetting of sons and daughters. So while single disciples may find themselves in an underappreciated minority within the family of Christ (reflecting somewhat the Jewish disdain for eunuchs), Jesus assigns to them a place of dignity and honor in service to his kingdom (like the stature of court eunuchs serving in royal administrations).[12]

Two things stand out from Jesus' instruction. The first is that the choice between marriage and singleness belongs to the individual disciple: some "became eunuchs." The second is the decisive reason for one's decision: "for the sake of the kingdom of heaven." Here we are reminded again of the priorities that are to govern the decision making of Christ's followers. One's marital status, as important as it is, should remain secondary to one's service and submission to the Lord.

Based on these comments by Jesus (reinforced by Paul's elaboration in 1 Corinthians 7), Vera Stinton developed her own answer to the questions she posed about how Christians should regard singleness.[13] Her options, you may recall, were: (1) singleness is a *pathological* condition requiring a cure, or (2) singleness is a *privilege*—the special vocation of super-devoted disciples. Her carefully crafted summary forms a fitting conclusion to this chapter:

> So the Christian perspective on the biblical material is that, while the first created beings, Adam and Eve, were a married couple, in the new creation the second Adam, Jesus Christ, was a single man. Singleness and marriage are parallel routes for loving and serving in the world and preparing us for life in the resurrection community. They are gifts from God to be accepted or to be chosen within the scope he gives us for choice.[14]

Questions for Reflection and Group Discussion

1. What is the most significant insight you have gained from reading this chapter?

2. Why was Jesus' practice and teaching about singleness noteworthy to the people of his day and culture? How does Jesus' decision to remain unmarried affect your view of singleness?

3. Why might a disciple choose to forgo marriage for the sake of the kingdom of heaven? What difference would it make whether one was married or not?

4. How do the prophecies of Isaiah bring together the negative connotation of eunuchs in Judaism and the positive picture of eunuchs in royal courts? Do you think both perspectives are in view in Jesus' statement, or just one?

5. How does Vera Stinton's concluding summary of the biblical material on singleness differ from the view that prevails in the church today?

For additional questions, go to www.TheMarriageDecision.com.

8
Singleness and the Will of God
(1 Corinthians 7)

In my preparation for writing this book, I met for an evening with nine mature Christian single adults ranging in age from late twenties to mideighties(!). The meeting was conceived as a think tank where thoughtful, seasoned singles could reflect and interact on issues related to single living.

One of my questions was, "Do you regard your single state as a burden or a blessing?" Their resounding, unanimous answer was, "Yes!" There are indeed pluses and minuses connected to the experience of celibacy.

This reality is aptly reflected in the answer Vera Stinton gives to her question cited in the previous chapter. That question, you will recall, was, what are we to make of the single condition? She concluded:

> Singleness and marriage are parallel routes for loving and serving in the world and preparing us for life in the resurrection community. They are gifts from God to be accepted or to be chosen within the scope he gives us for choice.[1]

Stinton's last sentence, in particular, will resonate with many single adults. The part that proves to be so perplexing is the dual reality that, on the one hand, either singleness or marriage may be chosen and, on the other, these gifts may be accepted "within the scope [God] gives us for choice." In other words, while there are two options in theory, at any given moment in life there is often only one.

Why do our lives unfold the way they do? As Christians, we do not believe that our experiences happen by chance or that our circumstances are the product of fate. As we saw in chapter 2, the dominant shapers of our destiny are the choices we make (on the human side) and the sovereign will of God (on the divine side). The question we are poised to consider is, how do God's moral will and God's sovereign will relate to our marital status, and how should we respond?

One passage in the New Testament speaks to this question directly—1 Corinthians 7. In fact, this is the one chapter in the New Testament that directly addresses whether one should marry or remain single.[2] It also provides a classic example of the principles of the Way of Wisdom elucidated in chapters 1 and 2.[3]

Because 1 Corinthians 7 is a lengthy chapter that presents the Bible student with several interpretive challenges, the next few paragraphs will not be light reading. But the payoff for a little hard work will be an understanding of God's will for singleness expressed in principles that have practical applications. So hang in there.

Reading Someone Else's Mail

It is ironic that the most complete apostolic guidance on marital decision making was likely written to address a circumstance that is almost exactly opposite what we find in the church today. While contemporary Christian singles feel a certain amount of social pressure to get married, influential elements within the Corinthian church were advocating a solitary life.[4] To be specific, *some people within the Corinthian church were promoting sexual abstinence as a means of advancing their standing before God.*[5] And they were seeking to impose this view on everyone, insisting on a celibate lifestyle, complete and permanent, for all believers: nevermarried, married, divorced, and widowed.

What were they thinking?

To get to that, we're going to need to track the story line and get oriented to a philosophical worldview very different from our own.

The apostle Paul founded the church in Corinth on his second missionary journey and spent eighteen months getting it established (Acts 18). On his subsequent mission trip, he established a base of operations in Ephesus, from which he evangelized and discipled believers throughout the region of western Turkey for about three years (Acts 19).

While he was in Ephesus, Paul would get news about the church in Corinth, much of which was disheartening (1 Corinthians 1:11). Then he received a letter from the church leaders asking for his advice on issues that were dividing the church (1 Corinthians 7:1). So Paul decided to address the problems he had heard about and the ones they were asking about in an extended epistle (1 Corinthians).

As we analyze a portion of that treatise, it will be important for us to remember that we are reading somebody else's mail. It was written two thousand years ago in a different language to people whose world-view seems foreign to us. And we have only Paul's half of the correspondence. So our understanding of the problems being addressed, and even the questions being answered, must be inferred from Paul's replies and our knowledge of history.[6]

In contrast to the Jewish milieu of Jesus' comments about eunuchs (Matthew 19), Paul was addressing a predominantly Greek audience. Though they may have become aware of the Hebrew scriptures from their Jewish brethren[7], most of the Corinthian converts were saved out of Greco-Roman paganism. And it took a while for them to recover from the mindset of a Greek worldview.

For example, one of the dominant features of the Greek picture of reality was a dualism that viewed spirit as good and matter as evil. This outlook originated in the philosophical teachings of Plato and exercised a profound influence on Western thought for centuries. One of the ethical dilemmas posed by dualism was the nature of the interaction between the soul of a person (which was spiritual) and his body (which was material). Bible scholar Craig Blomberg summarizes the debate:

> [Platonic dualism] drove a deep wedge between spirit and matter. Only the former was potentially good and redeemable; the latter was inherently evil. What then was to be done about bodily appetites and desires? A majority of the philosophers tried to deny them and became ascetic[8] in their morality. A majority of the common people took the opposite tack and indulged them. If matter was by nature irredeemable, if religion was primarily or exclusively a matter of the spirit, then why not enjoy sensual pleasure while one could?[9]

These opposite conclusions may well have been represented within the church at Corinth. On this scenario, the *hedonistic group*, which advocated fleshly indulgence and employment of the services of temple prostitutes, was addressed by Paul at the end of 1 Corinthians 6, a passage we will consider in chapter 11. The *ascetic group*, which believed that one's spiritual nature is inevitably contaminated by any sexual activity, elicited the apostolic response recorded in 1 Corinthians 7. Isn't it interesting that these conflicting points of view and ethical lifestyle emerged out of the same worldview?[10]

This, then, comprises part of the background to Paul's message in 1 Corinthians 7.[11] As I said earlier, some people within the Corinthian church were promoting sexual abstinence, presumably as a means of advancing their standing before God. And they were seeking to impose this view on everyone, regardless of their marital status.

According to these ascetics, single people (never-married, divorced, and widowed) should not wed, and married people should *become celibate within their marriage*. And if one's partner was unwilling to become abstinent, the "spiritual one" should take the radical step of divorce.[12]

As they sought to deal appropriately with this state of affairs, the leaders of the Corinthian church wanted to know: Paul, do you agree with the ascetics that all Christians should refrain from sex?[13]

Paul's Response to the Corinthian Ascetics

In his response, Paul addressed the marital situation of everyone in the Corinthian congregations. Though he was expounding one central principle, the application varied according to the diverse circumstances of the church members. To track the flow of Paul's argument, it will be helpful to arrange the biblical text in a way that demonstrates his outline.[14] (For the sake of space, I am printing only the paragraphs that have a direct bearing on the marital decisions addressed in this book.)

Part 1: Counsel to the Married and Previously Married (7:1-16)

1. *For the married: Maintain sexual relations (1-7).*

2. *For widowers and widows: Stay unmarried, unless... (8-9).*

3. *For Christian married couples: No divorce (10-11).*

4. *For Christians married to unbelievers: Stay in the marriage (12-16).*

Part 2: General Rule: Remain As You Were When Called (7:17-24)

> Nevertheless, *as the Lord has assigned to each one, as God has called each person, so must he live.* I give this sort of direction in all the churches. Was anyone called after he had been circumcised? He should not try to undo his circumcision. Was anyone called who is uncircumcised? He should not get circumcised. Circumcision is nothing and uncircumcision is nothing. Instead, keeping God's commandments is what counts. Let each one *remain in that situation in life in which he was called.* Were you called as a slave? Do not worry about it. But if indeed you are able to be free, make the most of the opportunity. For the one who was called in the Lord as a slave is the Lord's freedman. In the same way, the one who was called as a free person is Christ's slave. You were bought with a price. Do not become slaves of men. *In whatever situation someone was called,* brothers and sisters, *let him remain in it with God* (emphasis added).

Part 3: Counsel to the Never-Married and Widowed (7:25-40)

1. *For the never-married: Remain as you are (25-38).*

> With regard to the question about people who have never married, I have no command from the Lord, but I give my opinion as one shown mercy by the Lord to be trustworthy. *Because of the impending crisis* I think it best for you to remain as you are. The one bound to a wife should not seek divorce. The one released from a wife should not seek marriage. But if you marry, you have not sinned. And if a virgin marries, she has not sinned. But those who marry will *face difficult circumstances,* and I am trying to spare you such problems.
>
> And I say this, brothers and sisters: The time is short. So then those who have wives should be as those who have none, those with tears like those not weeping, those who rejoice like those not rejoicing, those who buy like those without possessions, those who use the world as though they were not using it to the full. For the present shape of this world is passing away.
>
> And I want you to be free from concern. An unmarried man is concerned about the things of the Lord, how to please the Lord. But a married man is concerned about the things of the world, how to please his wife, and he is divided. An unmarried woman or a virgin is concerned about

the things of the Lord, to be holy both in body and spirit. But a married woman is concerned about the things of the world, how to please her husband. I am saying this for your benefit, not to place a limitation on you, but so that without distraction you may give notable and constant service to the Lord.

If anyone thinks he is acting inappropriately toward his virgin, if she is past the bloom of youth and it seems necessary, he should do what he wishes; he does not sin. Let them marry. But the man who is firm in his commitment, and is under no necessity but has control over his will, and has decided in his own mind to keep his own virgin, does well. So then, the one who marries his own virgin does well, but the one who does not, does better (emphasis added).

2. *For widows: Remarriage permitted; though happier unmarried (39-40).*

A wife is bound as long as her husband is living. But if her husband dies, she is free to marry anyone she wishes (only someone in the Lord). But in my opinion, she will be happier if she remains as she is—and I think that I too have the Spirit of God!

As we prepare to unpack the content of this passage, the first thing to notice is the similarity of this exchange between Paul and the Corinthian ascetics to Jesus' response to his men in Matthew 19. In both cases, some disciples were suggesting that maybe marriage ought to be avoided, although for different motivations.[15] In both cases, the leader acknowledged that *some* disciples might well choose to remain unmarried, though for entirely different reasons from those advocated by their followers. Both Jesus and Paul were making the case that some should consider choosing the single life "for the sake of the kingdom" (Matthew 19:12; 1 Corinthians 7:35).

In Answer to Your Question...

The short answer to the question, "Should all Christians refrain from sex?" was no. Sexual abstinence is required of unmarried believers (1 Corinthians 6:12-21), but "marital celibacy" is an oxymoron (7:1-7). Sexual union is an integral part of a one-flesh relationship, and spouses may not unilaterally deprive their mates of their conjugal rights. So if some Corinthian believers had imposed a kind of sexual fasting on their partners, Paul ordered them to cease and desist. His warning was that the danger they incurred was the opposite of what was intended. Rather than attaining a higher spiritual state, the temptation enflamed by denying powerful urges might actually lead to sexual sin. Marriage is precisely where the desire that draws a man and woman together ought to be satisfied. It is part of the deal.

Principles for Marital Decision Making

But Paul was not given to short answers. The extended reply was intended to answer the question-behind-the-question. Paul recognized that the underlying issue requiring correction was the assertion that a Christian could attain a higher standing before God by altering some external life situation—in this case, rejecting marriage for singleness.[16] So he enunciated one general rule, which he then applied to the diverse circumstances of his readers. As we track his argument, his principles for marital decision making will emerge.

Remain as You Are

Paul's general rule, articulated in part 2 of his essay (verses 17-24), cannot be missed (he said it three times!): *"Let each one remain in that situation in life in which he was called"* (verse 20, echoed in verses 17 and 24).[17] Against the ascetics who were insisting that believers take extraordinary steps to change their life circumstances in order to attain a higher spiritual status, Paul counsels the opposite tack. Rather than being in a hurry to change one's status—whether ethnic (circumcised/uncircumcised), social (slave/free), or marital (single/married)—the believer should first learn how to live out his vocation as a servant-steward of Christ in the life situation he was in at the time of conversion.[18]

For our purposes, *the first principle* for marital decision making established in these verses is this:

> *Like other life situations, one's marital status at any given time is determined by the sovereign will of God.*

In a chapter devoted to marital decisions, Paul illustrates his main thought with two life situations that have nothing to do with singleness and marriage: namely, circumcision and slavery. Paul's opening statement makes clear that each of these external circumstances (ethnic, social, and marital) come to us as an assignment from God: "Each one must live his life in the situation the Lord assigned when God called him" (7:17 HCSB).[19] So if one believer was an unmarried Jewish slave and another was a married Gentile freedman, the respective components of each person's life situation constituted their current assignment from God.

The starting point for responding to God's sovereign will for one's marital status is to affirm the reality of it. Carolyn McCulley bravely declares this truth: *"Ultimately, we are single because that's God's will for us right now"* (italics hers). There may be other secondary reasons, but "they don't trump God's will."[20]

How is God's sovereign will implemented in our lives? At one level, we do not know—we're confronting mystery. But we experience it in the outworking of our circumstances. We all start out single. But whether we remain single or get married is controlled by God's sovereign will.

Are you single because of divorce? That painful reality is encompassed in God's sovereign will. Are you single because your spouse died? That grievous loss is governed by God's sovereign will. For many single people, the circumstantial reason for their state—a broken engagement, a failed marriage, a tragic death—is a source of great pain. Even so, as it passes through the hands of a sovereign God, he baptizes it with grace, directs it to his purposes, and instructs us to trust in his goodness.

Sometimes, later on, we are able to discern some of the beneficial results of God's plan (as Joseph did); in other cases, the positive outcome remains hidden from us (as was the case with Job). In either case, part of walking by faith is accepting our present status as an assignment from God and seeking to glorify him through the manner in which we faithfully exercise our stewardship within it. (For an expanded commentary on this paragraph, review chapter 2.)

Subject to Change

The *second principle*, embedded in verse 21, qualifies the first one by reminding us that our present appointments are not necessarily permanent:

Throughout the course of one's life, one's assignments are subject to change, sometimes through personal choice.

Most modifications of status come about through some change of circumstance plus whatever choices we make in response. The change may take the form of adversity or opportunity. This reality is illustrated in these verses by the institution of *slavery*. In antiquity, a person could become enslaved against his will through the (mis)fortunes of war. Or, being someone's slave, he might have the opportunity to gain emancipation. Even though Paul's essential counsel is "remain as you are," he makes allowance for prospects that would improve one's situation. And so he advised: "But if indeed you are able to be free, make the most of the opportunity" (7:21).[21] Similarly, throughout 1 Corinthians 7, Paul addresses the fact that some people are not locked in to their marital status. Change is possible and permissible—but only within the moral will of God (see below).

Guidelines for Decision Making

So how is the believer to respond to the current assignments of God's sovereign will? The *third principle* found in this passage is:

One's responses to their life situations must be directed by the moral will of God and wisdom.

This principle, which summarizes the first three precepts in the Way of Wisdom (explained in chapter 1), is clearly in evidence throughout 1 Corinthians 7. The determinative role of God's moral will is proclaimed in Paul's comments about circumcision: "Circumcision is nothing and uncircumcision is nothing. Instead, *keeping God's commandments is what counts*" (7:19, emphasis added).[22] As one makes decisions about staying single or getting married,[23] it is crucial to distinguish between what is permissible (within the area of freedom) and what is required (the moral will of God). Within the context of 1 Corinthians 6–7, the aspect of God's commandments that is being emphasized concerns sexual purity, whether one is unmarried (no fornication) or married (no adultery) (1 Corinthians 6:12–7:9).[24]

Within the moral will of God, plenty of latitude exists for the application of wisdom. And wisdom seeks to accomplish three practical goals:

(1) avoiding mistakes, (2) maximizing opportunities, and (3) managing difficulties.

Wisdom: Avoiding Mistakes

Paul's advice in the central segment, "remain as you are," is an instance of *mistake avoidance*. The original issue he was addressing—the assertion that all believers should become sexually abstinent—was based on the false premise that the repudiation of carnal pleasures would somehow exalt one's standing with God. In actual fact, any effort to elevate our spiritual status by changing an external circumstance (our present assignment from God) opposes God's grace and produces false pride. Such a step would prove to be spiritually damaging rather than enhancing. This is a mistake we should avoid.

Wisdom: Maximizing Opportunities

That doesn't mean that celibacy itself should be avoided by all believers. Paul denied that celibacy should be adopted as a means of elevating our spiritual stature. But he maintained that *some* already-single believers might choose to remain unmarried in order to more effectively advance the kingdom of God. This would be an exercise in *maximizing the opportunities*.

Paul's case[25] for continued singleness ("remain as you are") was spelled out in verses 25-35, and his reasons fall into two categories: (1) the urgency of the hour ("because of the impending crisis," v. 26),[26] which he elaborated in verses 29-31; and (2) the difficulties and distraction inherent in marriage ("those who marry will face difficult circumstances," v. 28), which he spelled out in verses 32-36.

First, Paul challenged the never-married to take the circumstances of the present age into consideration (7:29-31). He was acutely aware that he and the Corinthian believers were living during the third movement of the symphony. The fact that the world we live in is fallen changes things. We are at war. What would be unusual during a time of peace and prosperity becomes sanctioned in the prosecution of a strategic plan of battle. The status of singleness that would be abnormal in the pristine environment of Eden is normalized during the third movement. In the fight to bring all things under the headship of Christ, Paul wanted to mobilize unmarried believers as Special Forces who sensed the urgency of the hour and were available for unconventional duty.

One aspect of the mindset that enables single believers to forego the blessings of marriage is an eternal perspective.[27] In his recruiter's spiel, I could imagine Paul saying, "Hey, if you don't get married in this life, don't worry about it. You'll get in on the real thing during the fourth movement. Marriage can wait; we have work to do." What he actually said was, "the present shape of this world is passing away" (7:31).

This passage corresponds to Paul's explanation in Ephesians 5:16 that living wisely involves "taking advantage of every opportunity, because the days are evil." We can hear the ticking of an eschatological clock inside Paul's head—so much to do, so little time.[28] As stewards of the resources of grace, we need to be careful lest we invest too heavily in what is temporary. "Everything that belongs to this world is lame-duck, marriage included."[29]

The second category of reasons for preferring the single state emerges from a comparison of the relative freedom single people have to serve God with the limitations encountered by the married (7:32-35). It is better, in Paul's opinion, to give "undistracted devotion to the Lord" (7:35 NASB) than to have one's energies divided between attending to the needs of a spouse[30] and focusing on Christ. But, once again, he declined to bind his audience with a command one way or the other.[31] The bottom-line question the never-married person should ask is: *"In which state can I better exercise the stewardship of my walk with and service to God?"* Different people will come up with different answers. In fact, the same person may well come up with different answers at different times of life.

One thing this argument tells us about God's design for singleness is that it, like marriage, is intended to be a *ministry institution.* There is some irony here in that one of the reasons for considering marriage is the potential contributions a partner could make to one's work and one's spiritual growth. Here Paul exposes the other side of the coin. There are benefits to marriage, yes, but there are also distractions. In marital decision making, all of these factors must be weighed by wisdom.

Wisdom: Managing Difficulties

As much as Paul might favor his current status of singleness, he was profoundly aware that celibacy has its own distractions. One, in particular, might be so strong for some persons that it could single-handedly tip the scale in favor of marriage. For if the married person had to deal with the added burdens of family life, the single person had to contend with the greater susceptibility to sexual sin. And so wisdom seeks not only to maximize the opportunity, it also attends to *the management of difficulties.*

Temptation to sexual sin is the subject with which 1 Corinthians 6 ended (6:12-20) and 1 Corinthians 7 opened. In his refutation of the ascetics' insistence on celibacy within marriage, Paul countered that husbands and wives should not deprive one another sexually "because of immoralities" (7:2) and "so that Satan may not tempt you because of your lack of self-control" (7:5). When he subsequently counseled previously married singles[32] to "remain as I am" (i.e., single), he immediately issued this caveat: "But if they do not have self-control, let them get married. For it is better to marry than to burn with sexual desire" (7:9).

And this is where wisdom contends with reality by managing difficulties. Paul acknowledges that some among the formerly married may not only have strong urges for sexual intercourse, but may lack the self-control to practice abstinence. In such a case, it would be better for them to return to the state of marriage, which is where such drives may be legitimately channeled (7:9).

If I might expand on Paul's vocabulary of "good" (7:1), "better" (7:9,38), and "best" (7:8,26), his argument is that celibacy is *best* for giving undistracted devotion to the Lord. Giving in to the temptation to sexual sin would be "worst." So it would be *better* for some to marry than to be consumed by the distraction that attends single life. Singleness may be better for service to God, but marriage is better for managing sexual desires.

Sufficient Grace

Almost in passing, Paul gives a wistful aside: "I wish that everyone was as I am. But each has his own gift from God, one this way, another that" (7:7). Unlike the married couples he had been addressing (7:1-6), Paul, being a celibate single, did not have to contend with the negotiations of marital life. Thanks to God's gracious gifting, Paul was able to focus on "undistracted devotion to the Lord" (7:35 NASB), and he wished everyone else could too.

The precise meaning of Paul's statement in verse 7 is less than clear and has produced considerable debate. One group of interpreters take the expression "I wish that everyone was as I am" to refer to the *freedom from distraction* from sexual temptation he experienced, even though he was single, by virtue of the *spiritual gift of celibacy* he had received. On this view, he was reluctantly agreeing that other singles who had not been blessed with that particular gift should consider marriage.

Another group takes "the gift" to refer not to the *capacity* to live as an unmarried man but to the *status* of singleness itself. On this view, singleness and marriage are equal gifts that have been bestowed "one this way, another that." If one is single, they have received the "gift of singleness" by definition. "Gift" is another way of describing the sovereign will of God.

A third group stresses the grace aspect of the word *charisma* ("gift") and understands Paul to be talking about the enablement that God supplies for faithful living in whatever life situation one encounters. From this standpoint, "I wish that everyone was as I am" refers both to his singleness (because he wanted more undivided ministers) and *the self-control he exercised through the appropriation of God's sustaining grace*. "One this way, another that" means that this grace, which is available to everyone, not only energizes singles to maintain self-control, but also empowers spouses to manifest self-sacrifice. (For an extended evaluation of these three views, go to www.themarriagedecision.com.)

I am inclined to the third position, in part because it meshes well with so much of Paul's teaching elsewhere as well as the general rule of 1 Corinthians 7 to "remain as you are." Accordingly, the *fourth principle* attests:

> Whatever one's present life assignment, the provisions of God's grace are sufficient (1) to handle the difficulties attending it, (2) to live in obedience to the moral will of God, (3) to produce character growth toward Christlikeness, and (4) to fulfill one's vocation as a steward of God's resources for the advancement of his kingdom.

The elements in that principle are perhaps more clearly set out in other comments Paul made to his Corinthian correspondents.[33] Of course, the classic passage on the sufficiency of God's grace is 2 Corinthians 12:7-10:

Therefore, so that I would not become arrogant, a thorn in the flesh was given to me, a messenger of Satan to trouble me—so that I would not become arrogant. I asked the Lord three times about this, that it would depart from me. But he said to me, "My grace is enough for you, for my power is made perfect in weakness." So then, I will boast most gladly about my weaknesses, so that the power of Christ may reside in me. Therefore I am content with weaknesses, with insults, with troubles, with persecutions and difficulties for the sake of Christ, for whenever I am weak, then I am strong.

The relevance of Paul's thorn to our consideration of God's provisions for our life situations (including marital status) becomes apparent at several points.

- First, like our other assignments in life, this circumstance was sovereignly determined by God.

- Second, it was in some sense a gift. (The verb "was given" is the general word for giving.) Paul didn't receive it because he earned or deserved it, but because he apparently needed it.

- Ironically, this imposition included an element of satanic harassment. Just as Paul had been concerned about the vulnerability of Corinthian spouses to the temptation of Satan (1 Corinthians 7:5), so he had to contend with the devil's efforts to derail him from his calling.

- This thorn imposed a significant limitation on Paul's ability to minister—to such a degree that he earnestly sought its removal. One could say that it had become a "distraction," to borrow a key concept from 1 Corinthians 7. Furthermore, the word *thorn* connotes a significant degree of severity—greater, no doubt, than the variety of difficulties that typically occur in single or married living.

- Nevertheless, this thorny present proved to be ultimately beneficial, though the advantage may not have been immediately obvious. A gift doesn't have to be uniformly pleasant to be good for us. Like a parent's discipline, it may be experienced as a severe kindness with deferred benefits (Hebrews 12:5-15). In Paul's case, the thorn counteracted a besetting inclination toward arrogance, a toxic vice for a spiritual leader.

- Equally important, the presence of the thorn introduced Paul to an experience of God's grace that he would not have otherwise known. This goal-oriented apostle came to acknowledge that he was actually more productive with the thorn, because of the power of Christ, than he would have been without it. To say that the Lord's grace is "enough" or "sufficient" turns out to be an understatement.

- Finally, Paul's response provides a model for believers as we adapt to the sovereign will of God in our lives. His first reaction was typical of anyone who encounters frustration at the confining limits imposed by circumstances beyond one's control: "You are God. You can make this go away!" But over time, as Paul came to recognize the potential benefits of his sovereignly imposed constraint and the kind purposes of his Master, the bowed neck of resistance relaxed into reliance and contentment. And disgruntlement gave way to joy.

Bloom Where You Are Planted

All of this culminates in the *fifth principle*:

As one responds to the outworking of the sovereign will of God, God's moral will calls the believer to maximize the opportunities inherent in those circumstances to the glory of God.

The shorter version of this principle is: whatever your lot in life at the moment, make the most of it. In 1 Corinthians 7, this principle shows up at several points. The Christian married to a non-Christian is encouraged to stay in the marriage if the other is willing, for "how do you know... whether you will bring your [spouse] to salvation?" (7:16). The slave is reminded that though his situation is personally confining, there is no limit on his ability to serve Christ: "For the one who was called in the Lord as a slave is the Lord's freedman. In the same way, the one who was called as a free person is Christ's slave" (7:22). And, of course, the unmarried are challenged to capitalize on the freedoms of single living "so that without distraction you may give notable and constant service to the Lord" (7:35).

All of these instructions are applications of one of Paul's overarching goals for personal living expressed elsewhere: "So whether you eat or drink, or whatever you do, do everything for the glory of God" (1 Corinthians 10:31; see Colossians 3:17).

Singleness and the Will of God: Principles

1. Your current marital status is determined by the sovereign will of God.

2. God's sovereign assignments are subject to change.

3. Your response to your current assignment must be governed by God's moral will and wisdom.

4. God's grace is sufficient for your current assignment.

5. Goal: Maximize the opportunities of your current assignment to God's glory.

It is these principles, extracted from Paul's original instructions to his Corinthian audience, that contemporary Christian singles should seek to apply to marital decisions in the twenty-first century.

❖ ❖ ❖

Questions for Reflection and Group Discussion

1. What is the most significant insight you have gained from reading this chapter?

2. *Principle 1: Your current marital status is determined by the sovereign will of God.* If the observable reasons for one's singleness are painful (breakup, divorce, death), is the assertion of the first principle about the sovereign will of God helpful? Why or why not?

3. *Principle 2: God's sovereign assignments are subject to change.* Why is this an important qualification on Principle 1? How does it affect your attitude about your current circumstances?

4. *Principle 3: Your response to your current assignment must be governed by God's moral will and wisdom.* If Christian singles should seek to avoid mistakes, maximize opportunities, and manage difficulties, what are some examples of situations where wisdom could be applied in these ways?

5. *Principle 4: God's grace is sufficient for your current assignment.* How does Paul's response to his thorn in the flesh apply to Christian singles as they confront the difficulties of single living? For what, specifically, is the grace of God sufficient?

6. *Principle 5: Goal: Maximize the opportunities of your current assignment to God's glory.* What are some of the advantages that the single state has over marriage? Are you maximizing the opportunities of your single status presently? How?

7. This chapter is titled "Singleness and the Will of God." How does the will of God affect your experience of singleness? As a single person, what is your response to the will of God?

❖   ❖   ❖

For additional questions, go to www.TheMarriageDecision.com.

9

Single Choices

When we talk about the choice between singleness and marriage, this is not the sort of decision where we dispassionately try to choose between two untried options—like a pedestrian comparing a motorcycle to a car for transportation. No, we start out single. The question is: shall I *remain* single, or shall I get married?

But, of course, the question is not that simple. The meaning of one's inquiry is profoundly influenced by a number of factors, including one's stage of life. A twenty-one-year-old man who has just joined the Peace Corps is probably not entertaining plans for marriage in the immediate future. He has things to do, places to go, people to see. He's not ready to be tied down to domestic responsibilities. A thirty-five-year-old woman who postponed marriage to pursue her career (or who simply never encountered a qualified man to marry) may be tuned in to the ticking of the biological clock. She may be satisfied with her professional life, but she's wondering if marriage has been put off—or ruled out.

The meaning of the question is also affected by one's current prospects. If you are in a relationship, the question probably means, "Is *this* the person and is *now* the time?" That is, are you open to this relationship developing toward marriage, or should you pull back because of other priorities at this time in your life? On the other hand, if there is no candidate for matrimony on the horizon, the question would be, "Am I satisfied with my single state, or do I want to get married?" How active should you be in looking for a partner or exploring that option? Should you be taking initiative to find a marriage partner? What steps should you take?

When due allowance is made for the historical-cultural differences between Paul's world and our own, the principles we uncovered in 1 Corinthians 7 in the previous chapter provide a reliable framework for marital decision making today. For in this passage, Paul shows how God's sovereign will, God's moral will, and wisdom all impinge on marital decisions.

Decisions, Decisions, Decisions...

As we seek to apply the teachings of 1 Corinthians 7 to our own time, we will need to pay attention to three major differences between Paul's setting and our own. The first concerns the reason Paul wrote this discourse in the first place—the ascetics. As far as I can tell, no Christian singles today are under pressure from within the church to reject marriage on the grounds of spiritual defilement caused by sexual intercourse. If anything, they are pressured to get married. So the circumstances are almost the opposite.[1]

The second major difference relates to the decision-making process—specifically, the identity of the decision makers. However marriages were arranged in first-century Corinth, younger single women had no official say in their marital destiny. In a patriarchal society, the contracts were worked out by the men.[2] Widows apparently acquired the right to act on their own initiative,[3] so the counsel given to them in verses 39-40 more closely parallels our current practices. For in contemporary Western culture, most marital decisions lie exclusively in the hands of the men and women directly involved.

Third, there is likely less assurance in our day that the person who desires to get married will actually have the opportunity to do so. As Paul writes, it sounds as though the only choice to be made is whether one will marry. If the decision maker opts for marriage, it will be arranged. There is no discussion about how to find a mate.[4] That is very different from the experience of many contemporary singles. (I happen to think this is a significant difference.)

Applying Biblical Principles to Marital Decision Making Today

With these historical and cultural differences in mind, we can proceed to apply biblical principles to contemporary marital decisions.

Application 1

Christian single adults have the freedom and responsibility to make marital decisions.

By now it should be clear that you should not expect God to make these decisions for you or tell you what to do (see chapter 2). While you are to trust in God's sovereign will, you have a decisive role to play. On the one hand, you have *freedom* to choose. That fact is implicit in Paul's description of the pros and cons of singleness and marriage, as well as the complete absence of any exhortation to seek God's will on the matter. This freedom was also made explicit in some direct statements:

> If anyone thinks he is acting inappropriately toward his virgin...*he should do what he wishes;* he does not sin. Let them marry. But the man who is firm in his commitment, and is under no necessity but has control over his will, and *has decided in his own mind* to keep his own virgin, does well...
>
> A wife is bound as long as her husband is living. But if her husband dies, *she is free to marry anyone she wishes* (only someone in the Lord)" (1 Corinthians 7:36-37, 39, emphasis added).

Paul acts as though it is up to the responsible parties to make their decisions. And so, on the other hand, you have the *responsibility* to choose. Paul assumes that his readers have the ability to evaluate the various factors and come to a mature judgment. When he sets out a principle such as "remain as you are," and then tells slaves to claim their freedom if they get the opportunity, he is acknowledging that life is complex—you can't just create a list of rules that apply to every situation. When it comes to singleness and marriage, one size does not fit all. What all this underscores is that marriage is for grownups. And mature adults are capable of making good marital decisions.

Application 2

While marital decisions are not dictated by the moral will of God, they are regulated by it. Regardless of status, believers are obligated to know and obey the relevant rules.

For over twenty-six years, Garry Friesen and I were obligated to the same requirements imposed on our lives as single men by the moral will of God. And then, at 2:37 p.m. on Saturday, November 10, 1973, God's moral will for my life instantaneously changed. As I stood next to my bride and a man wearing a black robe said, "I now pronounce you husband and wife," the obligations of a whole bunch of verses that had not previously applied to me kicked in. In my personal dictionary, *chastity* was redefined. Before God, I assumed responsibilities I had formerly been free from.

Either marital status, singleness or marriage, entails duties mandated by God's moral will. Part of the decision making process involves identifying and accepting those imperatives.

Application 3

The factors that need to be weighed in marital decision making must be judged by wisdom. As with all non-commanded decisions, each option has pros and cons.

As we said in chapter 1, in non-commanded decisions, the believer's goal is to make wise decisions on the basis of spiritual usefulness. In 1 Corinthians 7, this principle is conveyed through descriptive words such as "good," "better," "best," "benefit," and "happier." Wisdom aims to avoid mistakes, maximize opportunities, and manage difficulties. The summary statement in verse 35 encapsulates practical wisdom: "I am saying this *for your benefit*, not to place a limitation on you, but so that without distraction you may give *notable and constant service to the Lord*." A wise decision will both advance God's purposes and prove to be personally beneficial.

There are advantages and disadvantages to singleness; there are benefits and costs to marriage. Some folks labor under the illusion that if they make the right decision, they will live happily ever after. But this choice should not be framed in terms of *right* and *wrong*, but rather *good* and *better*.[5]

The advantages of marriage follow from its design: relational companionship and vocational partnership. These benefits have been spelled out in some detail in chapters 3 and 5. The disadvantages of marriage are well-summarized by Paul in 1 Corinthians 7. It takes a lot of time and energy to manage a marriage and a family.

While I was working on this chapter (on a Saturday), I needed to talk with our church's youth pastor about our plans for Sunday. So I called John on the phone. When he answered, I said, "I have two quick questions to ask about tomorrow. Is this a good time to call?"

He replied, "Um, could I call you back in a second? I'm in the middle of changing Daisy's diaper."

I wanted to say, "No, just drop what you're doing and answer my questions. Where are your priorities?" Instead, I thanked him for the illustration and returned to this paragraph. The fact is, John doesn't have the freedom he used to have to "drop what you're doing" for the sake of ministry. He must balance his responsibilities as a husband and father with his duties as a pastor. And it's not easy. While many fathers or mothers neglect their families (often giving higher priority to a career, a pastime, or a cause), others make an idol of their family at the expense of ministry.

Most of the benefits of singleness fall under the heading of freedom. Paul's stress was on freedom from concern along with greater flexibility for ministry.[6] Albert Hsu expands on the opportunities of singleness as he identifies six categories of celibate freedom:

- freedom to follow Jesus
- freedom to show God's love
- freedom to experience personal growth
- freedom to find healing and wholeness
- freedom to marry
- freedom of childlessness.

In each of these areas, there are recognizable advantages of singleness over marriage.[7]

The disadvantages of singleness represent the flip side of the benefits of marriage. Relational challenges usually top most lists: vulnerability to loneliness and denial of sexual intimacy. While these downsides to singleness can be lessened by healthy friendships, the effort required to develop mutually edifying relationships is greater for those who are unmarried.

Application 4

For contemporary singles, Paul's admonition to "remain as you are" might be aptly paraphrased, "Don't be in too big a hurry to get married."

As we make the shift from Paul's world to our own, we must bear in mind a couple of important details. First, Paul's original exhortation to first-century Corinthian believers was *not a command;* it was spiritual counsel. And second, he was addressing two issues—one theological and one pragmatic—that were different from the ones we face.

The theological issue was the mistaken belief by some that a change in their external circumstances would advance their standing with God. (So, in particular, abstaining from sexual intercourse would make one holier. Therefore, Christian spouses should terminate their marriages.) Not so, said Paul. They should "remain as you are...*with God*" (1 Corinthians 7:24).

The practical issue stemmed from a circumstance described by Paul as the "impending distress" (7:26). We don't know specifically what Paul was referring to, but it gave him such a sense of urgency that he was actively recruiting celibate ministers.

So is Paul's advice ("remain as you are") applicable to contemporary singles? How is our social situation different from his? And what difference, if any, does our cultural context make in our application of his counsel?

Let's start with the practical concern. I don't know exactly what Paul meant when he cites the impending crisis as a reason to "remain as you are."[8] But Paul's sensitivity to this state of affairs points out at least one principle that we can apply to our current situation: *there are circumstances in life that may justify deferment (at least) of marriage.*

The contemporary situations calling for "not yet" could stem from disruptive circumstances in the wider culture—war, economic depression, natural disaster, and so on. But more often the reasons for deferment will be peculiar to the individual—a lack of readiness for marital commitment, a personal crisis that needs to be resolved, or other priorities (ministry, education, employment) that demand undivided attention for a period of time. This is the pragmatic consideration. (Some aspects of this idea are being debated these days, so I will give it more attention in chapter 14.)

Like Paul, I also have a concern that is theological. The problem he confronted was a kind of hyper-spirituality; the pervasive syndrome of our day is a form of idolatry. In our quest for self-fulfillment, we moderns turn to external things rather than God to find Life itself. Whereas folks in Paul's day were abstaining from sex to attain a spiritual high, our culture worships sex as the ultimate attainment. Corinthian believers were withdrawing from their marriages; contemporary Christian singles are more inclined to pursue marriage as the One Essential Thing Required To Make Life Worth Living.

This temptation is especially strong for single adults dealing with difficult personal circumstances such as loneliness, low self-esteem, damage from abusive family relationships, and the like. They have a tendency to view marriage as a panacea for all manner of unsatisfactory conditions. But moving hastily into a marriage is likely to be an exercise in jumping out of the proverbial frying pan into the fire. What many people find, to their great disappointment, is that marriage seldom solves problems; it tends to magnify them. A spouse may make a wonderful companion but usually lacks the credentials to be a savior.

For wounded singles, the counsel to "remain as you are" refers only to their marital status (single), not their condition (wounded). A single person recovering from relational damage needs to take time and initiative to become a functional, healthy adult. A person who is not emotionally needy is in a better position to wisely evaluate marital options.

But the counsel to "remain as you are" is not restricted to singles recovering from bad experiences. Laura Smit points out that Christian singles should not simply avoid marriage for bad reasons, but should pursue marriage only if they have biblically sound ones:

> Christians should be free to marry if marriage will make them better Christians. It does seem, however, that singleness must be the default choice for a Christian, given the clear preference for singleness expressed in [1 Corinthians]...In other words, the burden of proof is on the decision

to marry, not the decision to remain single. Christians should assume that they will be single unless and until they have a godly reason to marry. Christians should never marry out of insecurity, fear, a desire to escape the parental home, a need for affirmation, or a search for financial stability. Christians should marry only those who enhance their ability to live Christlike lives, those able to be true partners in Christian service, those who give them a vision of the image of God and the glory of Christ.[9]

I'm not sure I agree that singleness should be considered the default choice for the believer; after all, we are still wired for marriage. But Smit wonderfully reinforces a major point of this book: if a Christian chooses to marry, *the reasons for getting married are as important as the selection of the life partner.* In fact, one's reasons for pursuing marriage will largely determine the criteria one adopts for choosing a particular mate.

There are many valid reasons why Christian singles should not be in too big a rush to get married. You should "remain as you are" long enough to carefully evaluate and choose healthy and godly reasons to be open to marriage. Then, should the opportunity for courtship with a prospective mate materialize, you will have the freedom to move forward with a clear perspective on your options.

Application 5

In weighing the pros and cons of singleness and marriage, Christians should place a priority on their relationship to God.

In chapters 4 and 7, we learned that with the coming of Christ, the institution of marriage was relocated from a place of primacy in human relationships to a secondary level of status—alongside singleness—within the kingdom of God. According to God's design, both marriage and singleness are equally valuable means for carrying out the mission of the church. Neither status is to be regarded as an end in itself, but rather a complementary component of God's plan to effect the reconciliation and restoration of all things.

As those who have been reconciled and are being restored, Christians are members of Christ's family, stewards in God's household, soldiers in the Lord's army. As such, we are called to give attention, first and foremost, to God's perspective on singleness and marriage. In contrast to our neighbors whose chief motivation is often self-advancement, our *first* question is *not* to be, "How does this affect me personally?" (We do get to ask that question; it's just not first on the list.) In our decision making, we are to "seek first his kingdom and his righteousness" (Matthew 6:33 NIV). And so Paul makes his case for choosing celibacy because it better promotes "undivided devotion to the Lord" (1 Corinthians 7:35 NIV).

Paul is very careful to communicate that both singleness and marriage are acceptable to God. The apostle had a practical recommendation, but God has assigned these decisions to the individuals involved. The point I am underscoring here is not Paul's preference, but his *reasons* for it. He demonstrates how we are supposed to approach our marital choices. So the first question a believer should ask is, *In which state can I better exercise the stewardship of my walk with and service to God?*[10]

The experience of Marva Dawn provides an instructive example of a woman who followed this priority. When she was considering the marriage proposal of her dear friend, Myron, she was asked by another friend what her primary criterion was for making a decision. Marva replied, "Will marriage to Myron help me to serve God better?"

> But that question usually resulted in what seemed a tie—I could serve God better if I were free to travel to teach anywhere at any time or I could serve God more effectively if I were more deeply rooted in the home. Marguerite proposed that I should ask instead if marriage to Myron would enable me to *love* God better. That made an enormous difference and brought my questioning more thoroughly in line with the biblical picture of marriage as a symbol of God's faithfulness. There was no doubt about it: Myron's gentle care would certainly enfold me in, and constantly remind me of, God's grace and love, and consequently would set me more free to respond in love to God.[11]

Are there any guidelines for how one might implement this application? Here is one approach.[12] After John Piper had preached a stirring message on the blessings of singleness, he was asked, "What is at all compelling about marriage? Why would one even want to be married?" Piper's reply was very insightful: "The 'compelling' comes only from the right combination of internal realities and objective truths about God's design for marriage."

You start with the objective truths of God's design. Piper listed four aspects of God's design for each state. (I've placed them here side by side.)

God's Design for Marriage	God's Design for Singleness
1. To display his covenant keeping love between Christ and the church	1. To display the spiritual nature of God's family that grows from regeneration, not procreation and sex
2. To sanctify the couple with the peculiar pains and pleasures of marriage	2. To sanctify the single with the peculiar pains and pleasures of singleness
3. To beget and rear a generation of white-hot worshippers	3. To capture more of the single's life for nondomestic ministry that is so desperately needed in the world
4. To channel good sexual desire into holy paths and transpose it into worshipful foretastes of heaven's pleasures	4. To magnify the all-satisfying worth of Christ that sustains [long-term] chastity

Step two engages the "internal realities" of your own heart. Put simply, within which of these designs do you see yourself living most productively to the glory of God? If you have a strong inclination one way or the other, that is your preferred status at this point in your life. (PS: It is subject to change.)

So what do you do if your *preferred* status is different from your *actual* status? (If you are married, you should be reading a different book!) For single believers who would like to get married, the answer to this question has two parts. And they are addressed in the next two applications.

Application 6

It is perfectly legitimate for those who hope to get married to take initiative that might lead to that outcome.

When Paul propounded the principle "remain as you are," he was not slamming the door on change. This is implicit in the fact that singleness and marriage are both legitimate choices for believers. But he made this principle explicit in his parenthetical comment to slaves—"But *if indeed you are able* to be free, make the most of the opportunity" (7:21, emphasis added). Slaves, by definition, had the fewest opportunities for decision making. Any initiative they might want to take toward manumission was severely limited. But sometimes a master would offer freedom, and Paul didn't want his instruction to "remain as you are" to prohibit acceptance of a legitimate release from slavery. By the same token, the one who desired to marry had the freedom to do so "if indeed you are able."[13]

But what does "if you are able" mean to single adults in today's world? How much initiative is appropriate? The Corinthian slave was at the mercy of his master; he was powerless to extract his own freedom. Are you likewise obliged to passively wait until God sovereignly drops a suitable mate in your lap? No. The range of options available to the modern-day single adult is much broader than those accessible to the first-century slave. You have not only the opportunity to seek out and court a potential spouse, but in the absence of intervention on the part of outside parties (parents, matchmakers), your personal involvement in the process is all the more necessary. Sometimes an unmarried person meets their future spouse through a magical, serendipitous encounter. But most marriages come about as a result of conscious deliberations and intentional behaviors on the parts of those eventually united.

Counselor Larry Crabb strikes the biblical balance when he advises: *Pray for your desires; work for your goals.* In this instruction he makes an important distinction. A *goal*, in this instance, is an objective that is under my control. I can attain it by applying diligent effort. A *desire*, on the other hand, is something I want, but I cannot obtain it on my own. I need the cooperation of another person(s).

If I hope to get married, I can make it my *goal* to become a mature Christian who acts for the welfare of others. No one can keep me from doing that, and such growth and commitment may open the door to a significant relationship with marriage potential. My *desire* to find a potential mate who is on a similar trajectory in timing and availability is beyond my control. Since that outcome is ultimately governed by God's sovereign will, that is a legitimate subject for prayer (Philippians 4:6). "The proper response to a desire, then, is *prayer*. To a goal, the appropriate response is a set of *responsible actions*."[14]

This perspective corresponds to the principles of decision making set out in the first two chapters of this book. In non-commanded decisions, the believer is free and responsible to make choices within the moral will of God as directed by wisdom. In the interplay between my responsibility and God's sovereign will, I am free to make plans and execute strategies. But I must subject my plans to God's sovereign will (James 4:13-16) and trust him to bring about his purposes, which are also for my good (Romans 8:28). One way to express this submission is through prayer (Romans 1:10).[15]

So how much initiative is appropriate? I hope these observations help us to identify the balance between the extremes of passivity and preoccupation. On one end of the spectrum is inertness that evades responsibility or reflects resignation. At the other pole is an all-out campaign to which most of one's discretionary time is devoted. This goes beyond initiative to obsession and often resorts to manipulative tactics.[16]

The balance is found in the middle—a "relaxed engagement" that determines and carries out a course of action while resting and relying on the sovereign will of God. For the single believer who aspires to marriage, wisdom points to developing a strategy for finding a mate. A deliberate plan will not in itself accomplish the hoped-for result. But being proactive in that direction is clearly fitting.

(The specific actions a single person might take are discussed in more detail in Part 5: "Looking for a Mate," chapters 14-18.)

Application 7

For as long as one is unmarried, the single adult should cultivate the complementary attitudes of contentment and ambition in carrying out the ministry functions of singleness.

In the introduction to this section on God's design for singleness, I expressed the opinion that most folks within the evangelical church think of singleness as a temporary and incomplete condition, a transitional stage en route to the ultimate destination of marriage. I also suggested that this perspective is biblically defective and consequentially damaging. We should now be able to recognize correctives to our misconceptions.

The first step is to acknowledge the change that has taken place as a result of the Fall and God's subsequent action to reverse it. Jesus reordered the hierarchy of relationships within his spiritual family such that singleness is sanctioned as a ministry institution alongside of and of equal standing with marriage. Singleness has the stamp of legitimacy in its own right—not simply as a stage culminating in earthly marriage. The ramifications of this upgrading of singleness should affect your view of both the present and the future.

With respect to the future, your present experience of singleness will turn out to be a transitional and preparatory stage that culminates, not necessarily in marriage, but in *whatever comes next in the sovereign plan of God* (whether singleness or marriage).[17] If you hope to marry one day, this perspective will help you refrain from postponing real life to an undetermined future. You should instead regard your present circumstance as your existing assignment from God and concentrate on being faithful to your current calling.

And so, in the present, like their married counterparts, single believers are called to carry out the divinely designated functions of their state. So what are those functions?

Ministry Functions of Singleness

The ministry functions of singleness are not directly spelled out in the Bible the way marriage functions are. In the beginning there was only marriage. Later, in a fallen world, Jesus established singleness as an additional platform for the advancement of his kingdom. We must derive the ministry functions of singleness *by contrast* to those of marriage. If God's design for marriage is expressed in vocational partnership and relational companionship, we can deduce that the functions of singleness are vocational *freedom* and relational *community*.

The function of *vocational freedom* is the more evident of the two, being explicitly set forth by Paul in 1 Corinthians 7:32-35. As we noted earlier in this chapter, the counterpoint that singleness offers to marital partnership is freedom from concern along with greater flexibility for ministry—potentially developed in the ways outlined by Albert Hsu and others.[18]

Less obvious but no less real is the function that corresponds to relational companionship. Like Adam, the prototype single, unmarried persons are relationally incomplete. God's provision for all solitary persons is social intercourse with other humans. The difference is that Adam's initial need was met through the intimacy of a one-flesh union with one other person. The companionship needs of single adults today are met through multiple relationships with a network of friends. So the second function of singleness may be said to be *relational community.*

Just as married persons must attend to the relational dimension of their union, so single persons must acquire and cultivate meaningful friendships (Proverbs 12:16; 13:20; 17:17; 18:24).[19] Good friends add richness to life and are valuable resources in times of difficulty. I know of no better way to make this point than to return to Ecclesiastes 4:9-12, that passage so often quoted at weddings, and observe that the paragraph is not about marriage at all—it is about the companionship of friends!

> Two people are better than one,
> because they can reap more benefit from their labor.
> For if they fall, one will help his companion up,
> but pity the person who falls down and has no one to help him up.
> Furthermore, if two lie down together, they can keep each other warm,
> but how can one person keep warm by himself?
> Although an assailant may overpower one person,
> two can withstand him.
> Moreover, a three-stranded cord is not quickly broken.

Yes, two are better than one, and three are better than two. Just because you are single doesn't mean that you are expected to go it alone.

Ministry Attitudes

The effective accomplishment of the two ministry functions of singleness—relational community and vocational freedom—requires the exercise of two complementary attitudes: contentment and ambition.

Contentment is a fruit of the Spirit that is required in those life circumstances that are less than ideal—when we do not get everything we would like to have. Paul did not talk about contentment directly in 1 Corinthians 7, but his thrice-repeated counsel to "remain as you are" clearly implies the need for it. This is well expressed by Eugene Peterson's paraphrase of 1 Corinthians 7:17 (MSG): "Don't be wishing you were someplace else or with someone else. Where you are right now is God's place for you. Live and obey and love and believe right there. God, not your marital status, defines your life."

Books and sermons addressed to singles invariably get around to talking about contentment. They have to because of the lack that exists in the abnormality of the single state. The reality that unmarried persons do not get to have what most of us fervently want—an intimate bond with a counterpartner—cannot be sidestepped. The natural reaction to this disappointment is dissatisfaction with one's lot.[20] "Marriage has been likened to the situation of flies at a window: those on the inside want out, and those on the outside want in. Singles think the chief end of man is to get married, while many marrieds secretly long to be single again."[21]

The only deterrent to dissatisfaction is contentment. The word *content* means "to have enough," "to be satisfied." But Larry Richards explains how the apostles expanded this concept: "It is not simply that something is in sufficient supply. It is that we have an attitude that lets us be satisfied with whatever is available."[22] This is the attitude that Paul describes in the classic passage, Philippians 4:11-12: "I have learned to be content in any circumstance. I have experienced times of need and times of abundance. In any and every circumstance I have learned the secret of contentment, whether I go satisfied or hungry, have plenty or nothing."

The good news is that contentment can be learned. There are two aspects to the process. The negative component involves being alert to and combating the subverting temptations to *idolatry* (seeking for ultimate satisfaction in something other than God) and *envy*. When you have been invited to be a bridesmaid or groomsman in your umpteenth wedding, it's easy to give in to the feeling that you're being deprived of one of the Main Things in life. But you must stand your ground against the malevolent whispers of the green-eyed monster.

The positive side is indicated by Paul in his explanation of the source of his contentment: "I am able to do all things through the one who strengthens me" (Philippians 4:13). Like other divinely granted endowments, contentment comes to us as a *by-product of something else more fundamental*—our relationship with Christ. This truth is reinforced, just a few sentences later, by Paul's promise to his Philippian friends, "And my God will supply your every need according to his glorious riches in Christ Jesus" (4:19). It is through our experience of the sufficiency of Christ and the provisions of his grace that we learn contentment (see 2 Corinthians 12:9-10).[23]

(I hasten to repeat a point made earlier: one of the "provisions of his grace" is good friends. I am convinced that all of an individual's *actual* relational *needs* can be met through close, godly friendships.)

The extent of Christ's sufficiency is expressed by the apostle in vocabulary that is stunning in its boldness. In Philippians 4, he asserts that God's supply for "all your needs" is in accordance with "his glorious riches in Christ Jesus" (4:19). And in 2 Corinthians 12, Paul was not merely "*content* with weaknesses, with insults, with troubles, with persecutions and difficulties for the sake of Christ," he actually "*boasted most gladly*" about them (12:9-10, emphasis added). This is an extraordinary response to clarity regarding God's purposes and the provisions of Christ's grace. It debunks any notion that contentment is to be thought of as grim, clinch-jawed resignation. The real thing, which is clearly attainable, goes beyond satisfaction to joy. Don't settle for less.[24]

If the call to relational community challenges singles to grow in *contentment*, the corresponding attitude that will advance the cause of vocational freedom is *ambition*. The fifth principle derived from 1 Corinthians 7 states: "As one responds to the current particulars of the sovereign will of God, God's moral will calls the believer to maximize the opportunities inherent in those circumstances to the glory of God." The apostle's challenge to single believers could not be more clear: for as long as you are single, be ambitious in the use of your relative freedom to advance the kingdom of God. In fact, if you devote your emotional energy to positive ambition, contentment will likely follow in its wake.

Single Choices
Applications for Marital Decision Making

1. Christian single adults have the freedom and responsibility to make marital decisions.

2. While marital decisions are not dictated by the moral will of God, they are regulated by it. Regardless of status, believers are obligated to know and obey the relevant rules.

3. The factors that need to be weighed in marital decision making must be judged by wisdom. As with all non-commanded decisions, each option has pros and cons.

4. For contemporary singles, Paul's admonition to "remain as you are" might be aptly paraphrased, "Don't be in too big a hurry to get married."

5. In weighing the pros and cons of singleness and marriage, Christians should place a priority on their relationship to God.

6. It is perfectly legitimate for those who hope to get married to take initiative that might lead to that outcome.

7. For as long as one is unmarried, the single adult should cultivate the complementary attitudes of contentment and ambition in carrying out the ministry functions of singleness.

Recommended Reading

Singled Out: Why Celibacy Must Be Reinvented in Today's Church by Christine Colón and Bonnie Field (Brazos Press/Baker, 2009).

Now and Not Yet: Making Sense of Single Life in the Twenty-First Century by Jennifer A. Marshall (Multnomah Books, 2007).

❖ ❖ ❖

Questions for Reflection and Group Discussion

1. What is the most significant insight you have gained from reading this chapter?

2. Review Application 3. Can you think of advantages/disadvantages of singleness/marriage in addition to the ones noted in this chapter? How is identification of these pros and cons important for marital decision making?

3. Review Application 4. How does Laura Smit's approach to the marriage decision differ from that of most contemporary singles? What are the pros and cons of adopting Smit's conditions for getting married? In what ways would one's reasons for getting married determine the criteria for one's choice of a mate?

4. Review Application 5. When you reflect on the objective truths about singleness and marriage and monitor the internal realities of your own heart, what is your resulting preference between singleness and marriage? How strong is it? Has it changed over time?

5. Review Application 6. If a single person chose to take initiative in the direction of marriage, what kinds of actions would be appropriate? What would constitute illegitimate initiative? Why?

6. Describe the tensions that are likely to arise from an effort to put Applications 5, 6, and 7 into practice. How might single Christians address these tensions?

For additional questions, go to www.TheMarriageDecision.com.

Part 4

God's Design for Sex

❧✦❧

Modern Myth 4

The best way to determine compatibility with a prospective mate and reduce the likelihood of marital failure is to live together prior to marriage.

Introduction to Part 4

In the conduct of everyday life, one of the things I dread is waiting in line at the pharmacy. Since I renew my prescriptions by phone, my transactions are simple—pay for the meds and leave. But the people in front of me always have complicated problems. So when I arrived at the pharmacy this morning, I was encouraged to see only one customer in front of me. But when I heard what she said to the cashier, I knew I was in trouble.

"I have two prescriptions, but I'm not sure I want both of them. I know about one of them, and I would like to purchase that one. But I need to know more about the other one. I was wondering if you could give me the descriptive literature that's in the sack with the prescription so I could take it home and read it. Then if I decide I want that medicine, I'll come back tomorrow and pick it up. Could you hold that prescription for me until I decide whether I want it?"

Oh dear. I looked into the eyes of the cashier and my fears were confirmed—they were glazed over. Even though I found the customer's request to be reasonable, I could tell that the store clerk had mentally seized up halfway through the inquiry. No one had ever made this request before. She would have to go ask her supervisor. But first she would have to understand what the customer wanted. "You want to buy this one, but you don't want that one? You want to read some literature?"

As you read this, I am still standing in that line.

In a few paragraphs, I will refer back to this episode in support of my contention that humanity can be divided into two categories: "systems" people and "rules" people. I will also explain what all of this has to do with sex.

But first I need to explain why I'm including a mini-book on "God's Design for Sex" in the maxi-book on *Singleness, Marriage, and the Will of God.*

Managing Sexuality

The whole big book is about marital decisions. The two obvious ones are *whether* (should I marry?) and *whom* (should I marry so-and-so?). But, as we have seen, there are many other decisions to be made along the way: Who decides? How do I decide? What is God's role in the process? How do my expectations of marriage line up with God's design? What is God's design for singleness? In what state can I best serve God? Should I regard my current situation as long-term or temporary?

I have addressed these questions (and others) at some length in the preceding chapters. In part 5, I will address questions that are of concern to single adults who desire marriage, including the development of an approach for searching out and choosing a spouse.

This fourth part is about certain issues that emerge between the decision to pursue marriage and an eventual wedding. They also must be addressed by those who choose or otherwise experience long-term singleness. Regardless of one's intended destination, every person has to decide how they are going to manage their sexuality as a single adult. The choices involved are marital in that they inevitably affect—for good or ill—any subsequent marriage that may occur. And decisions about one's sex life are very definitely encompassed by the moral will of God.

When I have told folks that I am writing a segment on "God's Design for Sex," I have encountered a predictable response: "How many ways can you say, Don't!" This reaction is prevalent, superficial, dismissive—and not very helpful. It is superficial in that it regards sexual choices to be strictly behavioral. But, as we shall see, that is not the case. Of equal concern is a cynical attitude that regards biblical constraints as outmoded and hopelessly unrealistic. It is commonly accepted that single adults will not indefinitely restrain their sexual impulses, that sex is a biological imperative[1], and that even Christian singles are ultimately helpless to resist the overpowering combination of hormonal urges, peer influence, and external temptation.

If I accepted that assumption, this book would be shorter by four chapters. But I not only reject the prevailing pessimism, I find it insulting and dehumanizing.[2] The current trends may be alarming, but they are neither inevitable nor even historically conventional.[3] As Elizabeth Abbott notes in her book *A History of Celibacy*, "for at least 3000 years in most parts of the world, celibacy has been far from uncommon and rarely considered unnatural."[4] This generation needs to get a grip.

As you enter this challenging arena, you once again have to decide which point of view is going to shape your decision making—the culture's or the Creator's? For once again they are diametrically opposed. And Paul's counsel to Christian disciples merits careful consideration:

> Therefore I exhort you, brothers and sisters, by the mercies of God, to present your bodies as a sacrifice—alive, holy, and pleasing to God—which is your reasonable service. Do not be conformed to this present world, but be transformed by the renewing of your mind, so that you may test and approve what is the will of God—what is good and well-pleasing and perfect (Romans 12:1-2).

Systems v. Rules

In the pages that follow, I aim to discern and apply God's moral will to the sexual lifestyle of the Christian single adult. As you join me in that project, we need to review two things about the moral will of God. The first is that it encompasses *more than behavior.*

Remember, I believe there are two kinds of people in this world—those who operate on the basis of *systems* and those who just try to follow *rules.* The cashier at my pharmacy falls in the latter group. And so do those in my congregation who fold their arms during the first part of my sermon and attempt to influence me through mental telepathy: *Don't waste my time with all that theoretical doctrinal stuff. Get to the bottom line; just explain what I'm supposed to do.*

But that is just the approach that will not work. For one thing, as my cashier just discovered, you can't cover every contingency with a to-do (or a to-don't) list. And for another, rules fail to motivate. Rules are for children for whom the decisive reason for compliance is, "Because I said so."[5] But God doesn't treat us as little children. He gives us the bigger picture so we can understand his whys as well as his wherefores. And when we comprehend God's reasons for his instructions, we are much more inclined to carry them out.

So when it comes to singleness, marriage, and sexuality, we need to become systems people—like the manager of the pharmacy who could come to my rescue. Because they understand the design of the overall operation, systems people apply that knowledge to the situation at hand, intuiting the action that is in agreement with the purposes and structures of the governing framework. They don't violate the rules. But they know why they are there—and when and how to override them when necessary.

The good news for Christian singles is that God's moral will encompasses more than behavior. It includes the explanatory material on the nature and purposes of sex. Before we can adopt a personal *morality* of sex, we must have a proper *theology* of sex. (It turns out that that "doctrinal stuff" isn't just theoretical after all.) Further, the moral will of God addresses our attitudes, our goals, and our motives. For our behaviors to have integrity, they must be directed from the inside out. The activities of our bodies need to be governed by these dispositions of the heart. More than a list of dos and don'ts, we need a grown-up perspective on sexuality that allows us to harness the expressions of our maleness and femaleness to the glory of God.

The second thing we need to remember about God's moral will is that it is *good for us* (Deuteronomy 10:12-13; Psalm 1). That may not be the most important thing about the moral will of God, but we need to reaffirm it here. For just as God's goodness was called into question by the serpent in the Garden of Eden ("He's holding out on you"), so it is challenged by the Sirens of our own age ("If God created the appetite, does he seriously forbid you from indulging it?"). But our enemy is a liar. The Creator is a loving Father who has the best interests of his children at heart. Any boundaries he establishes are for our protection and ultimate good.

Supporting Testimony

In biblical days of yore, when the revelation of God's will elicited surprise from the recipients, they would ask, "How can we know this is true?" In response, God would provide a confirming miracle. In our time, the validity of God's moral will is being corroborated from a surprising source—the social sciences. In the wake of the relational and social chaos created by the Sexual Revolution, a great deal of study has been directed toward human relationships in general and marriage in particular. As the psychologists, sociologists, and counselors who have to deal with all the brokenness have compared notes, a striking pattern is emerging. The studies are substantiating the wisdom of God's moral will.

The developers of the divorce-prevention and marriage-enhancement program *Christian PREP* state that "revelation and sound research are consistently and amazingly consistent in those areas where they speak to the same phenomena."[6] Specifically, they show that the consequences of violating the moral will of God are counterproductive and damaging. On the other hand, those who live in accordance with biblical principles experience more satisfaction and fulfillment.[7]

The book of Proverbs says it twice (14:12; 16:25):

> There is a way that seems right to a person,
>
> but its end is the way that leads to death.

In the sexual realm, the positive opposite is also true:

> Trust in the LORD with all your heart,
>
> and do not rely on your own understanding.
>
> Acknowledge him in all your ways,
>
> and he will make your paths straight.
>
> Do not be wise in your own estimation;
>
> fear the LORD and turn away from evil.
>
> This will bring healing to your body,
>
> and refreshment to your inner self.
>
> (Proverbs 3:5-8)

Questions for Reflection and Group Discussion

[*Note to Group Leaders*: For many people, sexuality is a highly sensitive subject. Some members of your group may be reticent to discuss some questions, particularly in a mixed-gender setting. This will be acutely true for any who have suffered from sexual abuse, especially if their victimization remains secret. So refrain from probing individual members who appear reluctant to enter into the discussion. Where there is a high degree of openness among group members, it can be very beneficial for men and women to hear the perspectives of the other gender. But the depth of discussion may be greater if, for these chapters, you subdivide into two groups—male and female.]

1. Do you think that it is appropriate to include a segment on "God's Design for Sex" in a volume on *Singleness, Marriage, and the Will of God*? Why or why not? What topics do you think should be addressed in the following chapters?

2. In their consideration of single sexuality, what two aspects of God's moral will does the author exhort readers to remember? Why is this important?

3. What is the difference between "rules people" and "systems people"? With which group would you classify yourself?

4. Do you ever wonder if the biblical teaching on sexuality is outmoded or unworkable for contemporary Christian singles? What aspects of biblical instruction do you question?

10
God's Purposes for Sex(uality)

❧❧❧

A ll Christians, single and married, are called to lives of moral integrity. The ways that single and married adults respond to that call look pretty much the same in most areas of life, with one glaring exception—sex. At one level, the expectation for all believers is the same; both single and married adults are directed to live chaste lives. Stated positively, all are to be morally pure.[1] And while there is more to moral purity than abstaining from unlawful sexual intercourse, the activity that is avoided is often the defining component of chastity.

Of course, the nature of unlawful sexual intercourse is so vastly different for single and married adults. For the married believer, chastity is defined as sexual faithfulness to one's partner. For the unmarried, chastity is equated with celibacy (abstinence from sexual intercourse) and virginity (the state of being sexually inexperienced). If I may be permitted an understatement, those standards of chastity are not the same.

It is hard work to think straight about sex. Maybe it has ever been thus, but it seems as if sex has become the focal point of a united assault by the world, the flesh, and the devil. Our enemy lies to us in order to destroy us (John 8:44; 1 Peter 5:8). Our culture, in separating the physical from the relational, has perverted a wonderful means of intimacy into the indulgence of an appetite. It has elevated something that is good to the status of a god, enticing people into an idolatry that replaces what is real with a counterfeit that is both empty and harmful.

This seduction is perpetrated by a virtual tsunami of narcissistic rationalizations, titillating images, and exhibitionist models that flood our minds and senses from omnipresent media. To say that our culture is oversexed is a profound grasp of the obvious. And our carnal nature (what the Bible calls our "flesh") seems to be in cahoots with the enemies of our soul. For feelings of loneliness and the cravings of hormonally driven desire prompt us to dismiss biblical ideas of chastity as archaic, unrealistic expectations that should be discarded in favor of more enlightened practices.

There are other reasons why it is hard work to think straight about sex—not the least of which is the great mystery inherent in our makeup as male and female. And yet straight thinking is what is required if sexual sanity is to be restored. We don't have to be "conformed to this present world." We can be "transformed by the renewing of our minds" (Romans 12:2). Our hope lies in the fact that we can know the truth about sex. And, as good counselors often remind us, the truth is our friend.

What's It All About, Alfie?

As I indicated in the introduction to part 2, there was a time when the cultural rules of conduct supported the sexual standards of Bible-believing Christians. When those rules were broken by the defiant, the offenders were regarded as brazen rebels. Societal support of the ideal of premarital virginity made the standard of chastity easier to attain. By contrast, singles who seek to maintain sexual purity in our day find themselves swimming against a current that is raging in the opposite direction. Nonmarital sexual liaisons are now considered acceptable and normal in secular culture.

A national study conducted among twentysomething singles revealed that the sexual attitudes and practices of this generation fall into two categories: *relational* sex and *recreational* sex. The former describes the experience and intentions of two people who are attracted to each other, are building a relationship, and incorporate sex into that process. Recreational sex is sex-without-strings. It is considered a physical act in which two people provide mutual pleasure to one another without any commitment beyond the sexual encounter.[2]

The premise underlying both practices is that sex is no different, qualitatively, from any other bodily functioning. It can take place with or without emotional involvement. So long as both participants mutually agree about the nature of the relations (whether the intent is recreational or relational), no one will get hurt.

The biblical picture is very different, as we shall see. But even apart from divine revelation, we have evidence that challenges the notion that sex can be strictly physical.

One clue comes from a comparison of the mating behaviors of animals with those of Homo sapiens. Humans are the only species that commonly copulate face-to-face. The partners are able to look at each other and have full-body contact. In contrast to other social creatures, we prefer privacy for the act. Most other mammals have a specified time when the female is in heat; the human female can be receptive at virtually anytime. Husbands and wives continue to engage in sex long after they have stopped having children; much more is involved than reproduction.

Philip Yancey observes, "Unlike the Tasmanian ram who services every receptive female within sniffing distance, mating humans demand some sort of mutual consent. When none exists, we call that rape and punish it."[3] The point is that for animals, sex *is* strictly physical. It is an instinctive mechanism that propagates the species. For humans, sex is physical-plus. It is not without reasons that we refer to intercourse as "making love."

From a historical perspective, human societies have never treated sex as a merely physical act with no other intrinsic meaning. No matter how primitive, every tribe studied by anthropologists has set boundaries on who may have sex with whom and under what conditions. And the taboos are remarkably the same.

Another pointer is the impact of sexual abuse on the soul of the victim. Rape victims may recover relatively quickly from the physical violence, but the inward damage—manifested in depression, shame, sexual dysfunction, nightmares, and the like—may plague the person for years. Victims of incest or other forms of molestation know that the damage done to a child is far more than physical. There is an inner pain that often carries over into adulthood. More is going on in sexual interactions than the physical exercise of sex organs.[4]

Another indicator is the negative impact of premarital sex on subsequent marriage. John Van Epp cites scientific studies that demonstrate some of these damaging effects.[5] The first finding revealed that sexual involvement with persons other than one's eventual spouse significantly increases that individual's odds of divorce. A study of sixty-five hundred women who married between 1970 and 1995 demonstrated that a woman who had just one sexual partner other than her husband during the dating years was *three times* more at risk for divorce than a woman who had sex only with her husband. Other studies indicated that the more sexual partners one has, the less likely that person will be to remain faithful in marriage. In fact, the correlation is proportional—the more sexual partners one has, the greater the likelihood of infidelity. Apparently one's sexual practices prior to marriage have an effect on that relationship—not the sort of thing one would expect if sex is only physical.

Dr. Van Epp summarizes: "Sex is always relational…because you cannot separate your body from the rest of who you are; therefore, what your body does, you do. Sex and self are inextricably linked, and during a sexual encounter something happens that is more than just a physical act."[6]

Actually, the truth runs even deeper than that. The reason that sex is always relational is that God made it that way.

God's Design for Our Sexuality

Again, we are back to design. If we are going to maximize the role that our sexuality plays in healthy relationships, we need to see what the Creator had in mind. So once again we return to the Beginning.

> God created humankind in his own image,
> in the image of God he created them,
> male and female he created them.
> God blessed them and said to them, "Be fruitful and multiply! Fill the
> earth and subdue it!
> (Genesis 1:27-28a)

> That is why a man leaves his father and mother and is united to his wife,
> and they become one flesh (Genesis 2:24 NIV).

Male and Female

In the quest for insight into God's purposes for sex, it is important to make a distinction between God's design for our sexuality (what we *are* as male and female) and his design for sexual intercourse (what married people *do*). Stanley Grenz explains: "Sexuality comprises all aspects of the human person that are related to existence as male and female. Our sexuality, therefore, is a powerful, deep, and mysterious aspect of our being. It constitutes a fundamental distinction between the two ways of being human (i.e., as male or female)." Accordingly, human sexuality is not to be equated with or reduced to physical characteristics or the ability to procreate; "sexuality...is that dimension of human existence that lies behind" these expressions of it.[7] So before we explore God's design for our sexual *behavior*, we must understand his design for our sexual *nature*.

Based on the core passages above (and others), Stanton L. Jones extrapolates three implications for human sexuality—our maleness and femaleness.[8] First, *bodily existence or embodiment is a created good*. "Our bodies...were God's design from the very beginning. God looked upon Adam and Eve, sex organs and all, ready for sexual union and procreation, and declared them to be 'very good.'" This explicit biblical teaching corrects the faulty notion (emphasized in various philosophical systems such as Platonism) that there is something inherently bad about our physical makeup.

Furthermore, when we think about our bodies, we must not make the mistake of driving a wedge between our physical being and our souls. Genesis 2:7 narrates that "the LORD God formed the man from the soil of the ground and breathed into his nostrils the breath of life, and the man became a living being."[9] "Part of man's 'soulishness' was his physical existence. We do not just have bodies; we are bodies."[10] And that is a good thing.

Second, *the differentiation of the two genders is specified as intentional*. There is an emphasis on the distinction between the sexes: "male and female he created them" (Genesis 1:27). Both the female and the male bore the divine image; both were blessed and declared to be "very good"; both had a primary orientation to their Creator before whom they lived with equal worth and standing. Yet they were markedly, correspondingly different from each other. And this differentness served to enhance the third aspect of human sexuality that emerges from the creation narrative—*men and women were created by God's design to be relational beings*.

In the exposition of Genesis 1–2 (chapter 5) we learned that human beings by themselves are incomplete, and this incompleteness is intentional. The divine provision for the solitary man was another human being of the opposite sex—someone who corresponded to him but was different from him. And these two persons, who were separate from each other, were naturally drawn toward each other in relationship.

But the experience of opposite-sex relationship is not limited to marriage or spouses. This inbred recognition of relational incompleteness established a drive that impels men and women *to seek community through bonding.* At the human level, we seek resolution to our sense of incompleteness through the development of social communities, beginning with marriage and family and extending beyond to friends and societies.

But there is a spiritual dimension to this drive as well.

> The message of the Bible...claims that in the final analysis, the source of this completeness is found in the community that focuses on fellowship with the Creator...Just as God is the community of the Trinitarian persons, so also God has created us for the sake of community, namely, to find completion in community with each other and together in community with our Maker.[11]

Our sexuality, then, serves as a kind of built-in magnet to draw us toward relationship with other persons—a spouse (most intimately), but also fellow members of the family of Christ and, ultimately, God himself.[12]

God's Design for Our Sexuality

1. Bodily existence is a created good.

2. Differences between male and female are intentional and purposeful.

3. Our gender-based incompleteness prompts us to seek relationship.

God's Purposes for Marital Sex

These observations certainly do not represent an exhaustive treatment of our sexuality, but they do provide an important framework for identifying the purposes of sexual intercourse within the marital bonds. In the summary of God's design for sex that follows, I will elucidate three broad purposes.

Procreation: The Reproduction of Image-Bearers

The first purpose mentioned in Scripture is *procreation*: "Be fruitful and multiply," instructed the Creator (Genesis 1:28). It is certainly not coincidental that this assignment was given within the context of God's own creative activity and the description of the man and woman as image-bearers of God. What he had just done (producing creatures in his image), they were to replicate (see Genesis 5:3). "Healthy sexuality makes marriage the beginning of a family."[13]

In the course of history, the pendulum has swung regarding the significance of the link between sexual intercourse and procreation. As I noted in the introduction to part 3, the view of some of the early Church Fathers was that procreation is the *only* legitimate purpose for sex. Clement of Alexandria wrote:

> To have intercourse without intending children is to violate nature...Marriage is the desire for procreation, but it is not the random, illicit, or irrational scattering of seed. Sexual activity is to be limited to marriage, is to be engaged in solely for the sake of procreation, and is to be undertaken as a purposeful, reverent endeavor.[14]

This assessment, echoed by such spiritual stalwarts as Jerome and Augustine, became the prevailing view of the medieval church.

The opposite idea, that sex is mostly about pleasure, is a recent notion. Until the advent of modern contraceptives, the strongest deterrent to extramarital intercourse was fear of pregnancy. Now, singles are encouraged to have "safe sex," taking measures to prevent the "danger" of pregnancy as well as sexually transmitted diseases. Imagine that. What is described in Genesis (and throughout the Bible[15]) as a *blessing* of God is now regarded as an *undesirable consequence* to avoid.

One major implication of the purpose of procreation is that couples should not engage in sexual intercourse until they are prepared to welcome and care for children. In saying this, I am not agreeing with the position of the Church Fathers that procreation is the only valid purpose for sex. I am agreeing with this insight by R. Paul Stevens:

> It would be wrong to say that every act of intercourse must have procreation as its end. In the Genesis narrative the man and woman were in the image of God and enjoyed profound companionship before there were children. But to cut the tie between sex and children is to reduce sexuality. A childless marriage can be a godly community on earth. But a marriage that refuses procreation for reasons of self-centeredness is something less than the God-imaging community, male and female, that was called to "be fruitful and increase in number" (Genesis 1:28).[16]

One-Flesh Union: Five Ways God Unites Two Persons

The second divine purpose for sexual intercourse is the *experience and expression of one-fleshedness*. "That is why a man leaves his father and mother and is united to his wife, and they become one flesh" (Genesis 2:24 NIV). In contrast to the Church Fathers, Stanton Jones believes that this *unitive* function of sex is "most central, as our Lord made this notion of union central to his teaching on divorce and the nature of marriage (Mt. 19)."[17] This broad purpose of one-fleshedness is experienced in five interrelated ways.[18]

1. Relational union

The first way a husband and wife experience and express one-fleshedness is through *completion in relationship*. We have already noted that there is a sense in which individual humans are incomplete in themselves, and that this incompleteness exists by design. God intended that we should move beyond ourselves. This movement occurs at the most complete level in sexual intercourse. Sexual impulses drive us to join back together the union that has been severed. Richard Rohr explains this impact of sex:

God seemingly had to take all kinds of risks in order that we would not miss the one thing necessary: we are called and even driven out of ourselves by an almost insatiable appetite so that we could never presume that we were self-sufficient. It is so important that we know that we are incomplete, needy, and essentially social that God had to create a life-force within us that would not be silenced![19]

2. Complementary union

The second way one-fleshedness is experienced is through *completion in complementarity*. Men and women are different in their sexuality(!). This difference emerges immediately in the creation narrative. Adam's maleness is evoked by the arrival of Eve. By himself, he is just "the human" (*ha-adam*). After she is created, he is designated "the man" (male person, *ha-ish*). Likewise, Eve's distinctive nature as female is called forth by the process of her extraction and reconfiguring from Adam. As I observed in chapter 5, she is a "corresponding companion" (or "suitable helper," Genesis 2:18) who is the man's opposite in the sense of being complementary. And so he describes her as "woman" (female person, *ha-ishsha*) whose femaleness is recognized by means of contrast to her mate (Genesis 2:23).

The complementary nature of the sexes that is evident in the creative design of God continues to be exhibited in every act of sexual union. This is graphically explained by Dr. Stevens:

> In intercourse woman receives the man, letting him come inside her. In this act she makes herself extremely vulnerable. The man, on the other hand, is directed outward. While the woman receives something, the man relieves himself of something. It means something different to the man...A woman needs to be psychologically prepared for this self-abandonment, not only by the public commitment of her husband to lifelong troth but also by her husband's ongoing nurture of the love relationship...It is a gross but instructive overstatement to say that men must have sex to reach fullness of love while women must have love to reach fullness of sex.[20]

The point here is that in sexual intercourse, a man and a woman express and experience a sense of completion in a way that reinforces their complementary natures.

3. Union with distinctness

The third aspect of one-fleshedness manifested in sex is *union with distinctness*. When Jesus said of a husband and wife, "So they are no longer two, but one flesh" (Matthew 19:6), he was not describing a fusion in which the two partners lose their individuality.[21] He was describing the establishment of a community (*com* ["with" or "together"] plus *unity* equals "unity alongside another"). The sexual impulse is not "the urge to merge," as when a drop of water returns to the sea.

> Sexuality is the urge to be part of a community of two symbolized by the act of intercourse: one person moves in and out of another. The differences and uniqueness of both people are celebrated at the very moment of oneness and unity...Reverently we may speak of the ministry of one God in three persons; we know they are not merged. Nor do we merge in the human covenant. Partners should find, not lose, their identity.[22]

4. Consummation and renewal of covenant

Fourth, a husband and wife experience and express one-fleshedness through *consummation and renewal of covenant*. "The enjoyment of sex within the marital bond can become the reenactment, reaffirmation, and symbolic embodiment of the marriage vow."[23]

In antiquity, covenants were sealed and reaffirmed by special rituals and signs. These ritual acts underscored the solemnity of promises made and the seriousness of the consequences. The Creator invoked this practice when he constituted marriage to be a public covenant ("leave and cleave") ritually sealed in a private consummation ("become one flesh").

Jesus also drew on this tradition when he enacted the New Covenant. He gave the church rituals—baptism and the Lord's Supper—that serve these purposes with respect to the salvation he provided. We may say, by analogy, that sexual intercourse is to the marriage covenant what baptism and the Lord's Supper are to the New Covenant. Like baptism, the initial act of sexual union consummates and seals the wedding commitment. Like the Lord's Supper, each subsequent coition reenacts, reaffirms, renews, and celebrates the original heart covenant. "If the symbol is not backed by a full covenant, it is merely a powerless, graceless act."[24]

5. Physical joy in love

The fifth way a husband and wife experience and express one-fleshedness is through *physical joy in love*. Sexual intercourse is meant to be intensely pleasurable, and husbands and wives are given the delightful assignment to grant this pleasure to one another.[25]

The only hint we have of this function of sex in Genesis 1–2 is Adam's eruption of delight when he first encounters his bride: "At last!" (2:23 NLT). But other passages of Scripture are refreshingly frank in extolling the beauty of physical love. Proverbs 5:18-19 declares:

> May your fountain be blessed,
> and may you rejoice in your young wife—
> a loving doe, a graceful deer;
> may her breasts satisfy you at all times,
> may you be captivated by her love always.

That's a pretty good summation of another entire book in the Old Testament—the Song of Songs—which narrates powerfully the intoxicating bliss of romantic love and sensual enjoyment. The New Testament does not wax so poetic. In 1 Corinthians 7:1-9, Paul speaks in the most matter-of-fact way about sexual drive and the obligation of spouses to meet each other's needs.

In contrast to the pleasure sought by unattached singles who exploit one another for the sake of erotic stimulation, marital sex is enjoyed within the context of the divinely sanctioned covenant as an expression of committed love. It is, for this reason, all the more pleasurable. For the physical delight is enhanced by the emotional connectedness appropriate to the one-flesh relationship. And because such unions are favored with the blessing of God, spouses are free to enjoy one another without moral constraint—free from the guilt that attends violations of the divine will (Hebrews 13:4).

Illumination: Telling God's Love Story Through Our Love Story

Thus far I have identified and elaborated two primary functions for sex: procreation and one-flesh union. There is a third purpose that I will call *illumination*. To grasp what this means, we need to remember that people apprehend truth with varying degrees of comprehension. This third function of sex involves the communication of important truths at a deeper, experiential level.

This purpose is not easy to describe. Perhaps an analogy will be helpful. When I was a student at Wheaton College, the college community convened daily for a chapel service. One day, as the benediction was completed and the attendees started to exit the chapel, one of the students from the music conservatory began to play a postlude on the organ. Now this was no ordinary organ; it was a seven-manual, state-of-the-art, Schantz pipe organ. And, as it turned out, this was no ordinary postlude; the musician had launched into J.S. Bach's *Toccata and Fugue in D Minor*—one of the most powerful pieces ever composed for the organ. (It could serve as the sound track for Genesis 1.)

Arrested by the grand introduction to this masterwork, about half the student body turned around and sat back down to listen. *Toccata and Fugue* is complex and intricate and majestic—and the organist had mastered it. Time stood still as we were transported to some other realm. Seated as he was with his back to the auditorium, the musician was oblivious to the presence of an audience numbering several hundred appreciative listeners. So when the echo of the last thunderous chord was greeted with an explosion of applause, the organist levitated momentarily above his bench. As he turned, stunned, to acknowledge the ovation, my friend leaned over and said to me, "That guy must know what it feels like to be God."

All of us in that chapel had an encounter with Bach's *Toccata and Fugue*. We came to "know" how that piece sounds. But none of us who heard the performance would have claimed to have a level of understanding or appreciation equal to that of the organist. In translating Bach's musical score into an audible work of art that brought enjoyment, inspiration, even worship into the hearts of transfixed listeners, that musician fulfilled his design as an image-bearer emulating the creative, aesthetic nature of God. He brought beauty that had not previously existed into being. And yes, in a particular way that went beyond what all the rest of us had experienced, that organist knew what it felt like to be God.

In a similar manner, sex is designed to impart a level of apprehension that transcends the capacity of the intellect. As John White put it, "God designed us to learn in the body and through the body the intimacy of a close personal relationship."[26]

We witness this deepening comprehension and appreciation of "the other" in the experience of the first man. When the newly minted female was brought to Adam, he instantly recognized what a wondrous creature this was. But it was in the intimacy of sexual intercourse (meaning "communication between persons") that Adam came to truly "know" his wife (see Genesis 4:1 NKJV).

So what truth is sexual union designed to *illumine*? This purpose is linked to the picture-function of marriage. In chapter 6, we saw that marriage is a reflection, first of all, of the unity-in-diversity that exists within the godhead; and second, it is a metaphor or parable of the covenant relationship between Christ and his bride, the church. As Paul said in his quotation of Genesis 2:24: "*For this reason a man will leave his father and mother and will be joined to his wife, and the two will become one flesh. This mystery is great—but I am actually speaking with reference to Christ and the church*" (Ephesians 5:31-32). Doug Rosenau and Michael Todd Wilson summarize:

> Our sexuality was designed to be the greatest parable of the ultimate love story—God's great love for us. Sexual intercourse between husband and wife is to reflect God's love for us—pure, priceless, and protected from all who seek to destroy it...*God designed our love stories to tell his love story.*[27]

What marriage is designed to *portray,* Christian husbands and wives can actually *experience.* And when they experience what marriage was designed to convey, especially through the intensity and intimacy of sexual intercourse as the ultimate expression of "becoming one flesh," a doorway is opened into deeper insight. A never-married person can become theoretically knowledgeable about marriage (by reading this book, for instance). But spouses can know marriage—and another person—in a way that single people cannot. And they have the opportunity to appreciate the mysteries of Trinitarian communion and our bridal relationship to Christ at a deeper level than single, celibate people can.[28]

That is not to say that the illuminating purpose of intercourse is accomplished by sex in and of itself. The picture-function of marriage is conveyed by the totality of the one-flesh relationship described in Ephesians 5. The emphasis there is on the mutual upbuilding of husband and wife as they carry out their roles with an attitude of sacrificial servanthood empowered by the Holy Spirit. The only sex act that illuminates the picture-function of marriage is sex as an expression and symbol of the marital covenant. Sex without covenant tells a selfish tale; covenant-renewing sex discloses God's love story through our love story.

I hasten to add two additional disclaimers. First, this illuminating function of sex does not put married believers into a different spiritual class than single Christians. They are not, by virtue of their sexual experience, closer to God. They may have experiential insights into certain aspects of revealed truth, but they do not necessarily know God better. Indeed, there are other areas in which single believers have the subjective advantage.[29] In either event, there is not one kind of spirituality for married believers and another for the unmarried. "We *all*...are being transformed into the same image from one degree of glory to another, which is from the Lord, who is the Spirit" (2 Corinthians 3:18, emphasis added).[30]

Second, while the illuminating purpose of sex is part of God's design, it is not automatically experienced by all married couples—even Christian ones. It seems likely that many couples are oblivious to this aspect of God's intent. Either they are ignorant of God's revelation (in Genesis 1–2 and Ephesians 5) or they have failed to connect the dots between the text and their own experience.[31]

Those who get it might be likened to a couple admiring a painting in an art gallery. As they discuss those features of the composition that appeal to them, they are joined by another person who, it turns out, is the artist who painted the picture. In response to their interest, he interprets his work for them, explaining what he was attempting to convey through his presentation of the subject matter. With his exposition of his own work, their perception is vastly expanded and their appreciation is heightened. In the case of marriage, it is more accurate to say that the Holy Spirit connects the dots between his revelation and our experience of it.[32]

God's Purposes for Marital Sex

1. Procreation of children

2. The experience and expression of "one-fleshedness" (unity)

   • Relational union

   • Complementary union

   • Union with distinctness

   • Consummation and renewal of covenant

   • Physical joy in love

3. Illumination of the picture-function of marriage

Beyond Recreation to Meaning

Even this limited exposition of God's design for sexuality clarifies two important truths. First, it exposes the illegitimacy of the concept of nonmarital, recreational sex. Sexual intercourse is more than a physical act; it is more than the mutual stimulation of pleasure between consenting adults. "Sex may engage our bodies, but unlike such bodily functions as excretion, sneezing, and burping, it also touches our souls—as tenderly, and as precariously, as they can be touched."[33]

The reason this is true is that sex is a *meaning-laden* activity, given as a gift to human beings for divinely ordained purposes. And that meaning is hardwired into our makeup as men and women. All nonmarital sex not only perverts the divine purposes, it dehumanizes the participants who are treating one another merely as convenient objects for pleasure.[34]

Second, God's design for sexuality demonstrates both the necessity and appropriateness of the Bible's insistence on celibate chastity for unmarried persons. Stanley Grenz's summary is eloquent in its simplicity: "Sexual intercourse must be reserved for marriage, because single persons cannot express through this act the profound meanings intended by it."[35]

❖ ❖ ❖

Questions for Reflection and Group Discussion

[*Note to Group Leaders*: For many people, sexuality is a highly sensitive subject. Some members of your group may be reticent to discuss some questions, particularly in a mixed-gender setting. This will be acutely true for any who have suffered from sexual abuse, especially if their victimization remains secret. So refrain from probing individual members who appear reluctant to enter in to the discussion. Where there is a high degree of openness among group members, it can be very beneficial for men and women to hear the perspectives of the other gender. But the depth of discussion may be greater if, for these chapters, you subdivide into two groups—male and female.]

1. What was the most significant insight you gained from reading this chapter?

2. When you were growing up, did anyone convey to you that there was something bad about your sexual makeup? How do you think your current attitudes about sex are shaped by your upbringing? Is your adult perspective in harmony with biblical revelation?

3. R. Paul Stevens writes: "to cut the tie between sex and children is to reduce sexuality." What does that mean? How has that tie been cut in Western society? Can you identify any consequences?

4. What are the five aspects of the unitive function of sex? Which one strikes you as especially significant? Why?

5. Why is the experience of married sex potentially superior to that of nonmarried sex?

6. Stan and Carol have been dating for eight months and are "engaged to be engaged." One of them confides in you (as their best friend) that they are talking about engaging in sex because "it wouldn't be cheap recreational sex but a meaningful expression of our committed love." How would you respond?

❖ ❖ ❖

For additional questions, go to www.TheMarriageDecision.com.

Sex and the Moral Will of God

Behind my home in Klamath Falls, Oregon, is a large ditch filled with running water eight months out of the year. That ditch is part of a massive network of canals that convey water from Upper Klamath Lake to agricultural lands extending to the south. The floor of the Klamath Basin consists of nutrient-rich soil. But its elevation and location on the east side of the Cascade Range deprives it of sufficient rain to grow most crops. Our region is designated "high desert." For these reasons, the water that flows through our ditch and the interconnected canals is the lifeblood of a sizable agricultural community surrounding us. Access to that water is essential for viable farms and the amazing variety of crops they produce.

When our firstborn daughter began to crawl, I undertook a construction project—a wooden fence that enclosed the back of our property. It was a dual-purpose fence: I wanted to keep critters out; but mostly I wanted to keep my daughter in. The same water that was life-giving to our neighboring farmers could be life-threatening to our toddler. Because I loved her, I built a fence.

In the revelation of his moral will, God has placed fences around his gift of sex. They are for our benefit. When his spokesman warns, "Flee sexual immorality!" (1 Corinthians 6:18), he is not seeking to squelch our enjoyment of his gift. He is protecting us from its misuse and our injury.

Furthermore, God's boundaries are not arbitrary. His directions for our behavior are congruent with the way he has made us. "The body is not for sexual immorality, but for the Lord...Or do you not know that your body is the temple of the Holy Spirit who is in you...Therefore glorify God with your body" (1 Corinthians 6:13,19,20). The prohibition, "Don't," is simply one aspect of a more encompassing directive: "*Be* who you are. You are the very dwelling place of the Holy Spirit. Live like a temple!" God's warning to stay on the right side of the fence is intended to ensure that the purposes of his design are maximized in our lives.

So we are prepared to move from the *theology* of sex (chapter 10) to explore a biblical *morality* of sex. The negative summary of this ethic is succinctly stated by the apostle Paul: "The body is not for sexual immorality...Flee sexual immorality!" (1 Corinthians 6:13,18).

Locating the Fence

And what is sexual immorality? It is the violation of the limits set on permissible sexual activity—namely sexual intercourse within marriage (1 Corinthians 7:3; 1 Timothy 4:1-5; Hebrews 13:4). Prohibited behaviors and patterns spelled out in Scripture include, in rough order of their appearance: adultery (Exodus 20:14 and many other passages), incest (Leviticus 18:6-18; 20:11-22), homosexual intercourse (Leviticus 18:22; 20:13; Romans 1:26-27; 1 Corinthians 6:9), bestiality (Leviticus 20:15-16), rape (Deuteronomy 22:23-29), fornication (Acts 15:29; 1 Corinthians 6:9), and lust (Matthew 5:28).[1]

Stanton Jones summarizes the biblical revelation on sexual morality:

> The Christian sexual ethic...at its core [is] the teaching
>
> - that our sexuality—our embodiedness, our gender and all aspects of what it means to be men and women—is a precious gift from God;
>
> - ...that full sexual intimacy is properly experienced only between a man and a woman who are married;
>
> - ...that those who are not married should refrain from full sexual intimacy with others;
>
> - ...that all persons, married and unmarried, should be characterized by certain virtues that will guide and mold their living out of their sexual natures before God and their fellow men and women.[2]

At the outset, we need to observe three things about the Bible's perspective on sexual sin. First, it is not the singular preoccupation of Scripture, nor is it elevated to the chief of all sins.

On the other hand, it not only appears in virtually every list of vices, but is marked off by Paul as being in a category of its own (1 Corinthians 6:18). Dr. Jones correctly concludes: "Sexual purity was clearly a concern of the early church; over and over we are exhorted to pursue sexual purity."³

Finally, over against the naysayers, we must affirm that the moral purity required of all Christians, single and married, is *possible*. I appreciate the unequivocal assertion and testimony of lifelong celibate, John R.W. Stott:

> We Christians must insist that self-control is possible. We have to learn to control our temper, our time, our greed, our jealousy, our pride: why should it be thought impossible to control our libido? To say that we cannot is to deny our dignity as human beings and to descend to the level of animals, which are creatures of uncontrolled instinct.⁴

Problems with Sexual Sin: Biblical Reasons

I have already made several references to 1 Corinthians 6, a passage in which sexual sin was momentarily a singular preoccupation of Paul. In order to respond positively to the moral will of God, the single Christian must be acquainted with this entire segment (6:12-20).

> "All things are lawful for me"—but not everything is beneficial. "All things are lawful for me"—but I will not be controlled by anything. "Food is for the stomach and the stomach is for food, but God will do away with both." The body is not for sexual immorality, but for the Lord, and the Lord for the body. Now God indeed raised the Lord and he will raise us by his power. Do you not know that your bodies are members of Christ? Should I take the members of Christ and make them members of a prostitute? Never! Or do you not know that anyone who is united with a prostitute is one body with her? For it is said, *"The two will become one flesh."* But the one united with the Lord is one spirit with him. Flee sexual immorality! "Every sin a person commits is outside of the body"—but the immoral person sins against his own body. Or do you not know that your body is the temple of the Holy Spirit who is in you, whom you have from God, and you are not your own? For you were bought at a price. Therefore glorify God with your body.

The relevance of this passage to our presentation is underscored by an interesting detail of the immediate context. Apparently, some in the Corinthian church were arguing that one's sexual appetite is no different from one's appetite for food—the satisfaction of both hungers is natural and appropriate (6:13). In other words, they maintained, sexual intercourse is merely physical.[5]

The apostle's reply is both forceful and clear: the believer must "flee immorality."[6] And this is so for at least six reasons:

1. Sexual sin has an enslaving power (6:12; see John 8:34; Romans 6:6; 2 Peter 2:19). This is the dead opposite of the freedom deluded people think they are exercising.

2. Sexual sin is a violation of God's purpose (design) for the human body: "The body is not for sexual immorality, but for the Lord" (6:13).

3. Because the believer is united to Christ, when a Christian man hooks up with a prostitute (in this case), he is involving Christ in his sin (6:15).

4. Illicit sex creates a one-flesh union apart from covenant. As such it is a perversion of the divinely established marriage union.[7]

5. The body of the believer does not belong to himself but rather to Christ, who redeemed it with his blood (6:19-20). Faithful stewardship prohibits immoral behavior.[8]

6. Unlike other sins, sexual immorality constitutes a sin "against [one's] own body," which is the temple of the Holy Spirit (6:18-20).[9] Sexual immorality is thus a form of idolatry that constitutes sacrilege in the holy precincts of God's dwelling place.[10]

These same arguments stand behind other similar apostolic warnings against nonmarital sex, such as 1 Thessalonians 4:3-5: "For this is God's will: that you become holy, that you keep away from sexual immorality, that each of you know how to possess his own body in holiness and honor, not in lustful passion like the Gentiles who do not know God" (see also Ephesians 5:3).

The import of what I have been saying is well summarized by Lewis Smedes:

It does not matter what the two people [who are having sex] have in mind...The *reality* of the act, unfelt and unnoticed by them, is this:

it unites them—body and *soul*—to each other. It unites them in that strange, impossible to pinpoint sense of "one flesh." There is no such thing as casual sex, no matter how casual people are about it. The Christian assaults reality in his night out at the brothel. He uses a woman and puts her back in a closet where she can be forgotten; but the reality is that he has put away a person with whom he has done something that was meant to inseparably join them. This is what is at stake for Paul in the question of sexual intercourse between unmarried people.

And now we can see clearly why Paul thought sexual intercourse by unmarried people was wrong. It is wrong because it violates the inner reality of the act; it is wrong because unmarried people thereby engage in a life-uniting act without a life-uniting intent. Whenever two people copulate without a commitment to life-Union, they commit fornication.[11]

Problems with Sexual Sin: Experiential Consequences

At the beginning of chapter 10, I noted that observant people can recognize clues that point to the relational nature of sex. What we can now affirm is that biblical revelation provides the only complete explanation for those clues: the Creator's design. When we commend the moral will of God to Christians, we are not merely appealing to religious statements that are unrelated to life. *They are accurate descriptions of reality.* They account for the way things are. They do not give us an optional perspective that we may take or leave. And if we attempt to ignore or supplant them with some other opinion of how things seem to us or ought to be, there are predictable and unpleasant consequences.

We encounter the reality of God's design, for instance, when we seek the pleasure of sexual exercise apart from the intended *relational* purpose and context. John White, psychiatrist and author, points out that we experience genuine pleasure only when it comes to us as a *by-product* of some another, legitimate goal.

> When we devote ourselves to pursuing pleasure, pleasure ceases to be a delight. Our appetites grow jaded and require ever more stimulation. On the other hand when we devote ourselves to loving obedience to God and to serve one another, we find that the pleasures that eluded us when we made them our goal spring unbidden to surprise us. To seek pleasure is to find disenchantment. To seek God is to find (among other things) piercing pleasures.[12]

Like all counterfeits, recreational sex fails to deliver what it promises. James Emery White observes a pervasive sense of disillusionment among sexually active adults. "People are thinking, *Tell me there's more. I've taken this sexual thing as far as it can go, and...this is it?* They're finding it didn't have the payoff that it lured them into believing it would have spiritually and emotionally."[13]

Others crash into this reality when they experience the breakup of a romance in which sex was a prominent feature. Many women can relate all too well to the testimony of one young lady who wrote:

> After you've done it, you're really attached to that guy. It's as if he's your life; you feel really vulnerable. When the relationship ended, I felt really awful. I can't describe it. About a week after we had sex, we broke up because I found out he was dating other girls. It really hurt.

Counselors have long recognized that sex alters the relational dynamics of an unmarried couple. "Sex intensifies your experience of closeness, whether in a committed relationship or not." John Van Epp cites research that shows that one act of sex starts a chain reaction of several relationship activities. "One of the activities was a desire to open up and feel closer. At the same time, this was countered by an equally strong feeling of being more vulnerable to getting hurt by the partner, and an apprehension about letting down your guard." This confusion of contradictory feelings was the result of getting the sexual cart ahead of the commitment horse.[14]

But there is more to this sense of bonding than mere emotional attachment. Sexual coupling is a physical event with *physiological* effects that stimulate strong feelings of connectedness. Dr. Jennifer Roback Morse devotes an eye-opening chapter to the bonding impact of hormones that are released during sex (oxytocin in women, vasopressin in men). After reviewing the findings of physiological research, she concludes: "The human tendency to attach to our sexual partners is built into our biochemistry and is more than simply cultural conditioning... The basic desire to connect to one's sexual partner has deep physiological roots." Sexually involved individuals may intend to avoid or postpone commitment. "Few such couples realize that their hormones may create an 'involuntary chemical commitment.'" As a result, "We are not really capable of being indifferent to our sexual partners, nor are we really capable of calculating and recalculating our attachments to our partners."[15]

In the movie *Vanilla Sky*, Julie, the woman stalking David Aames (Tom Cruise), was espousing both the theology of the apostle Paul and the findings of scientific research when she said, "Don't you know that when you sleep with someone, your body makes a promise whether you do or not?"[16] Sometimes real wisdom pops up in surprising places.

These findings, both theological and scientific, provide a coherent explanation for the report published by the National Marriage Project in 2000. A study of never-married, twentysomething singles revealed that many sexually active women who had experienced a succession of breakups felt "burned, angry, betrayed when they are dumped." The result is a "cumulative negative attitude on subsequent relationships," expressed in a "global mistrust and antagonism toward men."[17] It turns out that sexual involvement between two consenting adults does not simply affect those two individuals. It generates emotional baggage that has a potentially damaging impact on at least two other people who are not yet on the scene—future partners of the current pair.

Questions for Reflection and Group Discussion

[*Note to Group Leaders*: For many people, sexuality is a highly sensitive subject. Some members of your group may be reticent to discuss some questions, particularly in a mixed-gender setting. This will be acutely true for any who have suffered from sexual abuse, especially if their victimization remains secret. So refrain from probing individual members who appear reluctant to enter in to the discussion. Where there is a high degree of openness among group members, it can be very beneficial for men and women to hear the perspectives of the other gender. But the depth of discussion may be greater if, for these chapters, you subdivide into two groups—male and female.]

1. What was the most significant insight you gained from reading this chapter?

2. What is the connection between the biblical *theology* of sex and the biblical *ethics* of sex?

3. Of the six reasons given by the apostle Paul to "flee sexual immorality," which ones are most persuasive to you personally?

4. What is the essence of Lewis Smedes's argument against fornication?

5. What are some consequences of sexual sin? Have you witnessed or experienced any of the consequences of violating God's design? What happened?

6. How committed are you to maintaining sexual purity as a single adult? What proactive steps will you take to achieve the success of this goal? Write them down.

❖   ❖   ❖

For additional questions, go to www.TheMarriageDecision.com.

12

Sex and the Single Christian

~~~~~~~

The need for moral guidelines in male-female relationships emerges fairly early in adolescence, as I discovered just a little over a decade ago. My teenage son, Mike, had discovered girls and, equally to the point, they had discovered him. It was a happy development on both sides, and Mike was enjoying the euphoric benefits of having a girlfriend. The opportunity for a father-son conversation on setting boundaries for expressing affection came during a drive through the woods. Mike was a Christian with high moral standards. But he was experiencing powerful feelings that were new, exciting, and disorienting. And he admitted to wondering what behavior was appropriate with the current love-interest.

"What do you think the chances are that you'll marry this girl?" I asked.

"Well, I really like her," Mike said. "But since we're only sophomores in high school, I guess it isn't very likely that this relationship would last that long."

"Do you think you'd want to get married someday?"

"Yeah, I think so."

"So that means the girl you're going to marry is out there somewhere. You don't know who she is or where she is, but she's alive somewhere on this planet. Right?"

"That's right."

"OK then, you should treat the girl you're dating now the way you want some other guy to be treating the girl you're going to marry."

Mike nodded. "That's good. That's what I'm going to do." And that's what he did.

(By the way, Mike's future wife was in Africa, which is, in fact, "somewhere on this planet." At the moment of our conversation, she was eleven years old.)

From Ethics to Strategy

This exchange between Mike and me illustrates the fourth point of Stanton Jones's summary of a Christian sexual ethic: "that all persons, married and unmarried, should be characterized by certain virtues that will guide and mold their living out of their sexual natures before God and their fellow men and women."[1] If Christian singles are going to be successful in honoring God with their sexuality, they must *prethink* how they are going to carry out their relationships. They need to decide in advance not only *how* they are going to behave, but more importantly *why* they are going to act in certain ways. And this deliberate decision making should encompass not only the negative (what I am not going to do), but the positive (how I am going to constructively express my sexuality in relationship).

A Strategy for Sexual Stewardship

So what would a proactive strategy for sexual stewardship look like? Here are seven components (adapted from *Soul Virgins*, the outstanding book by Doug Rosenau and Michael Todd Wilson).[2]

1. Diligently guard God's design for sexuality in oneself and others.

2. Distinguish between gender relating and erotic relating.

3. Identify stages of intimacy on the bridge between friendship and marriage. (I'll explain this bridge in a moment.)

4. For each stage on the bridge, determine what constitutes appropriate relational dynamics.

5. Prior to romantic involvement, learn how to relate with appropriate intimacy to God and fellow Christians.

6. Learn to discipline sexual energy through reframing and redirecting.

7. Be proactive in dealing with sexual temptation.

Let's briefly sketch out what is involved in each of these strategic elements.

1. Value, Celebrate, and Protect God's Design

An effective management plan begins with a commitment "to value, celebrate, and protect God's design for sexuality—body, soul, and spirit—in oneself and others."[3] Rosenau and Wilson carefully crafted this description of a "soul virgin." The verbs ("value, celebrate, protect") reflect the vocabulary of stewardship, reminding us that we are called to faithfully manage something of great value that actually belongs to Someone Else (1 Corinthians 4:2; 6:19-20). The focus is on God's *design*, and we are helpfully reminded that his purposes for our sexuality encompass not only our bodies, but our souls (mind, emotion, and will) and our spirits (capacity for relational intimacy with God and others). Finally, our responsibility is both personal ("in oneself") and communal ("in others"). Within the Christian community, we *are* our brothers (and sisters) keepers.

Every other component in our plan is a means to accomplishing this one. It all begins with a life-shaping decision and determination to be a person of virtue in whom God's intentions for sexuality are fulfilled. Apart from this mindset, there isn't much point in reading further.

2. Distinguish Between Gender Relating and Erotic Relating

Second, it is helpful *to distinguish between two categories of sexual relating: gender and erotic.* Gender relating includes the broad range of interactions we have with other people in which maleness and femaleness (both ours and theirs) come into play. Within a family, for instance, the males reflect their masculinity as fathers, sons, and brothers; the females express their femininity as mothers, daughters, and sisters. Such relationships are characterized by a love that is social and nurturing. Within the broader family of God, gender relating promotes healthy friendships between Christian brothers and sisters. So Paul wrote to Timothy, "Speak to younger men as brothers, older women as mothers, and younger women as sisters—with complete purity" (1 Timothy 5:1-2).

Erotic relating, on the other hand, is romantic and arousing. It includes such behaviors as amorous talk, holding hands, caressing, kissing, and, ultimately, intercourse. It is properly shared with one other person in an exclusive relationship within morally governed, mutually accepted limits. The ultimate purpose of erotic relating is true intimacy.

3. Identify Relational Stages: Connecting, Coupling, Covenanting

Third, it is useful *to identify distinctive stages of developing intimacy on a continuum between friendship and marriage.* In our culture, total strangers do not marry. Courtship moves through a sequence of phases from acquaintance to matrimony. Rosenau and Wilson distinguish between three broad stages: Connecting, Coupling, and Covenanting. To explain the distinctive characteristics of each relational phase, they utilize the imagery of crossing a bridge that links the starting point of casual friendship to the consummation of covenanted marriage.

The Relationship Continuum Bridge

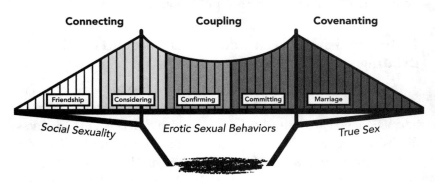

Copyright 2006 by Doug Rosenau and Michael Todd Wilson. Used by permission.

Connecting relationships include friendships and casual dating. The focus at this juncture is on building skills for interactions with opposite-sex friends. At the other end of the continuum is *Covenanting* or marriage. This is where an exclusive relationship with a single mate is formalized and lived out in one-flesh union.

Between the initiation (Connecting) and the consummation (Covenanting) of a marital relationship lies the bridge of *Coupling*. This is not the same as mating, as one sees in the animal kingdom; it is the process by which a man and a woman become an exclusive couple. This in-between phase has three substages.

1. Considering: The adventure of Coupling begins with the progression from friendship to romance. It includes a period during which the woman and man agree to date exclusively. Each begins the process of evaluating the other as a potential life partner.

2. Confirming: This is sometimes described as the stage when the couple is "engaged to be engaged." During this period, the couple should explore any and all issues that may affect a future marriage. This is most effectively accomplished with the help of a pastor or counselor through pre-engagement counseling.[4]

3. Committing: This is formal engagement. The intention to marry is publicly announced and plans are set in motion for a wedding.

An individual will start across the Coupling bridge with another person only a few times in life. Such a journey may be terminated at any point along the way for any number of reasons. But it is the right route to take with the person who will ultimately become one's spouse.

4. Predetermine Appropriate Relational Dynamics for Each Stage

The fourth step is *to determine what constitutes appropriate relational dynamics and behavior for each stage on the continuum.* All Connecting relationships (friendships and casual dating) that have not evolved into romance should feature *gender* relating that is nonerotic. Sexual intercourse must be reserved for the Covenanting phase (marriage). Intermediate erotic behaviors should be phased in as the couple advances in their level of commitment. This should be done on the basis of conscious mutual choice in a way that "values, celebrates, and protects God's design for sexuality."[5]

Three times in the Song of Songs, sexually mature adults are warned not to "awaken or arouse" erotic impulses prematurely (2:7; 3:5; 8:4). As a practical exercise, Rosenau and Wilson advocate setting up stop signs: "A *stop sign* is any behavior you choose, by the deliberate act of your will, not to engage in until you've reached a certain level of commitment in your relationship." Examples would include no kissing after midnight, no hands under clothing, no making out after a romantic movie. The next-to-last stop sign they suggest is the bikini line. This boundary says that parts of the body covered by a bikini should be reserved for Covenanting. "Yes, this eliminates any type of mutual orgasms, whether manual or oral, under clothing or on top of clothing."[6]

5. Cultivate Healthy Skills and Relationships

Fifth, before you become romantically involved with a specific someone, *learn how to relate with appropriate intimacy to God and fellow Christians.*[7] Many singles live under the illusion that the solution to their loneliness is marriage. But if two lonely singles marry, what they will likely experience is a lonely marriage. Our sense of isolation is not automatically removed by human coupling in marriage. Our experience of intimacy with another must begin with the One to which the parable of marriage points. We become relationally complete as we experience God's love, especially as it is conveyed in community with spiritual brothers and sisters (1 John 4:12-17). If one never marries, healthy, growing relationships with God and fellow Christians will be sufficient to overcome loneliness with companionship.[8] And those who marry will find that the unitive function of marriage will be experienced to the degree that intimacy needs are already being met through these two prior relationships.

One of the major developmental tasks of single adulthood (in particular) is the development of a vital sense of masculinity and femininity. A perception of one's sexual identity is shaped within the parental home. But it is refined and matured in the context of friendships with peers, as well as older and younger acquaintances, of both genders. This personal development is a prerequisite for a successful life, to say nothing of a healthy marriage. And so the cultivation of friendships, the development of relational skills, and the maturation of one's sexual identity should be a priority for Christian single adults.[9]

6. Constructively Discipline Sexual Energy

Sixth, understand that *the sexual ache* that you feel is more than physical and hormonal. *It is designed to motivate you toward intimate connection that is more than physical.* Unmarried persons will have greater success in rechanneling sexual energy when it is harnessed toward ends that are consistent with its purpose. We can do this because of our tripartite nature (body, soul, spirit). We are not animals who are in heat. We have the ability to feed our arousal or to discipline it. Two means for processing sexual ache are *reframing* and *redirecting*.

Reframing is mostly a mental exercise that involves looking at something in a different way. Our popular culture says that true love is about erotic connection, and we should exercise no restraint in indulging what is essentially a physical appetite. A biblical worldview acknowledges the reality and legitimacy of *eros* as a magnetic force that draws two people together. But it places greater emphasis on two other kinds of love that are distinguished in Greek vocabulary as *philos* (friendship love) and *agape* (a sacrificial, unconditional love that focuses on meeting the needs of another). *Philos* and *agape* are clearly appropriate expressions of gender relating between nonromantically connected friends. The single adult reframes his or her sexual ache when another person who might be thought of as an object of desire (a literal or imagined conquest) is mentally reconstructed into a subject for compassion.

Rosenau and Wilson give an example of one man's approach.

> [Jim had been] challenged at a seminar to treat women as three-dimensional people. Now when he noticed a sexy woman at the mall, he gave her a soul and a life as he noticed in her face that she was tired. He looked at the packages she was carrying and wondered what her life was like and who the packages were for. He thought about her desire to love and respect her husband, knowing fully that it wasn't him. He also prayed for her, that she would come to know Christ if she didn't already.[10]

Redirecting is more behavioral. It involves channeling sexual energies toward nonerotic activities and accomplishments. Sometimes this involves translating *eros* into *philos* or *agape*. Since *eros* is designed to motivate a person toward intimate connection, activities that pursue that purpose in nonerotic ways are certainly appropriate. You might overtly invest in your relationship with God through devotional disciplines such as Bible study, prayer, or other forms of personal worship. Connecting with a good friend for a time of in-depth conversation, enjoying fellowship with other Christians in a church group, or engaging in a compassion ministry in one's community enable the single Christian to move outward into the lives of other people.

Sometimes it's just beneficial to dissipate sexual energy through strenuous physical activity. Exercise, yard work, hiking, jogging, and team sports increase adrenaline and promote mental as well as physical health.

7. Deal Proactively with Sexual Temptation

Finally, the single adult who is committed to Christ must *be proactive in dealing with sexual temptation*.

At the outset, I must reiterate that sexual *desire* is not the same thing as lust (James 1:14-15). The temptation lies in the enticement to indulge erotic *thoughts* (Matthew 5:28) or engage in sexual *behaviors* that violate the boundaries of God's design (1 Corinthians 6:14)—to misuse what is otherwise good. In fact, those are the two categories—fantasy and behavior—in which single adults are likely to be repeatedly tested.

Temptations in the thought life may lead to an activity that does not directly involve another person—masturbation. On this sensitive subject, there is a collective and confusing ambivalence on the part of Christian counselors and writers. Some do not hesitate to label the practice as sin. They focus their attention on reasons and strategies for abstaining from it. At the other end of the spectrum are those who suggest that masturbation may occasionally and legitimately be utilized to calm intense urges and reduce the temptation toward improper sexual activity.[11] The reasons for this disparity of opinion are well-summarized by Mike Nichols:

> Since God created the male and female bodies for one another, for intimacy and relationship, masturbation by its very nature falls short of the full expression of sexuality God intended. Yet it is interesting that there are only two forms of sexual expression not prohibited in the Bible: sex

within the marriage relationship (by the Bible's overt affirmation) and masturbation (by the Bible's silence on the subject).[12]

The Bible's silence puts masturbation in the category of debatable matters (discussed by Paul in 1 Corinthians 8–10 and Romans 14–15).[13] And since there is no biblical law commanding or prohibiting the behavior, this issue falls within the jurisdiction of wisdom. Because our hormonal drives and propensity for pleasure are thrown into the mix, this is one of those areas where it is extremely hard to think clearly. But that is our assignment since this is not a theoretical matter, but is one about which we are each obliged to become "fully convinced" in our own minds (Romans 14:5).

As you deliberate on this, carefully consider the counsel of William Struthers:

> You may be asking the question "Is all masturbation a sin?" I suggest that this is the wrong question to ask…The better question to ask is "Does masturbation lead me toward sanctification?"[14]

What we can affirm, on the one hand, is that since there is no prohibition in Scripture, the physical act, in and of itself, is not sinful. This opens the door to the line of reasoning that judicious use of masturbation is preferable to obsession with lustful fantasies or inappropriate sexual involvement with another person. Identifying a permissible activity that is better than a prohibited or intolerable alternative follows the style of reasoning used by the apostle Paul in 1 Corinthians 7.[15]

But of course the moral will of God is not restricted to our behaviors. It is also concerned with our thoughts and motivations. And only the most naïve would deny that the likelihood of sinning mentally during masturbation is high. In order for self-stimulation to not be sinful, it must be done without entertaining lustful thoughts toward another person (Matthew 5:27-28), it must not become compulsive or addictive (1 Corinthians 6:12; 10:23), and it should not be practiced as an erotic effort to meet nonerotic needs such as loneliness, fear, grief, or boredom.[16]

Using masturbation to curb sexual impulses is an exercise in fighting fire with fire. It may be a legitimate tactic to use in some circumstances, but it can also backfire. It may quench the wildfire on the immediate horizon only to flare up into an inferno that consumes everything in its path.

If there is such a thing as "disciplined masturbation," the range of its utility is very narrow indeed.[17]

While our ambivalence about masturbation may be justified, the same cannot be said about pornography. This social and moral blight, which often feeds compulsive, lust-driven masturbation, is wholly destructive and ought to be treated as the toxic poison that it is.

Pornography is visual material, literary and pictorial, designed to produce erotic stimulation. It is both evil and destructive. The evil in it is displayed in the word itself. "Porno" refers to a prostitute. When Paul says, "Flee sexual immorality!" in 1 Corinthians 6:18, the word he uses is the common term for all unlawful sexual intercourse: *porneia*.[18] Pornography intentionally provokes lust and lures men and women away from God's intention and design for sex. If our supreme goal is to please God, we would do well to take to heart these words of Paul:

> For this is God's will: that you become holy, that you keep away from sexual immorality, that each of you know how to possess his own body in holiness and honor, not in lustful passion like the Gentiles who do not know God. In this matter no one should violate the rights of his brother or take advantage of him, because the Lord is the avenger in all these cases, as we also told you earlier and warned you solemnly. For God did not call us to impurity but in holiness (1 Thessalonians 4:3-7).

But there are moments when pleasing God is not the motivation that determines our choices. The siren song of sexual pleasure, easily obtained, is a powerful lure. If we are to avoid its seduction, we must *think*. We must remember that the one who offers what we think we want is a liar who seeks our destruction (John 8:44; 1 Peter 5:8). And one of the most destructive weapons in his armory is pornography. "Porn is a whispered promise. It promises more sex, better sex, endless sex, sex on-demand, more intense orgasms, experiences of transcendence."[19]

But it does not, cannot, deliver on its promises. On the contrary, when a man, in particular, becomes a regular consumer of pornography and acts out via masturbation, here's what porn actually does:

- It *counterfeits* God's design with an empty imitation. It replaces relational intimacy with solitary sensual pleasure and conveys a false message that sex is about personal gratification.

- It *dehumanizes* women, making them objects to be penetrated rather than lovely creatures in the image of God to be valued, honored, and appropriately known.

- It literally *reconfigures* a man's mind in destructive ways. The impact of pornography consumption on the operation of the male brain is dramatically documented by biopsychologist William M. Struthers in his book *Wired for Intimacy: How Pornography Hijacks the Male Brain.* Here is one summary of his findings:

  > Sexually acting out in response to pornography creates sexual associations that are stored as hormonal and neurological habits. These associations are seared into the fabric of the brain. These memories can then be pulled up at any time and replayed as private sexual fantasies. In sexual fantasy, the neurological circuit is replayed, further strengthening it. The result is an increase in autonomic sexual arousal, which requires an outlet. These memories and fantasies keep him in bondage and worsen the consequences of the earlier behavior.[20]

- Not surprisingly, pornography often *enslaves* the voyeur through escalation and addiction. Pornography has been called the crack cocaine of sexual addiction. Not only does the individual become hooked, but the need for increasing levels of stimulation[21] prompts the exploration of images that are increasingly perverse. What was once exciting becomes boring, and what was previously disgusting now becomes enticing.[22]

- If not overcome, pornography will *cripple* the individual depriving him of the ability to function in a sexually healthy way. It trains him to bond emotionally to an image rather than a person and prevents him from entering into the relational intimacy that sex is designed to promote. One man reported to his counselor that he had been unable to consummate intercourse with his wife after they were married because of his premarital masturbating. In order for him to come to climax, she had to play out the scenarios that had become ingrained in his mind, often including viewing pornography. This was, of course, degrading to her and destructive to their marriage.

- Episodes of engaging with pornography *haunt* those who would like to leave it in the past. Because of the formatting of the brain, images from past sexual fantasies intrude into the legitimate acts of lovemaking between spouses, disrupting the intimacy that such union is designed to produce.

- Thus, pornography *steals* from a future marriage the fulfillment and joy that is intended by God and anticipated by a bride and groom. The unwitting victim is one's beloved who pays for sins she has not committed. This is certainly an instance in which the "marriage bed" *is* "defiled" (Hebrews 13:4).

The long-term cost can be great indeed; this is not something to fool around with.[23]

I have been talking about the need to be proactive in dealing with sexual temptation in our thought life. The other area where a commitment to purity will be challenged is in a romantic relationship with another person. In this case the additional risk is that of going too far in expressing erotic passion.

So how does one become proactive in dealing with this sexual temptation? Our guidance from the moral will of God consists of a single summary statement fleshed out by powerful elaborations from four characters in biblical history.

The governing principle comes from the apostle Paul: "Put on the Lord Jesus Christ, and make no provision for the flesh to arouse its desires" (Romans 13:14).[24] This statement is like a two-sided coin. The positive side uses the metaphor of clothing to communicate the importance of our moment-by-moment dependence on and submission to the Lord. "We who are in Christ must envelop ourselves with him in such a way that he directs all our thinking and conduct."[25] The flip side presents the negative counterpoint: make no provision for the flesh to arouse its desires. The importance of both sides of the coin is evident in the biblical commentaries.

The first is the narrative of Joseph and Potiphar's wife.

> Now Joseph was well built and good-looking. Soon after these things, his master's wife took notice of Joseph and said, "Have sex with me." But he refused, saying to his master's wife, "Look, my master does not

give any thought to his household with me here, and everything that he owns he has put into my care. There is no one greater in this household than I am. He has withheld nothing from me except you because you are his wife. So how could I do such a great evil and sin against God?" Even though she continued to speak to Joseph day after day, he did not respond to her invitation to have sex with her.

One day he went into the house to do his work when none of the household servants were there in the house. She grabbed him by his outer garment, saying, "Have sex with me!" But he left his outer garment in her hand and ran outside (Genesis 39:6-12).

The second is the famous example of Job:

"I made a covenant with my eyes
   not to look lustfully at a young woman."
                (Job 31:1 NIV)

To this we add the wisdom of Solomon:

Do not lust in your heart for her beauty,
and do not let her captivate you with her alluring eyes;
for on account of a prostitute one is brought down to a loaf of bread,
but the wife of another man preys on your precious life.
Can a man hold fire against his chest
without burning his clothes?
Can a man walk on hot coals
without scorching his feet?
So it is with the one who has sex with his neighbor's wife;
no one who touches her will escape punishment...
A man who commits adultery with a woman lacks wisdom,
whoever does it destroys his own life.
(Proverbs 6:25-29,32)

And finally, the warning of Jesus:

"But I say to you that whoever looks at a woman to desire her has already committed adultery with her in his heart. If your right eye causes you to sin, tear it out and throw it away! It is better to lose one of your members than to have your whole body thrown into hell. If your right hand causes you to sin, cut it off and throw it away! It is better to lose one of your members than to have your whole body go into hell" (Matthew 5:28-30).

Retreat and Avoid

Admittedly, the most practical steps one can take to resist sexual temptation are negative actions. The first principle can't be missed: *when you first encounter temptation, run for your life!* Paul gives the exhortation: "Run from anything that stimulates youthful lusts" (2 Timothy 2:22a NLT); Joseph provides the example. You won't want to. You may not think you need to. But if you don't, you will succumb to the song of the Sirens. And you will suffer shipwreck.[26]

But that principle is *reactive*. And it assumes an attitude of alertness that, frankly, won't be there—apart from prior, deliberate preparation. So a second principle is, *avoid circumstances where you're sure to be tempted.* Minimize your vulnerability by staying out of harm's way.

When we were in seminary, there was a pharmacy located one block from the men's dorm that was open all night. That was a convenient resource when some ailment such as a cold or a headache prevented study or sleep. The medications were located toward the back of the store. A customer could take two aisles to that destination, one of which passed by the magazine section. I don't need to spell out the nature of the magazines in this context. Headache or no, I had to deliberately plot my course to avoid the pornographic minefield I stumbled into on my first visit.

Today, of course, the situation is far worse. The drugstore *was* a block away and the fear of being seen by a classmate was an additional incentive to avoid the dangerous territory. Now—well, I am typing these words on a laptop computer from which, with just a few keystrokes, I could access images far more graphic than anything I would have ever seen in that pharmacy. And chances are, no one else would ever know.

Well, Someone would know. But you get my point. It's easy, it's free, it's anonymous, it's safe. And it's deadly as hell.

That's what Jesus said. So he advised plucking out one's eye or cutting off one's hand if that's what it would take to remove enticements to lust— hyperbole to be sure, but it gets your attention. Jesus was directing disciples to deal drastically, through godly discipline, with the lethal threat of lust. The believer must hit this temptation so hard that it can't get up off the mat.

And what might that involve? Getting rid of the computer?[27] Unplugging the cable? Canceling *Sports Illustrated* before February? Staying out of video stores? Burning the romance novels? "I made a covenant with my eyes," said Job, "not to look lustfully at a young woman." What will it take to keep lust-inducing women out of a guy's field of vision or fantasies of modern-day Casanovas out of a woman's imagination?

Seriously!

In a romantic relationship, setting up stop signs (which we talked about above) is a stratagem designed to minimize a couple's vulnerability.

So the negative steps to proactive guarding against sexual temptation are 1) to actively avoid situations where you're sure to be tempted, and 2) to flee from it when it arises.

But while the avoidance tactics are the most concrete, the positive side provides the *motivation*. Listen carefully to Joseph: "How could I do such a great evil and *sin against God?*"

Garry Friesen tells his students at Multnomah University, "*Learn to love God more than you love sin.*" A horse with a wild heart will find a way to get over, around, or through any fence erected to corral it. It is the heart that must be tamed and transformed. We will do what we love most. So we must train our heart to love God and people more than sin.[28]

In his advice to his younger protégé, Timothy, the apostle Paul combined the negative and the positive: "Run from anything that stimulates youthful lust. Instead, pursue righteous living, faithfulness, love, and peace" (i.e., "put on the Lord Jesus Christ"). And then Paul added one more extremely helpful suggestion: "Enjoy *the companionship of those who call on the Lord with pure hearts*" (2 Timothy 2:22 NLT).

The constructive role of other believers in helping us grow and maintain purity is often underestimated. The grace that we need for spiritual transformation has its origin in God (1 Peter 5:10; 2 Peter 3:18). But he most often channels that grace through other people (Ephesians 4:16; 1 Peter 4:10-11). This is where loving accountability comes in. Sometimes we need discipline and structure; sometimes we need acceptance and support. These factors in spiritual health are best supplied by brothers and sisters with whom we experience mutual commitment, trust, and love.[29] When we avail ourselves of and contribute to that resource, the business of dealing with sexual temptation becomes a shared experience. And we all become stronger for the company (Ecclesiastes 4:9-12).

These reflections on the positive, motivating approach to purity elucidate the third principle for fending off sexual temptation: *Cultivate your relationship with God and with his people.* It is highly significant that a major part of God's design for our sexuality is to motivate relational intimacy. Sexual sin is inherently selfish, moving us away from God's purpose. Connecting with God and other believers is both the *goal* of that design and the best *means* for subverting temptation.

The final thing you will see in this chapter is a chart that summarizes our "Strategy for Sexual Purity." Perhaps it will be helpful. But professors Stanley Hauerwas and Allen Verhey are surely correct when they observe, "all of this may be a lot for young people to remember in the back seat of a Buick." It's hard to imagine Joseph saying to Potiphar's wife, "Could you hold that thought while I review my list of seven keys to godly sexuality?"

In the end, it is not the strategy that determines your behavior—it's your character. The focus needs to shift from "what acts we are ready to permit to what sort of people we would be and become, from rules to virtue." Rules are seldom persuasive.[30] "But," as Hauerwas and Verhey remind us, "a good character, a virtuous character, can usually do the right thing without having to think about it very much."[31]

Which means that, of all the things on the following chart, the very last principle is the most important.

A Strategy for Sexual Purity[32]

1. Diligently guard God's design for sexuality in oneself and others.

2. Distinguish between gender relating and erotic relating.

3. Identify stages of intimacy on the bridge between friendship and marriage.
   - *Connecting:* friendships and casual dating
   - *Coupling:* dating exclusively with a view to marriage
     - *Considering:* the beginning of a romantic relationship

    –*Confirming*: exploring issues that may affect a future
    marriage

    –*Committing*: formal engagement

- *Covenanting*: marriage

4. For each stage on the bridge, determine what constitutes appropriate relational dynamics.

5. Prior to romantic involvement, learn how to relate with appropriate intimacy to God and fellow Christians.

6. Learn to discipline sexual energy through reframing and redirecting.

7. Be proactive in dealing with sexual temptation, whether fantasy (lust) or behavior (fornication).

- When you first encounter temptation, run for your life!

- Avoid circumstances where you're sure to be tempted.

- **Train your heart to love God and people more than you love sin.**

❖ ❖ ❖

Recommended Reading

Dance of the Sexes: Celebrating the soul in Single Sexuality by Doug Rosenau and Douglas Wilson (published by author, 2012).

Sexual Character: Beyond Technique to Intimacy by Marva J. Dawn (Wm. B. Eerdmans Publishing Co., 1993).

Real Sex: The Naked Truth About Chastity by Lauren Winner (Brazos Press, 2005).

Smart Sex: Finding Life-Long Love in a Hook-Up World by Jennifer Roback Morse (Spence Publishing Company, 2005).

Sexual Ethics: A Biblical Perspective by Stanley Grenz (Word, 1990).

❖ ❖ ❖

Questions for Reflection and Group Discussion

[*Note to Group Leaders*: For many people, sexuality is a highly sensitive subject. Some members of your group may be reticent to discuss some questions, particularly in a mixed-gender setting. This will be acutely true for any who have suffered from sexual abuse, especially if their victimization remains secret. So refrain from probing individual members who appear reluctant to enter in to the discussion. Where there is a high degree of openness among group members, it can be very beneficial for men and women to hear the perspectives of the other gender. But the depth of discussion may be greater if, for these chapters, you subdivide into two groups—male and female.]

1. What was the most significant insight you gained from reading this chapter?

2. Why is it important to consciously develop a specific strategy for maintaining sexual purity? Why is the "why" of this plan as important as the "how"?

3. How does consideration of others play into the development of one's strategy for sexual management?

4. In a hook-up culture, why is it important to distinguish between categories or stages of developing intimacy between a man and a woman?

5. The author presents three principles for dealing proactively with sexual temptation. What are they? Can you amplify on the suggestions made in this chapter?

6. How committed are you to maintaining sexual purity as a single adult? What proactive steps will you take to achieve the success of this goal? (Return to the list that you began after reading the previous chapter. What do you need to add?)

For additional questions, go to www.TheMarriageDecision.com.

13

Cohabitation:
A Dangerous Liaison

~⟐~

In the prologue to this book, I narrated the dilemma encountered by Lorraine, the grad student whose roommate had to bail on their apartment-sharing arrangement. As she was evaluating her options (none of which looked promising), her boyfriend, Josh, popped the question. No, it was not a proposal of marriage. He suggested that she move in with him. "You're going to have to relocate in a couple of months anyway," he reasoned. And then he added this cryptic comment: "And who knows how things might play out?"

It was in the late 1970s that I assisted Garry Friesen in writing the original edition of *Decision Making and the Will of God*. When we applied the principles of the Way of Wisdom to the big issues of life, we devoted two chapters to singleness and marriage. But it never occurred to us to even mention cohabitation. That alternative was not even on the radar screen of our target audience.

My how things have changed! When we revised and updated the twenty-fifth anniversary edition of *Decision Making* (2004), the mushrooming prevalence of cohabitation was one of the new topics that required comment. We devoted almost two pages (311-13) to this rising phenomenon. The problem, apparently, is that Lorraine and Josh never read those two pages. Nor have a lot of others. For an option that would not have even been considered by most Christian singles in 1980 is now receiving serious attention, even implementation, in the second decade of the twenty-first century.

Anyone who comes to this chapter having read the previous twelve is not in suspense regarding the authors' bottom line on cohabitation. For while the Bible does not directly address cohabitation,[1] it clearly prohibits one of the defining features of cohabitation—nonmarital sex,[2] as the preceding chapters have demonstrated. So living together apart from matrimony is ruled out for committed believers on moral grounds.

So why are we including an entire chapter on cohabitation in a book on marital decisions and the will of God? There are two reasons.

The first is that even though cohabitation should not be an option for Christian couples, some professing followers of Jesus *are* cohabiting. Pastors are increasingly confronted with the awkward circumstance of being asked to perform weddings for self-described Christians who are living together. So this is one place where, for some folks at least, cultural norms are exerting a greater influence than biblical ones. Whether this state of affairs is due to ignorance (lack of instruction) or willful disregard of scriptural guidelines, the subject needs careful attention.

The second reason for including this chapter is that this book is addressed to adults who are capable of thinking things through. There is more to be said about cohabitation than simply stating, "The Bible says no." As I noted in the introduction to this section on single sexuality, we have access to a growing collection of findings from sociological research that sheds light on the consequences of a variety of relational choices, including cohabitation. A thoughtful adult should be able to consider the data and make mature decisions informed by the relevant information. My hope is that those who read these pages will give them careful consideration.

Additionally, this material could be useful to those who minister to single adults who have not read the previous twelve chapters.

A Cultural Revolution

On the subject of cohabitation, there may well be a generational divide. Many older folks might be surprised by how pervasive it is. Young adults who lack a strong sense of h–istory may not be aware how unusual the current cultural acceptance of cohabitation is. This divergence of perspective is due to the fact that within a single generation, a historic shift in attitude and practice has taken place.

Throughout human history, cohabitation has been taboo. As I noted in the introduction to part 2, virtually every society around the world has had a way of marking off the beginning of a marriage relationship, a way of saying, "This man and this woman are going to live together permanently in a relationship that is exclusive, and they are going to relate to one another in ways that they do not relate to any other persons." The message to outsiders has been, "Keep your hands off." The idea that it is permissible for a man and a woman to live together in a sexually active but uncommitted arrangement is radically novel.[3]

The magnitude and velocity of this dramatic change first came to light with the publication in 1999 of the landmark report by sociologists David Popenoe and Barbara Dafoe Whitehead, "Should We Live Together? What Young Adults Need to Know About Cohabitation Before Marriage."[4] Subsequently updated in 2002, this "Comprehensive Review of Recent Research" revealed the following:

- The frequency of cohabitation increased tenfold during the last four decades of the twentieth century. In 1960, only 430,000 couples lived together. That figure mushroomed to 4,236,000 by 1998. (This trend has continued. As of 2006, the number of cohabiting couples had risen to 5,368,000—a twelvefold increase since 1960.[5])

- About a quarter of unmarried women between the ages of 25 and 39 are currently living with a partner, and about half have lived at some time with an unmarried partner.

- Cohabitation precedes marriage over 50 percent of the time. This makes cohabitation the most common way couples in America begin life together.

- In representative national surveys over 60 percent of high school seniors indicated that they "agreed" or "mostly agreed" with the statement "it is usually a good idea for a couple to live together before getting married in order to find out whether they really get along." And three quarters of the students stated that "a man and a woman who live together without being married" are either "experimenting with a worthwhile alternative lifestyle" or "doing their own thing and not affecting anyone else."

- Half of all children will spend some time in a cohabiting family before they are 16.

Because of the "frog in the kettle effect," the enormity of this about-face in cultural attitudes and practices is difficult to grasp. For an individual, thirty years is a long time, and the change seems gradual. But from the standpoint of human history, this shift is both sudden and seismic. For thousands of years, the human race maintained a consensus on the appropriate social structure for a family (with variations). And then, a generation revolted. They looked at how things had always been and said, "We think there's a better way."

It Seemed like a Good Idea at the Time

Many factors combined to bring about the social revolution in which cohabitation is viewed as an acceptable practice (see the introduction to part 2).[6] But one dominant cause and one facilitating condition propelled the adoption of new approaches to male-female relationships.

The primary cause was a devastating divorce rate. The children of divorce, whose personal experience with marriage was profoundly painful, were actively seeking ways to avoid repeating similar trauma themselves or inflicting it on their own kids. Wouldn't it make sense for a couple that is considering marriage to live together for a time to see if they are compatible? Pamela Smock, a sociologist at the University of Michigan, sums up the conventional wisdom that was emerging: "Common sense suggests that premarital cohabitation should provide an opportunity for couples to learn about each other, strengthen their bonds, and increase their chances for a successful marriage."[7]

Why had previous generations not entertained this approach? Because of a powerful, two-pronged deterrent: the *moral/religious prohibition* against sex outside of marriage reinforced by *fear of pregnancy*. But the former was abolished by the Sexual Revolution when the latter was alleviated by the widespread availability of effective contraceptive resources, followed shortly by the legalization of abortion. This was the circumstantial condition that permitted the experiment with cohabitation to proceed.

In the 1970s, when the practice of cohabitation was beginning to spread, many social scientists expressed optimism about the potential benefits of this approach to mate selection.[8] Linda Waite, professor of sociology at the University of Chicago, summarizes their expectations:

> When social scientists first started studying cohabitation, they thought, "Oh, well, it's a way to gather information. You should see if you're compatible, if this is a good idea, if you're a good match. The people who find out that they really don't like living with this person should split up." So the only people who should go to marriage would be those who found out this was really what they wanted. They liked it. They like this person. This was going to work. So they ought to be less likely to divorce than people who married not having this information, right? Those marriages ought to be more stable.[9]

As the cultural acceptance of cohabitation grew, so did the reasons people found for practicing it. For those who were leery of or just not ready for matrimony, living together seemed to offer some advantages over marriage.

- Cohabitation is easier to begin and end than marriage. To live with someone does not require a wedding, and to stop living with someone does not require a divorce.

- It can be less expensive than living apart. Two can live more cheaply than one.

- It seems to be more loving because cohabitation does not rely on the external prop of marriage.

- It offers a relationship where sex roles are less stereotyped.

- It combines the sexual and emotional closeness of marriage with the autonomy (independence) of singleness. It's the kind of situation where you can have your cake and eat it too.

So How's That Working for You?

Let's let the social scientists explain their findings. Judith and Jack Balswick, authors of *Authentic Human Sexuality*:

> Taking current findings into account, we can conclude that contrary to predictions made in the 1970s, one's participation in premarital cohabitation

does not lead to better adjustment in marriage. In fact, evidence points to the contrary of this initial optimistic prediction. In McRae's...review of the relevant literature,[10] she concludes: "The results of research suggest that a strong negative association exists between premarital cohabitation and marital stability."[11]

Pamela Smock, sociologist at the University of Michigan:

Common sense suggests that premarital cohabitation should provide an opportunity for couples to learn about each other, strengthen their bonds, and increase their chances for a successful marriage...The evidence, however, suggests just the opposite. Premarital cohabitation tends to be associated with lower marital quality and to increase the risk of divorce, even after taking into account of variables known to be associated with divorce...The degree of consensus about this central finding is impressive.[12]

Linda Waite, professor of sociology at the University of Chicago:

In fact, every research project that's ever looked at the stability of marriages that were preceded by cohabitation has found that people who lived together before they get married are significantly more likely to divorce later. It's true in Canada. It's true in Sweden. It's true in the U.S. It's true wherever we've looked. So for some reason, living with somebody is just not a guarantee.[13]

David Popenoe and Barbara Dafoe Whitehead, directors of The National Marriage Project at Rutgers University:

The social science evidence challenges the popular idea that cohabiting ensures greater marital compatibility and thereby promotes stronger and more enduring marriages. Cohabitation does not reduce the likelihood of eventual divorce; in fact, it is associated with a higher divorce risk...Virtually all research on the topic has determined that the chances of divorce ending a marriage preceded by cohabitation are significantly greater than for a marriage not preceded by cohabitation.[14]

Excuse me for piling on, but I want you to see the remarkable degree of consensus on the findings. These experts have surveyed a vast array of research, and their conclusions are uniform: *As an alternative to or preparation for marriage, cohabitation is far from beneficial; it is, in fact, detrimental.* The serpent who beguiled Eve is still at it. The fruit of cohabitation is enticing, but its latent toxins will poison rather than prepare for the commitment that undergirds a healthy marriage.

Specific Problems of Cohabitation

The seriousness of the negative impact of cohabitation on many couples is amplified when we move from the general conclusions (as summarized above) to the specific problems that are often experienced.

Higher Likelihood of Breakup

Over half of cohabiting relationships do not transition into marriage but break up within fifteen months. And the idea that such a separation is painless ("If it doesn't work out, we'll just go our separate way") is far from true. When one member of a sexually bonded couple leaves the relationship, the impact on the abandoned partner (at least) is wrenching. Jennifer Roback Morse provides this striking explanation:

> Many people imagine that living together before marriage resembles taking a car for a test drive. The "trial period" gives people a chance to discover whether they are compatible. This analogy seems so compelling that people are unable to interpret the mountains of data to the contrary. Here's the problem with the car analogy: the car doesn't have hurt feelings if the driver dumps it back at the used car lot and decides not to buy it. The analogy works great if you picture yourself as the driver. It stinks if you picture yourself as the car.[15]

Those cohabiting couples who actually transition into marriage are hardly home free. In studies that compared the marital health of married persons who had cohabited when compared with noncohabiting couples, the cohabiters experienced lower levels of competency or satisfaction in four areas: they had less marital *interaction*, had more serious marital *disagreements*, were more prone to marital *instability*, and reported a higher incidence of *divorce*. Of course, the problems exhibited in the first three categories culminated in the outcome of the fourth. In fact, those who lived together before marriage had a 50 percent higher hazard rate of divorcing after marriage than couples who had not cohabited.[16]

When you combine the breakup rate for cohabiters who do not marry and the divorce rate of those who do, you get this sobering statistic: *only two out of ten cohabiting couples are able to build a lasting marriage.*[17] This stunning projection prompted Charles Colson to comment, "Cohabitation—it's training for divorce."[18]

Quality of Life Issues

In addition to the likelihood that cohabitation will fail to lead to a lasting marital commitment, cohabiters are more prone to various lifestyle liabilities than their married counterparts. For instance, cohabiters are much more likely to be unfaithful to their partners than married spouses.[19] This stands to reason in a relationship where commitment is intentionally diluted. Furthermore, the incidence of domestic abuse is three times higher among cohabiters than among married partners, and the rates for severe violence are nearly five times higher for cohabiters.[20]

Differing Expectations

Flash back to the saga of Lorraine and Josh. She needs a solution to her housing dilemma; he suggests that she move in with him. On the surface, this is a proposed solution to a knotty problem. But the outside observer immediately senses that these two aren't viewing the projected scenario in the same way. Lorraine sees a higher level of significance in the suggestion than Josh does, and she is conflicted. He's being practical, matter-of-fact, though he hints of deeper import—"Who knows how things might play out?" Subtly, he intimates an awareness of her hopes without crossing the line of commitment.

Studies indicate that it is not uncommon for men and women to have differing attitudes and expectations about the nature of their cohabiting arrangement. Women are more inclined to view moving in together as a stepping-stone to marriage, a precursor to engagement. Men don't tend to attach the same meaning to the event. They may be thinking about marriage, but they are further back in the process. The dominant motivation for many men is convenience—available sex and shared expenses. They may well be open to a deepening relationship ("Who knows?"), but their level of commitment will usually be lower. And they will regard their options as being more open than their live-in companion. Such divergent expectations are a prescription for trouble, all the more so since many couples are unaware of them.

It appears, then, that it's common for men and women who are in a cohabiting relationship to enter cohabitation with two different "blueprints" for the future. It is thus not surprising that many of these relationships end badly, particularly for the woman. Women who live with men more readily expect that at some point they will marry the men with whom they are living. But studies show that men move much slower and much less readily to marriage. It's been suggested, in fact, that men move toward marriage at the pace of a "wounded sloth." And when they do marry, they are more likely to be less committed to it than are women. Men do fear divorce more and are more likely to believe that living together is simply easier and less complicated. Women, who tend to display a greater willingness to sacrifice for others, tend to be the ones who get hurt.[21]

There can be little doubt that the number one reason why many couples continue in a cohabiting relationship or break up is that the man refuses to commit to marriage.[22]

Liabilities for Women

Apart from having her hopes of marriage perpetually deferred or dashed altogether, a woman faces other disadvantages in a cohabiting arrangement. Even though the initial agreement involves equal sharing of responsibilities and costs, the contributions to the relationship don't always remain fifty-fifty. Over time, the woman often finds she is doing more than her fair share of the housework and paying more than her half of the expenses. A lot of women support their live-in boyfriends. If the couple has a baby, the burden for childcare falls disproportionately on her. And if the cohabiting relationship breaks up, guess who gets to be a single parent!

These inequities stem from an unrecognized reality: in a relationship in which commitment is intentionally open-ended, "the balance of power tilts to the partner who is less committed and more likely to walk out."[23] This fact prompts a woman to make all kinds of sacrifices to motivate her man to stick around. And it puts her in a decidedly disadvantageous position. This disparity was recognized by Judith Krantz all the way back in 1976 when she described the high risk of cohabiting women in an article in *Cosmopolitan* magazine:

> When a woman lives with a man without…a marriage certificate, she immediately loses the following things: her independence, her freedom to make choices, her privacy, all of her mystery, any practical bargaining position in the power struggle of love…the prospect of having a child other than an illegitimate one, and the protection of the law.[24]

Accordingly, Laura Schlessinger lists cohabitation as one of the *10 Stupid Things Women Do to Mess Up Their Lives.*[25]

Children at Risk

Most cohabiters probably do not intend to have children outside of marriage, but women who engage in sex sometimes get pregnant. Some cohabiters (usually those who were previously married) bring their children with them into a nonmarried pairing. Intended or not, over 40 percent of cohabiting couples today have children, and the percentage is growing. This is not a good situation.

Children of cohabiting couples are at serious risk for a host of destructive circumstances and experiences. Ironically, the very people who have wanted to spare their children the pain of divorce place them in greater jeopardy. For "fully three quarters of children born to cohabiting couples will see their parents split up before they reach age sixteen, compared to a third of those born to married parents."[26] Even when the cohabiting couple manages to stay together, the family environment may not be conducive to the health and well-being of the child. Cohabiting families tend to have higher rates of child abuse and violence, for instance, and lower incomes than their married counterparts.[27]

David Popenoe, director of the National Marriage Project, concludes his report on "Cohabitation, Marriage and Child Wellbeing" (2008) with this sobering indictment:

> In the final analysis, the issue of cohabitation comes down to a conflict between adult desires and children's needs. It seems a tragedy that, with all the opportunities that modernity has brought to adults, it may also be bringing a progressive diminution in our concern for the needs of children—and thus for the many generations to come.[28]

The determined cohabiter might reply, "There's no reason to believe that *our* relationship will break up. Plenty of people who live together get married. In fact, it's pretty common." But the question remains, is cohabitation a good way to prepare for marriage? Does it reduce the likelihood of divorce? Does it equip future spouses to have more successful marriages? The research indicates that the answer to all of these questions is no.

Why Cohabitation Doesn't Work

Sociological research does an admirable job of describing the consequences of cohabitation but is severely limited when it comes to explaining the reasons for these consequences.[29] But those of us who come to the subject from the perspective of Scripture are not surprised by these findings. They are, in fact, predictable. And that is because of the fundamental flaw in the nature of the relationship: cohabitation is a violation of the Creator's design for relationships between men and women. As far as the Bible is concerned, *cohabitation is a corrupted hybrid of the two sanctioned states of singleness and marriage.* It seeks the autonomy of singleness and the sexual communion of marriage. But it replaces the true freedom of singleness with confinement, and it fails to give the security that marriage provides for genuine sexual intimacy.

Like any counterfeit, the deficiencies of cohabitation come into sharper relief when contrasted with the real thing—God's design for marriage. By way of review from chapter 3: "Marriage is an exclusive heterosexual covenant between one man and one woman, ordained and sealed by God, preceded by a public leaving of parents, consummated in sexual union, issuing in a permanent mutually supportive partnership, and normally crowned by the gift of children."[30] The two essential components of a marriage include the *public commitment* in which faithfulness is promised at the wedding ("leaving and cleaving"), and the *private consummation* ("become one flesh") in which faithfulness is kept and expanded into a fully shared life. Cohabitation tries to simulate the benefits of marriage (becoming one flesh) without accepting the responsibility of public commitment (leaving and cleaving).

Cohabitation Is Different from Marriage

Cohabitation differs from marriage in the following ways:

A distortion of love. Permanence is at the heart of the biblical understanding of the reliable love that should characterize marriage. Cohabitation, however, rarely involves a commitment to permanence. It is often chosen in preference to marriage precisely because no such commitment is involved. Quite often, a cohabiting relationship begins in a casual and indefinite way with no discussion about the likely duration of the relationship.

There may be genuine love between cohabiting partners that is enjoyable and fulfilling, but it is the conditional love of *eros* (desire/passion) and *philos* (friendship). Therefore, it must remain mutually satisfying for the relationship to continue. If either partner begins to feel unloved, the tacit understanding is that he or she can exit. Strikingly absent from the mix is *agapé* (commitment/sacrifice). Without this component, the "love" of cohabitation remains essentially narcissistic, falling far short of the self-giving, self-sacrificial commitment that sustains genuine marriage.

Absence of vows. Though vows are not explicitly mentioned in Scripture, they are implicit in the idea of leaving and cleaving. Wedding vows have two functions: to define the nature of the relationship and to declare future intent. While marriage is a commitment for the future as well as for the present, cohabitation tends to be a relationship just for the present with the future left deliberately open-ended.[31]

Isolation from community. Marriage in the Bible is more than a private contract between individuals. It unites families. It is something that society recognizes and respects. The community offers the married couple certain protections, and it places certain responsibilities on them. Cohabitation, however, is an essentially private relationship that is largely blind to this community dimension. Quite often, cohabitation is a secret relationship that is hidden from other members of the family, especially parents.

No place for children. By the Creator's design, the procreation and upbringing of children is one of the purposes of marriage. Children need to grow up in the security that a constant, permanent marriage relationship at its best affords. But pregnancy in a cohabiting relationship creates a crisis of decision making. What are we going to do about the baby? Is abortion appropriate? Should we get married? It changes everything.

Perversion of freedom. Cohabitation appears to offer more freedom than marriage. If things don't work out, either partner is free to leave. But this freedom to leave introduces fear and insecurity into the relationship. Such fear is destructive of real freedom, which grows best in the security of a loving, committed, permanent relationship. The Bible talks a lot about freedom, but more often it is describing not freedom *from* something but freedom *to* something—freedom to become fully what we were designed to be. Just as a fish is most free in the limitation of water, and a bird is most free in the limitation of air, so a man and woman are most free to become one flesh (in the fullest dimensions of that phrase) within the boundaries of marriage.

Cohabitation Is Dangerous for Marriage

These distinctions help us to see why cohabitation is actually dangerous to the health of a marriage.

First, *the idea of a trial is faulty simply because it is impossible.* G.J. Jenkins writes, "It is ironic that many people opt for cohabitation as a trial for marriage, because the one thing that you cannot have a trial for is a permanent relationship such as marriage."[32] The mentality between cohabiting partners and married spouses is completely different. Cohabiters are *testing* compatibility; spouses are *building* compatibility. Cohabiters focus on *obtaining satisfaction* from their partner; spouses focus on *giving satisfaction* to their partner. The dynamics of commitment are also opposite: "Till death do us part" creates a very different relationship from "as long as I'm happy" or "until I get bored." Therefore, even a successful cohabitation is not a reliable predictor of a successful marriage.

Second, *the experience of prior cohabitation introduces dynamics into a marriage that, left unattended, will undermine it.*

Lingering Mistrust

A fellow might think to himself, *If she gave in to moral temptation with me before marriage, how do I know she won't do it with someone else after we're married?* Sometimes, the connection between cause and effect isn't so obvious, but the mistrust is there. As a pastor, I have counseled many married couples over a span of several decades. And a frequent, behind-the-scenes issue is a couple's experience of premarital sex. The presenting symptom is an irrational sense of distrust by one partner of the other. And often, the insecure spouse can't put his or her finger on the reason for the lack of trust. It's only when the history of the relationship is unveiled that the culprit is exposed. As Pogo famously said, "We have met the enemy, and he is us."

Regret and Guilt

Even though cohabitation has wide cultural acceptance, individuals who live together may do so in violation of their own consciences. Maybe they are able to justify it, but they still sense there is something wrong about it. This could stem from their upbringing or an inborn sense of right and wrong. Guilt may even motivate a couple to "do the right thing" and get married.

The place where regret often intrudes is in the absence of a true honeymoon. This awareness may prompt one (or both) of the partners to realize how "opening the presents before Christmas" has taken away the wonder of what might have been. This sense of loss may develop into resentment toward one's spouse, especially if the other person initiated the cohabitation or applied pressure to secure agreement. Or it could be expressed in self-punishment where one psychically beats up on oneself for getting into this kind of situation.

Intruding Memories

If either spouse had sexual relationships or cohabited with one or more other partners, those experiences often invade and corrupt the experience of that partner in marriage. Stacy and Paula Rinehart, in their book *Choices*, describe one man's discovery of this. The young husband admitted that his relationship with his new wife wasn't what he had hoped it would be. "It's my fault," he admitted. "Before we were married I had several physical relationships with girlfriends. Now, whenever I kiss my wife or engage in love play, my memory reminds me that this girl could kiss better than my wife, that girl was better at something else and so forth. I can't concentrate on loving my wife with all that I am—there have been too many women in my life to be wholly committed to one."[33]

The Comfort Factor

Ironically, the very act of tying the knot causes some relationships to deteriorate. During cohabitation, each partner had to exhibit enough of their better side to keep the other from walking out. But after the wedding, some people take the marriage license as a license to "be myself." Dr. Jekyll morphs into Mr. Hyde; the fairy princess becomes the wicked witch. The person who was once kind and considerate under the pressure of maintaining approval relaxes their guard, and latent selfishness emerges because it doesn't matter like it used to.

Practiced Self-Withholding

Jennifer Roback Morse addresses the inclination that cohabiting couples have to guard themselves from the vulnerability of full disclosure in intimate encounters:

> When people live together, and sleep together, without marriage, they put themselves in a position that is similar to the person being asked to give a blank check. They either hold back on their partner by not giving the full self in the sexual act and in their shared lives together. Or, they feel scared a lot of the time, wondering whether their partner will somehow take advantage of their vulnerability.
>
> No one can simulate self-giving. Half a commitment is no commitment. Cohabiting couples are likely to have one foot out the door, throughout the relationship. The members of a cohabiting couple practice holding back on one another. They rehearse not trusting. The social scientists that gather the data do not have an easy way to measure this kind of dynamic inside the relationship. In my view, this accounts for the disappointing results of cohabitation.

And then Jennifer Morse adds:

> I am sorry to say that I learned this from experience. My husband and I lived together before we were married. It took us a long time to unlearn the habits of the heart that we built up during those cohabiting years.[34]

But ultimately the reason that cohabitation is dangerous to the health of your marriage is that *it is wrong*. It is wrong because it is a violation of God's design and limits on male-female intimacy. It is wrong because it elevates one's own judgments and desires over those of God. It is therefore an expression of defiance against his right to rule over our lives. It is wrong because it elevates personal happiness over holiness. It is wrong because it is motivated not by true love, which protects the lover from harm, but by self-centered love, which enters into a pact to produce mutual happiness.

God's response to rebellion in the lives of unbelievers is *judgment*— not just for sexual sin but for the spirit of independence that motivates it (1 Corinthians 6:9-11; Colossians 3:5-6). His response to rebellion in the lives of his children is *discipline* (Hebrews 12:5-11). And one form of this discipline lies in allowing the consequences of premarital cohabitation to be played out in the marriage. The intent of such discipline is not to punish but to correct. But rest assured, the damaging consequences of violating God's design and God's moral will are certain to emerge (Galatians 6:7-8). It is surely preferable to choose the path that avoids such consequences.

Cohabitation and You

At the beginning of this chapter, I asserted regarding cohabitation: "A thoughtful adult should be able to consider the data and make mature decisions informed by the relevant information." I trust that I have made the case for a clear verdict: if the evidence is taken seriously, even those who base their decision making strictly on self-interest would have to conclude that cohabiting with another person prior to marriage is foolish. To those who share Christian convictions, I hope this presentation has clearly demonstrated that both the moral will of God and wisdom converge in a shared conclusion: cohabitation is a bad idea and should be rejected as an acceptable alternative to or preparation for marriage.

My hope is that this chapter will be read by individuals who are single and solitary—that is, you have not become entangled in a cohabiting arrangement. And I hope what you have learned here (or elsewhere) will prompt you to pursue godly relationships that steer clear of cohabitation.

I realize, however, that for some who read these words, cohabitation is either a part of your past and you are now married,[35] or it is a part of your present and you find yourself in that specific situation. And you may be wondering, *What should I do about that?*

The Bible uses one word to describe our appropriate response any time we find ourselves walking outside of the moral will of God. And that word is *repentance*. The short answer is, you should repent and receive God's forgiveness. Speaking to Jewish people who had just heard the gospel message and were pierced by conviction, the apostle Peter said, "Repent and turn back so that your sins may be wiped out, so that times of refreshing may come from the presence of the Lord" (Acts 3:19-20).

If you are currently in a cohabiting relationship, my counsel to you will be hard to hear and harder to follow. For repentance to be genuine, it must be expressed in action. The apostle Paul stated that his consistent message to all sinners from every background was "that they should repent and turn to God, performing deeds consistent with repentance" (Acts 26:20; also see 2 Corinthians 12:21). So what should you do? *Stop the sex immediately and separate as soon as possible.*

In the Gospel of John, the story is told of a woman caught in adultery and brought before Jesus for judgment. Recognizing the evil motives of her accusers, Jesus issued this challenge:

> "Whoever among you is guiltless may be the first to throw a stone at her." Then he bent over again and wrote on the ground.
> Now when they heard this, they began to drift away one at a time, starting with the older ones, until Jesus was left alone with the woman standing before him. Jesus stood up straight and said to her, "Woman, where are they? Did no one condemn you?" She replied, "No one, Lord." And Jesus said, "I do not condemn you either. Go, *and from now on do not sin any more*" (John 8:7-11, emphasis added).

When we are involved in something contrary to the will of God, we are to repent of it—but we're also to put an end to it.

Am I counseling a complete severance of the relationship? It depends. If your cohabitation is an arrangement of convenience, then the answer is probably yes. I am assuming that the person you are living with lacks the qualities of a godly partner and there is no long-term future to this relationship.[36] Breaking up is hard to do.[37] But in this case, it is the price of foolish decision making in the past, and it is time to pay the piper.

It is also the cost of discipleship in the present, a concrete expression of your commitment to Christ. And if leaving the relationship is motivated by your determination to be obedient to the One who is your Lord, he will give you the strength to follow through. For the sake of your spiritual and emotional health, such a drastic step should be followed by an extended period of recovery in a supporting community of believers who can administer appropriate doses of truth and grace.

But what about cohabiters who intend to get married? I can imagine someone saying, "My fiancé(e) and I moved in together because we were clueless about the moral and practical ramifications of cohabitation. Do we need to break up? Wouldn't it just make more sense for us to go ahead with marriage?" In this case, you may not need to end the relationship. But you do need to *change* the relationship by stopping the sex immediately and separating as soon as possible. In my judgment, this action is required for four reasons.

- The first and most important reason is obedience. You need to replace a situation that is sinful with one that is morally acceptable. All of the comments already made about repentance above apply here.

- Second, the separation will allow you to create a disruption between the old arrangement and the new style of relating. It will allow you to prepare for your marriage by correcting the mistakes of your past and establishing new commitments and patterns for the future. To this end, premarital counseling with a wise and experienced pastor or counselor is strongly recommended.

- Third, separation will allow you to establish what some call "secondary virginity" based on God's forgiveness and restoration. This step will let him create a new thing in your life (Isaiah 43:19), and it will allow you to plan your wedding with a real honeymoon.

- Fourth, separation will give you a legacy from which one day you can instruct your children. If you do nothing, all you can say to them is, "Do as we say, not as we did." They may or may not learn from your failure. But they are more likely to be powerfully influenced by *corrected* failure. Such would be a heritage of righteousness and grace.

"Are you serious about this manner of expressing repentance?" I am asked. "Do you realize what you are asking? It would be very expensive to set up separate living quarters—to say nothing of complicated. All of our stuff is together. And total abstinence would be really hard after what we're used to. Are you serious?"

I am so serious that I will not perform weddings for cohabiting couples unless they separate for a significant period of time and engage fully in premarital counseling.[38] My contention is that a couple who isn't willing to endure this discipline isn't ready for marriage. And the reason is simple: the heart of married love is self-sacrifice. So if separation and abstinence are hard, that's not a bad thing. It not only represents a break with the past, but it is excellent preparation for the future.

Here's my advice to the man in this relationship: "It's time for you to man up. You allowed this situation to develop in the first place—you probably even suggested it. Now it's time for you to show spiritual leadership and take the initiative to make things right. If you truly love this woman, this is your best opportunity to prove it. Follow Christ in laying down your life for your bride. Show her the kind of husband you intend to be. Do the hard thing and build a lasting foundation for your marriage." A man who accepts that challenge will recognize that such words are not harsh but caring. And he will provide a basis for hope for a God-honoring, lasting marriage.[39]

Jesus once said, "If you continue to follow my teaching, you are really my disciples and you will know the truth, and the truth will set you free" (John 8:31-32). God's will is always for our benefit.

May God give you the grace to obey him, even if it is costly, and to recognize his blessing on your commitment to follow his ways.

❖   ❖   ❖

Recommended Reading

Living Together: Myths, Risks and Answers by Mike McManus and Harriet McManus (Simon and Schuster, 2008).

Living Together: A Guide to Counseling Unmarried Couples by Jeff VanGoethem (Kregel Publications, 2005).

❖   ❖   ❖

Questions for Reflection and Group Discussion

1. What was the most significant insight you gained from reading this chapter?

2. Do you understand the test-drive analogy as a rationale for cohabitation? Does that seem like a sound analogy or do you recognize some flaws in it?

3. The author maintains that *cohabitation is a corrupted hybrid of the two sanctioned states of singleness and marriage.* How is it different from singleness? From marriage? How are each of these states superior to cohabitation?

4. This chapter lists five dynamics of cohabitation that, left unattended, may well undermine a subsequent marriage. Which do you think would have the most severe impact? Can you think of others?

5. Many people have engaged in cohabitation in order to reduce the likelihood of divorce after marriage. Can you think of more effective preventative measures than cohabitation?

6. What do you think of the author's strong suggestion that a cohabiting couple should separate for a time before they get married?

For additional questions, go to www.TheMarriageDecision.com.

Part 5

Looking for a Mate

❧

Modern Myth 5

*The most important criterion for a good
marital match is chemistry.*

Introduction to Part 5

O ur church recently hired a youth minister.

What if we had asked you to serve on our search committee? How would you advise going about such a project? Should we have asked the members of our congregation if "they know a guy who loves God and is good with kids"? Or should our approach have been more deliberate?

As you might guess, we employed a more calculated process. Before we sought out and interviewed candidates, we took several preliminary steps. First, we defined the *mission* of our youth ministry so we could describe what we expect this ministry to accomplish. Next we developed a *philosophy of ministry* that explains how we expect this ministry to be carried out. Then we developed a *job description* detailing the responsibilities of the youth minister. And finally, we determined the specific *qualifications* of the sort of person who would be equipped to do the job we had described. Only when we knew what we were looking for did we actually begin our search.

Our approach required a lot of work. But we went through the process because, in view of our church's purpose and mission, the choice we were making *mattered*—every bit as much as David LeVine's nose mattered to him (see p. 13).

Throughout this book, I have been arguing that single believers who are interested in marriage should take a similar approach to looking for a mate. Do you remember how I tried to recruit you to become the director of player personnel for a professional cricket team? The point of the introduction to part 2 was, "You don't evaluate the players until you understand the game."

Well, we've spent the last thirteen chapters spelling out the rules of the game. And we've covered a lot of ground. So before you move forward with your personnel search, let's review the key elements of God's design that will shape your plan.

God's Design: Overview

1. God's design for decision making can be summarized in four principles:

- Where God commands, we must obey.

- Where there is no command, God gives us freedom and responsibility to choose.

- Where there is no command, God gives us wisdom to choose.

- When we have chosen what is moral and wise, we must trust the sovereign God to work all the details together for good.

Accordingly, Christians are called to make wise decisions within the moral will of God, trusting in the sovereign will of God to accomplish his good purposes in and through us.

2. The choices of singleness and marriage are non-commanded decisions. That is, no biblical passage directs the believer to stay single; no passage requires marriage. Therefore, each believer is free and responsible to make those decisions in harmony with God's moral will and wisdom. God should not be expected to dictate one's choice of a spouse.

3. We make our choices in partnership with God. But he is a silent partner, working behind the scenes to carry out his purposes. The believer can move forward with confidence in pursuit of wise plans, trusting that the sovereign God is working out his divine plan in ways that will promote our good. Prayer for wisdom and open doors of opportunity are certainly appropriate. But it is a mistake to attempt to read circumstances as a sign from God pointing to specific choices.

4. Sequences are important in decision making. Before the single adult decides what sort of person he or she would like to marry, it is first necessary to explore the purposes and merits of marriage and singleness. Before one considers the *who* question, one must answer the *whether* question. Both singleness and marriage are legitimate options for single Christians; both have their advantages and their limitations.

5. Marriage was God's idea. Contrary to popular opinion, marriage was not established simply for the mutual satisfaction of a husband and wife. It was designed to be a ministry institution. Its mission is to advance God's rule, both in the lives of the partners (and their offspring) and in the world the spouses (and their family) are to live in as salt and light. Those who marry are called to serve God by serving one another. As intimate allies, they are to invest in each other's personal growth, and they are to forge a partnership that makes an impact for good—through parenthood, occupations, and ministry—in the lives of others. God's intention is that each spouse be spiritually transformed by their mutual ministry and that the marriage be a transforming agent in the world God seeks to redeem.

6. Though marriage was to be the norm in a sinless world, both singleness and marriage are equally valid vocations in the age of redemption. Just as God has a design for marriage, so he has a design for the single state.

God's design for...	MARRIAGE	SINGLENESS
Mission:	To serve God by advancing his rule in my life and throughout my world	To serve God by advancing his rule in my life and throughout my world
Purpose:	To facilitate the mission through the implementation of the functions	To facilitate the mission through the implementation of the functions
Functions:	Relational companionship Vocational partnership (including physical procreation)	Relational community Vocational freedom (including spiritual procreation)

The single believer may choose either pathway and must apply wisdom to weigh the pros and cons of each option. The bottom-line question should be: *In which state, single or married, can I better exercise the current stewardship of my walk with and service to God?*

7. *While marital decisions are not dictated by the moral will of God, they are regulated by it.* All believers are called to sexual purity. While unmarried persons need to cultivate healthy friendships, they must reserve sexual relations for marriage. And those who actively seek a marital partner must do so in a way that applies wisdom within the moral will of God. Exploring sexual compatibility through cohabitation not only violates God's moral will, it is a foolish stratagem that actually contributes greatly to the likelihood of breakup or divorce.

8. *It is perfectly legitimate for those who hope to get married to take initiative that might lead to that outcome.* It is preferable to be proactive than reactive. It is wise to decide (in advance) with the mind what the heart is looking for. Establishing criteria for evaluating potential mates and devising a plan for meeting and courting a prospective spouse are advisable exercises. In that process, the single Christian should take into consideration the wisdom offered by qualified counselors.

The Wisdom of Counselors

As promised, the chapters that follow are devoted to fleshing out the final point (8). And as we do this, we move into a different category of content. Up to this point, we have focused considerable effort on exposition of the biblical text because there are key passages that address the topics of concern: decision making, marriage, singleness, and sexuality. But now we turn our attention to questions that are not always directly addressed by Scripture. So our search is not so much for the explicit moral will of God as it is for wisdom. And where is such wisdom to be found? The Bible emphasizes the role of wise counselors.

> When there is no guidance a nation falls,
> but there is success in the abundance of counselors.
> (Proverbs 11:14)

> The one who associates with the wise grows wise,
> but a companion of fools suffers harm.
> (Proverbs 13:20)

> Plans fail when there is no counsel,
> but with abundant advisers they are established.
> (Proverbs 15:22)

One of the advantages of living in the modern world is that we have access to the wisdom of counselors who have published their insights in books and articles. This can be very helpful because these are people who have devoted much time and energy to acquire expertise in areas where ordinary people need help. For every unmarried adult, the search for a prospective spouse is a new adventure in which he or she initially has no experience. Being a novice in addressing the most important decisions an adult will make ought to prompt one to seek guidance from those who know the ropes. This is no time to be reinventing the wheel.

As you consult with counselors, however, you need to keep three things in mind. First, *wisdom is not revelation.* The experts are not writing with divine authority, so you must be discerning in your evaluation of their input. Second, being human, *the counselors don't always agree with each other* in every area. Where there *is* unanimity of opinion, the neophyte should give that agreement considerable weight. Where there is divergence of opinion, the reasons and arguments for the respective points of view must be carefully assessed. Third, *the counselors cannot make your choices for you.* They can make helpful suggestions, but in the end, each person is responsible for their own decision making.

The chapters that follow represent my effort to summarize the key insights of experts in relationship formation and marriage. Some of their expertise is anecdotal—that is, they have formed conclusions based on years of counseling experience. But a lot of what they have learned is based on research, which provides a more objective basis for the conclusions reached. As I noted in the introduction to part 4, much of that research confirms the ancient wisdom found in the Scriptures. And so a good deal of the counsel offered in the following pages corresponds to and illustrates identifiable biblical principles. And some of it offers practical advice on how to implement those principles. As far as I can tell, nothing that is suggested violates the moral will of God.

The personal circumstances of readers of this material will vary greatly. Since I cannot know the situation of each reader, I am addressing those who are starting their search from ground zero—they have no immediate prospects but are interested in finding one. If you are in a relationship, these chapters can help you evaluate how things are going and determine whether any midcourse corrections are called for.

Remember, practical wisdom aims to maximize opportunities, manage difficulties, and avoid mistakes. Just for fun, we'll start with how *not* to do it.

❖ ❖ ❖

Question for Reflection and Group Discussion

1. Fourteen times in the Questions for Reflection at the end of the previous chapters, you have been asked: "What is the most significant insight you have gained from reading this chapter?" If you have been recording your thoughts in a journal, find your answers to that question and copy them to a single page. If you have been using a computer to record your answers, use the cut-and-paste function to compile a list of your responses. As you review those insights, which ones are especially pertinent as you think about looking for a mate?

14

Top Ten Missteps
to a Miserable Marriage

❖

As I write this chapter, one of the national cell phone companies is running an ad campaign in which they claim to be the network with the fewest dropped calls. The campaign consists of a series of commercials that feature two people talking on their cell phones. At a crucial juncture in the conversation, the call is dropped, and the listener misinterprets the silence to mean the opposite of what the caller is actually saying—with disastrous consequences. The episodes are humorous and effective at getting the point across—"If you don't sign up with our company, this (or something worse) could happen to you!"

In one of these commercials, Jennifer calls her mother to report that she is in Las Vegas with her boyfriend, Mike. "We just drove here on a whim," she says.

"City of Lights, heh, heh," responds her mother, keeping her cool. "Promise me you won't come back married, OK?"

(Dropped call. Jennifer is telling her mother that she doesn't have to worry about anything like that. But all Mom hears is silence. Panic is written on her face.)

"Jen. Jen! You're not getting married are you?" (Pause.) "Jennifer!" She glances over her shoulder toward the living room. Then she whispers frantically, "Jennifer, don't make the same mistake I made!"

❖   ❖   ❖

One wonders if the biblical author of the Proverbs might not be conveying a similar message when he wrote the following verses:

> It is better to live on a corner of the housetop[1]
> than in a house in company with a quarrelsome wife (21:9).
>
> It is better to live in a desert land
> than with a quarrelsome and easily-provoked woman (21:19).
>
> A foolish child is the ruin of his father,
> and a contentious wife is like a constant dripping (19:13).
>
> A continual dripping on a rainy day
> and a contentious wife[2] are alike (27:15).

On the basis of these passages and others like them, Bill Hybels wrote: "The first time I read the book of Proverbs, I was a little surprised by its straightforward manner in addressing the subject of marriage. After many years of study and analysis, I have concluded that the wisdom of Proverbs regarding the selection of a marriage partner can be condensed to four words: Don't mess it up."[3]

The problem, as we have seen, is that the prevailing system for mate selection actually promotes faulty decision making. It almost seems as though the shapers of contemporary culture got together in a boardroom somewhere and asked, "How can we best influence single adults to make choices that are most likely to produce marital failure?"

No one wants to have a miserable marriage. But what many do not realize is that there are certain choices, commonly made, that will likely yield that sad result. Experts who have studied the dynamics of human relationships and marriage have identified specific behaviors that yield predictable outcomes a high percentage of the time. If someone were to set out to create a miserable marriage, these steps would help them accomplish that goal.[4]

Misstep 1: *Marry Too Young*

While it is legally permissible for older teenagers to marry, it is not wise. "Marrying as a teenager is the highest known risk factor for divorce. People who marry in their teens are two to three times more likely to divorce than people who marry in their twenties or older."[5]

The reasons for this stunning statistic are not hard to understand. In our culture, few human beings reach psychological maturity before age twenty-five. During their late teens and early twenties, young adults are engaged in the intense work of identity formation. Bill Hybels identifies at least four components in this developmental task:

1. The process of *individuation*—becoming separate from one's parents and siblings

2. The determination of *core values*—the beliefs and priorities by which one will live

3. The development of *core competencies*—gifts, talents, abilities, and life skills that will be channeled through a career path

4. The work of *spiritual formation*—identifying and solidifying one's convictions about God and the role he will play in one's life

During such developmental flux, one doesn't know oneself well enough to choose a marriage partner, much less make a wise evaluation of someone else who is going through the same process. "One author said it is like shooting at a moving target from a spinning platform. It is nearly impossible."[6]

While I concur with the observations of Hybels and others,[7] some writers argue that more single Christians should get married at a younger age. They all point out, in the words of Gary Thomas, "You've been created by God with a body that is ready for sexual activity a decade before most people get married."[8] By delaying marriage to a later age, our culture has gotten out of sync with God's design.[9] The temptation and pressure to engage in sexual activity can feel overwhelming.[10] Since the God-ordained outlet for sexual desire is marriage, the best way to corral this impulse is to get married—sooner rather than later.[11]

What we have here is a tension between the onset of *physical sexual maturation* and a lagging *psychological development*. And this is a genuine problem with no easy answers. I think the arguments of the early marriage proponents should receive serious attention. However, to buck the statistical trend of a high divorce rate for those who marry young, a younger couple would have to be exceptionally mature, well-prepared for adult living, able to meet the financial requirements of a family, and surrounded by and responsive to a supportive network of family and friends. In today's world, that set of criteria is rare.

That said, I have other problems with the counsel to marry young. I have already expressed my strong disagreement with the assertion that contemporary Christian single adults are virtually helpless in the face of sexual temptation. This presumption excludes the possibility of long-term singleness for all but the supernaturally endowed. And, as a reason to marry, it elevates a hormonally driven motivation for marriage to a higher priority than is warranted. It seems to me that each person who marries should be ready not only physically, but psychologically, emotionally, and spiritually.

In my judgment, it is a misstep to marry too young. If you need a chronological guideline, this means postponing marriage beyond one's teens, at least. More important than a specific age, however, is maturity and the ability to function well in an adult world. So the corrective to marrying too young is, grow up first. Marriage is for adults.

Misstep 2: *Marry Too Quickly*

That is, have a really short courtship.

Any couple who plans marriage after dating for only a couple of months is demonstrating that they lack the very maturity required of marriage. They are long on fantasy, short on reality. I know this from working with people over many years. But a study done at Kansas State University demonstrated this reality.

> In their sample of 51 middle-aged wives, "a strong correlation was found between length of time spent dating their current spouses and current marital satisfaction."... This research found that "couples who had dated for more than two years scored consistently high on marital satisfaction, while couples who had dated for shorter periods scored in a wide range from very high to very low."[12] Thus, the risk of marital failure is significantly reduced by longer dating periods.[13]

How long should courtship last? For couples who have not known each other over a long period of time, it should last several months, not just several weeks. Courtship should last long enough to have some problems and work through them; long enough to become "experts" on the subject of marriage—together; long enough for those who know you best to observe you together and help you evaluate.

John Van Epp is one counselor who has worked with enough couples to recognize the Three-Month Rule: "It takes three months for many subtle but serious patterns to begin to surface." During the early stages of a relationship, both individuals are putting their best selves on display. Initial attraction can have an inebriating effect on the perceptions each is forming of the other. Typically it takes at least three months for imperfections to begin to surface, for patterns to begin to show through.[14] As a result, it's really hard to know what a person is really like during that early phase. Van Epp's advice: "Keep all of your bonding dynamics [trust, reliance, commitment, and sexual involvement] in check during the first three months."[15]

Ben Young and Sam Adams assert that it takes *more* than three months to discern the character qualities that one ought to require in a spouse—honesty, faithfulness, loyalty, commitment, forgiveness, self-control, discipline, endurance, and the like. "This bears repeating: these qualities are discerned over a *long period of time*. You cannot identify essential character qualities in the first three months of a relationship."[16] In another place, these same authors conclude: "We're convinced that the number one reason couples divorce is not money, sex, or infidelity, but rather the decision to get married was made too quickly."[17]

I'm not suggesting that three months is the minimum length for courtship. I'm agreeing with these authors that the Three-Month Rule argues for a much longer period of time to get to know another person.

Virtually all the authors I read set a minimum period of two years for an adequate courtship.[18] One speaker explains that if you meet a prospective mate in your midtwenties, it's as though you are stepping into a movie that has been running for a quarter of a century. It's going to take a while for you to get your bearings: to figure out the plot, to understand the history to this point, to become acquainted with the cast of characters, to appreciate the subtleties in the personality of the lead actor and how they relate to the other characters in the story. It's going to take a while.

The corrective to marrying too quickly is, go slow. Don't be in a rush. You've got the rest of your life to live with your decision.

Misstep 3: *Marry Too Eagerly*

This mistake often lies behind the first two. There are several reasons why people are in too big a hurry to get married. In some cases the eagerness is founded on an unrealistic view of marriage—a fantasy (shaped perhaps by too many Disney animated movies) that is out of touch with reality, believing that "Love will conquer all."

Others are anxiously eager because they are afraid their partner will have a change of mind.

Some are too eager to marry because they believe that marriage is going to extricate them from an undesirable situation and replace it with a better one. The classic example of this mindset is the woman who seeks to escape the control of her parents. Others who are overeager hope that marriage will compensate for a disappointing childhood. Still others turn to marriage to solve problems of loneliness or brokenness.

People who pursue marriage driven by fantasy, fear, or need are going to the wrong place to get their expectations met.[19] They will be doomed to disappointment. What many people find is that marriage seldom solves problems; it tends to magnify them.

The corrective: learn God's purposes for matrimony and get realistic about marriage.

Misstep 4: *Confine Your Courtship to a Narrow Range of Experiences*

A couple could spend a lot of time together and still be ill-prepared for marriage. One way this occurs is through superficial dating experiences that are long on fantasy but short on authenticity. If a couple's only significant exposure to one another occurs in the context of a romanticized dating environment—especially if they become entangled sexually—they experience a false sense of intimacy that fails to lay a solid foundation for marriage.[20]

Married life is not played out on a stage. It is not lived out in ideal circumstances where imperfections are hidden behind makeup and wardrobe. So courtship should provide opportunities for a man and woman to get to truly know one another through diverse experiences and in a variety of settings. A couple needs to see each other at work and at worship as well as at play. They need to serve God together in challenging circumstances. They need to experience hardship together, resolve conflict, negotiate competing values, sort out financial issues, weather some storms. They should become well acquainted with each other's families and friends.

The corrective: not just time but variety.

Misstep 5: *Test Compatibility by Living Together*

This is the opposite mistake from the previous one. Since I've devoted an entire chapter to this topic, I will not comment further here.

Corrective: maintain appropriate boundaries during each phase of courtship.

Misstep 6: *Marry to Please Your Father/Mother/Peers/Lover*

"So, when are you going to settle down and get married?" The question could come from your mother (who is anxious for grandchildren), a relative at the annual Thanksgiving get-together, or a former classmate at a class reunion. Most external pressure on single adults to get married is well-meaning, and not all of it is verbalized or even intended. Finding yourself in an adult Sunday school class populated by couples, or getting a wedding invitation or birth announcement from one of the old gang can make you feel like the odd (wo)man out.

Do people get married just because others expect them to? I didn't think this was a pervasive problem—until I met a newlywed couple honeymooning on a cruise ship. As they told me their story over breakfast, they were certainly happy to be married. But they expressed dismay over the number of their friends who had recently tied the knot because of peer pressure.

This is marrying because of the compulsion to please somebody else. Some people form their whole identity out of their need to make everyone else happy. Sometimes the person they are trying to please is the one they are dating. They go ahead with marriage because breaking up would hurt the other person's feelings. Not only is this need to please an unhealthy basis for a self-concept, it places the power for decision making into the hands of other people. This is a form of voluntary slavery, and the likely result will be a life sentence in an institution ruled by regret.

So there are two problems with this misstep. The first is that the wrong person(s) is controlling the decision making. For a covenant to have legitimacy, both partners to it must give willing consent. Husband and wife must have the ego-strength to choose for themselves. And second, the motivation for such marriage decisions is misplaced. Valid reasons for marriage should emerge from our understanding of God's design for marriage plus a mature evaluation of our situation in life. It's OK to want to please others within reasonable bounds; it's not OK to allow others to control our decisions.

I hasten to add that we should not err on the opposite side—failure to consult with others about marital decisions. Especially in matters of the heart, we need the counsel of family members and friends to identify blind spots in our relational perceptions. It's just that in the end, the decisions that potentially affect the remainder of our adult life should be made by the person who has to live that life.

The corrective: make deliberate, freely chosen decisions based on biblical reasons.

Misstep 7: *Make Assumptions Rather Than Mutual Decisions About Marriage Expectations*

When Louise and I first got married, we had one rather persistent problem—we had a dickens of a time getting the trash out of the house. We were both good at putting stuff in the trash bag, but often it would sit in the middle of the kitchen and we would both walk around it for a couple of days. And neither one of us really noticed that this was becoming a pattern. It was just something that went on for a while—until one day I tripped over the bag and kicked garbage all over the floor. Up until then, we both apparently expected that the other person was going to take the trash out.

Of course in most homes that assignment is allotted to the husband. So you're probably wondering what took me so long. But in my family, somebody else did it—it wasn't my job. Standing knee-deep in rubbish, I said to Louise, "Who took out the trash in your family?" And she said, "Charlie did." (Charlie was her younger brother.) And we realized that the problem in our family with the garbage was that Charlie wasn't doing his job. When our son, Michael, got old enough to take out the trash, we assigned the task to him, which didn't totally solve the problem. But it gave us someone else to yell at. When he went off to college, we were walking around the trash again. (Excuse me. I just remembered a chore I need to tend to.)

Every newlywed comes into marriage with expectations. Some of these expectations are overt. For example, the typical husband believes that his wife will never change. (She will.) The wife, on the other hand, expects that her husband—in response to her persistent, loving correction—*will* change. (He won't.) Such expectations are so deeply held that writing this paragraph was probably a waste of time.

But most of our expectations are subconscious and, therefore, unspoken. These are usually shaped by the homes we were raised in. All of us have a picture of how marriage works—or how we think it ought to work. That picture is formed mostly from watching our own parents (or the adults we lived with) and how they related. Over the years, we've made mental notes about things that we like and things we don't like about how our parents (and others) got along. And those notes have created a profile made up of the features of the kind of marriage we hope to have. The faulty assumption here is that *the person I'm getting married to is thinking pretty much the same way I am about how our marriage is going to work.* Or the man meets his fiancée's parents, observes how they relate, and thinks to himself, *Surely she doesn't want our marriage to be like that.* And he's wrong.

The problem in the preceding paragraph lies in the phrase *thinks to himself.* What the man needs to do is *speak right out loud* to his fiancée and ask, "Do you want our marriage to be like that?"

The corrective to this misstep: Explore and discuss expectations ahead of time. This is where premarital counseling becomes so important. Discussing expectations with a third party monitoring the conversation can be extremely valuable.[21] Also during courtship, watch the marriages of people that you know and analyze them together.

Misstep 8: *Marry Someone Who Does Not Share Your Commitment to Christ*

For generations, spiritual counselors have warned believers against becoming "unequally yoked" with unbelievers based on 2 Corinthians 6:14-16 and related passages:[22]

> Do not become partners with those who do not believe, for what partnership is there between righteousness and lawlessness, or what fellowship does light have with darkness? And what agreement does Christ have with Beliar? Or what does a believer share in common with an unbeliever? And what mutual agreement does the temple of God have with idols? For we are the temple of the living God.

While this passage does not speak directly about marriage, it certainly applies to that relationship. For marriage is the most binding of all human partnerships.[23] For a Christian to marry a non-Christian is to sow the seeds of conflict and to rule out the possibility of that marriage fully accomplishing its design. For a believer and an unbeliever are fundamentally different at the very core of their lives.

But this goes well beyond the prohibition against mating with an unbeliever. When one considers God's design for marriage—its mission, purpose, and functions—it should be obvious that a shared and growing commitment to Christ on the part of both partners is essential. The misstep here involves more than ignoring God's moral will about marriage to an unbeliever. It elevates a short-term desire to get one's needs met over the wisdom of waiting for a partner who has the spiritual maturity to pursue a godly marriage.[24]

Corrective: marry a committed Christian who is growing spiritually. (I will amplify this point in chapter 16.)

Misstep 9: *Ignore Unaddressed Personality and Behavioral Problems*

My mother, Willine, was an incest victim. The sexual abuse occurred during her teens, but our family didn't know about it until Mom was in her forties. She had repressed the traumatic memories, and they didn't come to light until she almost died from a toxic reaction to medication she was taking for insomnia. Her subsequent engagement in the process of recovery was nothing short of heroic, and part of her legacy to her children and grandchildren is a spirit of courage, grace, and hope. But I can tell you that my mother's experience of abuse took a toll on her, my dad, and our family.

Because of my mother's experience, I have had a special interest in the emotional and relational needs of abused women. Though I am not a professional counselor, I have learned about the dynamics of relational injuries of various kinds and their impact on subsequent adult relationships. As a pastor, I have walked with husbands through the process of their wives' recovery. And here is what I can tell you: *people do not simply outgrow childhood trauma.*

Growing up in a severely dysfunctional home inculcates unhealthy patterns of responding to others that become deeply imbedded in a person's psyche. These ways of relating become so normal to the damaged person that they aren't aware that anything is askew. Some of these learned behaviors appear positive to outsiders—high achievement, an extraordinary sense of compassion, a remarkable sense of humor. But eventually the detrimental, counterproductive nature of these learned patterns emerges, and the long-term impact on a marriage can be powerfully negative.

A lot of wonderful people have troubled pasts. A recent study by the U.S. Centers for Disease Control and Prevention reported that 60 percent of American adults say they had "difficult childhoods featuring abusive or troubled family members or parents who were absent due to separation or divorce."[25] Now the presence of problems should not automatically disqualify a person as a candidate for marriage. But if a troublesome history or a behavioral pattern comes to light, one should ask: has this situation been adequately addressed?

I have in mind two broad categories of problems. The first consists of *issues stemming from one's family of origin.* You should be especially alert for the Big Three: divorce, addiction, or abuse. Here's the bad news: the risk of divorce for children of divorced parents, children of substance abusers (drugs or alcohol), and children who have been emotionally, physically, or sexually abused is much higher than it is for the rest of the population. Here's the good news: the systems that children from dysfunctional families learn and apply to life are widely understood by relationship experts and can be comprehended by ordinary people. If your father was an alcoholic, you can gain much insight into yourself and the other members of your family by reading a book about adult children of alcoholics. If your fiancée's parents were divorced, you and she can learn about how divorce affects children like herself by reading a similar volume written for that audience. There's a lot of good help available.[26]

But there's a difficulty in dealing with one's past—it can be painful. So some people choose to deny the reality of their injury, hoping that time alone will heal the wounds and dim the memory. Pardon my French, but this approach will bite you (and your marriage) in the derrière. Marriage is for grownups, and you and your prospective mate need to be mature enough to face the past together in order to maximize the potential for a bright and healthy future. And reading is a good and relatively nonthreatening way to begin. It is also important to discuss these kinds of issues in premarital counseling. And if the effect of childhood wounding was severe, professional counseling may be required. Restorative therapy is one of the best investments a person can make.

The second category of red flag is *troubling behavior or personality patterns*. Is there any evidence of addiction in the life of the other person? Is there any history of substance abuse? What have they done about it? Do you recognize any extremes in the person's personality—reactions such as jealousy, anger, or stubbornness? Is there inflexibility? Is there dishonesty or irresponsibility? Can the person you are thinking of marrying get a job and hold a job? If they cannot now, they will not later.

The best time to deal with such issues is prior to marriage.[27] Rather than correcting such problems, marriage usually exacerbates them. If they remain unresolved, any flaws you recognize in the other person during courtship will likely become worse rather than better under the stresses of marriage. Plus the motivation for dealing with them will have diminished.

Recognizing any of these characteristics in a person's life does not disqualify that person as a candidate for marriage. Everyone has problems. The question is, have the problems been significantly addressed by the grace of God and have they been substantially resolved? Has the person grown as a result of having dealt with these dynamics or having lived in such an environment? If the answer to these questions is yes, you may have found an excellent prospect for marriage. But an unwillingness to address personal issues is a clear indication that this person is not ready for marriage. And if you ignore this warning, you will be doing some heavy-duty work in your marriage.

The corrective: unpack the baggage. Bring the issues to resolution. Get involved in counseling if that's what you have to do. Or run for your life.

(If you choose to disregard these observations as not applicable to your situation, please put an asterisk in the margin so you can return to this page later and read this message: "I told you so!")

Misstep 10: *Choose Your Spouse with Your Heart, Not Your Head*

Stephanie Coontz writes in her book *Marriage, a History*:

> George Bernard Shaw described marriage as an institution that brings together two people "under the influence of the most violent, most insane, most delusive, and most transient of passions. They are required to swear that they will remain in that excited, abnormal, and exhausting condition until death do them part."[28]

It is notoriously difficult to disabuse enraptured couples of the notion that, in the unforgettable lyrics sung by the Captain and Tennille, "Love Will Keep Us Together." As a relational glue, erotic love is next to useless.[29] In making this observation, I am not suggesting that romance is bad and ought to be discarded from the process of mate selection (as though that were possible).[30] But the influence of such strong feelings needs to be tempered with the passing of time, insight from wise counselors, and opportunities for shared life experiences that inject reality into the mix.

The remaining chapters in part 5 are addressed to those who seek to bring some objectivity to marital choices. Christians are to make non-commanded decisions on the basis of wisdom. In the acquisition of wisdom, the mind must be fully engaged. If it is, it can channel the passions of the heart to conclusions that are not only desirable in the short run, but beneficial over the long haul. If you want to be as glad on your twenty-fifth anniversary as you are on the day of your wedding, engage your mind.[31]

TOP TEN MISSTEPS TO A MISERABLE MARRIAGE

Missteps	Correctives
1. Marry too young.	1. Grow up. Marriage is for grownups.
2. Marry too quickly.	2. Court slowly. Get to know each other well.
3. Marry too eagerly.	3. Get realistic about marriage.
4. Confine your courtship to a narrow range of experiences.	4. Not just time, but variety.
5. Test compatibility by living together.	5. Set appropriate boundaries.
6. Marry to please someone else.	6. Make freely chosen decisions based on biblical reasons.
7. Make assumptions rather than mutual decisions about marriage expectations.	7. Explore and discuss expectations ahead of time in premarital counseling.
8. Marry someone who does not share your commitment to Christ.	8. Marry a committed Christian who is growing spiritually.
9. Ignore unaddressed personality and behavioral problems.	9. Unpack the baggage and bring issues to resolution.
10. Choose your spouse with your heart, not your head.	10. Engage your mind, preferably before you fall in love.

Get Healthy

When we step back and look at all ten missteps together, there are three clarifying points I need to make. The first is that all ten of these common mistakes should be taken seriously. This list is not like a pop quiz that is graded on the curve. A couple should not console themselves by saying, "Well, we're only doing three of those things, so that's not too bad." Any one of these missteps could have serious consequences for a future marriage. If you multiply the risk factors, you compound the likelihood of negative effects.

However, anyone who stumbles into one or more of these errors of judgment is not inevitably doomed to a miserable marriage or divorce. The mistakes I've been talking about are risk factors, not coffin nails. The authors of *Fighting for Your Marriage* explain:

> Our studies (and others) show that marital failure is predictable to a surprising degree, which means that for many couples, the seeds of divorce are present prior to marriage. It does not mean that we researchers are very good at predicting exactly which couples won't make it, but we have gotten pretty good at identifying the factors that greatly increase the odds of divorce.[32]

When I presented this material in a sermon, most of the people in the audience were already married. As I moved through the list, I could see individuals wince. These couples had made one or more of the missteps during their courtship, and they knew firsthand the difficulties they had experienced as a result. The most common response I got from that message was, "Where were you twenty [or thirty] years ago?" Having this information could have spared these folks a lot of grief. These missteps may not ruin a marriage, but they will likely result in marital stress that will have to be addressed. God's grace is sufficient, but it will be needed.[33]

Finally, and most important, all ten missteps may be symptoms of a pervasive underlying condition: emotional unhealth. "In 75 to 80 percent of all marriages that eventually end in divorce or separation, at least one of the partners suffers from an emotional health deficiency."[34] When asked what his one word of advice would be to someone who is about to get married, Neil Clark Warren replied, "Get yourself healthy before you get yourself married." One of Dr. Warren's mantras is: *"No marriage can ever be stronger than the emotional health of the least healthy partner"* (emphasis his). He explains:

> If you try to build intimacy with another person before you have done the hard work of getting *yourself* whole and healthy, all your relationships will become attempts to complete yourself. Moreover, if you are not healthy yourself, you will almost always attach yourself to another person in hopes of validating your self-worth.[35]

The importance of becoming emotionally healthy *before* one marries is stressed by virtually all the authors of books on dating and finding a mate. Apart from the obvious contribution of good health to the strength of a marriage, two other reasons for this critical task are given. First, *healthy people make healthy choices*.[36] So healthy persons would tend to avoid these ten missteps (and others), or would recognize the validity of the problems connected with them when they are explained. Second, *healthy people attract healthy people*.[37] Actually, this truism is often stated in the negative: unbalanced people attract unbalanced people. So one evidence of unhealth is the tendency to attract individuals who are not good for you.[38]

A comprehensive description of emotional health and the steps one could take to obtain it are beyond the scope of this book. Addressing single adults who are developing a plan for dating, Henry Cloud poses this question: "So what do you look like when you are healthy?" Then he offers this short list:

- You can make an emotional connection.

- You have self-respect and clear boundaries. People know where you stand and what you want.

- You are real and feel okay about yourself. You don't have to be perfect or find a perfect person.

- You are competent and have opinions and talents of your own, and you treat others as equals.

- You are comfortable with your sexuality, but not acting it out like a teenager.[39]

Les Parrott teamed up with Neil Clark Warren to write *Love the Life You Live*, a book pointing the way to emotional health. They identify three hallmarks of wholeness: 1) a profound sense of significance; 2) a lifestyle of unswerving authenticity; and 3) an attitude of self-giving characterized by generosity, truthfulness, and kindness. "At the risk of sounding too colloquial on such a meaningful matter, you can also think of health and wholeness as getting right with God (significance), getting right with yourself (authenticity), and getting right with others (love)."[40]

As I noted above, the reader who suspects they might need to address issues of emotional health, either because of circumstances related to their upbringing (such as divorce, addiction, or abuse) or current symptoms that crop up in relational problems, can begin that exploration by reading. (I call this bibliotherapy.) The books listed below (or at endnote 26) provide a place to start. Your pastor can refer you to other counseling resources in your geographic area.

❖ ❖ ❖

Recommended Reading

Love the Life You Live by Les Parrott and Neil Clark Warren (Tyndale, 2004).

Changes That Heal by Henry Cloud (Zondervan, 1997).

How People Grow by Henry Cloud and John Townsend (Zondervan, 2004).

❖ ❖ ❖

Questions for Reflection and Group Discussion

1. What was the most significant insight you gained from reading this chapter?

2. Have you or someone you know made any of these missteps? What happened?

3. Which of the ten missteps strike close to home for you at this point in your life? What are you going to do about it?

4. "Don't marry a project." What does that mean? Why is it good advice?

5. What is the bottom line of this chapter?

6. How would you rate your overall emotional health? Are there any issues you need to address? What steps will you take to do so?

7. *Bonus Question*: Which scenarios in the prologue to this book are addressed in this chapter? What counsel is offered to the individuals in those situations?

For additional questions, go to www.TheMarriageDecision.com.

15

Profile of a Keeper

＊＊＊

One of the authors of this book is married. On November 10, 1973, I took Louise Alleyne Bachman to be my lawfully wedded wife. But she wasn't exactly my first choice.

I hasten to explain. John Van Epp maintains that there are two ways to go about the business of falling in love. You can have chemistry first, relationship second. Or you can have relationship first, chemistry second.[1] Not having read Dr. Van Epp's book, I tried both approaches. In my opinion, one is preferable to the other.

Chemistry First

The first go-round began during the summer between my junior and senior year of college. I had a job in my home church in Southern California as an intern on the pastoral staff. I was responsible for the church's Christian education program. Shortly after I arrived home and started work, I met Cathy (not her real name). She had just graduated from high school, but she was very mature for her age, as we say. More to the point, she was cute and vivacious. Even more to the point, she set her sights on me and pretty much swept me off my feet.

This was chemistry first, relationship second—with chemistry overloading all the circuits. To say that this was new territory for me would be the epitome of understatement. My dating experience had been nothing less than pathetic. This was a classic instance of *Beauty and the Geek*, though we didn't use that word back then. And this geek was thoroughly, horribly, wonderfully twitterpated. It was a summer romance made in heaven—of this I was certain.

So when I returned to college for my senior year, I had this silly grin on my face and my feet weren't touching the ground. The photograph I was persuaded to display proved that Cathy was clearly out of my league. And it must have made my friends wonder, what does she see in him? That, as it turned out, was a good question.

They say that "absence makes the heart grow fonder." They also say "out of sight, out of mind." Those two sayings are not compatible—one or the other will prove true. And for Cathy, the separation of two thousand miles and four months (with no email, cell phones, texting, instant messaging, or Skype!) demonstrated the fragility of chemistry as a basis for lasting relationship. When I returned home for Christmas vacation, the fizz had gone out of the chemistry, and I found myself singing along with the Righteous Brothers, "You've lost that lovin' feeling."

What in the world had happened? I think a good case can be made for the theory that Cathy came to her senses. We were not, in fact, well-matched. They say[2] that opposites attract, and we were a case in point. Part of what Cathy saw in me (besides my innate charm and understated good looks) was my status as a leader in our Christian subculture. We were both Christians and we really hit it off, but we had precious little else in common. So lacking the time to cultivate the relationship, the chemistry just petered out. (Also, there was this other guy who came along who was actually handsome and had a nice car and didn't live two thousand miles away. So there's a competing theory that also has supporting evidence.)

The pain of rejection and the death of a dream were profoundly distressing to me. Yes, I had begun to formulate my thoughts about the future around Cathy. And I felt an acute sense of loss. It took several months before I could begin to appreciate how clouded my judgment had become. The mismatch had been clear as day to my grandfather, and probably a lot of other folks. But he had the moxie to write me a letter warning that Cathy would not be a good mate for me. That was one of the most courageous acts of love I have personally experienced. Of course, I disregarded his perspective at the time. (He was very old and not to be taken seriously.) But he was right. And I was spared. By the mercy of God and the severe kindness of Cathy, I was denied a marriage that almost certainly would have been difficult and may well have failed.

It took me four years to recover from my romance with Cathy.

Relationship First

At the beginning of my senior year of seminary, I began to take stock of my prospects for life beyond the cloistered walls. I would need to get a job, probably as a pastor. Would a church hire a single man as a pastor? Hmmm. Maybe I should think about finding a wife. How would I go about doing that? What sort of woman should I be looking for?

My experience with Cathy had taught me that that last question was really important. And I actually knew the answer. By this time I had taken a course in marriage and family from Prof. Howard Hendricks. So I had made The List. Mostly it consisted of character qualities with commitment to Christ at the top. But it would be nice if she was musically inclined, physically attractive, and reared in a godly, healthy family. The List was important because I didn't want to give my heart to another person like I had with Cathy only to experience, or inflict, the kind of pain I had experienced when the romance broke up. In other words, I had no intention of starting something I couldn't finish. My intention was that whomever I fell in love with next would be a woman I could and would marry.

I remember going for a walk one night and praying about my marital prospects. As I talked with God, I reviewed my List and used it to evaluate all the single women I knew who might conceivably be candidates for marriage. My goal was to winnow the field down to the Top Three. After thirty seconds of careful deliberation, I looked at the final cut and discovered there was only one name: Louise Bachman.

I knew that Louise matched up well with my List because, over the last three years, she had become a good friend. Whenever I went home from school, we would spend time together, often working together to lead music for the college group in my home church. Not only did I enjoy her company, but I had reason to believe that she might welcome some personal interest from me. As a candidate for marriage, she was almost perfect. There was only one drawback—the chemistry component was lacking on my part. And I really wanted chemistry. So I pointed out this detail to the Lord. And I said to him, *If you can light that particular fire inside me, I'll explore this relationship and see where it goes.*

(Upon receipt of that request, the corridors of heaven were filled with gales of laughter as angels winged each other and chortled, "That poor sucker doesn't stand a chance." Yes, the angels *chortled.* It doesn't happen very often.)

Little did I know that I was the last character to make an entrance in a drama that had been playing for some time. For her part, Louise too had made a List. And somehow, my name had made it to the top of the pile. (After we were married, she showed me an entry she had made in her journal during a college retreat I had spoken at. It read, "Make a point to marry Robin Maxson." My amazement melted into chagrin when I noticed that this item was written in pencil. I am not making this up.)

For her, the trick was to get the attention of this man who was away at school three-fourths of every year—and clueless about her considerable qualities when he was around. So she devised a strategy. When I was at home, she would place herself in close proximity through involvement with music. Most of the music we sang in those days was accompanied by guitars. She took the scholarship money she was awarded for being class valedictorian and bought a twelve-string guitar. She had the only twelve-string guitar in the college group. That put her on the worship team—right next to me. And she was a great guitarist.

When I was away at school, she wrote me letters and sent care packages on any holiday that provided an excuse. I appreciated this and said so in the *form* letters I sent back in response. (Yes, I know, I'm an idiot. Everybody has painful memories; this is one of mine.) She also courted and won over my entire family. When she spent a school term traveling around Europe and the Middle East, I didn't write to her—but my father did. If my parents had arranged my marriage, I would be married to the woman I am married to. Come to think of it, that's pretty much what happened. With Herculean patience, Louise worked her plan; and with corresponding restraint, my family allowed me to live under the delusion that I had some say in the outcome of what was about to unfold.

My little brother set and sprang the trap. A leader in his junior-high youth group, he recruited me to be the speaker at their upcoming retreat between Christmas and New Year's. Then when he saw Louise at church, he said, "Are you coming to our snow camp? Robin is." So she signed on as a counselor. Somehow, through planning meetings, prayer, conducting a retreat, sharing in trials and tribulation (junior highers, snow), and debriefing sessions (ah yes, debriefing sessions), a spark was ignited. And the rest, as they say, is history.

I must add one more detail about Louise's plan that proved to be helpful. She took intentional, specific steps (that I will not describe here) to maximize the potential of her physical appearance, and the results were impressive. She had on her own provided part of the answer to my prayer about chemistry. Suffice it to say, one of the great blessings of my life is that the lady who lights my fire is the woman I am married to. Amen.

Everyone's experience is different, but mine illustrates three themes that are prominent in this book. The first is the judgment-impairing effect of chemistry. Dr. Van Epp calls it "that intoxicating attraction." And he passes along four warnings: [3]

1. Chemistry is not always a good judge of character.

2. Chemistry sees what it wants to see.

3. Chemistry is not constant even in the best of relationships.

4. When chemistry precedes relationship, it prompts premature sexual involvement (which, as we observed in chapter 11, greatly complicates a relationship).

If you are already enmeshed in a romantic relationship, there are two things I hope for you. The first is that you have a "grandfather" in your life who can help you recognize any red flags in your relationship. (Several grandfathers would be better.) And second, that you will not disregard the counsel of anyone who knows you well and loves you enough to tell you something hard. If they are right, they may cause you grief in the short run but spare you from disaster in the long run.

The second theme illustrated in my experience is the preferability of relationship first, chemistry second. I will elaborate on that principle in the final chapter.

The List

The third point is the subject of the remainder of this chapter and the next: the benefit of developing a profile of the kind of person who would make a well-matched spouse—a keeper.[4] In both his books and his website, Neal Clark Warren advocates compiling a shopping list of criteria for the selection of a suitable spouse. Specifically, he recommends the careful and deliberate identification of one's top ten must-haves as well as one's top ten can't-stands. Then he advises that the single adult adopt a no-compromise policy for those criteria. "Don't marry a person who doesn't have *all* of your top-ten 'must haves'. Similarly, don't marry a person who has *any* of your ten can't stands."[5] No exceptions.

This is good advice,[6] which we apply in other areas of life. Whether we are choosing a college, shopping for a car, or seeking to recruit a youth pastor, we go to the trouble of establishing standards by which we will make an ultimate choice. Similarly, when the apostle Paul delegated the responsibility for the selection of elders and deacons to his protégés, Timothy and Titus, he enumerated the specific qualities required of those who would lead Christ's church (1 Timothy 3; Titus 1). The profile he established continues to provide criteria for churches in their choice of spiritual leaders.

Taking the effort to carefully think through and literally write down our specifications for a spouse was very helpful to Louise and me. The List I am talking about is not abstract and general. To be useful, it must be highly specific. So we'll explore the areas that should be considered momentarily.

But first we need to clarify the objective. What do we mean by a keeper? How would you recognize one if you saw one?

More Than a Soul Mate—a "Mission Mate"

The tendency at this point is to ask, "What do I want in a [wo]man?" The generic answer for many in the current generation is "a soul mate." Thus, The List might focus on those attributes that would maximize compatibility and a strong connection. A more sophisticated approach might involve the completion of an online survey designed to identify numerous dimensions that should be considered in defining the features of a good match.

One of the burdens of this book is to persuade Christians to begin their decision making further back. Before asking the question, "What do *I* want?" (which is a perfectly valid question), the believer is to ask, "What does God have in mind?" To repeat one of the major themes of the previous chapters, the proper starting point for the creation of a profile is God's design for marriage and, thus, for spouses.

Unless you have a photographic memory, it would be good to review the content of chapter 5. For that is where we fleshed out the two distinctive functions for marriage: vocational partnership and relational companionship. You may recall my campaign to correct our culture's conception of a soul mate while adding a renewed appreciation for the role of a teammate.

On the basis of my critique of the common quest for a soul mate, you might conclude that I am downplaying relational companionship as an important aspect of the profile. Actually, my intention is to do the opposite. I want you to recognize the true significance of the role of companionship in a healthy marriage. For as we noted, it has a biblical purpose that goes beyond the self-focused notion of a "roommate with privileges."

I see a good illustration of what I have in mind in the movie *As Good As It Gets*. Melvin (played by Jack Nicholson) is an isolated, self-absorbed, obsessive-compulsive writer who somehow develops a relationship with his waitress, Carol (Helen Hunt). In their conversations, his best efforts to say the right thing often come out sounding like insults. On their first date, one of his thoughtless comments hurts her feelings. But she gives him the opportunity to redeem himself with a meaningful compliment to her. He thinks very hard, sweating bullets. Finally, he explains that when she came into his life, he decided to start taking the medication prescribed by his shrink to hopefully improve his obsessive-compulsive disorder—even though he hates, *really hates* pills. Carol is bewildered. "I don't quite get how that's a compliment for me." Then Melvin explains: "You make me want to be a better man."

Henry Cloud maintains that someone who is good for you will have a threefold effect on you over time: 1) you end up closer to God; 2) you end up closer to others; and 3) you become more of yourself.[7] This is the value-added nature of a healthy marriage. What you're looking for, then, is an *intimate ally* who is good for you and who recognizes that in you they found someone who is, in those same ways, good for them.

But the point I want to reinforce here is that you should be looking for more than a companion. In the alternative terminology of "intimate ally," the noun is *ally*; the modifier is *intimate*. What you should be looking for is a partner-in-life you can join forces with to accomplish together what you could not achieve on your own. More than a soul mate, more even than a workmate, your search is for someone who qualifies in both categories—a *mission mate*. If the divine *mission* of marriage is the advancement of God's rule in your life and your world (chapter 9), your quest is to find a qualified partner in that enterprise.

Laura Smit summarizes it well: "Christians should marry only those who enhance their ability to live Christlike lives, those able to be true partners in Christian service, those who give them a vision of the image of God and the glory of Christ."[8]

That, in general, is the Bible's description of a keeper.

What About Compatibility?

But you are not looking for someone "in general." The profile you create will be specific, identifying qualities that maximize the potential for a harmonious match. The objective, in a word, is *compatibility*.

In the next chapter, we will explore key components of compatibility that ought to be included in a profile. But first, two personal observations.

First, I agree that compatibility, properly understood, is very important in marriages. As the prophet Amos famously said, "Can two walk together, unless they are agreed?" (3:3 NKJV). The two related functions of marriage—partnership and companionship—seem to require being "capable of living together harmoniously or getting along well together; in agreement, combine well, etc.," as the dictionary defines *compatible*.[9] If compatibility advances the effectiveness of any enterprise involving teamwork, it is especially advisable for marriage.

Second, however, I agree with H. Norman Wright's assessment of compatibility in marriage. In the second paragraph of his book *Finding the Right One for You*, he writes:

> Marriage. You want to be married or you wouldn't be reading this book. In fact, you're looking for that special someone who will be a wonderful companion, meet all of your needs, and totally complete you. *But you're not going to find such a person!* Every person you find will be flawed. But that's all right. All marriages begin with that condition. Keep searching, but realize that even with the best match you find, you won't really be 100 percent compatible in the beginning. However, you can *become* compatible. Plan on that as a major marriage goal for the first five to ten years [emphasis his].[10]

Later, he repeats: "You need the marriage relationship for the opportunity to learn to become compatible, and it takes the first decade of marriage for this to become a reality."[11]

I agree with him. While a couple may attain a certain level of affinity during courtship, true compatibility is forged in the furnace of marriage. No matter how well matched you might be in temperament, background, values, interests, and the like, one of you will be a man, the other will be a woman, and both of you will be sinners. Making a good match should reduce the level of difficulty, but there will still be plenty of work to do in the process of *becoming* one flesh.

Is this nuance of meaning significant? I believe it is. For it alters what you are looking for as you evaluate prospective mates. Rather than assessing the presence or absence of compatibility, you ought to be appraising the *potential* for compatibility. This difference is subtle, to be sure, but important for two reasons.

First, it injects a healthy dose of reality into the process. The existence of premarital harmony and chemistry do not guarantee success in the creation of a compatible marriage. The task of building compatibility will require intentional, sustained effort on the part of both spouses.

Second, it should help to refine your focus on what you should be looking for—the qualities that will *contribute* to compatibility. And the question changes from "Are we compatible?" to "Do we have what it takes to become compatible?"

One of the discoveries I have made in writing this book is that one of the things that distinguishes a *Christian* approach to marital decision making is asking the right questions. By defining a *keeper* as "an intimate ally," you keep before you the two essential aspects of marriage: vocational partnership and relational companionship.

As you consider the desired specifications for a potential mate, then, you should ask two questions:

1. What are the qualities of a person I could effectively join forces with in the pursuit of God's goals for our marriage?

2. What qualities in a candidate for marriage will contribute to compatibility?

Those are the right questions. And I think the answers to them will significantly overlap.

❖ ❖ ❖

Questions for Reflection and Group Discussion

1. What was the most significant insight you gained from reading this chapter?

2. Do you have any personal experience with "chemistry first, relationship second" v. "relationship first, chemistry second"? What did you learn?

3. What do you think of Dr. Warren's advice to create a shopping list of criteria for mate selection? Why does he insist on "No exceptions!"

4. How does Dr. Cloud's description of someone who is good for you correspond to the biblical design for marriage? What traits and behaviors would characterize a person who would affect another person in these three ways?

5. Dr. Wright maintains that compatibility is not something a couple starts out with, it's something they develop over time. Do you agree? Why or why not? Do you think the distinction is significant?

6. As you worked through the chapters of part 2 ("God's Design for Marriage"), you were given the assignment to begin creating a profile of a prospective mate. Based on what you have read so far, what are the key components of your profile?

❖ ❖ ❖

For additional questions, go to www.TheMarriageDecision.com.

16

Calculating Compatibility

∞❖∞

The search for a mate is an exercise in risk assessment. The objective is to find another person whose personal qualities offer the greatest possibility of a successful marriage. This description of the task at hand may sound more analytical than romantic, but I contend that this project is too important to be haphazard. I agree with those who advocate the creation of a profile of a keeper—preferably *before* you fall in love. Making a List of must-have qualities, can't-stand vices, and desirable bonus features could help you to recognize a keeper when you see one.

The starting point is the biblical design for spouses: vocational partnership (a teammate) and relational companionship (a soul mate). With a balanced view of the target in mind, you are well positioned to think about the details of The List. Two good questions to ask are:

1. What are the qualities of a person I could effectively join forces with in the pursuit of God's goals for our marriage?

2. What qualities in a candidate for marriage will contribute to compatibility?

The former question keeps the partnership requirement in view; the latter relates to companionship.

The wording of the second question reflects my perspective on compatibility. Since *compatibility* means being "capable of living together harmoniously or getting along well together; in agreement, combine well," true compatibility is not something a couple starts out with. It is better to think of it as something that will be created over time as the husband and wife become one flesh. So the task of the profiler is to identify those features in a prospective mate that would maximize the *potential* for compatibility.

It wouldn't hurt at this point to pull out a sheet of paper (or boot up the computer) and start writing things down. But eventually you will find it helpful to organize the profile into five ingredients in the recipe for compatibility: character, commitment, comparability, complementarity, and chemistry.[1]

Five Keys to Compatibility

Character

At the beginning of chapter 14, I quoted verses from Proverbs on the unhappy plight of the man married to a quarrelsome or contentious woman. You will be glad to know that the writers of the Proverbs also expressed admiration for wives of noble virtue.

> A noble wife is the crown of her husband,
> but the wife who acts shamefully is like rottenness in his bones.
> (Proverbs 12:4)

> A house and wealth are inherited from parents,
> but a prudent wife is from the LORD.
> (Proverbs 19:14)

> Who can find a wife of noble character?
> For her value is far more than rubies.
> (Proverbs 31:10)

One man who found a "wife of noble character" was Boaz. When, after an unconventional courtship, he accepted *her* (!) proposal of marriage, the reason he gave was that "everyone in the village knows that you are a *worthy* woman" (Ruth 3:11). ("Worthy" is the very same word translated "noble character" in Proverbs 31:10.) The narration of their story in the Old Testament book of Ruth gives a glimpse into what Boaz and Ruth saw in each other.

From observing her in the harvest fields, Boaz knew that Ruth was a hard worker. That was relevant because most of life involves work. They both saw each other getting the yield of the ground from the sweat of their brows (Ruth 2; Proverbs 31:13-16). Further, Boaz witnessed

Ruth's devotion to her mother-in-law, Naomi (Ruth 2:11), a woman who described herself as "bitter" (1:20-21). Boaz concluded that if Ruth could love an embittered mother-in-law, she could love him, warts and all. As she worked in the fields, Ruth noted that Boaz cared for his workers and they respected him as their foreman. Boaz and Ruth impressed each other with their diligence and their caring spirit. Finally, both were growing in faith. Boaz blessed Ruth for her faith (2:12; see Proverbs 31:30), and his workers blessed Boaz for his faith (2:4).

What Boaz and Ruth observed in each other's outward behavior was a reflection of who they were on the inside, their character. Character is one's moral nature—those convictions and traits that guide one's attitudes, motives, and actions. A New Testament synonym is "godliness" (1 Timothy 4:8; 6:6; 2 Peter 1:3,5-7). *When considering a prospective mate, character is the most important thing.*

The importance of character in the marital relationship is deeply imbedded in the very structure of God's design for marriage. As image-bearers, the first husband and wife were created and united to reflect the moral nature of their Creator. In a fallen world, one purpose of marriage is the growth of spiritual character in the lives of each family member. Each spouse is to intentionally build the other up in godliness. So it follows that the Christian single adult should be looking for someone of sufficient spiritual maturity and commitment to have the inclination and capacity to pursue those God-given purposes.

Further, character is that aspect of who we are that is most real and lasting. Henry Cloud says, "While you might be attracted to someone's 'outsides,' what you will experience over the long haul is their 'insides.' The only things that last are in a person's *character.* Or, I should say the only thing that makes a relationship able to last is a person's character."[2] The biblical author who extolled the "wife of noble character" in Proverbs 31 implied the same point: "Charm is deceitful and beauty is fleeting, but a woman who fears the LORD will be praised" (31:30).

Character is fleshed out in specific traits. The New Testament abounds in lists of desirable virtues: love, joy, peace, patience, kindness, goodness, faithfulness, gentleness, self-control, humility, compassion, integrity, forbearance, mercy, gratitude, endurance, contentment, generosity (Galatians 5:22-23; Ephesians 4:22-23; Colossians 3:12-17; 1 Timothy 3:1-7; 6:6,11,17-19; 2 Peter 1:5-8). Such a list may seem too abstract to be practical. But if you are trying to assess the character *of a specific person*, this inventory of spiritual qualities provides a ready-made checklist from a Reliable Source.

The Best and the Worst

In the estimation of relationship experts, certain virtues stand out as being especially valuable in marriage. When David LeVine sought advice from Orthodox Jewish rabbis, the most frequently mentioned quality was kindness. Rabbi Dov Heller explains: "In Judaism we say that if you have two people who are kind, there is no possibility of divorce. That's because a kind person is a giver."[3] Neil Clark Warren reinforces the importance of kindness: "It might surprise you to discover that in survey after survey, both men and women rate kindness as the second most important quality to look for in a mate."[4]

The other three virtues emphasized by the Jewish commentators were humility, responsibility, and contentment. Young and Adams highlight five character qualities: faithful, honest, committed, forgiving, and giving.[5]

Sometimes the most effective way to think about character is to reflect on what one *doesn't* want in a marriage—that is, the vices that correspond to desirable virtues. For example, you don't want to be tied for life with someone who is *dishonest*. Trust is absolutely indispensable in marriage, and you cannot trust someone who lies or cheats. Nor should you commit to someone who has not learned to manage his or her *anger*. If your partner is *irresponsible*, you will spend your life picking up the slack. Dr. Warren warns against *obstreperousness*—"a big word for a person who is harsh, critical, unappreciative, difficult to please, and never satisfied. An obstreperous person will drain you of every ounce of energy you have and will make life a living hell."[6]

The profile you develop for a future spouse needs to give careful attention to the character dimension. What are your must-haves? As you do this, there are a couple of things that are important to remember. First, nobody's perfect. Anyone you consider will be a work-in-progress. A realistic standard is *relative* maturity. Presumably, a mature fifty-year-old will exhibit greater spiritual development than a mature twenty-five-year-old. The question is not "Has he arrived?"; the question is, "Where is he headed?" You are looking for red flags on the one hand and evidence of *growth in the direction of godliness* on the other.

Second, according to the Bible, the production of godly character is a joint effort between God and the believer. The Christian is to take initiative to pursue Christlike virtues (Ephesians 4:22-32; Colossians 3:12-17; 1 Timothy 6:11; 2 Timothy 2:22; 2 Peter 1:5-8). Yet the resultant transformation is said to be "the fruit of the Spirit" that comes as we "remain" in Christ (John 15:1-5; Galatians 5:22-23; Colossians 3:10). Accordingly, you should pay attention to *the priority a prospective spouse places on the cultivation of their relationship with God.* Furthermore, since that relationship is best expressed and advanced in community, that person's involvement with a local church is highly relevant. Does she take initiative to engage with God through spiritual disciplines such as Bible reading, prayer, corporate worship, and service? Does he have an identifiable group of Christian friends with whom he enjoys fellowship, experiences support and accountability, and engages in ministry? Does this person "seek first the kingdom of God and his righteousness" (Matthew 6:33 ESV) out of personal conviction and desire, or is their religious involvement dependent on you? In short, who is their God, and how do you know?

My sister-in-law, Elizabeth, experienced the disappointment of a failed first marriage. As she experienced sufficient healing to begin considering marriage again, she attended a presentation I was giving at her sister's church on decision making. During the question-and-answer session, someone asked for my take on the Bible's perspective on mate selection. Apparently I said, "Find the most spiritually mature person who will have you, and marry them." I had forgotten about that comment, but Elizabeth wrote it down in the margin of her Bible next to 1 Corinthians 7:39-40. She took it to heart and before long she found her Boaz. That advice was much more succinct than this book, but it worked for her. As of this writing, she and Terry have been happily married for over thirty years.

Commitment

The couple standing before me look better than they have ever looked before—and it's not just because they are wearing very expensive clothes. They are simply radiant. They exude joy and enthusiasm and anticipation. They are getting married, and they are so rapture-filled they are about to explode. Love and solemn decision making have brought them to this place. But their hope for the future lies in the words of promise that they recite to each other:

> I, Steven, take you, Haley, to be my lawfully wedded wife.
> And before God and these witnesses,
> I promise to love you,
> To honor and cherish you,
> And leaving all others, cleave only to you.
> And to be to you in all things a true and faithful husband
> As long as we both shall live.

Marriage is a covenant between two people publicly declared. The willingness to stand before one's family and friends and make these *vows* is the fundamental factor that distinguishes marriage from cohabitation. For while cohabiters *test* compatibility, spouses *build compatibility*. One reason that husbands and wives become compatible is that, having made vows, no other option is entertained.[7]

The forging of compatibility happens when commitment is expressed in a determination to deal constructively with difficult problems.

> Commitment is more than continuing to stick it out and suffer with a poor choice of a spouse. It's not just maintaining; it's investing. It's not just enduring; it's working to make the relationship grow. It's not just accepting and tolerating negative and destructive patterns on the part of your spouse; it's working toward change. It's sticking to someone regardless of circumstances.[8]

So while a bride and groom on their wedding day are deeply, gloriously in love, they are not counting on that euphoria to bind them together permanently. When push comes to shove (or hopefully before), it is *troth* that keeps spouses together. "Troth is an Old Eng[lish] word for fidelity, truth, trust, love and commitment...Keeping the troth is counting on each other, giving the utmost, sharing deeply from inside, sticking together through thick and thin."[9] It refers to the commitment of the covenant; it is synonymous with *cleave* (another Old English word) in Genesis 2:24. Romantic love flows from emotion; troth is a decision of the will. It is a promise that is as trustworthy as the character of the one who makes it.

This linkage between character and commitment ought to be obvious. And as you construct your profile, you need to be looking for someone who is a promise keeper. As a criterion for mate selection, reliability is a better indicator of marital stability than romance.

Comparability (Similarities) and Complementarity (Differences)

For years one of Neil Warren's mantras has been: "Find somebody to love who is a lot like you."[10] The short version of his recommended approach to evaluating prospects is this: "If you find somebody who has good character and is emotionally healthy, and then you get somebody who is a lot like you, the two of you will have a tremendous chance to make that relationship work."[11]

While other authors agree about the importance of substantial comparability, they collectively add important qualifications. First, don't misread Warren's advice to mean find somebody who is *exactly* like you. "In most successful relationships, the two partners have a blend of similarities and differences in personalities, backgrounds, and lifestyles. The *balance* of this blend is what makes or breaks the couple."[12] This balance is evident in God's original design. When God introduced Eve to Adam, his response was, "Wow! She's just like me—only different." There were ways in which she was comparable to Adam, and ways that she was complementary. If the purposes of marriage are vocational partnership and relational companionship, and if you're looking for an intimate ally in fulfilling God's mission, then you're going to want your partner to be like you in ways that promote unity of purpose and perspective, while bringing distinctive characteristics and aptitudes that strengthen the team.

Constructive Similarities

Second, when it comes to comparability, it's not just the number of similarities that count but the *kind*. Some are more important than others. As you compile your profile, you will want to pay attention to the following five areas:

1. Where you have come from. As your two lives converge, the degree to which your *backgrounds* are similar will affect the ease with which you develop compatibility. This includes your parental and extended family, culture, socioeconomic class, ethnicity, geographic setting, and religious upbringing. One of the reasons that arranged marriages worked in bygone years is that these points of similarity were built in. If you have much divergence in any of these areas, you will have a lot of adjusting to do.

2. *Where you are going.* Our *goals* and dreams give direction to our lives. The questions here are: What do you hope to accomplish and what do you want to become? What are your respective goals for your education, your vocation, your family, your involvement in ministry, your financial security, and the like? These goals do not have to be identical, but they cannot be mutually exclusive. If you are going to travel together, you should have the same destination and be in agreement on the route you are taking to get there.

3. *What you are like.* Features of *personal makeup* where similarities are important include level of ambition, level of energy, level of intelligence (and even education),[13] sense of humor (do you laugh at the same things?), desire and ability for verbal intimacy, personal habits (punctuality, cleanliness, orderliness, social graces, weight management), work habits, and personal interests. These characteristics affect the level of comfort and enjoyment a couple finds in each other's company.[14] Since companionship is a major component of marriage, similarities in these areas (especially common interests) will advance the cause of compatibility.

4. *What matters to you.* Values are the convictions and principles that guide the way we live and make decisions. *This is the most important category where alignment between allies is required.* Most relational conflicts can be traced to clashing values. Our values tend to operate below the surface, and most people would be hard pressed to identify their own. But you can uncover a person's values, including your own, through careful observation. How does he spend his time, energy, and money? What does she like to talk about? What makes him angry? What makes her happy or excited? What motivates him? What makes her bored? What does he praise? Your answers to those questions will expose many of a person's core values.

5. *What you hope for.* Your *expectations* of what your marriage will be like are shaped by the previous four categories. As I said in chapter 14, the expectations of each prospective spouse need to be identified and

compared. Of particular importance is each person's assumptions about marital roles.[15] What will be the responsibilities of the husband? What are the anticipated duties of the wife? Does each person want children? How many? What parenting styles are preferred? Similar expectations bode well for compatibility. Dissonant expectations will produce a discordant marriage.

Complementary Differences

Earlier I said that it would be a mistake to look for someone who is *exactly* like you. Of course, there is no such person. Anyone you might find to marry will be significantly different from you in at least one respect—gender. As God was preparing to create the first woman, he said, "I will make a companion for him who corresponds to him" (Genesis 2:18). The word *corresponds* means "opposite" in the sense of "complementary." So the union of a man and a woman will, by definition, be characterized by substantive differences that are intended to strengthen the relationship. The whole is greater than the sum of its parts. As the French say, "Vive la différence!"

But other differences emerge as well. There is variety in the temperaments, aptitudes, skills, gifts, talents, abilities, and experiences that people bring to their relationships. In healthy friendships, families, and communities, we contribute our individual strengths to the well-being of others and are enriched in turn by those who have assets that we lack. This dynamic is particularly at work in a good marriage. In fact, we tend to be drawn to persons who possess what we do not have so that we can vicariously experience things that do not come naturally to us.[16] It is even possible to internalize and adopt the strengths of our partner as we become apprenticed to someone with distinctive capabilities.

Dangerous Differences

But not all of our differences are complementary. Some are contradictory and others are potentially destructive. Almost all relationship experts include a word of warning: "Beware when opposites attract." A normal appreciation for admirable distinctives becomes abnormal when one makes the opposing style or ability the *primary basis* for the relationship.

The problem with this kind of opposites-attract dynamic is that instead of fixing your emotional imbalance, you identify the opposite quality in someone else and think that *your relationship* will complete what is lacking. It doesn't! Instead, the relationship multiplies the problems and drives you further from center.[17]

Instead of a mutual relationship of love, an unhealthy dependency is established. "Dependency that does not lead to growth ultimately creates more immaturity in the person."[18] And unfortunately, unbalanced people have a knack for finding each other: addicts find codependents, abusers find the victimized, controllers find adapters, and the emotionally needy find rescuers.

Other noncomplementary differences are less serious, but will still bring challenges to a marriage. These are contradictory opposites that do not mesh well. Examples include the spendthrift and the tightwad or the social butterfly and the recluse. Such contradictory differences require negotiation and compromise on some middle ground that is less than satisfactory to either party. This sort of difference should be flagged before a couple makes a lifelong commitment. *If it bothers you when you're dating, it's going to drive you nuts when you're married.*

So how can you tell if a difference is complementary? John Van Epp gives three helpful guidelines: 1) complementarity exists when time ends up refining the blend of differences in mutually beneficial ways; 2) this produces a deep and mutual appreciation of differences; and 3) partners with true complementarity become less different and more alike over-time.[19] This is one evidence that they are *becoming* compatible.

Matching Temperaments?

Before we move on to the final ingredient in our recipe for promoting compatibility, I want to add a few thoughts about the role of temperament in evaluating prospective mates. Because our personalities are complex, the attempt to match them can get complicated. Should they be similar or complementary or both? Should an extrovert pair up with an introvert or would she find greater harmony with another extrovert? What about thinkers and feelers, realists and dreamers, disciplined and spontaneous? How should we factor in similarities and differences in personality as we construct the profile of a keeper?

A couple of months ago, our church staff went on a team-building retreat for a day. Each member of the staff had read the book *Understanding How Others Misunderstand You* by Ken Voges and Ron Braund.[20] This book utilizes the DiSC personality inventory to help individuals understand their behavioral styles, identify the distinctive patterns of others, and recognize how those variations affect their interactions. This format helped us to see both the similarities and differences we each had with our colleagues, and the effects these dynamics had on the ways we work together.

Working through several exercises in self- and other-discovery helped our staff members gain a greater appreciation for the diversity on our staff and, even more importantly, the *value* of that diversity. When people work in close proximity to each other, our differences can easily become a source of tension, even conflict. What this experience helped everyone to see is that those differences will make us more effective as a team—if we value and utilize the strengths of each type and make allowance for those tendencies that are different from ours.

Along the way we were reminded that temperaments are not right or wrong. Each style has strengths and weaknesses. That's why we need each other. We will become most effective in relating to and working with each other when we 1) understand each other's styles and perspectives, 2) appreciate the value of the other's distinctive makeup, 3) resist the impulse to try to change that person to become like us, and 4) show respect in every interaction. And what we are doing is building compatibility.

While there may be categories of temperament types, each person's personality is unique in ways that defy precise analysis. So I'm not convinced that it is very useful to try to predetermine a preferred personality type in one's profile of a keeper.[21] In their books on dating, Henry Cloud and John Townsend encourage singles to keep an open mind in this area. Sometimes people are too restrictive, limiting consideration of potential dates to those who are "my type." But one's type could be the product of some imbalanced or unhealthy complex of influences. For instance, some young adults are strongly imprinted by one (or both) of their parents.[22] ("I want a gal, just like the gal that married dear old dad.") That influence isn't necessarily pathological, but it could close off options that should otherwise be considered. A lot of happily married people who kept an open mind were surprised by the kind of person they ended up with.[23]

Chemistry

Chemistry is a powerful feeling of attraction for another person. It isn't the same as friendship, for a person can have all sorts of great friends who do not turn you on. It is a kind of emotional magnetism that draws two people toward one another. It creates the desire to be close, to hold hands, to kiss, to have sex. It is the sense of connectedness that is the *precondition* of falling in love.

When the experts on marital relationships talk about chemistry, there are common themes. The first is that no one knows what causes it. It appears to be a spontaneous response to a complex of factors that could include some combination of physical appearance, personality, sense of humor, charm, intellect, status, talents, spirituality, or the release of pheromones[24] (which, if true, would give *chemistry* another level of meaning). It is the most mysterious component in the recipe for compatibility.[25] "There are no 'Ten Steps to Developing Chemistry' with your partner. You either have it or you don't,"[26] some say.

I'm not ready to sign on to such a sweeping generalization. If there is absolutely no chemistry to start with, the statement may be true. But if, to change the metaphor, there are embers, there are ways to blow on them if there is a good reason. Millions of couples whose marriages were arranged have started by "rubbing two sticks together" with highly satisfactory results.[27] And, as I found out, one can always pray. Still, there is enough truth in the generalization to pay attention to it.

The second and third themes are warnings. The first warning is, "Chemistry: don't get married without it." This may sound like a profound grasp of the obvious, for the assumption of most people (and even the Bible) is that people who are getting married can hardly wait to consummate the wedding. For most engaged couples, lack of chemistry isn't their biggest problem. But for some it is. Marriage counselors work with couples for whom there was no spark during courtship, but they expected things to change when they got married—and that didn't happen. It remains true that sexual union is to be reserved for marriage; but in a culture where couples arrange their own marriages, they should experience some symptoms of the urge to merge.

The more prevalent warning is, "Don't get married because of chemistry alone." Neil Warren explains this caution well:

> While love without chemistry equals friendship, chemistry alone is not a foundational building block of your relationship. It is the icing, not the cake. If all you have is chemistry, that is not enough. Somebody said, "Passion, though a bad regulator, is a good spring." In other words, it is good at getting love going, but not so good at keeping it going. The chemistry of passion, without a base of deeper, more important compatibilities, typically lasts only about six to eight months.[28]

Marry a Friend

If chemistry is the icing, friendship is the cake. You need to *like* the one you love, or as Cloud and Townsend say, "Don't fall in love with someone you wouldn't be friends with."[29]

> A real and lasting relationship must be built upon friendship first. You are going to spend a lot of time with that person. As one friend of mine said about picking her mate: "He was someone I knew I could grow old with. I liked spending time with him. And he made me laugh." She also shared deep spiritual values and other commonalities with him as well, as she would with any other friend. They have been married for nearly 30 years.[30]

As I mentioned at the beginning of the previous chapter, John Van Epp says that couples fall in love in two ways. You can have chemistry first, relationship second. Or you can have relationship first, chemistry second. I also noted his cautionary words about chemistry, which bear repeating: 1) chemistry is not always a good judge of character; 2) chemistry sees what it wants to see; 3) chemistry is not constant even in the best of relationships; and 4) when chemistry precedes relationship, it prompts premature sexual involvement. The rest of the story is that Dr. Van Epp's own experience followed the "chemistry first, relationship second" pattern. Though that is not the logical order (and there is nothing logical about this kind of chemistry), it can be done.

> The building of a best-friends relationship between Shirley and me became the foundation of our future. Over the next two years, our in-love feelings were channeled into endless conversations and experiences that welded a bond of deeply knowing each other. We held back on indulging our passions and concentrated on becoming best friends.[31]

In fact, some observers of the American courtship scene maintain that one benefit of a romantic relationship is that it prompts a couple to focus their attention on one another long enough to actually get to know each other at much deeper levels.

The bottom line for the profiler: include chemistry and friendship on your list of must-haves.

Five Keys to Compatibility

- *Character:* Godliness that is the product of one's past and ongoing relationship with God reflected in specific, Christlike virtues.

- *Commitment:* Faithfulness to the marriage covenant underwritten by the reliability of the promise keeper.

- *Comparability:* Similarities that promote unity of perspective and purpose

  —*Where you come from*—background

  —*Where you are going*—goals

  —*What you are like*—personal makeup

  —*What matters to you*—values

  —*What you hope for*—expectations

- *Complementarity:* Differences that help each other grow, to be better than either could be on your own.

- *Chemistry:* A powerful feeling of attraction for another person.

Sketching the Profile

If we were to portray our recipe for compatibility as a mathematical formula, it would look something like this:

[Character + Commitment] + [Comparability + Complementarity + Chemistry] → **Compatibility**

The brackets mark off subsets to show that the first two ingredients relate to one another in a distinctive way, as do the last three. Specifically, character and commitment are reflections of what a person is in himself or herself. By contrast, comparability, complementarity, and chemistry have to do with the characteristics of a person *in relation to* another.[32] The practical significance of these subdivisions will be spelled out below.

When it comes to actually compiling The List, there are two extremes to avoid. The first is to create a profile that is too detailed, too idealistic. The mistake here is failure to distinguish between requirements and preferences. Some people put too many items from their wish list on their must-have list. Or everything on the list is must-have. In her insightful article, "Shopping for a Spouse? Why I Decided to Chuck My Mr. Right Checklist,"[33] Shana Schutte tells how she did this. The list she threw out contained her specifications for "the perfect guy." "My list was longer than Santa's," she admits. But the quest for perfection is not only unrealistic, it is unbiblical. If you were to find someone who is perfect, there would be no way for you to contribute to their spiritual growth, which is one of the primary missions of marriage. Besides, as a believer, you are already married to Jesus Christ. So you can afford to be a little less picky in selecting your earthly spouse.

The opposite error is to compromise on the must-haves and can't-stands. This happens when one settles for what is available rather than holding out for what really should be required. The idea behind the must-have and can't-stand lists is that every item included is essential. Disqualification by a prospect on *any single criterion* is a deal-breaker. You're not grading on the curve—it's all or nothing.

So you need to be precise in the construction of your must-have and can't-stand lists. It also means that most of the items on those lists should come from the first subset of character and commitment. Conversely most of the items on your like-to-have list will come from the second subset of similarities, differences, and chemistry. By the way, your spec-ifications for those you will date and the person you will marry are not identical (see chapter 18).

Are you going to make a list? I suspect that some who read this book will not bother—they will have too many other, more urgent things on their plate. But I hope you will. Here's a suggestion: go on a one-day retreat and get it done. Study, reflect, and pray. Make rough drafts and then refine your profile to a finished product. Write your requirements in ink; write your preferences in pencil (and keep an eraser handy). You will tweak your lists over time, maybe dramatically, as you grow. But you will find it helpful to have a place to start. And someday you may want to show your profile to the person it eventually described. That person will be overwhelmed. And that's a really good reason to have an actual list.

How Does This Affect Me Personally?

As I conclude this chapter on the profile of a keeper, I must not neglect to mention two corollaries. The focus of my attention has been on "the other person"—the theoretical marriage prospect. But the ingre-dients that lead to compatibility have ramifications for the one making the lists. The first is this: if you are going to evaluate similarities and dif-ferences, there must be a standard for comparison. And so the first cor-ollary is: *"Know yourself."* Before you can think of investigating some-one else's assets and liabilities, you need to become an expert on yourself.

Why? This principle becomes immediately apparent the moment you begin exploring the areas related to comparability and complemen-tarity: background, goals, personal characteristics, values, and expecta-tions. Do you know how your upbringing affects the way you live? Do you know where you want to go in life? Do you have ideas about how you plan to get there? Do you know your own inclinations and aptitudes, your abilities and gifts? Can you identify your interests and passions? Can you list the core values that motivate your actions and shape your decision making? Do you know your expectations of a future spouse, or of your-self as a spouse?

This is why marriage is for grownups. One measure of mature adult-hood is a sense of identity that is separate from your parents and your peers. Before you can take the measure of others, you must have clarity on your own goals, values, convictions, interests, and expectations. So when you go on that one-day retreat, you may need to spend the morning sorting out your own profile.[34] And if you can't do that, you are not ready to consider joining your life to someone else.

With respect to the first subset, character and commitment, the second corollary is: *"Become the profile."* In these areas, it is simply not legitimate to require qualities in a prospective mate that you do not have yourself. The ingredients that maximize the likelihood of building compatibility must characterize you as much as they do your marriage companion. Someone else may be looking for the very traits you would require in a teammate in vocational partnership.

In a provocative article titled "The Question That Could Save Your Marriage Before It Begins," Les Parrott dares the reader to ask: "How would I like to be married to me?"[35] His point is one that many others have made. While it is important to find the right person to marry, it is more important to *be* the right person to marry.

❖ ❖ ❖

Recommended Reading

How to Avoid Falling in Love with a Jerk: The Foolproof Way to Follow Your Heart Without Losing Your Mind by John Van Epp (McGraw-Hill, 2008).

❖ ❖ ❖

Questions for Reflection and Group Discussion

1. What was the most significant insight you gained from reading this chapter?

2. What are some practical ways to discern the true character of a prospective mate?

3. Have you ever seen or experienced a romantic relationship in which there was one or more glaring difference(s) between the people involved? Was the difference complementary, incompatible, or destructive? How did the relationship work out?

4. In what ways were your parents similar and different? How did those similarities and differences affect their marriage? What have you learned from their experience?

5. In the prologue, review the situations faced by Claudia and Carl (second vignette) and Mary and Jeff (last vignette). What counsel would you give to Claudia and Mary? How about Carl and Jeff?

6. Make a rough draft of a "keeper profile." Share your initial ideas with your study group or a trusted friend. Get their feedback. Ask them if they know anyone who matches your profile!

For additional questions, go to www.TheMarriageDecision.com.

17

Courtship: Getting Our Bearings

~~~✦~~~

M y wife, Louise, manages a used bookstore. As I was completing my research for this chapter (or so I thought), she came home from work with a book. "Someone traded this in today," she said, as she handed me the paperback. "I thought it might be relevant to your project." The title: *5 Paths to the Love of Your Life: Defining Your Dating Style.*[1] It took me a few moments to absorb the implications. Five paths. *Five* paths? The light at the end of the tunnel was morphing into the proverbial oncoming train. My research had only begun.

If you are a single person who eventually marries, you will go through some process of progressive knowledge, attraction, and commitment to another person that culminates in a wedding. In Western culture, that process has been referred to as courtship. Courting has usually involved dating, a term that is sometimes used as a synonym, but is actually a distinct activity that may or may not be directly related to courtship.

The metaphor of a journey seems apt enough.[2] And given the complexities of human personalities, the dynamics of interpersonal relationships, and the mystery of love, it comes as no surprise that the venture of getting from Point A to Point M ranges from challenging to daunting. Of course, it has not always been thus. Throughout much of human history, a prospective bride was introduced to her chosen groom and that was that. The journey more or less began at the altar, and the hard work was reserved for the marriage itself. But our culture has opted for freedom of choice. And part of the price we pay for this do-it-yourself approach includes labor and anxiety and the risk of a broken heart. It's like climbing on a roller coaster with the hope that you don't have to get off before it reaches its destination.

For modern singles, navigating the terrain between singleness and matrimony has never been easy. But in recent years, it has become even harder. In the subculture of my youth, there was a prescribed route to the objective of marriage. But things have changed, and that is no longer the case. Writing in 2000, University of Chicago professors Amy and Leon Kass observed:

> Until what seems like only yesterday, young people were groomed for marriage, and the paths leading to it were culturally well set out, at least in rough outline...Today there are no socially prescribed forms of conduct that help guide young men and women in the direction of matrimony...For the great majority the way to the altar is uncharted territory. It's every couple on its own bottom, without a compass, often without a goal. Those who reach the altar seem to have stumbled on it by accident.[3]

In the ensuing decade, that situation has not improved.

If you are a single Christian looking for a mate in the context of this cultural disarray, you have some important advantages over your secular counterparts. By virtue of the explanation provided by the Designer, you have a clearer picture than anyone of the *destination*. And while the choice of whether to go there is given to you, you are provided with the *criteria* for making that decision. Unlike your peers, you do have a *compass* that can keep you from getting lost—the moral will of God. You also have access to trustworthy *guides* (wise mentors) who can help you find your way along the path. And you have a *Travel Agent* who guarantees your safe arrival at the destination of his choosing as he secretly guides by means of his sovereign will.

The question is, what will you use for a *map*?

The professors Kass maintain that the map got lost. By contrast, the contributors to 5 *Paths* contend there is a reliable, sanctioned route to follow. But they argue among themselves as to which one it is. So the question before us is this: *Is there a biblically prescribed method for mate selection?*

That is an interesting question for lots of reasons. To me, the most interesting thing about it is that it is new. As far as I can tell, the question didn't really come up prior to the 1990s. It certainly wasn't under discussion when I was single and thinking about marriage. There's a reason this issue emerged among Christians, and it is best understood by tracing the story of the evolution of courtship in America.

Some More History[4]

As one might suspect, the history of courtship runs parallel to the history of marriage narrated in the introduction to part 2. As we noted, the biggest shift in patterns of mate selection began in Western Europe during the 1700s when, over time, the arranged marriage was replaced by individual freedom to choose or refuse a partner. During an extended period of transition, parents continued to hold veto power over their children's marital choices, but they were no longer the initiators of a wedded union.

In colonial and post-revolution America, there was no clear demarcation between home and commerce. Part of the national agenda was populating the huge continent. That called for adventurous men, strong women, and large families. Husbands and wives were coworkers—the husband was clearly the boss, and he chose his wife largely on the basis of her potential for productive labor (and producing more productive laborers). Most courtship consisted of the social interactions that were integrated into everyday life. Young people chose marital partners over the span of a decade as they grew up together. Love might be a factor in mate selection, but more often it was expected that love would grow as the natural expression of marriage.

With the development of a wage-based economy through the nineteenth century, gender roles began to change. Men and women moved into separate spheres as the husband became *the* breadwinner and the wife's domain was the home. Once children reached adolescence, boys and girls were socially separated as the young ladies entered the female world and were groomed for future housewifery. Courtship became more formalized. During this era the customs of formal engagement announcements and the giving of engagement rings began. This is also when brides began wearing white dresses and veils (symbolizing purity) in formal wedding ceremonies.

Calling (Women in Control)

Social perceptions of gender differences evolved as well, and romantic love came to be the dominant basis for marriage. Women were considered to be morally superior to men. In fact, toward the end of the century, men were viewed as depraved—they needed to learn to control their animal passions.[5] So women became the custodians of moral propriety and helped men govern their impulses by their modesty, distance, and restraint. Most courting was conducted in the girl's home under the watchful eyes and ears of parents.[6] The process was referred to as "calling," and the protocols became increasingly sophisticated with detailed rules of etiquette. Each step in the courtship was completely controlled by the young woman who instigated the visits by issuing an invitation (initially through her mother) to a prospective caller. And most of the courtship was conducted on her turf.[7] The end goal of this system of courtship was understood by everyone involved: marriage.

Dating (Men in Control)

The elaborate customs of calling were widespread, but not universal; they were limited to those upper- and middle-class families affluent enough to own a home with a parlor or front porch where the visits were conducted.[8] Since propriety forbade men from visiting a young woman in her apartment, boardinghouse, or dorm room, working-class youth became innovative and courted in public. So instead of him coming in, she went out with him to a restaurant, soda fountain, movie, or baseball game.[9] Over time, young adults from the upper classes recognized the fun and excitement of dating, and came to see the possibility of "privacy in the anonymous public."[10] As they emulated the more informal systems of their working-class counterparts, dating came to be widely practiced. By 1920, public dating had essentially supplanted private calling as the universal approach to courtship.

The shift from calling to dating changed more than the venue. It brought about a major realignment in the balance of power at two levels. One change was generational: the dating system lessened parental control and gave greater autonomy to the dating couple. But the more striking change was the reversal of roles between men and women. When courtship took place in the home, the woman was the hostess who entertained her guest. But the invitation to go out was an invitation into the man's world, not only because a date took place in the public sphere (man's territory), but because he was paying for it.[11] So he now took the initiative and exercised the prerogatives of a host. The advent of the automobile reinforced, accelerated, and expanded these trends in courtship.

For our purposes, it is worth noting that "there was some confusion caused by this reversal of initiative, especially during the twenty years or so when going out and calling co-existed as systems."[12] It may be some consolation that the simultaneous operation of two conflicting systems of courtship within one society is not unprecedented.

As the culture of dating evolved between the two world wars, dating came to be seen as distinct from courting. That is, dating became a vehicle for getting to know someone *before* pairing off with them in an exclusive relationship. This casual dating came to be more a function of acquiring social status (attaining popularity) than of pursuing a potential spouse. The transition to courtship was made when a couple began keeping "steady company." This system of dating, going steady, getting engaged, and getting married is the paradigm that governed the romantic progressions of young adults through the fifties and into the Sexual Revolution of the sixties.

Hanging Out and Hooking Up (No One in Control)

In the last third of the twentieth century, dramatic upheavals occurred in society that profoundly challenged the once-conventional views of human mating. One product of this social revolution is an alternative mating system that came into being alongside the established dating/courtship system that prevailed during the first two-thirds of the twentieth century. Social historian Barbara Dafoe Whitehead calls it a "Relationships System," and summarizes it in this way:

> It is not a romantic courtship and marriage system. It is designed to foster the romantic pursuits, not so much of the young, but of an older universe of dating singles. This universe is highly diverse. It includes senior citizens, the divorced, never-married single parents, gays and lesbians, as well as young never-marrieds. And like its universe, the purposes of this emerging mating system are more diverse: it is designed for a variety of intimate pair-bonded arrangements, from marriage to living together

to serial monogamy to sexual partnerings without any strings attached. This emerging mating system has no comprehensive "national" set of standards for romantic courtship. Nor is it likely that it ever will, given its diversity.[13]

So now the ways that men and women get together socially have greatly diversified. Alongside the more structured protocols of dating are less formal systems for connecting. Many singles are more inclined to "hang out" in groups at parties, clubs, and other social settings. Individuals within these groups may find a partner to "hook up" with—an ambiguous term that usually describes a one-time encounter that features erotic behavior at some level (not necessarily intercourse). Whereas dating may initiate a relationship that progresses in the expression of romantic intimacy over time, hooking up typically features overt sexual interaction, often between acquaintances or virtual strangers, and usually goes nowhere relationally.[14]

Christian Alternatives

Many Christians have rightly reacted to the rise of the Relationship System with alarm. Its goals, values, motivations, behaviors, and consequences stand in opposition to a biblical worldview. Any believer whose educational or vocational pursuits requires them to be immersed in that culture will be hard pressed to remain unaffected by those influences.

But even before the connecting patterns of secular culture degenerated to current levels of social acceptability, perceptive Christians began recognizing problems with traditional dating models widely practiced by believers. Some writers decried the artificiality of dating experiences that resulted in romantic bonding within superficial relationships.[15] Others protested the inappropriateness of serial recreational romances "in which each party intentionally endeavors to cultivate the other's desire, while recognizing the relationship is most likely temporary."[16] The erotic behaviors that typically characterize such relationships ought to be reserved for the person one ultimately marries, it was argued.

The deficiencies of the dating system *as practiced by Christians* prompted Joshua Harris to write *I Kissed Dating Goodbye* (1997)[17]. His critique of the dating system[18] and efforts to identify a more biblical approach to courtship resonated with a huge number of Christian singles. In some quarters, agreement with Harris's conclusions was so pervasive that the practice of dating was virtually shut down. Some went so far as to vilify dating as unbiblical, even sinful.

Courtship

Harris proposed replacing the culture of dating with a system of date-less courtship. It is distinguished from dating by its purpose: courtship is a process in which a man and woman of marriageable age intentionally explore the possibility of marriage. They do this by spending time together in a variety of settings, sharing in diverse experiences.

Practitioners of courtship do not engage in casual or recreational dating. They reserve any interactions that might lead to romance for one person who is a likely candidate for matrimony. While some of their activities might look like dates, they make a point to guard their hearts and avoid the pitfall of falling in love too soon. They are conscious of moving through phases in the development of their relationship—from casual friendship, to deeper friendship, to purposeful intimacy with integrity, to engagement.[19] The courtship process may be terminated by either party at any juncture prior to a wedding.

Harris's initiative prompted others to explore the Scriptures in an effort to identify a biblical approach to mate selection. A variation of the courtship approach adds one dimension—"the active, involved authority of the young woman's father (or head of the household) in the formation of her romantic attachments leading to marriage."[20] In this arrangement, the father functions as the guardian of his daughter's hand and heart. Any man interested in cultivating a personal relationship with her must gain the approval of her father. And the subsequent courtship will be carried out under his watchful eye. As the protector of his daughter's best interests, the father has veto power over any agreements she may be inclined to make; his blessing must be secured before an engagement can be declared.

Betrothal

In the "father-approved" version of courtship, the pendulum swings back in the direction of the arranged marriage. But for some, it doesn't swing far enough. And so a third system, called betrothal, has also been proposed. In this paradigm, the distinctive feature added to the mix is *front-end commitment*. If a man identifies a woman that he finds suitable or desirable as a wife, he approaches her father and expresses his interest. If the man passes muster with the father, the girl's parents approach their daughter, informing her of his interest and their approval.

After a time of thoughtful reflection and prayer, the girl decides how to respond to the proposal. If the answer is yes, the man and woman become betrothed, that is, decisively engaged to be married. It is understood by all involved that the betrothal is binding; this couple *will* marry at the agreed upon time. It is only after this commitment is made that the couple enter into the process that, in the other systems, would constitute courtship. The period of betrothal is seen as a time of preparation authorizing the couple to begin "releasing their hearts to one another."[21]

Dating Reconsidered

One other reaction to Harris's declaration of war against dating moved in a different direction. When counselors Henry Cloud and John Townsend read *I Kissed Dating Goodbye*, they identified with the pain and disillusionment of many singles who had been wounded through their experiences of dating. But while they validated the reasons behind the no-dating movement, they disagreed with the proposed solution. "This is a little like saying because there is divorce, no one should get married."[22] It isn't necessary to throw the baby out with the bath water, they argued. What Christian singles need to kiss goodbye is *defective* dating.

Taking Responsibility

If we rule out hooking up, the alternative pathways to marriage available to Christian singles appear to be some version of dating, courtship, or betrothal. (The book *5 Paths* discusses courtship, betrothal, and three perspectives on dating.) So now we return to our question: *Is there a biblically prescribed method for mate selection?*

The short answer is no.[23] It is true that there is one dominant approach throughout biblical history—the arranged marriage.[24] It is also true that the Mosaic Law regulated some behaviors connected with the acquisition of a spouse. But we do not find directives that require a specific approach to follow in mate selection. (In making this point, Ben Young and Samuel Adams provide a humorous list of "Top Ten 'Biblical Ways' to Find a Mate," starting with: "10. Find a prostitute and marry her" [Hosea 1:1-3].)[25]

The Bible provides a definitive explanation of what constitutes marriage. But it prescribes no system for choosing the person one marries. Rather than telling us what process to follow, the prophets and apostles gave instructions on how God's people should act as they applied the societal norms of the cultures they lived in. In the Old Testament, God's prophets set moral boundaries that restricted the potential for abuse by those who exercised power, while providing protections for the welfare and dignity of those in subjection. And in the New Testament, the apostles spelled out the ways in which righteousness and grace should affect the behaviors and characters of those who seek to please God in every arena of life.[26]

In the absence, then, of specific instructions on mate selection, the decision making involved in acquiring a spouse falls into the category of non-commanded decisions that entail personal freedom and responsibility. This situation corresponds to the choices of singleness and marriage as described in 1 Corinthians 7. Whatever approach you take must be consonant with the moral will of God and with wisdom.

"So if there is no biblically prescribed method for mate selection, what should I do?" you ask. R. Paul Stevens provides the answer: "In reality there are only two ways to get married: have an arranged marriage (someone else does the arranging) or arrange one yourself."[27] You must take the responsibility to develop a wisdom-shaped plan to guide your search for a mate. (I will try to help you. That's why there's one more chapter in this book.)

Imagining Courtship

Before you identify the specific elements of your plan, you need to determine the courting paradigm you intend to follow. But rather than attempting to choose between a dating model, a courtship model, or a betrothal model,[28] I believe it is preferable to incorporate key elements of all three approaches in an appropriate sequence.

The appropriate sequence is well-illustrated in the picture of crossing the bridge suggested by Doug Rosenau and Michael Todd Wilson. (We encountered this analogy in chapter 12 in the context of developing a strategy for managing single sexuality.) In their scenario, the mating journey involves movement through three stages: Connecting, Coupling, and Covenanting.

The Relationship Continuum Bridge

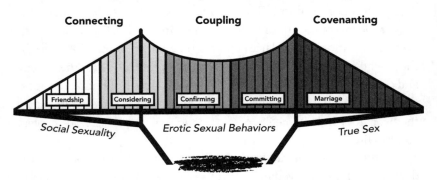

Copyright 2006 by Doug Rosenau and MIchael Todd Wilson. Used by permission.

The journey begins with the development of *connecting* relationships, which include friendships and casual dating. The focus at this juncture is on building skills for interactions with opposite-sex friends. At the other end of the continuum is *covenanting* or marriage. This is where an exclusive relationship with a single mate is formalized and lived out in one-flesh union. Bridging the initial and culminating stages is the intermediate *coupling* phase where a man and woman interact as an exclusive (yet unmarried) couple.

"Crossing the bridge" entails moving through three subphases: Considering, Confirming, and Committing.

- *Considering.* This stage begins when the woman and man agree to date exclusively. Now the process of evaluating the other as a potential life partner begins in earnest.

- *Confirming.* This is sometimes described as the stage when the couple is "engaged to be engaged." During this period, the couple explores any and all issues that may affect a future marriage.

This is most effectively accomplished through pre-engagement counseling.

- *Committing.* This is formal engagement. The intention to marry is publicly announced and plans are set in motion for a wedding.

It is not difficult to correlate the phases of this model with the functions of dating, courtship, and betrothal. In reverse order, betrothal is synonymous with engagement (*commitment*).[29] Courtship corresponds to the entire process of crossing the bridge (*coupling*), but most especially *considering* and *confirming*. Dating is distinctive in that it both precedes and initiates the journey (*connecting*). But it also plays a major role as one of the means by which *coupling* is advanced; and it enhances the marriage relationship on the other side of the wedding.

If we superimpose, then, the concepts of dating, courtship, and betrothal onto the steps involved in crossing the bridge, we see the following equivalencies:

- *Connecting* = casual dating

- *Coupling* =

    —*Considering*: dating/courtship

    —*Confirming*: dating/courtship

    —*Committing*: dating/betrothal

- *Covenanting* = dating/marriage

The Role of Dating

The adoption of this framework for courting presumes that it is not necessary to completely reject dating. I agree with Drs. Cloud and Townsend that there is such a thing as healthy dating that most couples can employ as they approach and cross the bridge.

In my advocacy of dating, I am assuming an encounter that is not sinful by definition. I think we will be on safe ground if we start with the broad definition extracted from the dictionary by Jeramy and Jerusha Clark: "a prearranged social engagement; a time set aside beforehand, social in nature."[30] In our culture, some purposeful, social, personal interaction appears to be required in order for a man and woman to explore and cultivate the kind of relationship that could develop into a courtship.

In evaluating the relative merits and liabilities of dating, we start with the moral will of God. Does the Bible command dating? No. Does the Bible forbid dating? No. Does the Bible say anything about dating? Not directly. There were no social categories in biblical culture that correspond precisely to the contemporary practice of dating. So once again we are talking about issues that lie within the area of freedom and responsibility.

However, that does not mean that the moral will of God has no bearing at all on dating. For Scripture has a lot to say about how men and women (even unmarried men and women) ought to relate to each other. This includes the Great Commandment, all of the "one another" passages, as well as the texts that address moral concerns. (We surveyed much of that content in the chapters on God's design for sexuality.) So while dating is a neutral activity as far as the Bible is concerned, those who practice it should do so wisely and Christianly.

The apostle Paul told the Corinthians that one way to evaluate the appropriateness of a morally neutral activity is to ask: "Is it beneficial? Is it constructive?" (1 Corinthians 6:12; 10:23). It is precisely in those terms that Cloud and Townsend make their case for healthy dating:

1. Dating gives people the opportunity to learn about themselves, others, and relationships in a safe context.

2. Dating provides a context to work through issues.

3. Dating helps build relationship skills.

4. Dating can heal and repair. (A date is not the proper venue for therapy, but a positive dating experience is good for the soul.)

5. Dating is relational and has value in and of itself.

6. Dating lets someone learn what he or she likes in the opposite sex.

7. Dating gives a context to learn sexual self-control and other delay of gratification.[31]

Dating in isolation from other forms of social interaction will not provide sufficient experience to get to know another person in-depth. But constructive and enjoyable dates can contribute a lot to the participants as well as to their relationship. As a couple proceeds to cross the bridge, their experience of dating will reflect their growing relationship and provide a context for increasing intimacy with integrity.

With your profile of a keeper in hand, and a functional framework for courtship in place, you are now in a position to consider the specific elements in your plan to look for a mate.

❖ ❖ ❖

Questions for Reflection and Group Discussion

1. What was the most significant insight you gained from reading this chapter?

2. Was the narrative on the history of courtship helpful to you? How so?

3. How would you describe the culture of dating in your setting? Do you find it easy or difficult to engage in dating? Why?

4. What is your assessment of Joshua Harris's critique of dating as he encountered it (see endnote 18)? Have you had any experiences that might confirm or challenge one or more of his assertions? Which suggested correctives do you think should be implemented by Christian singles?

5. If one adopts Rosenau and Wilson's analogy of crossing the bridge, what is the role of dating in each stage of courtship?

6. What is your assessment of Cloud and Townsend's case for healthy dating? Have you had any experiences that might confirm or challenge one or more of their assertions? Can you think of anything, positive or negative, they might have overlooked?

For additional questions, go to www.TheMarriageDecision.com.

18

Courtship: Devising the Plan

❧◆❧

I n *Get the Ring,* Sherry Zimmerman says, "Spouse hunting is very much like job hunting."

Rosie and I suggest that our audiences approach the search for a dating partner—the kind of partner with whom they would like to develop a good relationship that can lead to marriage—the same way they would approach the search for a job.

Let's say that my company was just taken over and my whole department was given pink slips. In two weeks I have to pack up my desk and move out to greener pastures. Will there be a greener pasture for me to go to? Not unless I make a major effort to find it. And so what do I do? I perfect my resume, I add information that is relevant to how my career has developed, and the kind of person I have become over the past few years. I polish my shoes, I make sure my suits look good, get a haircut.

I network with everyone I know to let them understand what has happened and ask them if they can refer me to a firm or an individual who might be interested in hiring someone with my qualifications. I scan the want ads and I register with headhunters. I research background information about possible employers, and I even practice how I am going to behave on a job interview. I try to be realistic. I know that I am not going to be hired on the first look-see. And I expect that if things are promising, I'll be called back a couple of times before the firm will make a decision. Nevertheless, even at the beginning, I try to make my best impression. I want to make my best effort to find the best possible job—one that has a good future so that I can support myself and maintain my sense of self-worth.[1]

Is that good counsel? Consider this wisdom from Proverbs 21:5 (NLT): "Good planning and hard work lead to prosperity, but hasty short-cuts lead to poverty." When it comes to marital decision making, I think that many people want the process to be easy, and they want the outcome to be good. But that's not how life works. "Prosperity" is more often the product of "good planning and hard work."

I ought to know. I had a ringside seat for a classic case in point.

On July 31, 1970, Louise Bachman wrote a reminder to herself in her journal: "Make a point to marry Robin Maxson." On November 10, 1973, she put a check mark next to that item on her to-do list. During the intervening months, she devised and executed the plan through which, ultimately, she attained her desired outcome. (Some aspects of her strategy and the way it unfolded are narrated in chapter 15.) When we married, I had no inkling that I would ever write a book like this. But it is certainly convenient that my own wife is one of the best illustrations of its principles. I can espouse the virtues of the divine design, in part, because I am the beneficiary of someone who has put them into practice.

I do not mean to imply, of course, that those who create and implement an effective plan are assured of achieving their desires. As we saw in chapter 2, the ultimate determiner of such outcomes is the sovereign will of God. But I think there is good reason to believe that Louise's marital hopes would not have come about apart from her creative initiative to encourage that outcome. If you want to find a mate, you should have a profile and you should develop a plan.

This chapter does not contain such a plan.

The circumstances of the readers of this book are too diverse to attempt a one-size-fits-all program. Some readers are in a relationship; others are at square one; others have been through a relationship and are back at square one. Even the narration of Louise's experience joins the story at the point where she found someone who matched her profile. She had taken other steps prior to that point to be in a position to assess potential candidates. But I can't know where *you* are in relationship to the bridge you want to cross.

What I intend to do is identify some of the tasks that you will need to include in your plan and make some suggestions about how to approach them.

Prerequisites for Crossing the Bridge

But first, you need to stop and assess whether you are ready to consider venturing across the bridge. For before you begin to seriously look for a mate, you need to become ready for marriage. The person who is prepared to take initiative in finding a mate should meet the following conditions (which have already been elaborated elsewhere in this book):

- You are a grown-up and growing adult.
- You are emotionally healthy.
- You have a life (you don't *need* to get married to be OK).
- You understand God's design for marriage and are committed to it.
- You know yourself well.
- You have established boundaries of moral behavior.
- You have constructed your profile of a keeper.
- You are pursuing godly character.
- You have good friends.

If any of these characteristics are not in place, you need to focus your energies on self-preparation rather than looking for Mr. or Ms. Right.

The Tasks of Courtship

Whatever systems of courting existed in the past, the reason they were followed is that they guided the participants in accomplishing the discrete elements required to get a man and woman married. The advantage of living in a time and culture where those processes were clearly spelled out and widely understood is that everyone knew what they were doing. The advantage of living in a time and culture where the procedures are in a state of flux is that men and women can create a plan that will work for them. In our setting, it is not the protocols that matter; it's the effectiveness of the measures taken to accomplish the intermediate objectives en route to the destination. In a context of freedom, there's plenty of room for creativity. What's required is the willingness to take personal responsibility for developing, implementing, and communicating the plan to whoever else may be involved.

What Christian women have to decide is how much initiative they are willing to take in exploring a relationship with a man. In my view, there are two ways to think about this. On the one hand, there is plenty of precedent for women setting the courtship process in motion. One biblical illustration is Ruth. And the whole system of calling in vogue at the turn of the nineteenth century gave control of the proceedings to women.

On the other hand, some women may be looking for a man who will show his willingness to lead in a relationship by taking the initiative. Such a woman is hardly without recourse in influencing a man in the direction he ought to go. (Just go back and read the story of why I am married.) Many men would eagerly respond to signals of interest on the part of enterprising women. But if "subtle" isn't working, you could always walk up to the guy and say, "If you ask me out for coffee, I would be glad to go." (That's coffee, not sex.)

Here are the tasks of courtship that I have identified.[2]

Task 1

You need ways to meet prospective mates.

If you attend a large church, are a student in a Christian college, or are involved in a campus ministry at a secular university, this may not be a huge problem for you. You may have an adequate pool of prospects available. This can be more challenging for that large segment of single adults who are out of school and pursuing a career or other life interests. Whatever the reasons, if your pool of contacts is too limited, you will have to do something to expand it.

Dating coach Henry Cloud offers this profound grasp of the obvious: *"People who meet people go where people are"* (italics his). Then, to be practical, he offers this list of places where singles have met their future spouse:[3]

1. Visit churches.

2. Talk to your friends (close and extended) about setting you up. (This is the most common means by which single people meet future spouses.)

3. Attend events sponsored by organizations.

4. Go to parties of all types.

5. Join organizations and activities related to your interests.

6. Check the newspaper and web. Most papers have postings of local activities.

7. Throw some parties.

8. Start something up. As an example, Cloud tells of a group of women who hosted a monthly event called SWARM (Single Women Actively Recruiting Men).

9. Seek out and attend cultural events.

10. Visit singles' vacation and recreational spots.

11. Exercise where singles are.

12. Take a class.

13. Join your coworkers when they go out.

My niece is one of the many Christian singles who have found the person they eventually married through an online dating or matching service. This doesn't work for everyone, but there is no reason not to investigate the possibilities that this modern-day phenomenon might open up. The first rule to practice in such exploration is safety. Find out the precautions that the service has established and go through the proper channels. Be cautious about giving out personal information, and conduct the first meetings in public places. The second rule is to be persistent. Most people don't find their keeper on the first match. It may take quantity to get quality.[4]

Task 2

You need ways to acquire the social skills necessary for relationship building.

Most of the required social skills are naturally developed in routine interactions with people at school, work, and church. We become more or less adept at communicating and connecting with people as we form friendships. Dating requires different nuances, however, that are best learned in the specific context and experience of dating. This may be the best reason for casual dating—just learning how to do it. If you actually were to cross paths with Mr. or Ms. Right, but you lacked the skills to express yourself and to actively engage with the other person's self-disclosures, you would miss the opportunity presented. So the message here is, practice, practice, practice.

Henry Cloud offers sage advice to singles who are at the front end of the connecting stage. One of his maxims is, "Dating is not about marriage." Those who submit to his tutelage must take the following pledge:

> I will date as an end in and of itself. I will no longer see dating as a place only to find a mate, but as a place to learn, grow, experience, and serve other people. It is my new laboratory of learning, growth, and experience.

The corollary to his understanding of dating is this follow-up advice: Go out with almost anyone once, and maybe again. At the beginning, the requirements one has for a date should not be as stringent as the specifications one has established for a mate. The main reason is simple: you can't know whether a date has a potential mate's qualities until you get to know that person. So on your first date(s), leave the profile at home. Just have fun![5]

This is one area where coaching, whether written, video, or personal, can be helpful. Dr. Cloud's book, *How to Get a Date Worth Keeping,* is remarkably practical and comprehensive.[6] Much of the content in that book is also available in brief video clips on the website of Drs. Cloud and Townsend (www.cloudtownsend.com).

For personal advice, you will need to recruit one or more mentors. Talking with experienced friends who will candidly share their insights could help you identify blind spots. Perhaps the best approach would be to find a friend who would be willing to read through Dr. Cloud's book with you and help you develop strategies for expanding your social skills and experiences.

Task 3

You need ways to get to know another person very well.

John Van Epp coined a term to describe this task: the "know-quo," or the quotient for knowing someone. He helpfully summarizes the component parts in a mathematical formula: $I = T + T + T$. Intimacy equals Talk (mutual self-disclosure) plus Togetherness (diversified experiences) plus Time. "A balance is necessary between what you know about a person from talking and what you learn from your experiences in a new relationship…Therefore, to truly know another person, you must engage in a deepening openness that is matched with a variety of experiences in which you see the other person 'in action.'"[7]

Consumer Alert: I am about to offer dating advice. In the interest of full disclosure, you should know (if you haven't already figured it out) that my experiential qualifications for this exercise are nil. I have been married for over thirty-five years, and I have pretty much given up dating my wife to write this book. So I'm out of practice.[8] Ordinarily, I would heed the proverb, "Fools rush in where angels fear to tread." But in my analysis of the current dating scene, I've come up with some ideas that, if I were single and searching, I would implement myself. As it turns out, someone else will have to field-test them.

Maxson's Maxims

My *first idea* has to do with actually making a date. I've heard that for some people, this comes easily. But a lot of singles are stuck in the starting gate. If you're one of them, here's my suggestion: *recruit a broker.* Ask someone you trust to act as your representative in communicating your invitation to a prospective date.[9] The involvement of a go-between should reduce the emotional risk of rejection on both ends of the inquiry, which is the threat that immobilizes many would-be daters. People use this approach in many avenues of life,[10] and some cultures employ the services of matchmakers. A date-maker would belong to that same genre of broker—just several notches down on the commitment meter.

My *second idea* is to establish and practice two categories of dating: *social* dates and *service* dates. These categories correspond to the two functions of marriage: relational companionship and vocational partnership.

The dominant pattern for contemporary dating is clearly social. Typical dates seek to create shared experiences of entertainment or recreation that offer the opportunity for advancing the relationship.

Such encounters are clearly appropriate and necessary for conversational interchange. If the chemistry is positive, romance may ensue. But this sort of interaction addresses only half of the marital equation and is insufficient to produce the degree of self-disclosure required for in-depth knowledge of another person.

The other dimension to be explored is suitability for partnership in mission. And this aspect can be addressed by *service* dates. Before we began going out, Louise and I worked together on a worship team. Then we were fellow staff members for a junior high snow retreat. In a variety of ways, we were able to observe one another and participate together in work and ministry situations. (The same was true, you may recall, for Ruth and Boaz.) I propose that men and women issue invitations for joint participation in service or ministry projects. Work together with a youth group, help out in the church nursery, volunteer for a community-service event, go on a short-term mission trip.

To take this idea a step further, I recommend that you give a priority to service dates over social dates for three reasons. First, you may find that an invitation to share in a ministry project is less threatening and easier to accept. Second, service dates provide a better setting for demonstrating and evaluating the more significant components of your profile—*character* and *commitment* (but also *comparability* and *complementarity*). And third, starting out with service-related interactions follows the sequence in the arranged marriage where a couple launches the vocational partnership first and grows the relational companionship over time.

The *third idea* is related to the second: whether a given date is social or service-oriented, approach it (and your date) with a *ministry mindset*. If I could paraphrase Jesus and his Sermon on the Mount: "You shall not be like the pagans who go on dates mainly to impress the other person and evaluate their suitability to meet their needs. Instead, seek to advance God's rule and righteousness in the life of your date, and these other things will be properly ordered in your relationship." Think of your date as a Christian and treat them accordingly, applying the "one another" commands to your relationship. Should you someday marry, you will be well practiced in one of the central purposes of your union. Also, you will probably be more relaxed and have more fun.

Whether you choose to follow Maxson's Maxims or not, you must find ways to enter into the other person's world—work, family, friends, recreation, service, and worship—in order to truly know (and be known by) him or her. You will learn a great deal about a person when you observe their interactions with their parents and siblings, as well as their friends. You need to see if you integrate comfortably into that world (and they into yours), because if you get married, those people will become part of your life. Furthermore, the way your prospect interacts with family members (especially the parent and siblings of the opposite gender) will give you a pretty good picture of how you can expect them to relate to you in your marriage. And their choice of friends will reveal a lot about their character.

In other words, you don't just court the individual; you must also court that person's family and friends.

Shared experiences, however they come about, are prime means of self-revelation and other-discovery. Within these shared experiences are two areas of behavior to pay special attention to: the situational and the relational. The *situational behavior* has to do with how the other person acts in various situations. One of your biggest questions should be, how does he react to crises? How does she respond to challenges? The *relational behavior* has to do with how the other person treats you in those shared experiences. Relational behavior during courtship is predictive of the dynamics you will experience in marriage. That's why it is so important to give the process plenty of time. The two-year rule isn't chiseled in stone, but it provides a benchmark that you should pay attention to. You need to be together with the other person long enough to get a realistic feel for how it's going to be over the long haul.[11]

If it looks like the relationship has the potential to culminate in marriage, pre-engagement counseling will provide an avenue for surfacing any background, emotional, or relational issues that need to be addressed. It should also provide a format for identifying relational skills that need to be learned as well as a guided opportunity to practice and grow in those abilities.

Task 4

You need strategies and structures to address and mitigate the judgment-impairing effects of romantic attachment.

One of the ways we have for distinguishing between the three dominant systems for mating is by locating the point on the continuum where the couple falls in love. In the traditional *dating* pattern, falling in love is the object—it happens before the couple begins a serious consideration of marriage. In fact, it is the reason why they begin to explore marriage. In the *courtship* paradigm, the prospect of marriage is broached toward the beginning of the process and romance is postponed until the couple is out in the middle of the bridge. One of the major objectives of the *betrothal* arrangement is to stave off romance as long as possible—until the period just before the wedding or, following the biblical pattern, after it. Proponents of courtship and betrothal are very aware of the twitterpating effects of romance on sound judgment, so they seek a structure that delays that influence on the decision-making process as long as possible.

The only thing wrong with those strategies is that the timing of Cupid's assault is often very inconvenient. The resultant inflammation of the heart is notoriously difficult to schedule. But while love's euphoria is very powerful, one's mind and will are not rendered helpless. And one of the ways to maintain sanity while under the influence is by taking preemptive steps before the arrow strikes.

Steps to Preempt Cupid's Assault

The first step is simply being aware of the potential problem. The number of people who are utterly convinced they are the first ones to have truly fallen in love is astounding. "Never has there been a love like this," they coo. Hello! This is the dominant theme of human literature, poetry, music, and drama. We've been down this road before, and we know what happens. Literally.

> Through brain-imaging studies, researchers at University College London found that "feelings of love lead to a suppression of activity in the areas of the brain controlling critical thought. It seems that once we get close to a person, the brain decides the need to assess their character and personality is reduced"…In addition, massive releases of oxytocin, dopamine, and other hormones and neuropeptides in the brain create euphoric feelings that further cloud analytic judgments.[12]

If you have read this far in this book and remain unconvinced of this point, there is nothing further I can do.

Second, while the feelings of attraction may be unruly, something can be done to manage the *expression* and *intensification* of those feelings. This involves setting boundaries at the beginning of a relationship about how affection is going to be expressed and phased in over the course of the relationship (see chapter 12).

The third step is to call in the cavalry. One of the biggest flaws in the romance-based dating system is the way that relationships are carried out and decisions are made in isolation from an engaged community. (Conversely, community involvement was one of the strengths of the arranged marriage.) Even though marital decisions lie in the area of freedom and responsibility, wisdom compels us to consult with counselors. So here is the suggested corrective: recruit a team of people you can trust to oversee your courtship.

> The team you assemble depends on what you need. It could be a therapist, a small group, recovery group, prayer partners, accountability partners, a therapy group, a mentor, or wise friends. There is no hard and fast rule. The only rule is that you must make yourself vulnerable to them, submit to them, put it all out there for them to see, and consider the wisdom, feedback, challenges, and correction they offer you.[13]

Do people actually do this? Marva Dawn and her fiancé, Myron, did. Here is her description of their process:

> When my dear friend of seven years proposed, we decided to spend two weeks gathering the input of the Christian community before we made a final decision. What a wonderful process that was! We asked many people—single and married, those who might be opposed to the idea, even someone who was also dating me who had jokingly insisted that if Myron ever proposed he wanted to have a chance to make a counter proposal! How helpful it was to us—as we contemplated such issues as my many physical handicaps, our differences in education, our age, and our diversities of interests—to know that our friends and colleagues in the Church were praying with us and for us. We asked them to give us specific advice and to ask us questions that would help us to think more clearly.[14]

As you consult counselors, do not overlook the potential benefit of giving your parents a prominent role, if that is possible, as members of that supervising team. It was ancient and enduring wisdom that, in previous eras, gave the assignment of mate selection to them. Even if the systems of parent-directed courtship and betrothal are not biblically mandated, one should not ignore the sensibleness of paying heed to the counsel of those who know us best and truly have our best interests at heart.

There is a fourth thing you can do to constructively channel the power of passion. But that step is part of a broader task that is comprehensive enough to warrant its own task number.

Task 5

You need to learn how to balance and manage agapé, philos, and eros.

When a couple comes to see me for premarital counseling and I ask them why they want to get married, their first answer is often, "Because we love each other." From a biblical perspective, that is not a bad place to start. For the New Testament is clear that husbands are to love their wives (Ephesians 5:25,33), and wives are to love their husbands (Titus 2:4).

But as the ancient Greeks perceptively discerned, love is multidimensional. So they had a distinctive word for each nuance. *Eros,* a word not found in the biblical text (probably because of its self-serving connotation), stands behind the notion for *erotic passion* (which we just discussed in Task 4). *Philos* is the term that most closely corresponds to the mutual affection expressed and enjoyed in friendship (Titus 2:4). The apostles co-opted the word *agapé* to describe sacrificial, self-giving love bestowed with no thought of a return from the other (Ephesians 5:25,33).

It is too simplistic to slice-and-dice these notions of love to say that *agapé* impels our partnership, *philos* warms our companionship, and *eros* drives the lovemaking that results in procreation. But it is hard to dismiss the triadic correspondence. And it is clear that a good marriage is enriched by all three shades of love as they become interwoven in the fabric of life. One of the tasks of courtship is to cultivate the integration of all three aspects of love in a way that strengthens the relationship and prepares for marriage.

In my warnings about the intoxicating effects of passion, I may have inadvertently conveyed a disparaging view of romance. Lauren Winner restores an appreciative perspective by pointing out that "the exhilarating experience we call falling in love, can actually teach us something about loving our neighbor." Then she cites theologian Diogenes Allen:

> When falling in love, we seem to float on air. The whole world seems wonderful, and we take in stride people who normally irritate us and the things that normally frustrate us...A particular person's idiosyncrasies, which normally rub us the wrong way, no longer affect us adversely. For a while, we simply seem to be able to love anyone—to love our neighbor—without any effort at all. These momentary occasions can...give us a glimpse of what it would be like to love our neighbor all the time.[15]

Having said that, *agapé* protects the loved one from the abuses of unfettered *eros* during courtship and superintends its expression during marriage. *Agapé* guards the heart and allows *philos* to grow into a devoted companionship that will sustain a marriage for a lifetime.

And so, even as a couple grows in the deepening of their friendship and delights in the measured enjoyment of burgeoning romance, each must give due diligence to cultivating the undergirding *agapé* that will sustain the commitment of the covenant. This quality of selflessness cannot be produced by sheer determination or effort. It is a fruit of the Spirit. And so the highest form of devotion that one person can show another is to pursue the higher love that enables such love. One's growing relationship with God will be the most important aspect of a courtship that results in a godly and fulfilling marriage.

Task 6

You need to keep the "find a mate" project in proper perspective and balance with the rest of your life.

Two biblical passages in particular sound a cautionary note against allowing this quest to take over your life. The permission to take initiative in looking for a mate comes from 1 Corinthians 7:21: "Were you called as a slave? Do not worry about it. But if indeed you are able to be free, make the most of the opportunity." By analogy, unmarried believers who desire a mate are free to "make the most of the opportunity" to find one. But the main thrust of Paul's argument in the immediate context (7:17-24) is the thrice-repeated admonition: "Remain as you are." Don't be overeager to change your status in life, he said. Do not fail to maximize the benefits of your current gift of singleness

The reader is reminded here of our extended discussion in chapter 9 of the ramifications of this passage. The middle ground between a resigned passivity and self-reliant orchestration of events is a "contented initiative" or "relaxed engagement" that determines and carries out a course of action while resting and relying on the sovereign will of God.

The second passage is that statement by Jesus intended to direct disciples in their choice of life-governing priorities: "But above all pursue [God's] kingdom and righteousness, and all these things [food, drink, clothing] will be given to you as well" (Matthew 6:33). The reign of God in his life and world, and the right relationship and conduct that ensues, is to be the foremost ambition of the disciple. All other pursuits are to have a subordinate status in the ordering of one's life. An important implication of the words "above all" is that one may have secondary goals that are perfectly legitimate. But they must contribute to the governing priority and not usurp it.

It may be that looking for a spouse resembles the search for happiness. When pursued for its own sake, happiness proves elusive and illusory. Our greatest experiences of happiness come to us as a by-product of something else—holy, love-giving living. It is not usually the person who is fixated on finding a mate who gets one. Rather the individual who focuses on being God's person in relationships is often the one who ends up getting married.

Task 7

You need to get your person of interest on board with your approach so that you are traveling together.

One way to do this is to ask him or her to read a copy of this book and then discuss how the principles and insights are going to shape the conduct of your relationship.

Seven Tasks of a Highly Effective Plan

- *Task 1:* You need ways to meet prospective mates.

- *Task 2:* You need ways to acquire the social skills necessary for relationship building.

- *Task 3:* You need ways to get to know another person very well.

- *Task 4:* You need strategies and structures to address and mitigate the judgment-impairing effects of romantic attachment.

- *Task 5:* You need to learn how to balance and manage *agapé, philos,* and *eros.*

- *Task 6:* You need to keep the "find a mate" project in proper perspective and balance with the rest of your life.

- *Task 7:* You need to get your person of interest on board with your approach so that you are traveling together.

❖ ❖ ❖

Recommended Reading

How to Get a Date Worth Keeping by Henry Cloud (Zondervan).

❖ ❖ ❖

Questions for Reflection and
Group Discussion

1. What was the most significant insight you gained from reading this chapter?

2. Do you know of anyone who attempted to cross the bridge before they had met the stated prerequisites? How did that turn out? How do you account for the outcome?

3. Have you considered signing up for eHarmony.com? Do you know of anyone who has used an online dating or matching service? How did it work out for them?

4. What are the merits of Maxson's Maxims? Have you seen any of these ideas implemented? What happened? Do you see any problems with his suggestions? What are your best ideas for getting to know another person well?

5. Were you aware of the distinctive connotations of *agapé*, *philos*, and *eros*? What contribution would each make to a healthy marriage? Why would it be important to manage and balance these three expressions of love during courtship?

6. The author lists seven tasks that need to be addressed in a courtship plan. Can you think of any more? How will you address each of the tasks you have identified? Write down the specific components of your plan for looking for a mate. Share your ideas with your study group or a trusted friend. Get their feedback.

For additional questions go to www.TheMarriageDecision.com.

Afterword

In a book this long, you could easily lose sight of the forest for all the trees. Of all the things we have said, what is most important?

At the outset, I declared that the purpose of this book is to equip unmarried Christians to make wise marital choices according to the will of God. In the pursuit of this objective, you need to remain clear about three things: 1) the *framework* for marital decision making, 2) the *requirements* for making wise choices, and 3) the proper *attitude* for this pursuit.

Framework

Christians should carry out marital decision making within the larger context of their allegiance to the kingdom of God. As important as it is, your marital status is not the main thing about your life. As a child of God and a disciple of Jesus, the choices you make about singleness and marriage should be viewed in terms of your stewardship of a life-on-loan. As long as you view your marital status as part of the avenue along which you walk with God, and by which you serve him, you will be moving in the right direction.

Requirements

To make wise marital decisions according to the will of God, you should do five things:

1. You need to pray *for* wisdom and *about* your desires.

2. You need to understand and commit to God's design.

3. You need to grow up and become a healthy, maturing adult.

4. You need to make relational choices that are moral and wise.

5. If you find a suitable prospect for marriage, you need to prepare well together.

There's also one advisable option: if you want to get married, create a profile and devise a plan.

Attitude

I close with this disclaimer: following the principles and counsel in this book does not guarantee any specific outcome. You can do everything in your power to apply the moral will of God and wisdom and still end up with a result that falls short of what you hoped for. Sometimes our fallenness, or the circumstances we have no control over, overwhelm our best intentions.

That said, I am convinced that applying the principles in this book will provide the best chance of fulfilling God's design for your life whether you remain single or marry. The thing to remember is that your decision making is not the only factor in the outcome of your choices. The ultimate determiner of the course your life takes is God's sovereign will. And because God is good, his plans for you are good.

So the appropriate attitude for marital decision making is *trust*. Trust in the goodness of God's character, the wisdom of his timing, and the sufficiency of his power should give you confidence that your plans and efforts will lead to an outcome that brings benefit to you and glory to God. For as you devise and implement your plan, you can count on God to bring about his purposes in, through, around, and beyond it.

The believer's point of contact with God's sovereign will is prayer. Recall the advice of counselor Larry Crabb: "Pray for your desires; work for your goals." It should be your goal to live in a way that honors God whether through singleness or marriage. It should be your goal to "become the profile." But what is your desire? A godly mate? Your heavenly Father is eager to hear what is on your heart.

Do not be anxious about anything. Instead, in every situation, through prayer and petition with thanksgiving, tell your requests to God. And the peace of God that surpasses all understanding will guard your hearts and minds in Christ Jesus (Philippians 4:6-7).

I close this book with the prayer that you will find great blessing in God's personalized provisions for your life.

Soli Deo Gloria!

Appendix
Divorce, Remarriage, and the Moral Will of God

⁂

As of this writing, over 27 percent of the adults who are single in our country are divorced. So for a substantial segment of our target audience, one issue of burning interest remains that I have not addressed in this book: What is God's moral will regarding divorce and remarriage? Does God permit divorced believers to marry again? And if so, under what conditions?

Those who have explored the biblical passages that address these questions know that this is a complex subject. Capable Christian scholars giving diligent study to this matter have come to differing conclusions. And it is beyond the scope of this book to provide a thorough and definitive answer to these questions. In the end, each believer is responsible to come to informed convictions on this matter (Romans 14:5), and each church must determine how divorce and remarriage are going to be administered within the accountability structures of their fellowship.

Garry Friesen is an elder at Imago Dei Community, an evangelical fellowship of faith in Portland, Oregon. A few years ago, Dr. Friesen and his fellow elders undertook careful study of the Scriptures on divorce and remarriage, and he took the lead in drafting documents that summarized their conclusions. The first, a statement of position, sets out their collective understanding of what the Bible teaches. The second describes the policies by which church leaders seek to implement those positions in the life of the church. Because these statements closely reflect our shared conclusions on this challenging subject, we have decided to append them to this book. We hope they will serve as a helpful starting point for those who need to determine their personal convictions on these issues.

(The following statements of position and policy are published with the permission of the elders of Imago Dei Community. Because they have not read this book, the inclusion of these statements as an appendix does not constitute an endorsement of the preceding pages by the elders or the Imago Dei Community. These statements should be read as stand-alone documents addressing only divorce and remarriage and no other aspects of this book's content.)

Divorce and Remarriage

Imago Dei Community
Portland, Oregon
July 16, 2008

Position

I mago Dei Community seeks God's help to build strong marriages and families. Marriage is God's gift for believers and unbelievers (Genesis 2:24) but in a broken world, marriages will fail, and we must be ready to respond with grace and truth.

Marriage is a God-ordained, public covenant between a man and a woman that results in a "one flesh" relationship (Genesis 2:24; Proverbs 2:16-17; Ezekiel 16:8; Malachi 2:14). God's design is that every marriage be faithfully permanent. God loves covenant keeping, and His strength is sufficient to enable husband and wife to be faithful. His redeeming grace gives us hope that even the most broken marriage can be restored.

Our position allows divorce and remarriage for either of two valid causes: sexual immorality (Matthew 5:31-32; 19:9)[1] or desertion by an unbelieving spouse (1 Corinthians 7:15). This has been called the Erasmian view, the traditional Protestant view, and is the most common view among evangelicals. Divorce and remarriage is a debatable issue and we respect believers who differ with us.

The Mosaic Law brought the death penalty for certain sexual sins, including adultery, incest, homosexual behavior, and bestiality. Capital punishment showed the seriousness of sexual sin and allowed the innocent surviving spouse to remarry. God hates divorce (Malachi 2:16), but He allowed it because of the hardness of people's hearts (Deuteronomy 24:1-4; Matthew 19:8).

Jesus said, "whoever divorces his wife, except for sexual immorality, and marries another, commits adultery" (Matthew 19:9 ESV; see also 5:32). The exception clause ("except for sexual immorality") refers to adultery and probably covers all the cases of sexual sin that deserved capital punishment in the Old Testament. Matthew records Christ's most detailed teaching on divorce and remarriage (Matthew 5:27-32; 19:3-12). Mark 10:2-12 and Luke 16:18 do not include the exception clause because they are a summary of Christ's teaching.

The New Testament allows, but does not require, divorce for sexual unfaithfulness. God's grace encourages us to forgive and have hope that God's transforming power can redeem even the most broken marriage. However, when there has been sexual unfaithfulness, divorce and remarriage are allowed, and do not constitute adultery. The marriage bond includes a covenant and then uniting sexually in "one flesh" (Genesis 2:24). Biblically, a marriage is viewed as ending when one spouse dies (Romans 7:2). It also ends when two things occur: (1) the one flesh has been violated (sexual unfaithfulness), and (2) the legal covenant has been revoked (divorce); if only one of these two things has occurred, the marriage continues to exist.

If someone divorces without a valid cause, they are still married in God's sight. If one of them remarries, their new sexual union is adultery against their former spouse, and the first marriage is ended. Their union forms a new marriage. The new couple should repent of adultery, receive God's forgiveness, and seek to make their marriage faithfully permanent. The former spouse is now single and free to remarry (Matthew 19:3-12).

One further exception is the so-called "Pauline privilege" in 1 Corinthians 7:15 (the believer "is not under bondage in such cases" NASB). The "bound" condition is best understood as the marriage bond (1 Corinthians 7:39). In a marriage of believer and unbeliever, the believer should seek to preserve the marriage (1 Corinthians 7:13-14; 1 Peter 3:1-2). However, if the unbelieving spouse deserts, the believer, after patient prayer, may divorce and remarry.

There are many destructive behaviors that can threaten the safety of family members and jeopardize the health of a marriage. Even when sexual addiction does not include physical adultery, it is still a form of evil destructive lust (Matthew 5:27-28) and worthy of church discipline. Abuse of spouse or children cannot be tolerated. It is not, in itself, automatically grounds for divorce, but such abuse is so serious that it can result in church discipline and excommunication for the unrepentant abuser. Refusal to provide for one's family (1 Timothy 5:8) is a form of denying the faith and desertion. In these and other destructive situations we will: (1) seek to remove family members from physical danger, (2) follow required legal reporting, (3) confront the abuser, (4) provide a care team to nurture the couple, and (5) bring church discipline and excommunication when appropriate. When excommunication occurs, the case will be treated as desertion by an unbeliever (Matthew 18:17).

Unmarried sexual cohabitation is an expression of sexual sin that seeks intimacy without commitment. The couple should either separate or make a marriage covenant in harmony with Scripture and state law (Hebrews 13:4; Romans 13:1).

Qualifications for church leadership involve one's current lifestyle. No one is disqualified because they did not meet the requirements in the past. The "husband of one wife" qualification for elders and deacons (1 Timothy 3:2; 3:12 ESV) requires a person to have a reputation of living faithfully with their current spouse. The qualification is an idiom meaning a "one wife kind of man," not someone who has never been divorced or never remarried. For a single person this would require a reputation of sexual purity. Taking the phrase literally results in the unlikely view that it excludes single men like Paul, and those who have remarried for any cause.[2]

Church Policy

In harmony with our theological understanding, Imago Dei leadership will follow these guidelines:

> We will discourage and be unwilling to perform the wedding of a believer to an unbeliever (1 Corinthians 7:39; 2 Corinthians 6:14).

> We will encourage believers to give all effort to preserve their marriages with love, grace, and forgiveness. Sometimes temporary separation is appropriate, especially for protection of family members, but always with the goal of restoration.

> Our position allows divorce and remarriage only for the valid causes of sexual unfaithfulness or desertion by an unbelieving spouse. When

divorce occurs without valid cause, neither husband nor wife should remarry but should seek reconciliation.

We are willing to perform the wedding of a divorced person when there is clear evidence of either valid cause for divorce. The person performing such a wedding must have a clear conscience that the evidence is sufficient.

We will select elders, deacons, ministry leaders, and the main leader of a home community who have a reputation of faithfulness to their current spouse. When there has been divorce and remarriage, this fact alone will not disqualify someone. In such a case, extra caution will be taken to assure that the candidate has a history of being faithful to their current spouse.

A believer should seek reconciliation if they divorced as an unbeliever without valid cause and neither committed adultery or remarried. If their reconciliation effort is refused, their situation will be treated as the desertion of an unbeliever.

We welcome to membership all who have repented of past failures and wish to follow Christ through commitment to community.

Elders will seek God's wisdom and grace when dealing with cases that are not covered in this policy.

Unity

We welcome to Imago Dei those who differ with this position, but we ask that you do not allow your viewpoint to create division and that you speak in love about those who differ with you. Our differences will give us the opportunity to show unity and love within our diverse opinions.

For Further Study (the most helpful are listed first):

Andreas J. Kostenberger, *God, Marriage, and Family*, especially chapters 11-12.

John Stott, *Involvement: Social and Sexual Relationships in the Modern World*, vol. 2, chapter 6.

D.A. Carson, *Matthew, The Expositor's Bible Commentary,* vol. 8 (see Matthew 19).

John Murray, *Divorce,* especially chapter 2.

Craig L Blomberg, "Marriage, Divorce, Remarriage, and Celibacy." *Trinity Journal* 11 (1990): 161-96.

H. Wayne House, editor, *Divorce and Remarriage: Four Christian Views.*

Acknowledgments

In a project that spans seven years, the number of people who have made significant contributions is considerable. While fearful that a defective memory may have deleted some important contributors, I am eager to thank the following people for their substantial assistance.

- The boards and members of United Evangelical Free Church, Klamath Falls, Oregon, for your prayerful support and commitment to serving the larger Body of Christ through this project; and the college group of UEFC who sat through the first verbal presentation of this material with apparent interest and good humor, for your earnest encouragement and thought-provoking questions.

- The pastoral and administrative staff of United Evangelical Free Church—Rick Sonerholm, Sally Ritter, Doug Hallock, Aaron Knapp, John Kupitz, Charlene Rott, Nadine Ekstrom, and Pat Carpenter—for picking up the slack when I was away at class, away on writing assignment, or just mentally away. This wouldn't have happened without you.

- Dr. John Reed, director of the doctor of ministry program at Dallas Theological Seminary, for your enthusiastic permission to pursue an unconventional research project; and Dr. Jerry Wofford and Dr. Gary Barnes, faculty advisors, for your expertise and patience in shepherding my work through to an acceptable conclusion.

- Biblical scholars and researchers who pore over the documents in your offices and libraries and share your insights in theological journals and reference volumes—most of which are unnoticed by the public at large—for your immense contribution to the edification of the Body of Christ. We are in your debt.

- My research project proctors—Jon Bachman, Rebekah Crooks Horowitz, Karil Dodds Kottke, Todd Malone, Laurie McCoy, Palmer Muntz, Martin Schlomer, Katie Schnell, and Dan Sieker—who recruited and monitored readers across the country and around the world; and the thirty-five anonymous readers who worked through the original manuscript, for your effort and constructive feedback that greatly improved the final product.

- The Portland area "Eunuchs for Yeshua"—a multi-generational group of spiritually mature, unmarried Christians, who devoted time and energy to share insights with me and Garry on the realities of single life—for your practical wisdom, openness, and kindness.

- Pastors Clay Bynum, Steve Flecken, Kevin Drake, John Kays, Kevin Kroeker, David Loser, Ray Orndoff, Duane Pooley, Mark Pounds, Denny Roberts, and Don White—fellow shepherds of the flock in Klamath Falls who have met weekly for prayer, for your friendship and faithful intercession on behalf of me and this project.

- Jim and Marcy Kelly and Barney and Rhea Simonsen, for making available the cabin, the lake house, and the "prophet's chamber"—places of retreat where I contemplated deep thoughts and wrote profound sentences. Your generosity is appreciated.

- My agent of the year, Sandra Bishop, for exploring the options, giving wise counsel, and tending to details I know nothing about; and Chip MacGregor of MacGregor Literary Agency, for choosing to represent an obscure writer of nonfiction.

- Harvest House editor Rod Morris, for cheerleading this book and removing obstacles to comprehension. You are the readers' best friend.

- My daughter, Rachel Maxson, who challenged me to write this book, alerted me to resources that profoundly shaped its content, and served as a research assistant; and my son, Mike Evans-Maxson, who has been teaching this material in his life-skills class at Dakar Academy (Senegal, West Africa), for faithfully modeling the principles presented in this volume.

- My wife, Louise, whose commitment to and sacrifice for this book are appreciated by me, but truly known only by God and herself. Those who have benefited from this book have her to thank.

- The makers and distributors of Dr. Thunder soft drinks and San Francisco Bay coffee beans (French roast) for your contribution to my mental alertness. If you ever need a spokesperson for your products, I'm your man.

Endnotes

Introduction

1. David LeVine, *Get the Ring: How to Find and Keep the Right One for Life,* audio CD (Bradenton, FL: Warm Wisdom Press, 2003).

2. Stephanie Coontz, *Marriage, a History: From Obedience to Intimacy or How Love Conquered Marriage* (New York: Viking Penguin, 2005), 2.

3. Stephanie Coontz, *The Christian Science Monitor,* June 28, 2005, online: www.stephaniecoontz.com/articles/article19.htm, accessed 6 June 2009.

4. The approach of Orthodox Jews to courtship and marriage, which incorporates biblical principles, is narrated in the interviews contained in the audio series that Levine produced, *Get the Ring.* There is much helpful insight in these recordings. For more information, go to www.warmwisdompress.com.

5. To be precise, what he actually wrote was: "Pigmaei gigantum humeris impositi plusquam ipsi gigantes vident."

Introduction to Part 1: God's Design for Decision Making

1. In 2000, WaterBrook Press commissioned an opinion study conducted by Barna Research Group. In a nationwide sample, 1020 American adults were asked questions focused on their perceptions of finding God's will. The results were published in an appendix to Robert Jeffress's book, *Hearing the Master's Voice: The Comfort and Confidence of Knowing God's Will* (Colorado Springs, CO: WaterBrook Press, 2001). To each of seven statements, each participant was asked, "Do you agree or disagree; strongly or somewhat?" The third statement read: "You believe that if God intends a person to be married, God has only one specific marriage partner for them." Of those respondents identified as "evangelical," 52 percent agreed.

2. H. Norman Wright, *Finding the Right One for You* (Eugene, OR: Harvest House, 1995), 217-22. This book offers excellent guidance on marital mate selection. It is justly recognized as a classic.

3. Derek Prince and Ruth Prince, *God Is a Matchmaker* (Old Tappan, NJ: Chosen Books, 1986), 55-57. The conviction that Christians should let God determine their marital decisions is shared by Tim LaHaye, *Finding the Will of God in a Crazy Mixed-Up World* (Grand Rapids, MI: Zondervan Publishing House, 1989); and Elisabeth Elliot, *Passion and Purity: Learning to Bring Your Love Life under Christ's Control* (Grand Rapids, MI: Fleming H. Revell, 2002), among others.

4. Rick Stedman, *Your Single Treasure* (Chicago: Moody Press, 2000), 182-83.

5. Ben Young and Samuel Adams, *The One: A Realistic Guide to Choosing Your Soul Mate* (Nashville, TN: Thomas Nelson Publishers, 2001), 23. Other Christian writers who indicate that

marital decision making should be done by the persons involved include Stephen Arterburn and Margaret Josephson Rinck. *Avoiding Mr. Wrong (and What to Do If You Didn't): Ten Men Who Will Ruin Your Life* (Nashville, TN: Thomas Nelson Publishers, 2000); David Nicholson, *What You Need to Know before You Fall in Love* (Nashville, TN: Thomas Nelson Publishers, 1995); and Neil Clark Warren, *Finding the Love of Your Life: Ten Principles for Choosing the Right Marriage Partner* (New York: Pocket Books, 1992).

6. Fortunately, in the actual case, mature counselors eventually addressed the issues with Tom and Sandee, and they were persuaded to take a more deliberate and reasoned approach to their relationship.

7. Rachel wrote the Foreword to the revised and updated edition of *Decision Making and the Will of God* (Sisters, OR: Multnomah Publishers, 2004), 8-9.

8. Readers who find themselves challenged, if not convinced, by the content of Part 1 (chapters 1-2) are invited to read *Decision Making and the Will of God*, revised and updated edition. That is where the principles (and biblical support) for the Way of Wisdom are developed comprehensively. Many readers have found the study of that book to be a life-changing experience.

Chapter 1: Obeying God's Moral Will

1. This is one of two ways the phrase is used by biblical writers. The other usage is the *sovereign* will of God, discussed in chapter 2.

2. In addition to Colossians 1:9-10, some other passages that refer to "God's will" in this sense include Romans 2:18; 12:2; Ephesians 5:15-17; Colossians 4:12; 1 Thessalonians 4:3; 5:18.

3. The Christian's goals should reflect God's stated purposes for his life: to glorify God in all things (1 Peter 4:10-11; 1 Corinthians 10:31; 2 Corinthians 5:9; Colossians 1:10), to minister to others (1 Corinthians 10:23; Romans 14:19), to fulfill God-given responsibilities (Ephesians 5:22–6:9; Galatians 6:9-10), to evangelize lost people (1 Corinthians 10:31-33; 2 Peter 3:9), to do good works (Ephesians 2:10; Titus 3:8), to produce spiritual fruit (John 15:8; Colossians 1:10). It's not hard to imagine how a self-centered person, on the one hand, and a God-glorifying individual, on the other, would approach the same decisions. They would likely make very different choices about the use of time, expenditure of money, needs of others, and even the selection of a spouse.

4. A partial listing of God's will for this area of our lives would include: love (Mark 12:28-31), trust (Proverbs 3:5-6), humility (Philippians 2:5-8), gratitude (Colossians 3:17), integrity (Colossians 3:22), diligence (Colossians 3:23), eagerness (1 Peter 5:2), generosity (1 Timothy 6:17-19), courage (John 16:33), submission (Ephesians 5:21), contentment (Hebrews 13:5), and joy (James 1:2). A list of corresponding vices would include lust, independence, pride, presumption, irresponsibility, laziness, compulsion, selfishness, self-advancement, cowardice, and greed.

5. The moral will of God for divinely approved actions may be summed up in two broad principles: first, our choices must be biblically *lawful*—that is, they may not be forbidden by the revealed moral will of God (Ephesians 5:1-14); second, they must be *wise*—that is, the believer may not make a decision he knows to be foolish (Ephesians 5:15-17; Luke 14:28-32).

6. The source of this information, as I have noted, is the Bible. The process for gaining an understanding of God's moral will includes reading (1 Timothy 4:13), careful consideration (2 Timothy 2:7), search and inquiry (1 Peter 1:10-11), diligence in study (2 Timothy 2:15),

meditation (Psalm 1:2; Joshua 1:8), memorization (Psalm 119:11), and learning from gifted Bible teachers (Philippians 4:9; 1 Corinthians 12:28-29; Galatians 6:6).

7. Chip and Dan Heath, *Made to Stick: Why Some Ideas Take Hold and Others Come Unstuck* (New York: Random House, 2007), 25-26.

8. Colonel Kolditz gives an example: "Suppose I am commanding an artillery battalion and I say, 'We're going to pass this infantry unit through our lines forward.' That means something different to different groups. The mechanics know that they'll need lots of repair support along the roads, because if a tank breaks down on a bridge the whole operation will come to a screeching halt. The artillery knows they'll need to…generate smoke in the breach area where the infantry unit moves forward, so it won't get shot up as it passes through. As a commander, I could spend a lot of time enumerating every specific task, but as soon as people know what the intent is they began generating their own solutions." Ibid., 25-27.

9. Many examples could be supplied from both testaments. For instance, see 1 Corinthians 10:27 and 2 Corinthians 9:7. For amplification, see chapter 9 of *Decision Making and the Will of God*, revised edition.

10. A detailed critique of this view may be found in chapters 3-7 of *Decision Making and the Will of God*, revised edition by Garry Friesen with J. Robin Maxson (Sisters, OR: Multnomah Publishers, 2004).

11. It is truly providential that one of the central passages on singleness and marriage—1 Corinthians 7—is also a classic chapter of instruction on decision making within the moral will of God! We will explore that chapter carefully in part 3 of this book.

12. This is well-illustrated by a proverb in Ecclesiastes: "If an iron axhead is blunt and a workman does not sharpen its edge, he must exert a great deal of effort; *so wisdom has the advantage of giving success*" (Ecclesiastes 10:10).

13. J. I. Packer, *Knowing God* (Downers Grove, IL: InterVarsity Press, 1973), 80.

14. In a widely read article, A.W. Tozer described wisdom as "sanctified common sense." He argued that for many decisions the goal of the believer is a wise choice, rather than making the one "right" choice. A.W. Tozer, "How the Lord Leads," *The Alliance Weekly*, January 2, 1957.

15. See the book of Proverbs. For the teaching of Jesus see Matthew 7:24-27; 10:16; Luke 14:25-32. The pervasive scope of the Bible's instruction on wisdom in decision making is expounded in chapters 10 and 11 of *Decision Making and the Will of God*, revised edition.

16. Psalm 19:7; 119:97-100; 2 Timothy 2:7; 3:15-17; 2 Peter 1:19; Nehemiah 2:11-16; Luke 1:3; 14:28-32; Proverbs 6:6-11; 11:14; 13:20; 15:22; 30:24-28.

Chapter 2: Trusting God's Sovereign Will

1. These plans are further elucidated in Romans 15:20-28.

2. This fascinating case history in decision making is developed in detail in Garry Friesen with J. Robin Maxson, *Decision Making and the Will of God*, revised edition (Sisters, OR: Multnomah Publishers, 2004).

3. Other passages that refer to the sovereign will of God include Daniel 4:35; Proverbs 16:33; 21:1; Revelation 4:11; Ephesians 1:11; Acts 2:23; 4:27-28; Romans 9:19; 11:33-36.

4. This mystery may well be one of the "secret things" (Deuteronomy 29:29) that is simply beyond the grasp of finite minds.

5. A more thorough treatment of these points may be found in *Decision Making and the Will of God*, chapter 12: "God…the Only Sovereign."

6. The only exceptions to the secrecy of God's plan are statements of prophecy in which events are foretold (Amos 3:7; 1 Thessalonians 4:13-18), and explanations of the destinies of the saved and the lost (John 3:16, 36; Revelation 20:11-15; 21:8).

7. The existence of tension between biblical doctrines is not an unusual feature of Christian theology. We encounter seeming contradictions, for instance, within the doctrines of the Trinity and the Incarnation. Kenneth Boa's book *Unraveling the Big Questions About God*, previously titled *God I Don't Understand* (Grand Rapids, MI: Zondervan, 1988), provides an excellent treatment of the tension between truths that are both biblically necessary but appear mutually contradictory. He and other theologians call these mysteries "antinomies."

8. Os Guinness, *In Two Minds: The Dilemma of Doubt and How to Resolve It* (Downers Grove, IL: InterVarsity Press, 1976), 255 (italics his).

9. J.I. Packer, *Knowing God* (Downers Grove, IL: InterVarsity Press, 1973), 246.

10. See chapter 13, "God's Sovereign Will and Decision Making," in *Decision Making and the Will of God* for further elaboration of this material.

11. Job's comforters, Eliphaz, Bildad, and Zophar, tried to turn the interpretation of providence into an art form, but they were most helpful when they sat silently (Job 2:13). For nine chapters they expounded on providence (Job 4–5, 8, 11, 15, 18, 20, 22, 25). In their interpretations of Job's situation, they were wrong nine chapters out of nine! Only God really knew what was going on, and Job never did receive the divine interpretation of his troubles. During his earthly life, the most he could say was, "The LORD gives, and the LORD takes away. May the name of the LORD be blessed!" (Job 1:21).

12. There are two exceptions to this prohibition. The first occurred in the Bible when God himself interpreted the meaning of an event. For instance, Israel's crop failures and plagues were often the result of God's judgment—judgment announced in advance by his prophets (Deuteronomy 11:17; Amos 4:6-8; Joel 2). Apart from such divine commentary, a famine is just a famine, a plague is just a plague. The second kind of event that Scripture indicates is capable of communicating truth is the divinely wrought miracle (John 2:11; 5:36; see Deuteronomy 13:1-5; 18:20-22). Apart from these two exceptions, attempts to read messages from God in circumstances are invalid.

13. This application holds true for so-called "open doors" and "fleeces." See the discussion in chapter 13 of *Decision Making and the Will of God*.

Introduction to Part 2: God's Design for Marriage

1. The generations-old double standard that censured "tainted" girls but overlooked the coming-of-age exploits of boys continued to govern societal perspectives.

2. "For most of history, marriage was not primarily about the individual needs and desires of a man and woman and the children they produced. Marriage had as much to do with getting good in-laws and increasing one's family labor force as it did with finding a lifetime companion and raising a beloved child." Stephanie Coontz, *Marriage, a History: From Obedience to Intimacy or How Love Conquered Marriage* (New York: Viking Penguin, 2005), 5-6.

3. "Marriage before the seventeenth century was arranged by the parents, and the motives were the economic and political benefit of the kin group, not the emotional satisfaction of the individuals. As the concept of individualism grew in the seventeenth and eighteenth centuries,

it slowly became accepted that the prime object was 'holy matrimony,' a sanctified state of monogamous married contentment. This was best achieved by allowing the couple to make their own choice, provided that both sets of parents agreed that the social and economic gap was not too wide, and that marriage was preceded by a long period of courtship. By the eighteenth and nineteenth centuries, individualism had so far taken precedence over the group interest of the kin that the couple were left more or less free to make their own decision...Today individualism is given such absolute priority in most Western societies, that the couple are virtually free to act as they please, to sleep with whom they please, and to marry and divorce when and whom they please to suit their own pleasure. The psychic cost of such behavior, and its self-defeating consequences, are becoming clear, however, and how long this situation will last is anybody's guess." Lawrence Stone, "Passionate Attachments in the West in Historical Perspective," in *Wing to Wing, Oar to Oar: Readings on Courting and Marrying*, ed. Amy A. Kass and Leon R. Kass (Notre Dame, IN: University of Notre Dame Press, 2000), 42.

4. Coontz, *Marriage, a History*, 146.

5. Stone, "Passionate Attachments in the West in Historical Perspective," 40.

6. David Popenoe and Barbara Dafoe Whitehead, "The State of Our Unions: The Social Health of Marriage in America, 1999," The National Marriage Project, Rutgers, The State University of New Jersey, 1999, online: http://marriage.rutgers.edu/publicat.htm, accessed 8 February 2006.

7. Andrew J. Cherlin, *The Marriage-Go-Round: The State of Marriage and the Family in America Today* (New York: Knopf, 2009). In this recent best seller, Cherlin, a sociologist at Johns Hopkins University, maintains that the widespread commitment to individualism is the reason for the unprecedented rate at which Americans couple and uncouple, cycling through a sequence of short-lived marital and cohabiting relationships. The operational corollary of individualism is that if a given relationship becomes unsatisfying or burdensome, it can be— even *should* be—dissolved. This trend, which is more prominent in the U.S. than anywhere else in the world, has devastating consequences for children.

8. Popenoe and Whitehead, "The State of Our Unions: The Social Health of Marriage in America, 2007." See also Scott M. Stanley, "What Really is the Divorce Rate?" PREP, Inc., 2003, online: http://prepinc.com/main/Docs/what_really_div_rate.html, accessed 19 March 2008.

9. Neil Clark Warren and Ken Abraham, *Falling in Love for All the Right Reasons: How to Find Your Soul Mate* (New York: Warner Books: Center Street, 2005), 2. This projection is supported by research conducted by University of Texas sociologist Norval Glenn and reported by Howard J. Markman, Scott M. Stanley, Susan L. Blumberg, *Fighting for Your Marriage: Positive Steps for Preventing Divorce and Preserving a Lasting Love* (San Francisco, CA: Jossey-Bass, 2001), 7.

10. Markman, et al., *Fighting for Your Marriage*, 39.

11. Popenoe and Whitehead, "Ten Important Research Findings on Marriage and Choosing a Marriage Partner," The National Marriage Project, Rutgers University, 2004, online: http://marriage.rutgers.edu/Publications/pubtenthingsyoungadults.htm, accessed 19 March 2008. Jim Conway, *Adult Children of Legal or Emotional Divorce: Healing Your Long-Term Hurt* (Downers Grove, IL: InterVarsity Press, 1990), 111.

12. Judith S. Wallerstein, Julia M. Lewis, Sandra Blakeslee, *The Unexpected Legacy of Divorce: A 25 Year Landmark Study* (New York: Hyperion, 2000), 150, 332.

13. Lauren Winner, "Desperate Times," *Leadership Journal* 28, no. 1 (Winter, 2006): 31.

14. Popenoe and Whitehead, "The State of Our Unions: The Social Health of Marriage in America, 2007." The total population increased less than 1.7 times over the same period.

15. Popenoe and Whitehead, "Should We Live Together? What Young Adults Need to Know about Cohabitation before Marriage—A Comprehensive Review of Recent Research (Second Edition)," The National Marriage Project, Rutgers, The State University of New Jersey, 2002, online: http://marriage.rutgers.edu/publicat.htm, accessed 19 March 2008.

16. Barbara Dafoe Whitehead, *Why There Are No Good Men Left: The Romantic Plight of the New Single Woman* (New York: Broadway Books, 2003), 13. The component parts of this emerging pattern may be seen in this chart, which has been extrapolated from Whitehead's chapter, "The Rise of a Relationships System," 98-126.

Two Parallel Mating Systems		
	The Marrying System (Established)	The Relationships System (Emerging)
Target population	Never-married young	Diverse singles population (including senior citizens, gays, divorced, widowed, never-married)
Purpose	Pair off people for lifelong marriage	Pair off people for intimate relationships (marriage, cohabitation, serial monogamy, casual sexual partnerings)
Sex and marriage	Links sex, childbearing, and parenthood to marriage	Treats sex, childbearing, parenthood separate from marriage
Nature of commitment	Anchors commitment in a legal contract or religious covenant with publicly made vows	Reduces commitment to private understandings and mutual consent
Duration	Hopefully lifelong	Short-term, shallow relationships
Pattern	Climbs a sequence of rungs toward marriage: casual dating → exclusive dating → engagement → marriage	Cycles through a series of relationships that form and break up with no necessary connection to marriage
Initiative	Mostly male	Whoever wants attachment (often female)
"Signature" union	Marriage	Cohabitation
Society's interest	Maximize stability of family for child rearing	Minimize disorder, gender conflict, and couple violence

17. According to a Pew Research Center analysis of U.S. Census data, the median age at first marriage for women is 26.5 years, and for men, 28.7. This is the oldest average age for marriage for both men and women in American history. D'Vera Cohn, Jeffery S. Passel, and Wendy Wang, "Barely Half of U.S. Adults Are Married—A Record Low," *Pew Research Center: Social and Demographic Trends*, December 14, 2011, online: www.pewsocialtrends.org/files/2011/12/marriage-decline-final.pdf, accessed 2 January 2012. Some ramifications of this trend toward marrying at increasingly older ages are discussed in chapter 14 under "Misstep 1."

18. Ibid. Carolyn A. Koons and Michael J. Anthony place this data in historical context by reporting that the single adult population in 1900, and again immediately following World War II, was less than 5 percent of all adults! *Single Adult Passage: Uncharted Territories* (Grand Rapids, MI.: Baker Book House, 1991), 48-51.

19. That's not to say that it hasn't been tried. Paul Pearsall explains that in ancient Roman society, there were three levels of marriage—*confarreatio, coemptio,* and *usus*—with decreasing degrees of commitment. *Usus* amounted to a trial marriage for one year. If it worked out, the couple progressed to the permanent and legally binding status of *confarreatio*. Pearsall notes, "the *usus* marriage failed the Romans because only a small percentage of these marriages survived the one-year trial period." This arrangement was abandoned in the third century. *Ten Laws of Lasting Love* (New York: Simon and Schuster, 1993), 50-51, cited in Mike and Harriet McManus, *Living Together: Myths, Risks and Answers* (New York: Simon and Schuster, 2008), 73-75.

20. Barna Group, "Born Again Adults Less Likely to Co-Habit, Just as Likely to Divorce," *The Barna Update*, August 6, 2001, online: www.barna.org/barna-update/article/5-barna-update/56-born-again-adults-less-likely-to-co-habit-just-as-likely-to-divorce, accessed 11 January 2010.

21. Martinez, G. M. et al, "Fertility, contraception, and fatherhood: Data on men and women from Cycle 6 (2002) of the National Survey of Family Growth," National Center for Health Statistics, Vital Health Stat., 23 (26), 2006.

22. Christine A. Colón and Bonnie E. Field, *Singled Out: Why Celibacy Must Be Reinvented in Today's Church* (Grand Rapids, MI: Brazos Press/Baker Publishing Group, 2009), 85. Additionally, a Gallup Youth Survey found that 49 percent of religious teenagers (defined as those who have attended church or synagogue in the last seven days) approved of couples living together before they get married. This was in contrast to an 86 percent approval rate among nonchurch-attending teens. Linda Lyons, "How Many Teens Are Cool With Cohabitation?" *The Gallup Youth Survey*, April 13, 2004, online: www.gallup.com/poll/11272/How-Many-Teens-Cool-Cohabitation.aspx, accessed 25 February 2008. This trend was confirmed in a survey conducted in England by the Evangelical Alliance (the counterpart to the National Association of Evangelicals in the U.S.) targeting evangelical youth between the ages of eighteen and thirty-five. One-third of those questioned "have no problem with cohabitation." The researchers found this report "even more shocking" when compared to a similar survey taken six years previously in which 28 percent of young evangelicals approved of couples living together without marriage. Ted Olson, "One-Third of Young British Evangelicals Approve of 'Living in Sin'," *Weblog Christianity Today,* May 1, 2001, online: www.christianitytoday.com/ct/2001/mayweb-only/5-7-12.0.html, accessed 25 February 2008. Also, see endnote 3 in the introduction to part 4.

23. Disclaimer: It is, of course, presumptuous to make the claim that one is setting forth the definitive statement of "God's design for [whatever]." Only Holy Scripture can legitimately

make such a claim in a literal sense. So what I am explaining is my understanding of his design. And given the limitations of space, I have had to be content with a survey. My hope is that I have gotten enough of it right to provide a starting point for others who don't have the time or resources to conduct their own original study.

24. John Stott died July 27, 2011.

25. The term *celibate* is often used as a synonym for *single*. The meaning of the word actually includes the added dimension of a commitment to moral purity expressed in abstinence from sexual intercourse. In part 4 of this book, I will seek to expand on the idea of celibacy in a way that enriches the concept for Christian single adults.

26. Albert Y. Hsu, *Singles at the Crossroads: A Fresh Perspective on Christian Singleness* (Downers Grove, IL: InterVarsity Press, 1997), 176-77.

Chapter 3: Marriage in a Perfect World

1. The analogy of cricket was suggested by Dr. Del Tackett in the second lecture ("Philosophy and Ethics: Says Who?") of the DVD series *The Truth Project* (Colorado Springs, CO: Focus on the Family, 2006). He tells a similar story to make a different point.

2. See the summary by social scientists David Popenoe and Barbara Dafoe Whitehead in my introduction to part 2: God's Design for Marriage, under the heading "Who Wants to Live in an Institution?"

3. Throughout this (and subsequent) chapters, I relate the biblical narrative from the standpoint that its depiction of an original couple is factual. That is, I presume that the human race is descended from Adam and Eve who were real people, and that the human story begins with them. My presumption is strongly influenced by my reading of Jesus (Matthew 19:3-9; 23:35; John 8:44) and Paul (1 Corinthians 15:20-23,42-49; Romans 5:12-19; Acts 17:26), who apparently held the same view. This position is not shared by all Christian scholars and a lively debate is enjoined (See Richard N. Ostling, "The Search for the Historical Adam," *Christianity Today,* June 2011, 23-27, 61). Regardless of the view one holds on the historicity of Adam and Eve, it is evident from Matthew 19:3-9 that Jesus regarded Genesis 1-3 as an authoritative and reliable description of the Creator's original intent for marriage, as well as the definitive explanation of what went wrong. For a thorough, accessible presentation and defense of the traditional view on Adam and Eve, see C. John Collins, *Did Adam and Eve Really Exist? Who Are They and Why Should You Care?* (Wheaton, IL: Crossway, 2011).

4. This phrase is repeated seven times in 1:20-25.

5. "Humans are far more than animals. The text shows that human life was set apart in relation to God by the divine plan ('let us make man'), by the divine pattern ('as our image'), and by the divine purpose ('let him have dominion')." Allen P. Ross, *Creation and Blessing: A Guide to the Study and Exposition of Genesis* (Grand Rapids, MI: Baker, 1988), 112.

6. E. H. Merrill, "Image of God," *Dictionary of the Old Testament: Pentateuch*, ed. T. Desmond Alexander and David W. Baker (Downers Grove, IL: InterVarsity Press, 2003), 441, 443.

7. "In the ancient world an image was believed in some ways to carry the essence of that which it represented. An idol image of deity would be used in the worship of that deity because it contained the essence of the deity. This would not suggest that the image could do what the deity could do nor that it looked the same as the deity (even though the idol was a physi-

cal object). Rather, the deity's work was thought to be accomplished through the idol...In Mesopotamia one significance of the image can be seen in the practice of kings setting up images of themselves in places where they wanted to establish their authority...The Hebrew word *selem* ["image"] is a representative in physical form, not a representation of the physical appearance. The image is a physical manifestation of divine (or royal) essence that bears the function of that which it represents; this gives the image-bearer the capacity to reflect the attributes and act on behalf of the one represented." J. H. Walton, "Creation," *Dictionary of the Old Testament: Pentateuch*, 160-61.

8. John H. Walton, *The NIV Application Commentary: Genesis* (Grand Rapids, MI: Zondervan, 2001), 136.

9. Later, in Genesis 2:18 and 20, we will read that the woman "corresponded to" the man. But this is preceded in the narrative by the "correspondence" between both human beings and their Creator. "It is significant that the man and woman are not first defined by their sexuality or gender; they are first defined by the fact that together they are created in the image of God." R. G. Branch, "Eve," *Dictionary of the Old Testament: Pentateuch*, 240.

10. This priority of allegiance is precisely the principle that was violated by Adam and Eve in the fall (Genesis 3:17).

11. "A royal statue at a distant corner of the empire represented the king's authority when the ruler could not be physically present. So also, at the completion of God's creation, he left *adam* as his image to represent his authority on earth. This suggests that the function of the image is to reflect the divine will on earth in such a way as to extend God's kingdom into every area of nature, society and culture." R. H. Hess, "Adam," *Dictionary of the Old Testament: Pentateuch*, 18.

12. "It probably is this inbreathing that constitutes humankind as the image of God." Allen P. Ross, *Creation and Blessing*, 123.

13. "These two verbs are used throughout the Pentateuch for spiritual service...Whatever activity the man was to engage in in the garden...it was described in terms of spiritual service to the Lord." Ross, *Creation and Blessing*, 124. Professor Ross further explains the meaning of the two verbs: "'Keep'...is used for keeping the commandments and taking heed to obey God's Word; 'serve'...describes the worship and service of the Lord, the highest privilege a person can have."

14. Walton, *The NIV Application Commentary: Genesis*, 176.

15. "*Ezer* appears twenty-one times in the Old Testament. Twice, in Genesis, it describes the woman (Gen. 2:18, 20), but the majority of references (sixteen to be exact) refer to God, or Yahweh, as the helper of his people" [Ex. 18:4; Deut. 33:7, 26, 29; Ps. 20:21; 33:20; 70:5; 89:19; 115:9, 10, 11; 121:1, 2; 124:8; 146:5; Hos. 13:9]. Carolyn Custis James, *When Life and Beliefs Collide: How Knowing God Makes a Difference* (Grand Rapids, MI: Zondervan, 2001), 181, 252.

16. Carolyn Custis James also points out that military imagery is used for women elsewhere in the Bible—most notably in Proverbs 31. "She [the woman] is a valiant warrior conscripted by God, not to fight against the man but to fight at his side as his greatest ally in the war to end all wars...In the Garden, God...was building an army, and the enemy was waiting to launch his first assault." *When Life and Beliefs Collide*, 186-87, 253.

17. There is much debate among scholars as to whether Genesis 2 delineates gender roles, and if so, what they are. The particulars of that debate, though interesting, go beyond the scope of this book. If you find a candidate for marriage, it will be important for the two of you to be in essential agreement on *your* gender roles in marriage. This matter should be explored and resolved during premarital counseling. For a summary of the representative viewpoints currently held in the evangelical community (egalitarianism and complementarianism), see chapter 16, endnote 14.

18. "I would choose a translation such as 'partner' or 'counterpart.' The former better reflects the 'helper' part of the combination, while the latter better reflects the compound word. If we could make up words, 'counterpartner' would be a great one." Walton, *The NIV Application Commentary: Genesis*, 177.

19. Thus, Adam later observed that she was taken from his "bone *and* flesh" (Genesis 2:23).

20. Walton, *The NIV Application Commentary: Genesis*, 177.

21. "'Taking in marriage' was the action of a husband...; 'giving in marriage' was the action of a father." Craig A Keener, *A Commentary on the Gospel of Matthew* (Grand Rapids, MI: Wm. B. Eerdmans Publishing Co., 1999), 528.

22. John Stott, *Decisive Issues Facing Christians Today* (Old Tappan, NJ: Fleming H. Revell Company, 1990), 288.

23. The Hebrew word for "woman," *ishshah*, is a feminization of the word for "man," *ish*.

24. One version of this aphorism was written by the English commentator, Matthew Henry (1662-1714): "Observe...that the woman was *made of a rib out of the side of Adam;* not made out of his head to rule over him, nor out of his feet to be trampled upon by him, but out of his side to be equal with him, under his arm to be protected, and near his heart to be beloved." *Matthew Henry's Commentary on the Whole Bible, Volume I (Genesis to Deuteronomy)*, accessed at www.ccel.org/ccel/henry/mhc1.Gen.iii.html.

25. "The Lord God created a woman from the life of the man to be his corresponding partner in the service of God." Ross, *Creation and Blessing*, 121.

26. Dan B. Allender and Tremper Longman III, *Intimate Allies: Rediscovering God's Design for Marriage and Becoming Soul Mates for Life* (Wheaton, IL: Tyndale House, 1995).

27. The NET Bible reads: "That is why a man leaves his father and mother and unites with his wife, and they become a new family."

28. This conclusion to the creation narrative doesn't say everything God wants us to know about marriage, but it is foundational to everything else. So fundamental is this description, it is quoted verbatim three times in the New Testament (Matthew 19:5; Mark 10:7-8; and Ephesians 5:31) and partially cited one other time (1 Corinthians 6:16).

29. It may appear, at first glance, that there are three elements. But leaving father and mother to be united to one's mate are two parts of one action—namely, establishing an allegiance to one's spouse above all other human relationships. Blomberg, "Marriage, Divorce, Remarriage, and Celibacy", 166-67; Stott, *Decisive Issues Facing Christians Today*, 288.

30. The wife was not instructed to leave her parents in this statement because that went without saying.

31. David J. MacLeod, "The Problem of Divorce, Part 2," *The Emmaus Journal*, Vol. 2, No. 1 (Summer 1993), 25; Blomberg, "Marriage, Divorce, Remarriage, and Celibacy", 167.

32. Raymond C. Ortlund Jr., *God's Unfaithful Wife: A Biblical Theology of Spiritual Adultery* (Downers Grove, IL: InterVarsity Press, 1996), 21.

33. "It [marriage] can be compared to two objects that have been glued together, each maintaining its distinctive features. It is not the same as an alloy, an admixture of metals, because in that case the distinctiveness of each person would be lost." Harold W. Hoehner, *Ephesians: An Exegetical Commentary* (Grand Rapids, MI: Baker Book House, 2002), 775. "This phrase suggests both passion [see Genesis 34:3] and permanence." Gordon J. Wenham, *Word Bible Commentary: Genesis 1-15* (Waco, TX: Word Books, 1987), 70.

34. MacLeod, "The Problem of Divorce, Part 2," 26.

35. "A [biblical] covenant is a solemn, sacred agreement, in which persons bind themselves to certain obligations, swearing an oath and signifying in a ceremony the total commitment to fulfill the obligations. The promise is made under God's watchful eye. He is witness as to whether the obligations are completed or not." Jeff VanGoethem, *Living Together: A Guide to Counseling Unmarried Couples* (Grand Rapids, MI: Kregel Publications, 2005), 99.

36. This passage describes the marriage covenant as something undertaken by the woman. As such, it confirms that marriage was a matter of mutual consent—not simply a unilateral action on the part of the husband.

37. "A general characteristic of the OT [covenant] is its unalterable and permanently binding character." G. L. Archer, Jr., "Covenant," *Evangelical Dictionary of Theology*, ed. Walter A. Elwell (Grand Rapids, MI: Baker Book House, 1984), 277.

38. "Sex is not technically necessary to create marriage—Joseph did not have sexual relations with Mary until after Jesus' birth, yet Matthew says they were married (Matthew. 1:24-25). But apart from exceptional circumstances, Scripture simply does not picture marital union without physical union." Steve Tracy, "The Marriage Mystery," *Christianity Today*, January 7, 2002, 63.

39. This is the case, of course, if the groom and bride have remained chaste prior to the wedding—as is expected. It is very significant, in today's context, that the divinely ordained order is covenant first, followed by consummation. For it is the covenant that marks marriage off from cohabitation. People who live together apart from marital commitment experience bonding without the benefit of commitments which bind them. Thus the elements of trust and security, which marriage was designed to ensure, are absent. The consequences of getting the cart before the horse are predictably pernicious.

40. The equation of "one flesh" with sexual intercourse is clear from Paul's citation of Genesis 2:24 in his dire warning against sexual immorality in 1 Corinthians 6:15-16.

41. "'Flesh' here implies kinship or fellowship with the body as a medium, thus setting forth marriage as the deepest corporeal and spiritual unity of man and woman." L.I. Granberg, "Marriage, Theology of," *Evangelical Dictionary of Theology*, 694. "It incorporates every aspect of intimacy and interdependence which should ideally render the married couple a unified entity at the deepest levels of interpersonal communion." Blomberg, "Marriage, Divorce, Remarriage, and Celibacy," 167.

42. "The retention of the word 'flesh'…in the translation often leads to improper or incomplete interpretations. The Hebrew word refers to more than just a sexual union. When they unite in marriage, the man and woman bring into being a new family unit…The phrase 'one flesh' occurs only here and must be interpreted in light of v. 23. There the man declares that the woman is bone of his bone and flesh of his flesh. To be one's 'bone and flesh' is to be related by blood to someone. For example, the phrase describes the relationship between Laban and Jacob (Genesis 29:14); Abimelech and the Shechemites (Judges 9:2; his mother was a Shechemite); David and the Israelites (2 Sam 5:1); David and the elders of Judah (2 Sam 19:12); and David and his nephew Amasa (2 Sam 19:13, see 2 Sam 17:2; 1 Chronicles 2:16-17). The expression 'one flesh' seems to indicate that they become, as it were, 'kin,' at least legally (a new family unit is created) or metaphorically. In this first marriage in human history, the woman was literally formed from the man's bone and flesh. Even though later marriages do not involve such a divine surgical operation, the first marriage sets the pattern for how later marriages are understood and explains why marriage supersedes the parent-child relationship." *The NET Bible*, first edition (Biblical Studies Press, L.L.C., 1996-2007), 10, translation note 6.

43. "The term for joining or uniting ['what God has joined together'] is literally 'yoked together'…and portrays a married couple as partners working in tandem for a common cause." Blomberg, "Marriage, Divorce, Remarriage, and Celibacy," 169.

44. In the U.S. at the present time, every wedding is also a civil ceremony that changes the legal status of the husband and wife. A wedding confers specific privileges and obligations assigned by the state. With its focus on the divine design for matrimony, this chapter is concerned with what constitutes marriage in the eyes of God. But due application of Romans 13:1 (and related passages) requires believers to adhere to the statutes of civil authority as well. Historically, the people of God have sought to live out their marriages according to the guidelines of divine revelation within the framework of a given culture. That approach remains appropriate for Christians today.

45. Stott, *Decisive Issues Facing Christians Today*, 289.

Chapter 4: The Marring and Makeover of Marriage

1. My eighty-something-year-old father recalls that the brand name was Webers.

2. The NET Bible gives an interpretive translation of Genesis 3:16. Literally, the second sentence reads, "toward your husband [will be] your desire, and he [will] rule over you." The meanings of "desire" and "rule" are the subject of scholarly debate. In the traditional view, the "desire" of the woman is thought to be a kind of *yearning*, whether psychological or sexual (or both), for her husband. This may be a longing for intimacy (damaged in the Fall), or an expression of the woman's maternal instinct that overrides the daunting pain of childbirth. A more recent interpretation (reflected in the translation of the NET Bible) views "desire" as a drive on the part of the woman to be independent of or to control her husband. This understanding is based on semantic parallels with the structure and terminology of a statement in Genesis 4:7, which refers to sin's desire to control and dominate Cain. A woman's desire to control her husband would reflect a dramatic reversal of the wife's designated role as his helper. In their interpretation of "rule," some commentators point to this verse as the basis for male headship in marriage. But most view it as a sin-infected domination that subjugates the woman to the husband's purposes (as in the NET Bible). Many (if not most) commentators find resonance

with Derek Kidner's summary of the bottom line: "'To love and to cherish' becomes 'To desire and to dominate'" (*Genesis*, [Downers Grove, IL: InterVarsity Press, 1967], 71).

3. Raymond C. Ortlund Jr., "Man and Woman," *New Dictionary of Biblical Theology*, 652.

4. "The domestic happiness commended by the sages (Proverbs 5:15-23), the excellent wife of Proverbs 31:10-31 and the marital bliss of the Song of Solomon indicate that the prefall ideal is not completely out of reach." Ibid.

5. "Through his atoning sacrifice on Calvary, Christ set humankind free by taking the retribution of sin upon himself. He suffered the agony and shame that we deserve to suffer because of our sin. He thereby satisfied the just requirements of the law of God and at the same time turned away the wrath of God from fallen humankind. His sacrifice was both an *expiation* of our guilt and a *propitiation* of the wrath of God. It also signifies the *justification* of the sinner in the sight of God in that Christ's righteousness is imputed to those who have faith. Likewise, it represents the *sanctification* of the sinner by virtue of his being engrafted into the body of Christ through faith. The cross and resurrection of Christ also accomplish the *redemption* of the sinner, because he has been brought back out of the slavery of sin into the new life of freedom." D.G. Bloesch, "Sin," *Evangelical Dictionary of Theology*, ed. Walter A. Elwell (Grand Rapids, MI: Baker Book House, 1984), 1015. As the basis for this summary of the nature of the atonement, Bloesch cites the following biblical passages: John 3:16-17; Acts 20:28; Romans 3:21-26; 5:6-10; 2 Corinthians 5:18-19; Colossians 2:13-15.

6. Matthew 7:28; 8:27; 9:33; 12:23; 21:20; 22:22; Mark 1:22,27; 2:12; 5:20; 9:15; 10:24,32; 12:17; Luke 2:33,47; 4:32; 8:25,56; 9:43; 11:14; 20:26; 24:22; John 3:7; 4:26.

7. Stanley Grenz, *Sexual Ethics: A Biblical Perspective* (Dallas, TX: Word, 1990), 22.

8. The significance and ramifications of the shift in the role of marriage brought about by the coming of Christ is discussed by the following authors: Christine A. Colón and Bonnie Field, *Singled Out: Why Celibacy Must Be Reinvented in Today's Church* (Grand Rapids, MI: Brazos Press/Baker Publishing Group, 2009), 158-63; Laura A. Smit, *Loves Me, Loves Me Not: The Ethics of Unrequited Love* (Grand Rapids, MI: Baker Publishing Group, 2005), 61-83; Grenz, *Sexual Ethics*, 21-23,45-47; John Piper, *This Momentary Marriage: A Parable of Permanence* (Wheaton, IL: Crossway Books, 2009), 105-16; Barry Danylak, *A Biblical Theology of Singleness* (Cambridge, UK: Grove Books Limited, 2007). Piper's sermon, "Single in Christ: A Name Better Than Sons and Daughters," can also be accessed online at: www.desiringgod. org/ResourceLibrary/Sermons/ByDate/2007/2162_Single_in_Christ_A_Name_Better_ Than_Sons_and_Daughters/, as can Barry Danylak's paper, "A Biblical-Theological Perspective on Singleness," at www.desiringgod.org/ResourceLibrary/Sermons/ByDate/2007/2162_ Single_in_Christ_A_Name_Better_Than_Sons_and_Daughters/ (accessed August 5, 2009).

9. "Although the New Testament maintains that after the coming of Christ the church replaces the family and tribe as the central expression of the establishment of community, marriage is not for this reason rejected. Nor is it afforded an unimportant status. On the contrary, it retains a vital, albeit different role in the light of God's saving work. Specifically, marriage continues to be important for the *ongoing development and expansion of the divine community as it is focused in the church*. This role, however, is no longer to be understood in terms of bringing the community of God into the world, as in the Old Testament era. Rather, it is

now to be viewed from within the context of that community. Marriage is an expression of the expansive nature and outreach mandate of the church, and it functions quite naturally *as a vehicle of that mission.*" Grenz, *Sexual Ethics,* 45 (emphasis added).

Chapter 5: Balancing Marriage

1. Les and Leslie Parrott, *Saving Your Marriage Before It Starts* (Grand Rapids, MI: Zondervan, 2006), 102, 160. In an endnote, the Parrotts add: "This simplistic distinction is actually derived from studying a vast assortment of biological, hormonal, anatomical, neurological, psychological, and social differences. See Julio Wood, *Gendered Lives: Communication, Gender, and Culture* (Belmont, California: Wadsworth 1994) and Susan Basow, *Gender: Stereotypes and Roles,* third edition (Pacific Grove, California: Brooks/Cole, 1992)."

2. Stephanie Coontz, *Marriage, a History: From Obedience to Intimacy or How Love Conquered Marriage* (New York: Viking Penguin, 2005), 68.

3. Katie Couric in a report on "The History of Marriage," airing February 17, 2005 on the *Today Show,* NBC. http://video.msn.com/video/p.htm?m=Home%20and%20Living&mi=NBC%20Today&i=58ac6c66-a846-45a9-8202-40ccec633875,edf7865a-cf0e-4f52-bc78-9690ae60bcd3&p=Living_NBC%20Today&rf=http://www.msn.com/, accessed 21 February 2005.

4. Generally speaking, books written before 2000 that address mate selection from a Christian perspective don't use the term *soul mate.* This includes Neil Clark Warren's books, *Finding the Love of Your Life* (1992) and *How to Know if Someone Is Worth Pursuing in Two Dates or Less* (1999) and H. Norman Wright's classic, *Finding the Right One for You* (1995). *Soul mate* shows up in the titles or chapter headings of Christian books written after 2000, such as Young and Adams's *The One: A Realistic Guide to Choosing Your Soul Mate* (2001), John Van Epps's *How to Avoid Marrying a Jerk* (2006), Neal Clark Warren's *Falling in Love for All the Right Reasons: How to Find Your Soul Mate* (2005) and, notably, the revised edition of Dr. Warren's previous book, *Date or Soul Mate?: How to Know if Someone Is Worth Pursuing in Two Dates or Less* (2005).

5. David Popenoe and Barbara Dafoe Whitehead, "Who Wants to Marry a Soul Mate?" in the report, "The State of Our Unions: The Social Health of Marriage in America, 2001," 6-8, http://marriage.rutgers.edu/Publications/SOOU/NMPAR2001.pdf.

6. Ben Young and Samuel Adams, *The One: A Realistic Guide to Choosing Your Soul Mate* (Nashville, TN: Thomas Nelson Publishers, 2001), xvii-xviii.

7. Neal Clark Warren with Ken Abraham, *Falling in Love for All the Right Reasons: How to Find Your Soul Mate* (New York: Center Street, 2005), 30.

8. Young and Adams, *The One,* 190.

9. Neal Clark Warren, "The Soul Mate Solution: Is There One Perfect Person for You?" www.neilclarkwarren.com/article/soulmatesolution.html, accessed 16 February 2007.

10. Stanley Hauerwas and Allen Verhey, "From Conduct to Character: A Guide to Sexual Adventure," *Christian Perspectives on Sexuality and Gender,* ed. Elizabeth Stuart and Adrian Thatcher (Grand Rapids, MI: Eerdmans, 1996), 180.

11. Significantly, in the sociological studies that evaluate the components of successful marriages, the dominant criterion is "marital satisfaction."

12. Lawrence J. Crabb Jr., *The Marriage Builder: A Blueprint for Couples and Counselors* (Grand Rapids, MI: Zondervan, 1982), 31-32.

13. Cited in Paddy Ducklow, "Marriage," *The Complete Book of Everyday Christianity*, ed. Robert Banks and R. Paul Stevens (Downers Grove, IL: InterVarsity Press, 1997), 608-9.

14. Ben Patterson, *The Grand Essentials* (Waco, TX: Word, 1987), 20.

15. Ibid., 47. Ben Patterson's explanation of the Christian's vocation and work in the first five chapters of The Grand Essentials is superb and highly recommended for further study. See also Doug Sherman and William Hendricks, *Your Work Matters to God* (Colorado Springs, CO: NavPress, 1987).

16. Joseph was a literal steward, serving first Potiphar, then Pharaoh. Paul used the figure of a steward to describe his assignment as an apostle. Several of Jesus' parables expounded on the faithfulness, diligence, and integrity expected of stewards (Matthew 25:14-30; Luke 12:35-48; 16:1-13).

17. "Caring for children appears to be a physical and psychological drain that can be detrimental to intimacy and self-actualization in today's marital relationships…When spouses consider the goal of self-actualization as primary, they do not want to make the necessary sacrifice in time, money, and energy that the rearing of children requires in our culture." Diana S. Richmond Garland and David E. Garland, *Beyond Companionship: Christians in Marriage* (Philadelphia, PA: Westminster Press, 1986), 84.

18. The characteristics of *Christian* workers are established by analogy from the instructions given by the apostles to Christian slaves (Colossians 3:22-25; 1 Peter 2:18-25). For an extended treatment of biblical perspectives and guidelines for the Christian's stewardship of work, see Garry Friesen with J. Robin Maxson, *Decision Making and the Will of God*, revised and updated edition (Sisters, OR: Multnomah Publishers, 2004), 342-54. Also see the excellent books referenced above in endnote 15.

19. "The conviction of the Christian workman is that every single piece of work he produces must be good enough to show to God." William Barclay, *The Letters to the Galatians and Ephesians* (Philadelphia, PA: Westminster Press, 1958), 215; cited in Patterson, *Grand Essentials*, 63.

20. Patterson, Grand Essentials, 20.

Chapter 6: The Ultimate Marriage

1. For the record, our son, Michael, also briefly took art lessons. His preferred medium was colored pencil. His drawing of a bald eagle likewise won "Best of Show" at the Tulelake (CA) Fair. And that eagle also occupies a place of prominence in our living room. After winning his award, Mike abandoned art as "not challenging enough," and moved on to other pursuits involving pyrotechnics and sports. He will no doubt be bemused to find himself referenced as a footnote, once again, to his sister's prowess. (It's OK. His self-image is very healthy.)

2. Indeed, with the hindsight afforded by New Testament revelation, Christians have long recognized that a healthy human marriage reflects the unity-in-diversity that exists within the

Godhead. It is not unreasonable to infer a hint of this intention in the Creator's statement in Genesis 1:26, "Let us make humankind in our image, after our likeness." Christians have always recognized that the plural pronouns and verb make room for the plurality that exists within the unity of the Godhead, a doctrine explicitly revealed with the coming of Christ and the sending of the Holy Spirit. When the Creator extracted the female human from the male human and then reunited them in a one-flesh relationship (Genesis 2:22-24), the resulting community was a reflection of the divine unity-in-diversity. When two spouses harness their diversity in service to an observable oneness of heart and purpose, they represent the mystery intrinsic to the interrelatedness of multiple persons within one essential Being. See Wayne Grudem, *Systematic Theology: An Introduction to Biblical Doctrine* (Grand Rapids, MI: Zondervan, 1994), 227; Allen P. Ross, *Creation and Blessing*, 112.

3. Harold W. Hoehner, *Ephesians: An Exegetical Commentary* (Grand Rapids, MI: Baker Book House, 2002), 775-81.

4. John Piper, *This Momentary Marriage: A Parable of Permanence* (Wheaton, IL: Crossway Books, 2009), 75-76.

5. This current mission of Christ is described in more detail in chapter 2.

6. Piper, *This Momentary Marriage*, 11.

7. "Once individuals have received glorified bodies no longer subject to death, the need for procreation, one of the basic purposes for marriage, will no longer exist. Believers...will be like the angels in that regard, for angels do not reproduce themselves." Louis A. Barbieri, "Matthew," *The Bible Knowledge Commentary: New Testament*, ed. John F. Walvoord and Roy B. Zuck (Wheaton, IL: Victor Books, 1983), 72.

8. In retrospect, the temporal limitations of earthly marriage can be recognized in the bonding of the first couple into a one-*flesh* relationship. "Any union defined in terms of *flesh* must be acknowledged to be less than ultimate in nature. It extends for the full length of this mortal life, but it cannot transcend this life...Marriage is profound, but not ultimate." Raymond C. Ortlund Jr., *God's Unfaithful Wife: A Biblical Theology of Spiritual Adultery* (Downers Grove, IL: InterVarsity Press, 1996), 23.

9. Michael J. Wilkins, *The NIV Application Commentary: Matthew* (Grand Rapids, MI: Zondervan, 2004), 724. D.A. Carson adds this helpful analogy: "as a good mother today loves all her children and is loved by them." "Matthew," *The Expositor's Bible Commentary: Volume 8*, ed. Frank E. Gaebelein (Grand Rapids, MI: Zondervan, 1984), 462.

10. "Shadow-Lands" is the term coined by C.S. Lewis in his Chronicles of Narnia to refer to the physical world in the present age in contrast to the real world of the new heaven and the new earth. C.S. Lewis, *The Last Battle* (New York: Macmillan Publishing Co., 1956), 173.

11. Piper, *This Momentary Marriage*, 106.

12. Raymond C. Ortlund Jr., "Marriage," *New Dictionary of Biblical Theology* (Downers Grove, IL: InterVarsity Press, 2000), 657.

13. Raymond C. Ortlund Jr., "Man and Woman," *New Dictionary of Biblical Theology*, 654.

14. If I am wrong in trusting in this promise, then I am wrong in believing that faith in Christ brings eternal life. The two guarantees are tied up together.

Introduction to Part 3: God's Design for Singleness

1. "The One Where Mr. Heckles Dies," *Friends*. Written by Michael Curtis and Greg Malins, NBC, October 5, 1995. This episode is recounted by Christine Colón and Bonnie Field, *Singled Out: Why Celibacy Must Be Reinvented in Today's Church* (Grand Rapids, MI: Brazos Press/Baker Publishing Group, 2009), 33.

2. U.S. Census Bureau, "American Community Survey: 2003 Data Profile," www.census.gov/acs/www/Products/Profiles/Single/2003/ACS/Tabular/010/01000US2.htm, accessed on February 16, 2006. According to this survey, 46 percent of American adults were unmarried or separated in 2003. But since "the 2003 American Community Survey universe is limited to the household population and excludes the population living in institutions, college dormitories, and other group quarters" the actual percentage of single adults is even higher. Carolyn A. Koons and Michael J. Anthony place this data in historical context by reporting that the single adult population in 1900 (and again immediately following World War II) was less than 5 percent! *Single Adult Passages: Uncharted Territories* (Grand Rapids, MI.: Baker Book House, 1991), 48-51.

3. Actually it was John Stott, a single man, who used the term to describe bachelorhood. I just quoted him (page 72).

4. V.M. Stinton, "Singleness," *New Dictionary of Christian Ethics and Pastoral Theology*, ed. David J. Atkinson and David H. Field (Downers Grove, IL: InterVarsity Press, 1995), 790.

5. Albert Y. Hsu, *Singles at the Crossroads: A Fresh Perspective on Christian Singleness* (Downers Grove, IL: InterVarsity Press, 1997), 10. This is a superior guidebook to life as a single adult.

6. Rodney Clapp, *Families at the Crossroads* (Downers Grove, IL: InterVarsity Press, 1993), 95.

7. Hsu, *Singles at the Crossroads*, 32-33. In his second chapter, "A Brief History of Singleness," Hsu provides an excellent survey of this history.

8. J.S. Wright and J.A. Thompson, "Marriage," *The New Bible Dictionary*, ed. J.D. Douglas (Grand Rapids, MI: William B. Eerdmans Publishing Co., 1962), 787.

9. William A. Heth, "Unmarried 'For the Sake of the Kingdom' (Matthew 19:12) in the Early Church," *Grace Theological Journal*, vol. 8, No. 1, Spring 1987, 59. Heth documents the pervasive nature of the negative attitude toward singleness: "Both the secular society at large and the Christian church as a whole treat singleness, practically speaking, as something of an accursed condition (to overstate the case). The same seems to have been true in ancient times as well. A Sumerian proverb from ca. 2600 B.C. states: 'He that supports no wife, he that supports no son, may his misfortunes be multiplied.' We read in the intertestamental Jewish literature that 'He who acquires a wife gets his best possession, a helper fit for him and a pillar of support. Where there is no fence, the property will be plundered; and where there is no wife, a man will wander about and sigh [Sir 36:24-25].' 'A daughter keeps her father secretly wakeful, and worry over her robs him of sleep; when she is young lest she do not marry, or if married, lest she be hated [divorced]; while a virgin, lest she be defiled or become pregnant in her father's house; or having a husband, lest she prove unfaithful, or, though married, lest she be barren (Sir 42:9-10].'"

10. As I noted in chapter 5, *celibacy* is often used as a synonym for *singleness*. The meaning of the word actually includes the added dimension of a commitment to moral purity expressed in

abstinence from sexual intercourse. Later in this book, I will seek to expand on the idea of celibacy in a way that enriches the concept for Christian single adults.

11. Stinton, "Singleness," 792.

12. Ascetics practice strict self-denial for spiritual benefits. In this case the discipline took the form of sexual abstinence.

13. Craig Blomberg, *The NIV Application Commentary: 1 Corinthians* (Grand Rapids, MI: Zondervan, 1995), 25. David E. Garland, on the other hand, lists twelve possible sources of this ascetic bent. *1 Corinthians, Baker Exegetical Commentary on the New Testament*, ed. Robert W. Yarbrough and Robert H. Stein (Grand Rapids, MI: Baker Book House, 2003), 263-66.

14. Rebecca Harden Weaver, "Yes, But...Early Christian Teaching on Marriage, Sex, and Family," *Christian History and Biography,* July 1, 1995, accessed at www.ctlibrary.com/30953 on February 17, 2006.

15. Steven Ozment, *Protestants: The Birth of a Revolution* (New York: Doubleday, 1993), cited in "Reinventing Family Life" *Christian History and Biography,* July 1, 1993, accessed at www. ctlibrary.com/3971 on February 17, 2006. "A vernacular catechism from 1494 elaborates the third deadly sin (impurity) under the title, 'How the Laity Sins in the Marital Duty.' According to the catechism, the laity sin sexually in marriage by, among other things, having sex for the sheer joy of it rather than for the reasons God has commanded, namely, to escape the sin of concupiscence and to populate the earth."

16. "Reinventing Family Life" *Christian History and Biography.*

17. Ruth Tucker, *Women in the Maze* (Downers Grove, IL: InterVarsity Press, 1992), 239, cited in Albert Y. Hsu, *Singles at the Crossroads,* 46. Rebecca Hardin Weaver concurs: "Protestant views about marriage, sexuality, and family are deeply colored by Reformation zeal. Sixteenth century Protestants sought to eliminate monasticism, clerical celibacy, and burdens on the Christian conscience that resulted from ecclesiastical regulation of conjugal sex. Family life, they insisted, was precisely the arena in which Christian obedience was to be expressed. Almost five centuries later, I wonder whether we've taken this rather fervent affirmation of family life too far." "Yes, But...Early Christian Teaching on Marriage, Sex, and Family."

18. Most notably, Colón and Field, *Singled Out.*

Chapter 7: Eunuchs for Yeshua

1. Made you look, didn't I? Sorry. You'll have to make up your own.

2. William A. Heth, "Unmarried 'For the Sake of the Kingdom,'" 58-59. "In the Talmudic period, at the end of the first century, A.D....there was only one known instance of a celibate rabbi: *Ben 'Azzai.* Yet even *Ben 'Azzai* proclaimed the duty to marry as a command."

3. "It would be impossible to stress too strongly the shock caused to the people of Israel and the total innovation for orthodox Jews of the saying of Jesus concerning voluntary celibacy for the kingdom of heaven's sake." Max Thurian, *Marriage and Celibacy* (London: SCM Press Ltd., 1959 [English translation]), 46.

4. See chapter 4.

5. William A. Heth, "Unmarried 'For the Sake of the Kingdom,'" 59.

6. Thena Ayres, "Singleness," *The Complete Book of Everyday Christianity* (Downers Grove, IL: InterVarsity Press, 1997), 903.

7. Origin (ca. 185–ca. 254), one of the church fathers of the Greek church, took Jesus' words literally. He castrated himself so he could teach his female students without fear of scandal. C.C. Kroeger, "Origin," *Evangelical Dictionary of Theology*, ed. Walter A. Elwell (Grand Rapids, MI: Baker Book House, 1984), 803.

8. Craig S. Keener, *A Commentary on the Gospel of Matthew* (Grand Rapids, MI: Wm. B. Eerdmans Publishing Co., 1999), 472; David L. Turner, *Baker Exegetical Commentary on the New Testament: Matthew* (Grand Rapids, MI: Baker Academic, 2008), 463; Michael J. Wilkins, *The NIV Application Commentary: Matthew* (Grand Rapids, MI: Zondervan, 2004), 645.

9. Keener, *A Commentary on the Gospel of Matthew*, 471-72.

10. Albert Y. Hsu, *Singles at the Crossroads*, 36.

11. John Piper put these related passages from Isaiah together in a landmark sermon, "Single in Christ: A Name Better Than Sons and Daughters," preached April 29, 2007. This message is available online at: www.desiringgod.org/ResourceLibrary/Sermons/ByDate/2007/2162_Single_in_Christ_A_Name_Better_Than_Sons_and_Daughters/. It is also included as chapter 9 in his book *This Momentary Marriage*.

12. The meaning of the statement, "Not everyone can accept this statement, except those to whom it has been given," and the concluding admonition, "The one who is able to accept this should accept it," is not obvious. Some understand Jesus to be qualifying the option of singleness by limiting it to those "to whom it has been given"—that is, those who have received the gift of celibacy. More likely he is referring to the radical idea ("this statement") of singleness as a viable option for disciples. Coming as it does from the mouth of Messiah, it has his full authority. Therefore, his teaching should be accepted as true, and some should feel free to take the path of singleness. The apostle Paul is one who made such a choice (see 1 Corinthians 7:7; 9:5).

13. See Introduction to Part 3, page 128.

14. V.M. Stinton, "Singleness," *New Dictionary of Christian Ethics and Pastoral Theology*, ed. David J. Atkinson and David H. Field (Downers Grove, IL: InterVarsity Press, 1995), 791.

Chapter 8: Singleness and the Will of God

1. V.M. Stinton, "Singleness," *New Dictionary of Christian Ethics and Pastoral Theology*, ed. David J. Atkinson and David H. Field (Downers Grove, IL: InterVarsity Press, 1995), 791.

2. In 1 Timothy 4:3, Paul makes a passing reference to false teachers who "forbid people to marry."

3. Though it contains much relevant apostolic advice, it is curiously neglected (or misapplied) by many popular books written to explain how God's will relates to these decisions.

4. The argument that highly devoted disciples should remain unmarried continues to be made in some quarters today, but it is relatively rare, especially in comparison with the opposite perspective.

5. Richard B. Hays, *First Corinthians*, Interpretation: A Bible Commentary for Teaching and Preaching (Louisville, KY: John Knox Press, 1997), 114.

6. It is not necessary (or even possible) to have a precise understanding of the specific issues and perspectives being addressed by Paul in order to have a credible interpretation of his meaning. But the historical background information available to us may help us to understand why and how these were issues to the Corinthian believers. Further, knowledge of the cultural setting can help the interpreter to identify differences of perspective between the audience Paul was addressing and those of us who read this passage today. Making these distinctions can help us apply Paul's principles in our own setting with greater validity.

7. Plus the instruction of Paul, Aquila, and Priscilla (Acts 18:1-8).

8. Ascetic individuals practice rigorous self-denial, abstaining from any indulgence of the flesh, for purposes of religious or spiritual advancement.

9. Craig Blomberg, *The NIV Application Commentary: 1 Corinthians*, 24.

10. "All of the major problems in the Corinthian church can thus be viewed as stemming from one or the other of these two outworkings of dualistic thought—either asceticism or hedonism." Craig Blomberg, *The NIV Application Commentary: 1 Corinthians*, 25.

11. Again, there is a certain amount of speculation in this suggested reconstruction of the circumstances being addressed by Paul. Commentator David Garland cites twelve possible philosophical-theological-historical influences on the Corinthian believers and warns against being overly invested in any single explanation (*1 Corinthians*, [Grand Rapids, MI: Baker Book House, 2003], 246, 263-66). The presence of an ascetic group within the Corinthian church appears obvious; the reasons behind their viewpoint are less clear. That said, the likelihood that some within the church were significantly affected by a dualistic worldview is high.

12. "[Some members of the church] found their spouses withdrawing from the physical relationship or perhaps even separating from marriage altogether (cf. 7:10-11) in the interests of holiness. Perhaps this is part of the reason that some of the Corinthian Christians were going to prostitutes." Hays, *First Corinthians*, 115-16.

13. Paul did not precisely identify the question he was answering. Interpreters have to reconstruct it from what he says in reply. The starting point is the opening statement, which translated literally reads: "It is good for a man not to touch a woman" (NKJV). If Paul was expressing his own view (NASB, NKJV, NLT), he would be affirming qualified support for celibacy (explained in verses 28-35). In the opinion of most modern commentators (and several translations—HCSB, ESV, NET, NRSV, and the latest edition of the NIV), it is more likely that he was quoting from the letter he had received and may have had in front of him as he wrote. Since "touch" is a Jewish euphemism for sexual intercourse, the translation of the New International Reader's Version expresses the likely meaning: "Now I want to deal with the things you wrote me about. Some of you say, 'It is good for a man not to have sex with a woman.'" The ascetic party may have believed that Paul would support their doctrine since he was celibate. Gordon D. Fee, *The First Epistle to the Corinthians*, The New International Commentary on the New Testament (Grand Rapids, MI: Wm. B. Eerdmans Publishing Co., 1987), 275; Hays, *First Corinthians*, 113-18; Garland, *1 Corinthians*, 247-54.

14. The outline that follows has been modified from Hays, *First Corinthians*, 112-30.

15. Jesus' disciples appeared to be worried over the prospect of getting trapped in a miserable marriage without the escape hatch of divorce. The Corinthian ascetics believed that Christians would advance their standing before God by avoiding the "contamination" of sexual intercourse.

16. The ascetics' premise (dualism) was fallacious, so their conclusion (universal celibacy) was invalid. And so was the related inference that one's standing before God can be advanced by changing an external life circumstance. It is this latter inference that Paul addressed directly.

17. "The section has the structure of a club sandwich: in between the three-layered repetition of the maxim (vv. 17, 20, 24), he inserts two illustrative analogies, implicitly comparing the married/unmarried distinction to the circumcised/uncircumcised (vv. 18-19) and slave/free distinctions (vv. 21-23). All these distinctions, he declares, are unimportant before God." Hays, *First Corinthians*, 122.

18. The distinctive term *called* (which occurs eight times in this paragraph) refers to one's call to conversion. The Greek actually reads, "as God called him." The "calling" is not to the life situation (which is changeable), but to faith in Christ. The "assignment" is the circumstance one was in at the time of conversion. Blomberg, *The NIV Application Commentary: 1 Corinthians*, 145. David K. Lowery correctly summarizes, "The call to conversion radically altered an individual's spiritual relationship but need effect no changes at all in physical relationships that were not immoral." "1 Corinthians," *The Bible Knowledge Commentary: New Testament*, ed. John F. Walvoord and Roy B. Zuck (Wheaton, IL: Victor Books, 1983), 519. For a summary of the usage of *call* in the New Testament, see Garry Friesen with J. Robin Maxson, *Decision Making and the Will of God*, revised and updated edition (Sisters, OR: Multnomah Publishers, 2004), 318-20.

19. The Greek word *merizō* literally means "to divide" or "to distribute." So the NKJV renders the phrase, "as God distributed to each one." In his *Notes*, Matthew Henry explains: "Our states and circumstances in this world are distributions of divine Providence." Most modern translations use the verb "assigned."

20. Carolyn McCulley, *Did I Kiss Marriage Goodbye?*, 30.

21. A parallel illustration is Paul's decision to circumcise Timothy so the young man could join him and Silas on their missionary journey (Acts 16:1-3). Timothy had been uncircumcised when he was "called" to Christian faith. Circumcision did not improve his spiritual status, but it removed a potential obstacle to the proclamation of the gospel to the Jewish communities in Asia Minor and Greece. Being free to change his condition, he did so for the sake of the gospel ministry.

22. Under the Old Covenant, circumcision was included in the moral will of God. It was required of all males in order to be included in the community of the people of God (Genesis 17:9-14). Under the New Covenant, which fulfilled and supplanted the Old Covenant, believers in Christ have been brought into the community of faith by the Holy Spirit apart from circumcision (Acts 15:3-21; Galatians 3:1-5; 5:1-6; 6:15). In Christ, the spiritual reality to which circumcision pointed has been applied to the hearts of all believers (Colossians 2:11-12). Therefore, the physical rite has become a matter of indifference. T. R. Schreiner, "Circumcision," *Dictionary of Paul and His Letters*, ed. Gerald F. Hawthorne, Ralph P. Martin, Daniel G.

Reid (Downers Grove, IL: InterVarsity Press, 1993), 137-39; M.H. Woudstra, "Circumcision," *Evangelical Dictionary of Theology*, ed. Walter A. Elwell (Grand Rapids, MI: Baker Book House, 1984), 245.

23. "Paul could have gone on to say, 'Marriage is nothing, celibacy is nothing, neither commends us to God,' but he leaves it for the Corinthians to make the application." Garland, *1 Corinthians*, 305.

24. In addition, God's moral will prohibits: (1) imposed sexual abstinence via divorce of a believing spouse (7:10); (2) remarriage to a different spouse by a Christian husband or wife who separated for such reasons (7:11); (3) divorce by a believer of an unbeliever who is willing to continue in the marriage (7:13-15); and (4) marriage of a believer to an unbeliever (7:39).

25. Let us note, again, that this was a preference, not a command. For "if you marry, you have not sinned" (7:28).

26. Paul does not explain what he means by "the impending crisis." It could have been some current circumstances being experienced by the Corinthians. But there is nothing in the available historical record or within this letter suggesting social or physical upheaval. When linked to the statement, "Time is short" (7:29), it seems more likely that Paul is referring to the imminent return of Christ, which will prove to be the ultimate crisis for unbelievers.

27. Other biblical passages that exhort believers to adopt an eternal perspective are 2 Corinthians 4:14-16; Colossians 3:1-4; and Hebrews 11:13-16.

28. Craig Blomberg summarizes: "Paul is well aware that distractions of marriage may temper this urgency. So those who choose to wed must not become so preoccupied with their families that they can no longer effectively serve Christ (v. 29b). The same is true with other normal human activities—celebrations and wakes, commerce and shopping (vv. 30-31). All are legitimate endeavors, but all remain fleeting. The Christian should therefore be less involved in the affairs of this world than the non-Christian." *The NIV Application Commentary: 1 Corinthians*, 152.

29. Garland, *1 Corinthians*, 317.

30. He doesn't even mention the distraction of children!

31. The phrase "not to place a limitation on you" is literally "not to throw a noose around you."

32. Though English translations of verse 8 indicate that Paul is addressing "the unmarried and widows," I believe that his audience was narrower: *widowers* and widows. That Paul is addressing widowers rather than the broader group of the "unmarried" in verses 8-9 is not apparent from English translations. But several commentators argue persuasively that *agamois* in this context refers to men whose wives have died. If this is correct, those individuals for whom marriage may be preferable to the burning of sexual desire were people who *had been sexually awakened*—adults who had become accustomed to the rhythm of conjugal experience. They would also be those persons within that culture who were more in charge of their own marital destiny (in contrast, for instance, to the never married). If the apostle Paul was himself a widower (and that is an intriguing possibility), then he would be expressing his hope that others who found themselves in his position would be able to "remain as I am." In his case, the transition from married life to singleness had not been problematic; but that might not be the experience of all widowers and widows. Gordon D. Fee, *The First Epistle to the Corinthians*, 287-88; Blomberg, *The NIV Application Commentary: 1 Corinthians*,

133-34; Hays, *First Corinthians*, 118-19; and William A. Heth, "Unmarried 'For the Sake of the Kingdom'" (Matthew 19:12) in the Early Church," *Grace Theological Journal*, Vol. 8, No. 1, Spring 1987, 66; Garland, *1 Corinthians*, 276-77; Craig S. Keener, *The IVP Bible Background Commentary: New Testament* (Downers Grove, IL: InterVarsity Press, 1993), 469.

33. See for instance 1 Corinthians 10:13: "No trial has overtaken you that is not faced by others. And God is faithful: He will not let you be tried beyond what you are able to bear, but with the trial will also provide a way out so that you may be able to endure it."

Chapter 9: Single Choices

1. Of course single Christians are continually challenged to abstain from sexual activity so long as they are single. But this appeal to celibacy is very different from what Paul was addressing—and very appropriate.

2. This is the circumstance addressed by Paul in 1 Corinthians 7:36-38. This passage is notorious for being one of the most difficult texts in the New Testament to translate, much less interpret. What is clear is that Paul was addressing men who, in that culture, had the final say on whether the unmarried women in their charge would wed. What is not clear is whether the men being addressed were the *fathers* or the *fiancés* of the virgins in question. The New American Standard Bible presents Paul as addressing the father. In the New Revised Standard Version, he is addressing the fiancé. The New International Version adopts the fiancé translation in the main text, but offers the father version as an alternate reading in a footnote. The ambiguity is fairly well maintained in the NET Bible cited in chapter 8. As one might deduce, there is evidence supporting each translation, and there are problems with each translation. For a brief explanation of the alternatives and issues involved, see note 29 appended to 1 Corinthians 7:38 in the online edition of the NET Bible: http://net.bible.org/bible.php?book=1Co&chapter=7#n29, accessed 27 June 2010.

3. Craig S. Keener, *The IVP Bible Background Commentary: New Testament* (Downers Grove, IL: InterVarsity Press, 1993), 469.

4. It is possible that Paul neglects that aspect of the process because that goes beyond the scope of the questions he is answering. But it sounds like he is assuming that if one were to decide to marry, a partner would materialize.

5. The only ways that individuals can make wrong choices is by violating the moral will of God or by acting foolishly. I will talk about foolish choices in chapter 14, "Top Ten Missteps to a Miserable Marriage."

6. Rodney Clapp observes, "The married Christian has the missionary advantage of hospitality...The single Christian has the missionary advantage of mobility." His entire chapter, "The Superiority of Singleness," is very thought-provoking. *Families at the Crossroads* (Downers Grove, IL: InterVarsity Press, 1993), 107.

7. Albert Y. Hsu, chapter 5: "Freedom and Opportunity," *Singles at the Crossroads*, 83-98.

8. He may have been referring to a specific situation that was temporary in nature. Or he may have been speaking of the ongoing urgency of the church's current mission and our expectation of Christ's return that should put all believers on crisis footing.

9. Laura A. Smit, *Loves Me, Loves Me Not: The Ethics of Unrequited Love* (Grand Rapids, MI: Baker Academic, 2005), 77.

10. This question is very carefully worded. See the next endnote.

11. Marva J. Dawn, *Sexual Character: Beyond Technique to Intimacy* (Grand Rapids, MI: Wm. B. Eerdmans Publishing Company, 1993), 51-52. Dawn's original question, "Will marriage to Myron help me serve God better?" reflects the emphasis of 1 Corinthians 7:35 in the NET Bible and New Living Translation: "I want you to do whatever will help you *serve* the Lord best, with as few distractions as possible." But other English translations (HCSB, ESV, NASB, NIV) use the terminology of undivided or undistracted "*devotion* to the Lord." While the thrust of Paul's argument may emphasize service, *devotion* adds the nuance of relationship—an idea that is also in the context of 1 Corinthians 7:32-35 where the motivation for service is the desire to "please the Lord." Similarly, the goal of advancing the kingdom of God is not just about external ministry but internal sanctification—i.e., the advancement of God's rule *within* the believer. So the expanded question, "Will marriage to Myron enable me to *love* God better," is a legitimate amplification of this priority.

12. John Piper, "Married or Single: For Better or Worse," May 3, 2007. Online: www.desiringgod.org/ResourceLibrary/TasteAndSee/ByDate/2007/2163_Married_or_Single_For_Better_or_Worse/, accessed 5 September 2009.

13. Readers who have an eye for irony will enjoy the comparison between the freedom to be released from the bonds of slavery, on the one hand, and the freedom to assume the obligations of marriage on the other. Some will find that juxtaposition more than ironic.

14. Lawrence J. Crabb Jr., *The Marriage Builder: A Blueprint for Couples and Counselors* (Grand Rapids, MI: Zondervan Publishing House, 1982), 70-75; Lawrence J. Crabb Jr. and Dan B. Allender, *Encouragement: The Key to Caring* (Grand Rapids, MI: Zondervan Publishing House, 1984), 52-53.

15. We fleshed out these points in chapter 2, "Trusting God's Sovereign Will."

16. A classic example of manipulative strategies is found in Ellen Fein and Sherrie Schneider, *The Rules: Time-tested Secrets for Capturing the Heart of Mr. Right* (New York: Warner Books, 1995). An instructive critique of this best-seller is provided by Barbara De Angelis in *The Real Rules: How to Find the Right Man for the Real You* (New York: Dell Publishing, 1997). Neither of these books claims to be presenting a biblical perspective.

17. The same is true, of course, for those who are married.

18. See page 165. Albert Y. Hsu, chapter 5: "Freedom and Opportunity," *Singles at the Crossroads*, 83-98.

19. I do not mean to imply that all relational needs of married couples should be met by the spouses themselves or that married people do not need friends. In fact, the relational needs of a husband and wife cannot be met by the other spouse alone; solid friendships are essential to the health of a good marriage. The point I am making here is that the development of friendships needs to be a priority for single persons as one aspect of their calling by God.

20. The alternatives to contentment are negative attitudes and feelings that motivate destructive behaviors. Resentment can easily degenerate into bitterness that is eventually expressed in a defiant involvement in counterfeit (and counterproductive) relationships. But the only route to true peace and joy is through contentment.

21. Robert Hicks, *Uneasy Manhood* (Nashville: Nelson Publishers, 1991), 78, cited in Hsu, *Singles at the Crossroads*, 61.

22. Lawrence O. Richards, *Expository Dictionary of Bible Words* (Grand Rapids, MI: Zondervan, 1985), 189.

23. This idea is conveyed by Paul, perhaps less explicitly, in 1 Corinthians 7:24: "In whatever situation someone was called...let him remain in it *with God*" (emphasis added).

24. The brevity of these comments on contentment may leave the impression that gaining contentment is simple or that my explanation is simplistic. My belief, and experience, is that when one is grappling with a strong desire that concerns a consequential aspect of life, the contest for contentment is usually prolonged and hard-fought, often involving tears. I have found substantial help in the experience of Jesus in Gethsemane (Matthew 26:36-46; Luke 22:39-46) and Paul's narrative in 2 Corinthians 12:7-10. But both Jesus and Paul affirm that our struggles with contentment are good for us. For in our search for soul-satisfaction, they compel us to look beyond our circumstances, which cannot satisfy, to Christ who does.

Introduction to Part 4: God's Design for Sex

1. See the excellent discussion of this assumption by Christine Colón and Bonnie Field in chapters 1 and 5 of their landmark book *Singled Out: Why Celibacy Must Be Reinvented in Today's Church* (Grand Rapids, MI: Brazos Press/Baker Publishing Group, 2009), 21-36, 55-56, 99-121.

2. "Unlike those in the animal kingdom, humans *make choices* to create erotic arousal. We can pursue sexual feelings or not." Doug Rosenau and Michael Todd Wilson, *Soul Virgins: Redefining Single Sexuality* (Grand Rapids, MI: Baker Books, 2006), 219.

3. The most complete and current empirical assessment of the sexual practices of adolescents and young adults is provided by sociologist Mark Regnerus in two recently published books: *Forbidden Fruit: Sex and Religion in the Lives of American Teenagers* (New York: Oxford University Press, 2007), and with coauthor Jerry Uecker, *Premarital Sex in America: How Young Americans Meet, Mate, and Think About Marrying* (New York: Oxford University Press, 2011). The data points in two directions. On the one hand, while there is some difference between the amount of sexual activity on the part of practicing evangelicals versus single adults in the population at large, it is not great. In an interview, Regnerus cites one telling statistic: "41 percent of churchgoing, conservative Protestant men's relationships become sexual within one month, barely lower than the national average of 48 percent." ["Match-making Ministry?" *Leadership Journal*, December 13, 2010, Vol. 31, No. 4.] In actual practice, a majority of Christian teenagers and young adults are not remaining sexually chaste—and the trend is in the wrong direction. On the other hand, while they represent a small minority of eighteen to twenty-three-year-olds (16 percent), "plenty of young adults are still virgins, and these shouldn't be thought of as abnormal or sexually stunted" (*Premarital Sex in America*, 28). In the 2002 National Survey of Youth and Religion, "44 percent of respondents who had not yet had sex cited religion and morality as their primary reason for abstaining. It was by far the most common answer" (*Premarital Sex in America*, 31). The dynamics of sexual purity are not simple, but the evidence supports our contention that those who are serious about a biblical, evangelical faith and stay connected to a supportive fellowship of like-minded believers, are experiencing success in their commitment to chastity (*Premarital Sex in America*, 31; *Forbidden Fruit*, 42). It is not easy, but it can and is being done.

4. Elizabeth Abbott, *A History of Celibacy* (Cambridge, MA: Da Capo, 1999), 426, cited in Christine Colón and Bonnie Field, *Singled Out*, 23.

5. In fact, our typical reaction to rules is resistance—see Romans 7:7-8.

6. "Christian PREP: Integration Model," PREP Inc., P.O. Box 4793, Greenwood Village, CO 80155-4793, 1996-2007, accessed at: www.prepinc.com/main/cprep_integration_model.asp.

7. C. Gary Barnes, associate professor of biblical counseling at Dallas Theological Seminary, put it this way: "Small 't' truth [scientific research] is proving to be congruent with large 'T' Truth [divine revelation]." Class lecture, July 27, 2006.

Chapter 10: God's Purposes for Sex(uality)

1. The word *chastity* comes from the Latin *castitas*, which means "pure, morally clean, unpolluted."

2. John Van Epp, *How to Avoid Marrying a Jerk* (New York, McGraw-Hill, 2006), 287-88.

3. Philip Yancey, *Rumors of Another World* (Grand Rapids, MI: Zondervan, 2003), 75-76. Chapter 5, "Designer Sex," was adapted for an article in *Christianity Today* (October 2003) and retitled, "Holy Sex." It can be accessed online at: www.ctlibrary.com/10850.

4. Yancey, *Rumors of Another World*, 77.

5. "These studies have been replicated over and over and need to be brought to the forefront because of how they challenge our contemporary dating beliefs." Van Epp, *How to Avoid Marrying a Jerk*, 294-95.

6. Ibid., 289.

7. Stanley Grenz, *Sexual Ethics: A Biblical Perspective* (Dallas, TX: Word, 1990), 9.

8. Stanton L. Jones and Mark A. Yarhouse, *Homosexuality: The Use of Scientific Research in the Church's Moral Debate,* chapter 6: "Toward a Christian Sexual Ethic" (Downers Grove, IL: InterVarsity Press, 2000), 21-22, 153-83. With his wife, Brenna, Stanton is also coauthor of *How and When to Tell Your Children About Sex: A Lifelong Approach to Shaping Your Child's Sexual Character* (Colorado Springs, CO: NavPress Publishing Group, 1993), as well as a four-book series for parents on "God's Design for Sex" (NavPress).

9. "The Hebrew term *nefesh* ('being') is often translated 'soul,' but the word usually refers to the whole person. The phrase *nefesh khayyah* ('living being') is used of both animals and human beings (see 1:20, 24, 30; 2:19)." NET Bible.org, Genesis 2:7, note 23.

10. Jones, "Toward a Christian Sexual Ethic," 160.

11. Grenz, *Sexual Ethics*, 21.

12. "Our sexual longings can be about more than procreation; they can drive us toward intimacy with another human being and offer a taste of the transcendence found when we are in communion with God. Just as our needs for food, water, clothing and shelter point us toward the deeper needs whereby God sustains, covers and protects us, our sexuality also points us toward God as the one who meets our needs for intimacy and transcendence." William M. Struthers, *Wired for Intimacy: How Pornography Hijacks the Male Brain* (Downers Grove, IL: InterVarsity Press, 2009), 121, 157-58, 162.

13. R. Paul Stevens, "Sexuality," *The Complete Book of Everyday Christianity*, ed. Robert Banks and R. Paul Stevens (Downers Grove, IL: InterVarsity Press, 1997), 882.

14. Rebecca Harden Weaver, "Yes, But...Early Christian Teaching on Marriage, Sex, and Family," *Christian History and Biography*, July 1, 1995, accessed at www.ctlibrary.com/30953 on November 17, 2006.

15. See, for example, Psalm 127:3-5.

16. Stevens, "Sexuality," 882.

17. Jones, "Toward a Christian Sexual Ethic," 21.

18. Though the terminology is not identical, I am indebted to R. Paul Stevens and his excellent article on "Sexuality" in *The Complete Book of Everyday Christianity* for many of the insights in this segment. He is the professor of applied theology at Regent College and one of the editors of that very practical volume.

19. R. Rohr, "An Appetite for Wholeness," *Sojourner*, November 1982, 30. Cited in Stevens, "Sexuality," 880. Biopsychologist William Struthers points out: "It is important to note that the sexual drive is located in the same region [of the brain] as the centers for eating and drinking. Thus the sexual/reproductive drive is experienced as a survival need similar to the drive for eating and drinking." Then he adds, "However, while you can die from not eating or drinking, you can't really die from lack of sexual activity." Struthers, *Wired for Intimacy*, 92.

20. Stevens, "Sexuality," 881-82.

21. "[Marriage] can be compared to two objects that have been glued together, each maintaining its distinctive features. It is not the same as an alloy, an admixture of metals, because in that case the distinctiveness of each person would be lost." Harold W. Hoehner, *Ephesians: An Exegetical Commentary* (Grand Rapids, MI: Baker Book House, 2002), 775.

22. Stevens, "Sexuality," 881.

23. Grenz, *Sexual Ethics*, 66.

24. Stevens, "Sexuality," 880. See also Grenz, *Sexual Ethics*, 66-67.

25. Grenz correctly observes: "In contrast to popular misconceptions, the Bible presents a pleasure-affirming, not a pleasure-denying message." Part of the pleasure derived from sex stems from the Creator's design of male and female genitalia. "This biological design is not limited to the male, as is sometimes suggested, but includes the female as well. In fact, as Letha Scanzoni pointed out...'only women have a sexual structure that has no other function than to provide sexual delight'" [*Sexuality* (Philadelphia, PA: Westminster, 1986), 35]. *Sexual Ethics*, 70.

26. John White, *Eros Defiled: The Christian and Sexual Sin* (Downers Grove, IL: InterVarsity Press, 1977), 19.

27. Doug Rosenau and Michael Todd Wilson, *Soul Virgins: Redefining Single Sexuality* (Grand Rapids, MI: Baker Books, 2006), 69-70.

28. Gary Thomas devotes a chapter ("Sexual Saints") to the notion that "Marital Sexuality Can Provide Spiritual Insights and Character Development." *Sacred Marriage* (Grand Rapids, MI: Zondervan, 2000), 199-226.

29. For instance, it seems likely that single Christians would recognize, experience, appreciate, and promote the concept of "church as family" better than married persons. Spouses who are also parents tend to be more focused on the physical family. Singles more readily relate to fellow believers as spiritual siblings, and are more available to fulfill the "one another" exhortations in the apostolic writings.

30. The caution offered by Christine Colón and Bonnie Field against the "dangerous message" that "sex is sacred and necessary for spiritual maturity" is noteworthy. *Singled Out: Why Celibacy Must Be Reinvented in Today's Church* (Grand Rapids, MI: Brazos Press/Baker Publishing Group, 2009), 126-32.

31. In some cases, dysfunctional relational or sexual dynamics may intrude into the couple's experience, blurring the picture and thus obscuring their apprehension of the ultimate reality that sex is intended to portray.

32. On the other hand, the reality of the illuminating function of sex explains why *all* married persons who enjoy a healthy sexual relationship recognize *something* of the wonder of their union. To return to the art analogy, even those who do not have the benefit of the artist's explanation still recognize form, beauty, and even meaning in the painting. As they hold one another in the conjugal embrace, husband and wife intuitively recognize that married sex entails much more than physical copulation. They may be unaware that their union reflects God's unity-in-diversity or portrays the relationship between Christ and the church, but they sense the mystery of marriage nonetheless. This apprehension of wonder is inexplicable on naturalistic grounds, but is accounted for by God's design.

33. Yancey, *Rumors of Another World*, 77.

34. Grenz, *Sexual Ethics*, 64.

35. Ibid., 181.

Chapter 11: Sex and the Moral Will of God

1. Stanton L. Jones and Mark A. Yarhouse, *Homosexuality: The Use of Scientific Research in the Church's Moral Debate*, chapter 6: "Toward a Christian Sexual Ethic" (Downers Grove, IL: InterVarsity Press, 2000), 168. While it is appropriate to include lust in a catalog of sexual sins, it is in a different category from the listed variations of "immorality" (*porneia*), and should be distinguished from them. As coveting is the internal sin that may lead to theft, so lust is the mental preoccupation that could (but does not always) result in wrong sexual activity. While Jesus didn't want disciples to think that immoral *acts* were all that mattered before God and that lust is no big deal (Matthew 5:27-30), it is highly doubtful that he regarded lust as grounds for divorce (Matthew 5:31-32).

2. Jones, "Toward a Christian Sexual Ethic," 157-58.

3. Ibid., 158.

4. Albert Y. Hsu, *Singles at the Crossroads: A Fresh Perspective on Christian Singleness* (Downers Grove, IL: InterVarsity Press, 1997), 179.

5. An explanation of the dualistic worldview behind this viewpoint is given in chapter 8. See also Stanley Grenz, *Sexual Ethics: A Biblical Perspective* (Dallas, TX: Word, 1990), 63-64.

6. Some may wish to limit Paul's exhortation to a prohibition of linking up with *prostitutes*. But the central imperative, "Flee sexual immorality!" refers to the most generic term that encompasses all sexual intercourse outside of marriage (*porneia*). In Corinth, employing the services of the priestesses of Aphrodite would have been the most prominent, and culturally accepted, expression of sexual sin.

7. "When one has sex with a prostitute, what God intended to be a means of sharing one's life with another is dehumanized into a momentary coupling for the sole purpose of sexual release. It leaves a legacy of alienation and guilt rather than loving intimacy and mutual commitment." David E. Garland, *1 Corinthians* (Grand Rapids, MI: Baker Book House, 2003), 237.

8. This is not to say that a person's body is distinct from the person's self. (See Romans 12:1 where the presentation of our bodies to God as "a living sacrifice" is seen as consecration of one's entire being.) Biblical anthropology does not make a dualistic separation between the body and the soul. As Stanton Jones put it, "We do not just have bodies; we *are* bodies." This stands in contrast both to the Greek worldview of the first century and the assumptions of contemporary naturalism. In the biblical explanation of human nature, there is no disconnect between the actions of one's body and the participation of one's inner person. What my body does, *I* do. So the stewardship of my body is a stewardship of myself.

9. So while the believer does not inhabit his or her body (see endnote 8), God does.

10. Richard B. Hays, *First Corinthians*, Interpretation: A Bible Commentary for Teaching and Preaching (Louisville, KY: John Knox Press, 1997), 106, 108. The equation of fornication with idolatry, both in a literal and an analogical sense, is a prominent theme that runs through the Bible. See Francis A. Schaeffer, "Adultery and Apostasy: The Bride and Bridegroom Theme," *The Church at the End of the Twentieth Century* (Downers Grove, IL: InterVarsity Press, 1970), 113-29; Raymond C. Ortlund Jr., *God's Unfaithful Wife: A Biblical Theology of Spiritual Adultery* (Downers Grove, IL: InterVarsity Press, 2003).

11. Lewis Smedes, *Sex for Christians,* revised edition (Grand Rapids, MI: Wm. B. Eerdmans Publishing Co., 1994), 109-10.

12. John White, *Eros Defiled: The Christian and Sexual Sin* (Downers Grove, IL: InterVarsity Press, 1977), 11.

13. James Emery White in "Desperate Times" (*Leadership Journal,* January 1, 2006).

14. John Van Epp, *How to Avoid Marrying a Jerk* (New York: McGraw-Hill, 2006), 290-91.

15. Jennifer Roback Morse, *Smart Sex: Finding Life-Long Love in a Hook-Up World* (Dallas, TX: Spence Publishing Company, 2005), 48, 50, 57. Dr. Morse is a research fellow with the Hoover Institution at Stanford University. She has written an insightful book.

16. This startling line was noticed by Lauren Winner and included in her book *Real Sex: The Naked Truth About Chastity* (Grand Rapids, MI: Brazos Press, 2005), 87-88.

17. David Popenoe and Barbara Dafoe Whitehead, "The State of Our Unions: Sex Without Strings Relationships Without Rings, 2000," 16. Accessed at http://marriage.rutgers.edu/publicat.htm.

Chapter 12: Sex and the Single Christian

1. Stanton L. Jones and Mark A. Yarhouse, *Homosexuality: The Use of Scientific Research in the Church's Moral Debate*, chapter 6: "Toward a Christian Sexual Ethic" (Downers Grove, IL: InterVarsity Press, 2000), 157-58.

2. Doug Rosenau and Michael Todd Wilson, *Soul Virgins: Redefining Single Sexuality* (Grand Rapids, MI: Baker Books, 2006). This book is highly recommended.

3. Ibid., 21.

4. Many couples schedule premarital counseling after they have formally announced their engagement. This level of commitment makes it extremely difficult to reverse course if issues arise during the counseling that ought to be regarded as deal breakers for a prospective marriage. Rosenau and Wilson offer wise counsel in their recommendation to pursue premarital counsel during the Confirming stage.

5. See chapter 18 for further insights on sequences in courtship.

6. Rosenau and Wilson, *Soul Virgins*, 212-19.

7. Of course, this is a worthwhile endeavor whether one is romantically involved or not.

8. Marva Dawn argues that the failure to develop healthy friendship relationships prompts many to illegitimately seek intimacy through sexual encounters. "Without affection, approval, and the knowledge that one belongs in some sort of community, a person might become desperate and falsely assume that what is needed is genital sexual expression rather than social affection...I am convinced that, if the Church could provide more thorough affection and care for persons, many would be less likely to turn falsely to genital sexual expression for the social support they need." Marva J. Dawn, *Sexual Character: Beyond Technique to Intimacy* (Grand Rapids, MI: Wm. B. Eerdmans Publishing Co., 1993), 11-12.

9. For a helpful picture of healthy masculinity and femininity, see chapters 7 and 8 of Rosenau and Wilson's *Soul Virgins*: "Soul-Sexy Masculinity" and "Soul-Sexy Femininity."

10. Rosenau and Wilson, *Soul Virgins*, 45.

11. The full range of contemporary opinion is provided by Rick Stedman in thirteen quotations supplied to him by Harold Ivan Smith. He declines to mention names or references because "I have known many singles who are unduly swayed by certain personalities that are popular today." We will follow his example. He also provides an interesting summary of the history of the church's attitude toward masturbation. *Your Single Treasure* (Chicago, IL: Moody Press, 2000), 195-206.

12. Mike Nichols, "Masturbation," *The Complete Book of Everyday Christianity* (Downers Grove, IL: InterVarsity Press, 1997), 611.

13. For an extended treatment of "debatable matters" see Garry Friesen with J. Robin Maxson, *Decision Making and the Will of God: A Biblical Alternative to the Traditional View*, Revised and Updated Edition (Sisters, OR: Multnomah Publishers, 2004), chapters 24-25.

14. William M. Struthers, *Wired for Intimacy: How Pornography Hijacks the Male Brain* (Downers Grove, IL: InterVarsity Press, 2009), 169.

15. On the one hand, it might be argued that Paul's alternative to unrelenting sexual pressure was marriage. He did not say, "It is better to masturbate than to burn." On the other hand, Paul was not addressing young adults who reached their sexual peak in their late teens or early

twenties but did not marry until their late twenties or beyond. And while the Corinthian culture was sexually permissive, it is not likely that Paul's audience had to deal with the same level of pervasive erotic stimulation one encounters today at every turn.

16. Stanton and Brenna Jones provide a thorough and reasoned analysis of masturbation. Their cautious response to the question, "Is masturbation sin?" is "It all depends." Then they elaborate: "What does the morality of masturbation depend upon? The worst kinds of masturbation would seem to us to be those that cultivate a heart of selfish preoccupation with *my* pleasure, those that involve a fantasy about clearly immoral and degrading acts with others, those that channel one's energies away from loving relationships with others, those that make one more rather than less preoccupied with sex, those that drive a wedge between the person and God by becoming a focus of guilt and shame. The least questionable kinds of masturbation would seem to be those that are a phase in adolescence rather than a life practice, those that do not use mental images of immoral acts, those that somehow contribute to the person maintaining his resolve to stay chaste, those that contribute to the person's positive appreciation of her body and sexuality as a gift from God, and those that help the person positively anticipate his eventual sexual union with a spouse in marriage." Then they add, "There is probably more suffering caused in Christian circles by overreactions to masturbation than there is by the practice itself." *How and When to Tell Your Kids About Sex: A Lifelong Approach to Shaping Your Child's Sexual Character* (Colorado Springs, CO: NavPress, 1993), 196.

17. This approach may be analogous to recommending a glass of wine, which "gladdens human hearts" (Psalm 104:15 NIV) and settles a sensitive stomach (1 Timothy 5:23), to someone who is genetically predisposed to alcoholism. A thing that is good when utilized according to its design becomes destructive when indulged inappropriately or in excess.

18. The word *prostitute* found in the preceding verses (15-16) is *porné*.

19. Struthers, *Wired for Intimacy*, 69.

20. Ibid., 59.

21. "Pornography is a tickle-and-tease….But tickle-and-tease gets you nowhere except hankering after more tickle-and-tease…It is the itch you can never scratch enough…Let me go further. Experiments show that the relationship between sensory stimulation and pleasure is not static. The more sensual stimulation we are exposed to, the greater our tolerance of it becomes. And the greater our tolerance of stimulation, *the more of it we require to achieve pleasure.*" John White, *The Race: Discipleship for the Long Run* (Downers Grove, IL: InterVarsity Press, 1984), 201-2.

22. James Emory White tells of participating in a radio interview along with a producer of pornography, who said: "There are things I'm doing now that sicken me. It's almost like we're having to get harder core and we're having to get more base in order to keep up the titillation because the more people are exposed to pornography, the less it titillates, and the more we have to go into shock, gore, crude value." And then he said, "I wish I could just have an erase button for my memory." "Desperate Times," *Leadership Journal*, January 1, 2006.

23. Sexual addiction already afflicts thousands of people. Circumstances that heighten one's risk for sex addiction include: inability to form healthy relationships (loneliness), coming from a family in which one member is an addict (of any kind), coming from a hyperreligious family

where all sex is seen as bad, and having been abused as a child (in any way). If you think that you or someone you know is enslaved to pornography, here are the online addresses of some ministries where help can be found: www.puredesire.org; www.pureintimacy.org; www.xxx-church.com; www.nationalcoalition.org; www.newlifepartners.org; www.purelifeministries. org; www.bebroken.com; www.freedomeveryday.org; and www.operationintegrity.org.

24. This statement is the culminating summary to two chapters of instruction on Christian lifestyle (Romans 12–13).

25. Douglas J. Moo, *The NIV Application Commentary: Romans* (Grand Rapids, MI: Zondervan, 2000), 441.

26. In Greek mythology, the Sirens were sea nymphs who used the enchantment of their musical voices to lure mariners to destruction on the rocks surrounding their island.

27. If the Internet is too hot to handle on your own, you can build some accountability into your use of it through websites such as CovenantEyes.com. It guarantees that if you go to the "magazine rack," one of your "seminary classmates" will see you. Your pastor can help you with other resources.

28. In a gut-wrenching exposé in *Leadership Journal*, a pastor wrote anonymously of his personal experience with the tenacity and destructiveness of sexual addiction. His efforts to obtain deliverance through prayer, repentance, and self-discipline always fell short. Breakthrough insight came from the memoirs of François Mauriac who concluded, "There is only one reason to seek purity. It is the reason Christ proposed in the Beatitudes: 'Blessed are the pure in heart, for they shall see God.'" The truth that broke the bondage for this pastor was his awareness that by continuing to harbor lust, "I was limiting my own intimacy with God." "The War Within: An Anatomy of Lust," *Leadership Journal* (Fall 1982, Vol. 3, No. 4), 30.

29. Henry Cloud and John Townsend, *How People Grow: What the Bible Reveals About Personal Growth* (Grand Rapids, MI: Zondervan, 2001), 117-46.

30. "Though an ethics of character makes use of the same biblical commandments as part of the narratives which form our character, its focus is not on the rules themselves but only the kind of people we want to be. Moreover, the motivation lies, not in the rules as laws for behavior, but in the positive invitation of God's grace and the delightful results of obedience." Marva J. Dawn, *Sexual Character: Beyond Technique to Intimacy* (Grand Rapids, MI: Wm. B. Eerdmans Publishing Co., 1993), 51.

31. Stanley Hauerwas and Allen Verhey, "From Conduct to Character: A Guide to Sexual Adventure," *Christian Perspectives on Sexuality and Gender*, ed. Elizabeth Stuart and Adrian Thatcher (Grand Rapids, MI: Wm. B. Eerdmans Publishing Co., 1996), 181.

32. For a more comprehensive exploration of strategies for sexual purity, read the appropriate volume in the Every Man Series from WaterBrook Press. Each of the following books is well-suited to group study and has a corresponding workbook: *Every Man's Battle* and *Every Young Man's Battle* (two different books) by Stephen Arterburn and Fred Stoeker with Mike Yorkey; *Every Woman's Battle* and *Every Young Woman's Battle* by Shannon Ethridge and Stephen Arterburn.

Chapter 13: Cohabitation: A Dangerous Liaison

1. The Bible talks about marriage and singleness, but cohabitation simply did not occur to people in the biblical world. In the Old Testament era, if a couple cohabited, they would have been stoned—which would have greatly discouraged consideration of such an arrangement.

2. Cohabitation is a situation in which a heterosexual couple consistently share a common residence and regularly engage in sexual relations without the formality of marriage. It is theoretically possible for members of the opposite sex to live together without having sex. But the research indicates what most people suspect—celibate cohabitation is the rare exception to the rule. For purposes of this chapter, then, my references to cohabitation assume sexual involvement.

3. See the introduction to part 2, endnote 19.

4. David Popenoe and Barbara Dafoe Whitehead, "Should We Live Together? What Young Adults Need to Know about Cohabitation before Marriage—A Comprehensive Review of Recent Research (Second Edition)," The National Marriage Project, Rutgers, the State University of New Jersey, 2002, http://marriage.rutgers.edu/publicat.htm.

5. David Popenoe and Barbara Dafoe Whitehead, "The State of Our Unions: The Social Health of Marriage in America, 2007," The National Marriage Project, Rutgers, the State University of New Jersey, 2007, http://marriage.rutgers.edu/Publications/SOOU/TEXTSOOU2007 .htm.

6. See also the excellent summary by David Popenoe, director of the National Marriage Project, in "Cohabitation, Marriage and Child Wellbeing: A Cross-National Perspective" (2008), www.virginia.edu/marriageproject/pdfs/NMP2008CohabitationReport.pdf, accessed January, 2010.

7. Pamela Smock, "Cohabitation in the United States: An Appraisal of Research Themes, Findings, and Implications," *Annual Reviews Sociology* 26 (2000): 6. Cited in Mike McManus and Harriet McManus, *Living Together: Myths, Risks and Answers* (New York: Howard Books [Simon and Schuster], 2008), 70.

8. Judith K. Balswick and Jack O. Balswick cite the conclusions of J. Trost ["Married and Unmarried Cohabitation: The Case of Sweden, With Some Comparison," *Journal of Marriage and Family* 37:677-2 (1975)], C. Danzinger [*Unmarried Heterosexual Cohabitation* (San Francisco, CA: R&E Research Associates, 1978)], and D.J. Peterman ["Does Living Together Before Marriage Make for a Better Marriage?" *Medical Aspects of Human Sexuality* 9:39-41 (1975). *Authentic Human Sexuality: An Integrated Christian Approach* (Downers Grove, IL: InterVarsity Press, 2008), 170.

9. Linda Waite, *Marriage—Just a Piece of Paper?*, ed. Katherine Anderson, Don Browning, and Brian Boyer (Grand Rapids, MI: Wm. B. Eerdmans Publishing Co., 2002), 164.

10. S. McRae, "Cohabitation: A Trial Run for Marriage?" *Sexual and Marital Therapy*, 12:259-73 (1997).

11. Balswick and Balswick, *Authentic Human Sexuality*, 172.

12. Smock, "Cohabitation in the United States," 6.

13. Waite, *Marriage—Just a Piece of Paper?*, 164-65.

14. David Popenoe and Barbara Dafoe Whitehead, "Should We Live Together?"

15. Jennifer Roback Morse, "Why Not Take Her for a Test Drive?" *Boundless Webzine* (2001), www.boundless.org/2001/departments/beyond_buddies/a0000498.html, accessed January, 2010.

16. Balswick and Balswick, *Authentic Human Sexuality*, 163, 172. This same statistic is reported by McManus and McManus, *Living Together*, 61, 69.

17. McManus and McManus, *Living Together*, xii, 60.

18. Cited in McManus and McManus, *Living Together*, 58.

19. Balswick and Balswick, *Authentic Human Sexuality*, 171. McManus and McManus, *Living Together*, 48-49.

20. Jan E. Stets, "Cohabiting and Marital Aggression: The Role of Social Isolation," *Journal of Marriage and the Family*, 53 (1991): 674; Linda J. Waite and Maggie Gallagher, *The Case for Marriage: Why Married People Are Happier, Healthier, and Better Off Financially* (New York: Doubleday, 2000), 155; Kersti Yllo and Murray A. Strauss, "Interpersonal Violence Among Married and Cohabiting Couples," *Family Relations* (1981): 30, cited in McManus and McManus, *Living Together*, 39-40.

21. Jeff VanGoethem, *Living Together: A Guide to Counseling Unmarried Couples* (Grand Rapids, MI: Kregel Publications, 2005), 75. He cites the following journal articles: A. DeMaris and W. MacDonald, "Premarital Cohabitation and Marital Instability: A Test of the Unconventionality Hypothesis," *Journal of Marriage and Family* 55 (1993), 404; P.G. Jackson, "On Living Together Unmarried," *Journal of Family Issues* 4 (1983), 41; P.R. Newcomb, "Cohabitation in America: An Assessment of Consequences," *Journal of Marriage and the Family* 41 (1979), 559; Karen S. Peterson, "Cohabiting Can Make Marriage an Iffy Proposition," *USA Today*, 8 July 2002, 2.

22. David Popenoe and Barbara Dafoe Whitehead list ten reasons why young men (in particular) refuse to commit to marriage: 1. They can get sex without marriage more easily than in times past; 2. They can enjoy the benefits of having a wife by cohabiting rather than marrying; 3. They want to avoid divorce and its financial risks; 4. They want to wait until they are older to have children; 5. They fear that marriage will require too many changes and compromises; 6. They are waiting for the perfect soul mate and she hasn't yet appeared; 7. They face few social pressures to marry; 8. They are reluctant to marry a woman who already has children; 9. They want to own a house before they get a wife; 10. They want to enjoy single life as long as they can. "Why Men Won't Commit: Exploring Young Men's Attitudes about Sex, Dating, and Marriage," *The State of Our Unions: The Social Health of Marriage in America, 2002* (The National Marriage Project), www.virginia.edu/marriageproject/pdfs/print_menwont commit.pdf, accessed January, 2010.

23. Waite, *Marriage—Just a Piece of Paper?*, 149.

24. Judith Krantz, quoted in Michael J. McManus, *Marriage Savers: Helping Your Friends and Family Avoid Divorce*, rev. ed. (Grand Rapids, MI: Zondervan, 1993, 1995), 40; cited in McManus and McManus, *Living Together*, 35-36.

25. Laura Schlessinger, *10 Stupid Things Women Do To Mess Up Their Lives* (New York: Villard Books, 1994).

26. Waite, *Marriage—Just a Piece of Paper?*, 149. David Popenoe cites another study that reports "children born to cohabiting versus married parents have over five times the risk of experiencing their parents' separation." "Cohabitation, Marriage and Child Wellbeing," 4.

27. Popenoe, "Cohabitation, Marriage and Child Wellbeing," 4.

28. Ibid., 22.

29. There are currently two prevailing theories: (1) The "selection effect" hypothesizes that certain traits in people (less traditional, more independent) not only prompt people to cohabit but also make them less well-constituted to sustain the relationship long-term; (2) The "cohabitation effect" suggests that the very experience of living together, with its casual, impermanent bonding, affects the couple's attitudes and perspectives in ways that diminish respect for lifelong commitment and increases the propensity for divorce. In the former theory, it is the *kind* of people involved that undermine permanence; in the latter, it is the *nature* of the relationship itself that is the root problem. McManus and McManus, *Living Together*, 71-73; Balswick and Balswick, *Authentic Human Sexuality*, 172-73; Waite, *Marriage—Just a Piece of Paper?*, 165-66.

30. John Stott, *Decisive Issues Facing Christians Today* (Old Tappan, NJ: Fleming H. Revell Co., 1990), 289.

31. See David Blankenhorn, *Marriage—Just a Piece of Paper?*, 204-6.

32. G.J. Jenkins, "Cohabitation," *New Dictionary of Christian Ethics and Pastoral Theology* (Downers Grove, IL: InterVarsity Press, 1995), 238-39 (emphasis his). See also R. Paul Stevens, "Cohabiting," *The Complete Book of Everyday Christianity* (Downers Grove, IL: InterVarsity Press, 1997), 168-71.

33. Stacy and Paula Rinehart, *Choices: Finding God's Way in Dating, Sex, Singleness, and Marriage* (Colorado Springs, CO: NavPress, 1982), 94.

34. Morse, "Why Not Take Her for a Test Drive?"

35. If you are married and cohabitation is part of your past, you should seek forgiveness not only from God, but you should also seek the forgiveness of your mate. It would be entirely appropriate for you to confess your regret to your partner and hopefully receive forgiveness. And you will need to address issues that may have begun to surface. I don't have space to develop this point at any length, but there is a manual that can lead you through the process and it is found in Ephesians 4:17-25. It's as though the apostle Paul saw this kind of situation coming and told us exactly what we should do about it.

36. This is hardly a sanctioned context for evangelism, so don't use that justification as an excuse to maintain a relationship that is morally wrong. You need to get your life back on track before attempting to address someone else's spiritual issues (Matthew 7:3-5).

37. Helpful advice on how to disengage from a relationship is provided by Ben Young and Samuel Adams, *The One: A Realistic Guide to Choosing Your Soul Mate*, chapter 9: "Are You in Love with the Wrong One?" (Nashville, TN: Thomas Nelson Publishers, 2001), 149-59; and H. Norman Wright, *Finding the Right One for You*, chapter 9: "When You're Dating the Wrong Person—How to Get Out of a Relationship" (Eugene, OR: Harvest House Publishers, 1995, 2003), 181-97.

38. How long should the separation last?" inquiring minds want to know. "How long have you been living together?" we reply. We don't set rules that create hoops for couples to jump

through. There is a symmetrical justice to matching the length of the separation to the duration of the cohabitation. But it is more important to have enough time to do the work of preparing for the marriage. This isn't about punishment; it's about constructive discipline and growth.

39. Authors who have studied cohabitation in much greater depth than I concur with the counsel for engaged cohabiters to separate before marrying. For a more complete explanation of the rationale for this difficult step see VanGoethem, *Living Together*, 185-87; and McManus and McManus, *Living Together*, 96-100, 110-14. All of these authors strongly recommend premarital counseling as well.

Chapter 14: Top Ten Missteps to a Miserable Marriage

1. In that time and place, the houses had flat roofs, and people built little guest rooms up there. A modern version of this proverb might say that if you have a quarrelsome wife, you're better off just going and staying in the guest room—and watching Monday Night Football.

2. The Hebrew Proverbs may seem chauvinistic to modern readers for their criticisms of domestic discord are uniformly directed at contentious or quarrelsome wives. We must understand that the Proverbs were not only written by men, they were addressed to young men who were in training for leadership. See David Atkinson, *The Message of Proverbs: Wisdom for Life* (Downers Grove, IL: InterVarsity Press, 1996), 23. Given equal opportunity, Israelite women could no doubt identify corresponding foibles in the character of Jewish husbands. Today, we would not be out of line to mentally substitute the word *spouse* every time we read *wife* in the text.

3. Bill Hybels with Lynne Hybels, *Making Life Work: Putting God's Wisdom into Action* (Downers Grove, IL.: InterVarsity Press, 1998), 114. Hybels amplifies this point in the following paragraph: "I think the writer of Proverbs would tell us not to worry if we shank a golf shot, lose a family heirloom, burn the Thanksgiving turkey, dent a fender on the car, flunk a pop quiz, or say something stupid to our boss. Don't sweat the small stuff. But don't make a mistake when you're choosing a marriage partner. Don't subject yourself to years of heartache and pain. Don't mess it up."

4. This approach was borrowed from Neil Clark Warren, *Finding the Love of Your Life: Ten Principles for Choosing the Right Marriage Partner* (New York: Pocket Books, 1992), and includes many of his insights.

5. David Popenoe and Barbara Dafoe Whitehead, "Ten Important Research Findings on Marriage and Choosing a Marriage Partner: Helpful Facts for Young Adults," The National Marriage Project, Rutgers, the State University of New Jersey, November, 2004, accessed at: http://marriage.rutgers.edu/Publications/pubtenthingsyoungadults.htm.

6. Hybels, *Making Life Work*, 117-18.

7. According to Neil Clark Warren, "The divorce rate for those who marry at twenty-one or twenty-two is exactly *double* that of those who marry at twenty-four or twenty-five" (italics his). *How to Know If Someone is Worth Pursuing in Two Dates or Less* (Nashville, TN: Thomas Nelson Publishers, 1999), 28. John Stott gives this counsel: "Don't be in too great a hurry to get married. We human beings do not reach maturity until we are about twenty-five.

To marry before this runs the risk of finding yourself at twenty-five married to somebody who was a very different person at the age of twenty." Quoted in Albert Y. Hsu, *Singles at the Crossroads: A Fresh Perspective on Christian Singleness* (Downers Grove, IL: InterVarsity Press, 1997), 181.

8. Gary Thomas, "Get Married! (Sooner Rather Than Later)," 2006, online: www.trueu.org/dorms/menshall/A000000501.cfm, accessed November 2007.

9. "We've created this incredible span of time where sexual passion is ignited but there is no holy means for it to be fulfilled." Albert R. Mohler, "The Mystery of Marriage," 2004 New Attitude Conference, online: http://albertmohler.com/audio_archive.php, accessed May 23, 2008. Cited in Christine Colón and Bonnie Field, *Singled Out: Why Celibacy Must Be Reinvented in Today's Church* (Grand Rapids, MI: Brazos Press/Baker Publishing Group, 2009), 90.

10. "I am suggesting that when people wait until their mid-to-late 20s to marry, it *is* unreasonable to expect them to refrain from sex. It's battling our Creator's reproductive designs." Mark Regnerus, "The Case for Early Marriage," *Christianity Today,* August 2009.

11. Frederica Mathewes-Green notes that "through much of history, teen marriage and child-bearing was the norm." And, "In fact, in the days when people married younger, divorce was much rarer." "Let's Have More Teen Pregnancy," *National Review Online,* September 20, 2002, online at: www.frederica.com/writings/lets-have-more-teen-pregnancy.html, accessed January, 2010. Colón and Field point out, conversely, that the eras in which men and women married in their teens were also characterized by much shorter lifespans. *Singled Out,* 112.

12. Kelly Grover et al, "Mate Selection Processes and Marital Satisfaction," *Family Relations,* vol. 34, 1985, 383-86.

13. Warren, *Finding the Love of Your Life,* 9.

14. H. Norman Wright calls this "the three-to-sixth-month syndrome." *Finding the Right One for You* (Eugene, OR: Harvest House Publishers, 1995), 84-85.

15. John Van Epp, *How to Avoid Marrying a Jerk* (New York McGraw-Hill, 2006), 70-71.

16. Ben Young and Samuel Adams, *The One: A Realistic Guide to Choosing Your Soul Mate* (Nashville, TN: Thomas Nelson Publishers, 2001), 74-75 (emphasis theirs).

17. Ben Young and Samuel Adams, "Commandment Four: Thou Shalt Take It Slow," *The 10 Commandments of Dating* (Nashville, TN: Thomas Nelson Publishers, 1999), 53-69.

18. This suggestion applies to a new relationship where the individuals have just met or are not well acquainted. Good, long-term friends whose relationship is moving to a new level may not require as much getting-to-know-you time.

19. See Henry Cloud's chapter, "Do You Have to Get Married?—Dating is Not for the Lonely," in *How to Get a Date Worth Keeping* (Grand Rapids, MI: Zondervan, 2005), 204-8.

20. R. Paul Stevens, "Dating," *The Complete Book of Everyday Christianity* (Downers Grove, IL: InterVarsity Press, 1997), 267.

21. The *PREPARE/ENRICH* Program of premarital counseling produced by Life Innovations, Inc. is especially effective in guiding couples through this process. It must be administered

by a counselor trained by Life Innovations. For more information, see their website: www .prepare-enrich.com/indexm.cfm.

22. A thorough treatment of the principle "marry only a believer" requires exposition of these relevant passages: Deuteronomy 7:1-6; 1 Kings 11:1-8; Nehemiah 13:23-27; Malachi 2:1-12; 1 Corinthians 9:5, and the passage we have already studied, 1 Corinthians 7:39. The strong sanctions in the Old Testament against intermarriage with unbelievers were given for two primary reasons: (1) intermarriage would compromise God's holiness (Deuteronomy 7:6); and (2) it would inevitably destroy the experiential holiness of God's people (Deuteronomy 7:4).

23. In 2 Corinthians 6:14, Paul employed an agricultural metaphor of an ox and a donkey (Deuteronomy 22:10) harnessed together in a double yoke. No believer is to be so "mis-mated" with an unbeliever. Not only are the believer's values, goals, motivations, and enablement for living incompatible with those of an unbeliever; they are diametrically opposed! They are serving two different lords that are archenemies of one another. See Murray J. Harris, "2 Corinthians," *Expositor's Bible Commentary*, vol. 10, ed. Frank Gaebelein (Grand Rapids, MI: Zondervan, 1976), 359.

24. Significantly, sociological research confirms the detrimental effect on marriage of "having different religious backgrounds" or "not practicing faith together." These are among the risk factors that "greatly increase the odds of divorce." Howard J. Markman, Scott M. Stanley, Susan L. Blumberg, *Fighting for Your Marriage: Positive Steps for Preventing Divorce and Preserving a Lasting Love* (San Francisco, CA: Jossey-Bass, 2001), 17, 38-42.

25. Steven Reinberg, "CDC: Majority of U. S. Adults Had Troubled Childhoods," *USA Today,* December 12, 2010, online: www.usatoday.com/yourlife/parenting-family/2010-12-17-adult-majority-troubled-childhood_N.htm?csp., accessed August 23, 2011.

26. A good place to start would be the relevant articles in *The Complete Life Encyclopedia* by Frank Minirth, Paul Meier, and Stephen Arterburn (Nashville, TN: Thomas Nelson Publishers, 1995). Here are some other helpful resources. For adult children of alcoholics: Charles Sell, *Unfinished Business: Helping Adult Children Resolve Their Past* (Portland, OR: Multnomah Press, 1989); for adult children of divorce: Jim Conway, *Adult Children of Legal or Emotional Divorce: Healing Your Long-Term Hurt* (Downers Grove, IL: InterVarsity Press, 1990); for victims of sexual abuse: Dan B. Allender, *The Wounded Heart: Hope for Adult Victims of Childhood Sexual Abuse* (Colorado Springs, CO: NavPress, 1990); and Steven R. Tracy, *Mending the Soul: Understanding and Healing Abuse* (Grand Rapids, MI: Zondervan, 2008).

27. Young and Adams, "Commandment Nine: Thou Shalt Not Ignore Warning Signs," *The 10 Commandments of Dating*, 131-47.

28. Stephanie Coontz, *Marriage, a History: From Obedience to Intimacy or How Love Conquered Marriage* (New York: Viking Penguin, 2005), 15.

29. James Peterson enumerates the problems: First, romance results in such distortions of personality that after marriage the two people can never fulfill the roles that they expect of each other. Second, romance so idealizes marriage and even sex that when the day-to-day experiences of marriage are encountered, there must be disillusionment involved. Third, the romantic complex is so short-sighted that the premarital relationship is conducted almost

entirely on the emotional level and consequently such problems as temperamental or value differences, religious or cultural differences, financial, occupational, or health problems are never considered. Fourth, romance develops such a false ecstasy that there is implied in courtship a promise of a kind of happiness that could never be maintained during the realities of married life. Fifth, romance is such an escape from the negative aspects of personality to the extent that their repression obscures the real person. Later in marriage these negative factors to marital adjustment are bound to appear, and they were not evident earlier. Sixth, people engrossed in romance seem to be prohibited from wise planning for the basic needs of the future even to the point of failing to discuss the significant problems of early marriage. *Manual for Group Premarital Counseling*, ed. Lyle B. Gangsei (New York: Association, 1971), 56-57.

30. Tim Stafford identifies a significant value of being in love: "Romantic feelings do, as if by magic, make us want to be what we ought to be: entirely giving, thoroughly concerned with someone other than ourselves and wondrously joyful." "So Which *Is* Better?" *Marriage Partnership*, Summer 1988, 78.

31. Young and Adams, "Commandment Two: Thou Shalt Use Your Brain," *The 10 Commandments of Dating*, 19-35.

32. Markman, Stanley, Blumberg, *Fighting for Your Marriage*, 17. These developers and directors of PREP (Prevention and Relationship Enhancement Program) have identified two categories of risk factors: static (relatively unchangeable) and dynamic (subject to change). The *static* factors include: having a personality tendency to react strongly or defensively to problems and disappointments; having divorced parents; living together prior to marriage; being previously divorced (yourself or your partner); having children from a previous marriage; having different religious backgrounds; marrying at a very young age; knowing each other only for a short time before marriage; and experiencing financial hardship. The *dynamic* factors are: negative styles of talking and fighting with each other, like arguments that rapidly become negative, put-downs, and the silent treatment; difficulty communicating well, especially when you disagree; trouble handling disagreements as a team; unrealistic beliefs about marriage; having different attitudes about important things; a low level of commitment to one another, reflected in such things as not protecting your relationship from others you are attracted to or failing to view your marriage as a long-term investment; and failing to practice faith together. *Fight for Your Marriage*, 38-42.

33. I got similar responses from readers who field-tested an earlier version of this book.

34. Warren, *How to Know If Someone is Worth Pursuing*, 112.

35. Warren and Abraham, *Falling in Love for All the Right Reasons*, 35, 61, 63.

36. Van Epp, *How to Avoid Marrying a Jerk*, 32-50.

37. Henry Cloud and John Townsend, *Boundaries in Dating* (Grand Rapids, MI: Zondervan, 2000), 146. Cloud, *How to Get a Date Worth Keeping*, 208.

38. Cloud, *How to Get a Date Worth Keeping*, 179-86.

39. Ibid., 178.

40. Les Parrott and Neil Clark Warren, *Love the Life You Live* (Wheaton, IL: Tyndale House Publishers, 2004), 11.

Chapter 15: Profile of a Keeper

1. John Van Epp, *How to Avoid Marrying a Jerk* (New York: McGraw-Hill, 2006), 79-87.

2. I'm not sure who "they" are, but I quote them so much it seems they should get credit with their own endnote.

3. Van Epp, *How to Avoid Marrying a Jerk*, 77-78, 84.

4. We live in the Pacific Northwest where fishing is more than a form of casual recreation, it is a way of life. In fishing parlance, a *keeper* is a fish that is of sufficient size to be caught and retained without violating the law. Another fishing phrase, "catch and release," is an apt description of some dating patterns that precede engagement or marriage.

5. Neal Clark Warren with Ken Abraham, *Falling in Love for All the Right Reasons: How to Find Your Soul Mate* (New York: Center Street, 2005), 226. Dr. Warren's most complete development of this idea is found in *How to Know If Someone Is Worth Pursuing in Two Dates or Less* (Nashville, TN: Thomas Nelson Publishers, 1999) where he lists the twenty-five most popular must-haves and the twenty-five most prevalent can't-stands. A brief article, "Your Must-Haves and Can't-Stands: Make Your List Before You Go Shopping for a Partner," may be found on the eHarmony website: www.eharmony.com/singles/servlet/ncw/articles/makeyourlist. H. Norman Wright offers similar advice suggesting the creation of a checklist subdivided into three categories: Optional, Would Like to Have, and Must Have. He offers a starter list of twenty-eight items. *Finding the Right One for You* (Eugene, OR: Harvest House Publishers, 1995), 79-80.

6. Similar counsel is offered by Ben Young and Samuel Adams in *The One: A Realistic Guide to Choosing Your Soul Mate* (Nashville, TN: Thomas Nelson Publishers, 2002), 79. Changing the metaphor, they speak of "constructing your love target." "It will require careful self-analysis and serious introspection over a period of time as you consider the things you most value in a future partner." Henry Cloud and John Townsend concur in their outstanding chapter, "What You Can Live With and What You Can't Live With," in *Boundaries in Dating* (Grand Rapids, MI: Zondervan, 2000), 91-106.

7. Henry Cloud, *How to Get a Date Worth Keeping* (Grand Rapids, MI: Zondervan, 2005), 225-26.

8. Laura A. Smit, *Loves Me, Loves Me Not: The Ethics of Unrequited Love* (Grand Rapids, MI: Baker Academic, 2005), 77.

9. *Webster's New World Dictionary, Third College Edition*, ed. Victoria Neufeldt (New York: Harrington Park Press, 1986), 153-54, adapted. Cited in H. Norman Wright, *Finding the Right One for You*, 199, 248.

10. Wright, *Finding the Right One for You*, 5.

11. Ibid., 199.

Chapter 16: Calculating Compatibility

1. As a persistent proclivity, the propensity (or, more precisely, penchant) for alliteration on the part of preachers is probably pathological. Sometimes it's perturbing.

2. Henry Cloud, *How to Get a Date Worth Keeping* (Grand Rapids, MI: Zondervan, 2005), 221-22.

3. Dov Heller, *Get the Ring: How to Find and Keep the Right One for Life* (audio CD), ed. David LeVine (Bradenton, FL: Warm Wisdom Press, 2003), disc 5. Also see "Never Get Married Because You Are in Love," accessed at: www.warmwisdompress.com/dating-love/Never_ Get_Married_Because_ You_Are_In_Love.aspx.

4. "Men worldwide...most often rate vitality as the number one trait they are looking for in a mate, while women consistently rate security as the number one quality they are looking for in a husband. Both men and women, however, want a mate who is kind." Neal Clark Warren with Ken Abraham, *Falling in Love for All the Right Reasons* (New York: Time Warner Book Group, 2005), 192.

5. Ben Young and Samuel Adams, *The 10 Commandments of Dating* (Nashville, TN: Thomas Nelson Publishers, 1999), 157-62.

6. Warren, *Falling in Love for All the Right Reasons*, 81.

7. Ironically, one result of such commitment is freedom. "It allows you to be yourself at the deepest of levels, to risk and grow, to be absolutely authentic without any fear of being abandoned." Neil Clark Warren, *Finding the Love of Your Life: Ten Principles for Choosing the Right Marriage Partner* (New York: Pocket Books, 1992), 141.

8. H. Norman Wright, *Finding the Right One for You* (Eugene, OR: Harvest House Publishers, 1995), 15.

9. J. H. Olthuis, "Marriage," *New Dictionary of Christian Ethics and Pastoral Theology*, ed. David J. Atkinson and David H. Field (Downers Grove, IL: InterVarsity Press, 1995), 566. The only place that obscure word is likely to appear these days is in traditional wedding vows that conclude, "and thereunto I plight thee my troth."

10. This sentence is the title of chapter 3 in Warren's first book on mate selection, *How to Find the Love of Your Life* (1992). It is a prominent theme in all of his books addressed to marriage-minded singles.

11. Warren, *Falling in Love for All the Right Reasons*, 42.

12. John Van Epp, *How to Avoid Marrying a Jerk* (New York, NY: McGraw-Hill, 2006), 77.

13. "Years ago, I could build a strong case that as long as individuals were similar in their intelligence levels, their actual formal education would not make a big difference to them. Over the years, as I've confronted the clinical evidence of couples in my office on the brink of calling it quits, I've had to change my thinking on this dimension. I am now convinced that having similar educational backgrounds does indeed matter. If you are not closely matched in your levels of education, at the very minimum you should have a similar appreciation for the value of education and the hard work that it requires." Warren, *Falling in Love for All the Right Reasons*, 114.

14. Sociologists explain this by means of the "equity/exchange (or social-exchange) theory." "What these fancy-sounding words mean is that you will probably not feel totally comfortable with your partner unless you have obtained a fairly equal exchange with your beloved in most of these areas. In other words, you will just naturally feel more at ease with a partner who is similar to you in level of attractiveness, social status, educational background, and so on. If my spouse were much 'better' than me in some of these areas—for instance, if she had a graduate degree while I had dropped out of high school—I would probably feel bad about the match, and believe that I wasn't contributing my fair share to the situation." David

Nicholson, *What You Need to Know before You Fall in Love* (Nashville, TN: Thomas Nelson Publishers, 1995), 119-20.; Wright, *Finding the Right One for You,* 85-88.

15. With regard to biblical teaching on gender roles, two competing viewpoints have substantial representation in the evangelical church. *Complementarianism,* the more traditional view, asserts that the Bible teaches ontological equality on the part of men and women—that is, they are of equal worth, dignity, and responsibility before God. But the Bible also teaches that men and women have different roles to play in the family and church. Husbands are called to be servant-leaders; wives are called to be supporting partners. These roles do not compete but complement one another. *Egalitarianism* denies a biblical distinction between roles, and it denies that a default authority is assigned to the husband. Rather, men and women are seen to be equal in *all* respects. In marriage, they are called to mutual submission (Ephesians 5:21). Marital roles should be mutually determined on the basis of aptitude and giftedness rather than gender.

Scholars and church leaders who promote the *complementarian* position are represented by the Council on Biblical Manhood and Womanhood (www.cbmw.org). An expanded summary of their position may be found in an essay, "Summaries of the Egalitarian and Complementarian Positions on the Role of Women in the Home and in Christian Ministry," (www.cbmw.org/Resources/Articles/Summaries-of-the-Egalitarian-and-Complementari-an-Positions). A representative book-length development of their view is *Recovering Biblical Manhood and Womanhood: A Response to Evangelical Feminism,* ed. John Piper and Wayne Grudem (Wheaton, IL: Crossway Books, 2006).

Scholars and church leaders who promote the egalitarian position are represented by Christians for Biblical Equality (www.cbeinternational.org). An expanded summary of their position is found in an essay, "Men, Women and Biblical Equality" (www.cbeinternational. org/?q=content/men-women-and-biblical-equality). A representative book-length development of their view is *Discovering Biblical Equality,* ed. Ronald W. Pierce and Rebecca Merrill Groothuis (Downers Grove, IL: InterVarsity Press, 2005).

If you find a candidate for marriage, it will be important for the two of you to be in essential agreement on *your* gender roles in marriage. This matter should be explored and resolved during premarital counseling.

16. "It almost seems to us that couples in some way find each other on the basis of their potential to induce change…Their search for a mate is not haphazard, but rather based on some kind of deeply intuitive homing device that relentlessly and purposely pursues exactly the kind of person who will provide them with the stimulation for the growth they are seeking." Robert F. Stahmann and William J. Hiebert, *Premarital Counseling* (Lexington, MA: Lexington Books, 1980), 20-21. Cited in Wright, *Finding the Right One for You,* 90-91.

17. Van Epp, *How to Avoid Marrying a Jerk,* 43.

18. Henry Cloud and John Townsend, *Boundaries in Dating* (Grand Rapids, MI: Zondervan, 2000), 144 (emphasis theirs). Cloud and Townsend devote an entire chapter (9) to "Beware When Opposites Attract."

19. Van Epp, *How to Avoid Marrying a Jerk,* 91-92.

20. Ken Voges and Ron Braund, *Understanding How Others Misunderstand You* (Chicago, IL: Moody Press, 1990).

21. "Instead of looking for specific personality traits, we suggest that you…look for someone who wants the same general things in life that you do. Your lives should move in the same

general direction." Rosie Einhorn and Sherry Zimmerman, *Get the Ring: How to Find and Keep the Right One for Life* (audio CD), part 3, ed. David LeVine (Bradenton, FL: Warm Wisdom Press, 2003).

22. Nicholson, *What You Need to Know before You Fall in Love*, 125-29.

23. See Henry Cloud's chapter 13, "Don't Limit Yourself to a Type," in *How to Get a Date Worth Keeping* (Grand Rapids, MI: Zondervan, 2005), 91-97. Also Cloud and Townsend, *Boundaries in Dating*, 91-96.

24. A pheromone is "a chemical secreted by an animal, especially an insect, that influences the behavior or development of others of the same species, often functioning as an attractant of the opposite sex." pheromone. Dictionary.com. *The American Heritage Dictionary of the English Language*, Fourth Edition (Boston, MA: Houghton Mifflin Company, 2004). http://dictionary.reference.com/browse/pheromone (accessed: November 01, 2007). Some research has been conducted in an attempt to determine whether humans communicate via pheromones, but nothing conclusive has been established.

25. "Frankly, trying to define chemistry is like trying to nail fog to the wall." Warren, *Falling in Love for All the Right Reasons*, 201.

26. Young and Adams, *10 Commandments of Dating*, 141.

27. People from non-Western cultures, whose marriages are arranged by family members, shake their heads at our mantra: "first comes love, then comes marriage." An Indian man who did not even see his wife until the day of their wedding observed, "After seven years of marriage, I think we have a happier marriage than many couples we hear about in the West…We put cold soup on the fire and it becomes slowly warm; you put hot soup into a cold plate and it becomes slowly cold. You marry the girl you love. We love the woman we have married." Ingrid Trobisch, "Kahlid's Mystery Bride," *Marriage Partnership*, Summer 1988, 75.

28. Warren, *Falling in Love for All the Right Reasons*, 203-4.

29. Cloud and Townsend, *Boundaries in Dating*, 107.

30. Ibid., 118.

31. Van Epp, *How to Avoid Marrying a Jerk*, 81-82.

32. I am indebted to John Van Epp for the second constellation of comparability, complementarity, and chemistry. "The soul mate you need is a person with whom you have a rich chemistry, whose differences make you better than you could be on your own, and who shares many of your core values and life goals, as well as some of your personality qualities and lifestyle preferences." *How to Avoid Marrying a Jerk*, 77.

33. Shana Schutte, "Shopping for a Spouse? Why I Decided to Chuck My Mr. Right Checklist," *Today's Christian Woman*, September/October 2004, 72ff, accessed at: www.christianitytoday.com/tcw/2004/sepoct/16.72.html, November, 2007.

34. One resource to assist in such self-evaluation is Neil Warren's chapter 2, "Know Yourself," in *How to Know If Someone Is Worth Pursuing in Two Dates or Less* (Nashville, TN: Thomas Nelson Publishers, 1999), 25-41. He has an abbreviated version of the same content in *Falling in Love for All the Right Reasons*, 217-20. In fact, just filling out the questionnaire for eHarmony.com is a major exercise in self-awareness and self-disclosure.

35. Les Parrott, "The Question that Could Save Your Marriage Before It Begins," 2003, accessed at: www.christianitytoday.com/singles/eharmony/03jun-2.html, November, 2007.

Chapter 17: Courtship: Getting Our Bearings

1. *5 Paths to the Love of Your Life: Defining Your Dating Style*, ed. Alex Chediak (Colorado Springs, CO: Th1nk [NavPress], 2005).

2. Barbara Dafoe Whitehead has chosen the analogy of climbing the rungs of a ladder, which is also an apt description. *Why There Are No Good Men Left: The Romantic Plight of the New Single Woman* (New York: Broadway Books, 2003), 107-10.

3. *Wing to Wing, Oar to Oar: Readings on Courting and Marrying*, ed. Amy A. Kass and Leon R. Kass (Notre Dame, IN: University of Notre Dame Press, 2000), 2, 23.

4. Primary resources for this section include: Rodney M. Cate and Sally A. Lloyd, *Courtship* (Thousand Oaks, CA: Sage Publications, Inc., 1992); Stephanie Coontz, *Marriage, a History: From Obedience to Intimacy or How Love Conquered Marriage* (New York: Viking Penguin, 2005); Beth L. Bailey, *From Front Porch to Back Seat: Courtship in Twentieth-Century America* (Baltimore, MD: Johns Hopkins University Press, 1989); *Wing to Wing, Oar to Oar*, ed. Amy A. Kass and Leon R. Kass; Whitehead, *Why There Are No Good Men Left*; Lauren Winner, "The Countercultural Path," *5 Paths to the Love of Your Life*, ed. Alex Chediak; Kathleen A. Bogle, *Hooking Up: Sex, Dating, and Relationships on Campus* (New York: New York University Press, 2008).

5. This represents a complete reversal from the prevailing view of the Middle Ages when women were "considered the lusty sex, more prey to their passions than men." Female purity came to be idealized in a manner unique to the nineteenth century. "Whereas women had once been considered snares of the devil, they were now viewed as sexual innocents whose purity should inspire all decent men to control their own sexual impulses and baser appetites." Coontz, *Marriage, a History*, 159.

6. Readers familiar with the classic Christmas movie *It's a Wonderful Life* may recall a scene that illustrates this custom. When George Bailey comes calling on Mary Hatch, her mother (who does not approve of George) repeatedly intrudes upon their parlor room conversation.

7. Winner makes this pointed observation: "The unquestioned patriarchy of current Christian courtship, then, is actually something of an innovation. This, perhaps, is something that current-day advocates of courtship should bear in mind before appealing to tradition as a means of shoring up a system of gender roles in which men are always to pursue and women are always to wait and be pursued." "The Countercultural Path," *5 Paths to the Love of Your Life*, 22.

8. Cate and Lloyd add this pertinent endnote: "The history of courtship is limited largely to the history of white, middle-class and upper-class customs (Rothman, 1984). Information on courtship patterns among ethnic families (particularly black families under slavery), working-class families, and poor families is rather sketchy." *Courtship*, 22, endnote 1.

9. This new social custom was immortalized in the original first verse of a song that is now sung during the seventh-inning stretch of many baseball games. "Take Me Out to the Ball Game" was written by Jack Norworth in 1908 while riding on a subway train in New York City. He

had never attended a baseball game, but he understood the social dynamics of young men and young women.

> Katie Casey was baseball mad,
> Had the fever and had it bad.
> Just to root for the home town crew,
> Ev'ry sou, Katie blew.
> On a Saturday her young beau
> Called to see if she'd like to go
> To see a show, but Miss Kate said "No,
> I'll tell you what you can do:
>
> "Take me out to the ball game,
> Take me out with the crowd;
> Buy me some peanuts and Cracker Jack,
> I don't care if I never get back.
> Let me root, root, root for the home team,
> If they don't win, it's a shame.
> For it's one, two, three strikes, you're out,
> At the old ball game."

10. Bailey, *From Front Porch to Back Seat*, cited in *Wing to Wing, Oar to Oar*, 32.

11. In fact, the origin of *date* as a descriptor of these social outings probably stems from the economic exchange involved in obtaining the services of a prostitute. To "make a date" was to secure an appointment on the calendar of the woman one was purchasing sexual favors from. It apparently didn't take very long for the word to gain respectability in the common vernacular. Bailey, *From Front Porch to Back Seat*, cited in *Wing to Wing, Oar to Oar*, 35.

12. Ibid., 34.

13. Whitehead, *Why There Are No Good Men Left*, 13. For a side-by-side comparison of the respective features of the traditional marrying system and the emergent relationship system, see the introduction to part 2, endnote 16.

14. Bogle, *Hooking Up*, 42.

15. See R. Paul Stevens's critique of dating in chapter 14.

16. Jonathan Lindvall, "The Dangers of Dating: Scriptural Romance—Part 1," 2004. www.bold-christianliving.com/index.php?option=com_content&task=view&id=3&Itemid=25.

17. Joshua Harris, *I Kissed Dating Goodbye* (Sisters, OR: Multnomah Books, 1997).

18. Harris's criticisms of dating are enumerated in his second chapter, "The Seven Habits of Highly Defective Dating" (pp. 29-43):

    1. Dating leads to intimacy but not necessarily to commitment.
    2. Dating tends to skip the "friendship" stage of a relationship.
    3. Dating often mistakes a physical relationship for love.
    4. Dating often isolates a couple from other vital relationships.
    5. Dating, in many cases, distracts young adults from their primary responsibility of preparing for the future.

6. Dating can cause discontentment with God's gift of singleness.

7. Dating creates an artificial environment for evaluating another person's character.

19. Harris, *I Kissed Dating Goodbye*, 205.

20. Douglas Wilson, "The Courtship Path," *5 Paths to the Love of Your Life*, 85.

21. Jonathan Lindvall, "The Betrothal Path," *5 Paths to the Love of Your Life*, 144.

22. Henry Cloud and John Townsend, *Boundaries in Dating* (Grand Rapids, MI: Zondervan, 2000), 16.

23. Not all proponents of a particular approach to courtship maintain that their preference is the biblically prescribed one. Harris, for instance, does not make such a claim. Some advocates for courtship and betrothal do believe that they have identified *the* biblical approach. But, in my judgment, they fail to make their case. For a more complete critique of these alternative views, see my essay, "Dating, Courtship or Betrothal? Is There a Biblically Prescribed Method for Mate Selection?" at www.TheMarriageDecision.com.

24. Outside of cults, I know of no one who argues that this approach is biblically prescribed for believers today. The betrothal system modifies the practices of the biblical era, reducing the level of parental authority.

25. Ben Young and Samuel Adams, *The One: A Realistic Guide to Choosing Your Soul Mate* (Nashville, TN: Thomas Nelson Publishers, 2001), 27.

26. J. W. Drane, "Family," *New Dictionary of Biblical Theology*, ed. T. Desmond Alexander et al. (Downers Grove, IL: InterVarsity Press, 2000), 494.

27. R. Paul Stevens, "Dating," *The Complete Book of Everyday Christianity*, ed. Robert Banks and R. Paul Stevens (Downers Grove, IL: InterVarsity Press, 1997), 268.

28. Many single adult readers will wonder what to make of the authoritative role of the father that is central to the patriarchal versions of courtship and betrothal described. Proponents of these approaches are sincerely attempting to understand and apply biblical teaching. But they appear to overlook two significant factors. First, the absolute authority assigned to fathers in the Bible pertains to dependent children living in the home. All children are required to honor their parents (Exodus 20:12; Mark 7:9-13; Ephesians 6:2), but only minors are required to obey (Ephesians 6:1-4; Colossians 3:20-21). Second, in antiquity, girls usually became brides in their teen years, often upon the onset of puberty. A girl whose marriage was arranged by her father would be obedient to him, in part, because she was a dependent child until she became another man's wife. Marriage was the means by which a girl became an adult woman. Most brides in contemporary culture are adult women living independently of their parents. Such independence is regarded as desirable, for it demonstrates that the woman has acquired the maturity and life-skills to be a capable spouse. So the patriarchal authority attending proposed approaches to courtship are neither biblically demanded nor culturally applicable. On the other hand, many single adults would be well-advised to pay more attention to *parental counsel* in their marital considerations.

29. As I explained earlier, contemporary advocates of the betrothal system place commitment at the *beginning* of the process. They point out that this is the sequence in arranged marriages. The purported benefit of that sequence is that it keeps romantic attachment in its place. That is, it prevents the cart of romance from driving the horse of courtship. My contention is that

commitment must be preceded by in-depth knowledge. The acquiring of that knowledge is the task of courtship. The influence of romance does need to be reined in, but other measures will need to be taken to accomplish this.

30. "Date," *Random House Webster's Collegiate Dictionary,* 2nd ed. cited in "The Purposeful Path," 5 Paths to the Love of Your Life, 158.

31. Cloud and Townsend, *Boundaries in Dating,* 17-21. The developers of the PREPARE/EN-RICH program provide a similar list of the advantages of dating:

1. Learning about differences in people

2. Getting to know ourselves better

3. Learning about our likes and dislikes

4. Learning relational skills

David H. Olson, John DeFrain, Amy K. Olson, *Building Relationships* (Minneapolis, MN: Life Innovations, Inc., 1999), 24-25.

Chapter 18: Courtship: Devising the Plan

1. Rosie Einhorn and Sherry Zimmerman, *Get the Ring: How to Find and Keep the Right One for Life* (audio CD), part 3, ed. David LeVine (Bradenton, FL: Warm Wisdom Press, 2003).

2. The material that follows may prove to be elementary for relationally advanced readers. But if you get a couple of good ideas to refine your plan, that would be worthwhile.

3. Henry Cloud, *How to Get a Date Worth Keeping* (Grand Rapids, MI: Zondervan, 2005), 63-67.

4. Ibid., 61-75. For additional ideas on how to meet prospects, see H. Norman Wright's chapter 5, "Where Do I Meet Them and What Do I Say?" *Finding the Right One for You* (Eugene, OR: Harvest House Publishers, 1995), 95-118.

5. These ideas are developed in chapter 4, "Dating Is Not About Marriage," and chapter 16, "Go Out With Almost Anyone Once, and Maybe Again," in Cloud's book, *How to Get a Date Worth Keeping* 31-38, 106-8.

6. A valuable alternative is Neil Clark Warren's book *How to Know if Someone Is Worth Pursuing in Two Dates or Less* (Nashville, TN: Thomas Nelson Publishers, 1999) 173-76. Dr. Warren's perspective may be more relevant to experienced daters who are further along the path. He offers practical ideas on how to figure out if a casual date has the potential to become a keeper. Yet Warren also realizes that some people don't make good first impressions. So he warns against jumping to a hasty conclusion lest you miss a diamond in the rough. So "if a person has none of your can't-stand qualities, but you're unsure if he or she has your must-haves, take your time!"

7. John Van Epp, *How to Avoid Marrying a Jerk* (New York: McGraw-Hill, 2006), 58.

8. That circumstance will change soon. This is the last chapter!

9. There are actually businesses called "It's Just Lunch" or "It's Only Lunch" that arrange dates for busy professionals. Somebody else thinks this is a good idea.

10. When our children were preschool age and we wanted to attend a week-long conference, Louise and I would commission a broker to secure in-home childcare. On the one hand, it was easier for folks who really didn't want to accept that responsibility to decline the inquiry when it came from Anne. On the other hand, those who were willing appreciated being asked by her. That system worked out very well for us.

11. See Van Epp, *How to Avoid Marrying a Jerk*, 53-73, 109-28.

12. Ibid., 27-28.

13. Cloud, *How to Get a Date Worth Keeping*, 82-90.

14. Marva J. Dawn, *Sexual Character: Beyond Technique to Intimacy* (Grand Rapids, MI: Wm. B. Eerdmans Publishing Co., 1993), 51.

15. Diogenes Allen, *Love: Christian Romance, Marriage, Friendship* (Cambridge, MA: Cowley Publications, 1987), 28-29. Cited in Lauren Winner, "The Countercultural Path," *5 Paths to the Love of Your Life*, 36-37. See her insightful discussion of "Love and Christian Dating," 35-39.

Appendix: Divorce and Remarriage

1. In this position statement "sexual immorality" and "sexual unfaithfulness" are translations of the Greek word *porneia* (Matthew 5:32; 19:9). In a marriage context it refers to the sins of adultery, homosexual behavior, incest, and bestiality.

2. Kostenberger, *God Marriage and Family*, chapter 12; Alexander Strauch, *Biblical Eldership*, 189-93.

To learn more about Harvest House books and
to read sample chapters, log on to our website:

www.harvesthousepublishers.com

HARVEST HOUSE PUBLISHERS
EUGENE, OREGON